Add in Retail Market
M 301
11:30 - 12:20 MWF
Rm 105

ADVERTISING

ADVERTISING

James S. Norris

Reston Publishing Company, Inc.
A Prentice-Hall Company
Reston, Virginia

Library of Congress Cataloging in Publication Data

Norris, James S   1915-
    Advertising.

    Bibliography: p.
    Includes index.
    1. Advertising.   2. Advertising—United States.
I.   Title.
HF5823.N65   659.1'0973   75-43727
ISBN 0-87909-004-9

© 1977 by Reston Publishing Company, Inc.
A Prentice-Hall Company
11480 Sunset Hills Road
Reston, Virginia 22090

10   9   8   7   6   5   4   3   2   1

Printed in the United States of America

To Katie, Chris, Jim, and Harriet,
with Love

Contents

Preface

This book was written for the benefit of the thousands of young people who, each year, leave colleges and universities and very quickly find themselves involved with the problems of advertising and sales promotion.

Most of these young people are not headed for Madison Avenue. They are going back home; therefore, this book was written with Main Street in mind and deals with the realities of advertising as they exist in 90 percent of America. It "tells it the way it is"—not just for the 100 leading advertisers, but for the hundreds of thousands of retailers, regional manufacturers, and small businessmen across the face of the nation.

In this book I have tried to show how advertising works on both sides of the street—on the big national advertiser's side, and on the side where $300 a week is an important promotional budget.

This is a "how to" book. Advertising problems come quickly to the young business person without the cushion of corporate responsibility. In their new jobs they very soon want to know, "Where do I get it?" "How much will it cost?" "Who should I talk to?" This book tells them.

I respect advertising. I want other people to understand and respect it. The world of American business is full of executives who know a great deal about insurance, banking, and how to grill a T-bone steak in the back yard. But they don't know anything about advertising. That is why the young business executive who *does* know is worth his or her weight in gold. The business world needs young executives who can recognize advertising for what it is—a difficult, demanding form of salesmanship that calls on the skills and expertise of a dozen different kinds of professionals.

I hope that this book will give its readers a respect for advertising, and the facts and techniques to make it work for them.

Thanks . . .

I want to express my gratitude to the many men and women in my hometown who work in all phases of advertising and its many related fields. All were generous with their advice and patient in their explanations.

I am grateful, too, for the great response from so many agencies around the country. They were not only most generous in sharing the work they have done for their clients; but they also have been perceptive in expressing their ideas and feelings about advertising in America today.

I am also indebted to that flower in the garden of publishing, Ms. Dorothy Werner, for her help and guidance.

And this book would never have been finished, I am sure, without the editorial and moral support of my wife, Katie.

JAMES S. NORRIS

ADVERTISING

chapter one

Putting Advertising in Perspective

*As you begin to examine how advertising works, and
how you may best make it work for you, it is important
that you first view in proper perspective this marketing
activity that has been going on for so many centuries.*

*In this chapter we will look at advertising in the past,
at the part it has played historically in our lives. You
will see how advertising is always a reflection of the age
in which it exists. It has changed, as we have changed.*   **1**

If you had been a young Roman soldier in the occupation army in Gaul, spending an afternoon at the chariot races at the stadium at Nimes, you would have been exposed to advertising.

If in your former life you were a tall straight-nosed Grecian beauty strolling the streets of Corinth, with your market basket on your arm, you would certainly have been aware of all the advertising around you.

Whether Roman soldier or Grecian homemaker, your ears would have been assailed by the cries of street vendors broadcalling their wares for sale. On walls and buildings you would have read advertisements of a wide variety of products and, most likely, there would have been some "lost-and-found" notices too. Hanging from the fronts of the stores you would have observed signs identifying the place of the perfume merchant, the rug weaver, and the fish vendor.

Because the notices on Roman walls often began with the Latin words *si quis* (If anyone) as in "If anyone has information," or, "If anyone wishes to obtain," for many centuries afterward any poster advertisement in England or in America was known as a *siqui*.

Here is an actual Roman advertisement similar to those our soldier might have seen on his way to the races:

There Will Be a Dedication or
Formal Opening of Certain Baths
Those Attending Are Promised Slaughter
of Wild Beasts, Athletic Games,
Perfume Sprinkling, and
Awnings to Keep off the Sun

3

The slaughtering of wild beasts and perfume sprinkling may strike you as being a little unusual. But I think you will admit that this Pompeian sign of 2,000 years ago and the posters that sprout in your town just before the circus or the county fair arrives have something in common.

Although the voice of the street vendor in America grows fainter with each passing year, it is still possible to hear the mournful call and tinkling bells of the old-clothes and junk man, the call of the itinerant fruit peddler with his pushcart, or the street-corner vendor of hot chestnuts. And what would a football game be without the kids hawking pennants, peanuts, and soft drinks? Much the same calls, in a different language, echoed in the streets and stadia of the Mediterranean countries.

Again, if you will glance down the length of your Main Street, you will notice that the storekeepers of your town have taken some pains to make sure they are not unobserved—just as the marketkeepers have done in Corinth and Rome.

So you see what we call broadcast advertising, point-of-purchase advertising, and outdoor advertising have all been around for a long time. But it wasn't until the Middle Ages, with the world-shaking advent of the printing press and movable type, that advertising began to take the form most familiar to us today.

Advertising in Merrie England

Let us say you were a young blood in the London of Shakespeare and Marlowe in the 16th century. London was an exciting town; lively with soldiers and nobles, artists, politicians, scamps, and adventurers. As you sat in your favorite tavern discussing the latest gossip of the city and swapping epigrams with Ben Jonson and his circle, you would surely have been aware of all the advertising around you.

By now the building and designing of shop signs had become very specialized. The proprietor of the tavern in which you sat, the "Boar's Head," was rightfully proud of the beautifully carved and painted sign that hung above his doorway.

So handsome and colorful were many of these signs that you will find them preserved in museums of folk art and reproduced over the shop fronts in restored towns such as Williamsburg, Virginia, or Mystic, Connecticut. In Paris, in a very old part of the city called Le Marais (The Swamp) there is a little museum, Le Carnavelet, in which you can see French shopkeepers' signs from the 12th and 13th centuries.

If you live on the east coast of the United States, you may be familiar with one of those old turnpike inns the Conestoga wagons used to creak past on their way west. The "Spread Eagle," the "Black Horse," and the

In Europe and America in the 1800s, the use of advertising was unrestrained. Every available space was covered.

By permission: Henry Sampson *A History of Advertising*. London: Chatto and Windus Ltd., 1875.

"King of Prussia," still proudly wear the signs once sought by weary colonial travelers. And I'm sure you are familiar with the sign of three gold balls that hangs in front of the pawnship in your town, where you might have gone to pick up an inexpensive watch or guitar. This sign traces its ancestry right back to the coat of arms of the famous Medici family, who were successful moneylenders in the Florence of the 15th century.

The town criers, with their bright-red coats and big brass bells, would have been a familiar part of your London life. You often depended on them for news and official announcements as well as paid-for commercial messages.

By now, too, the warning "post no bills" had become a familiar sight. But despite the warning, the walls of London were plastered with the ever-present *siquis* offering goods for sale. Many of them were printed, and youngsters picked up a few pennies distributing printed handbills. The "sandwich-board man" had also made his apppearance—usually a poor old fellow down on his luck, who trudged the streets carrying signs, front and back, suspended from straps over his shoulders.

The street vendors, with their raucous, humorous, sometimes plaintive cries, were as much a part of your life as the foggy, smoky London air you breathed. Probably you were familiar with the cry of "Sweet Molly Malone" with her melodious "Cockles and mussels alive, alive-O!" The Cockney of London, an irrepressible fellow, took pride in the inventiveness of his street cries and filled them with humor and impromptu rhymes.

The Beginning of Newspapers

For you, advertising became even more pervasive when in 1625 your newspaper, the *Weekly News of London*, began to carry small advertisements of a personal and retail nature closely resembling today's classified ads. Many of these ads appeared on the front page of the paper, as later they would appear in many American newspapers of the 19th century—as in fact they did appear in the dignified and venerable *London Times* until a short time ago.

Daily newspapers, filled with ads and public notices, appeared a little later. The first was the *Daily Courant* in 1702, followed by the *Revue* in 1704, and the *Examiner*, the *Tatler*, and the *Spectator*. These were edited by famous literary figures such as Jonathan Swift, Daniel Defoe, and Joseph and Sir Richard Steele.

Advertising in the American Colonies

If you had been a young Englishman living in one of the outposts of the empire, such as Baltimore, Philadelphia, or Boston in Colonial days, you would have found the means and methods for offering goods for sale not much different from what they were back in the Old Country. Street criers, bills and posters, and store signs were just about the same as in Britain.

You would have had a variety of newspapers and periodicals from which to choose although these seemed to suspend publication with alarming regularity. Perhaps because the publishers were more concerned with editorial comment than advertising lineage, in Colonial America periodicals had a life span of less than a year.

In Philadelphia, center of early printing and publishing, you might have had a choice of Andrew Bradford's *American Magazine*, or *A Monthly Review of the Political State of the British Colonies*. The already well-known Mr. Benjamin Franklin published his *General Magazine and Historical Chronicle*, and William Bradford put out the short-lived *American Magazine and Monthly Chronicle*.

During those days in Colonial Philadelphia or Boston, you and your friends would have lived in a state of constant frustration—a frustration born of your inability to grow and prosper, to look forward to becoming an affluent consumer or a successful businessman. You were bound by

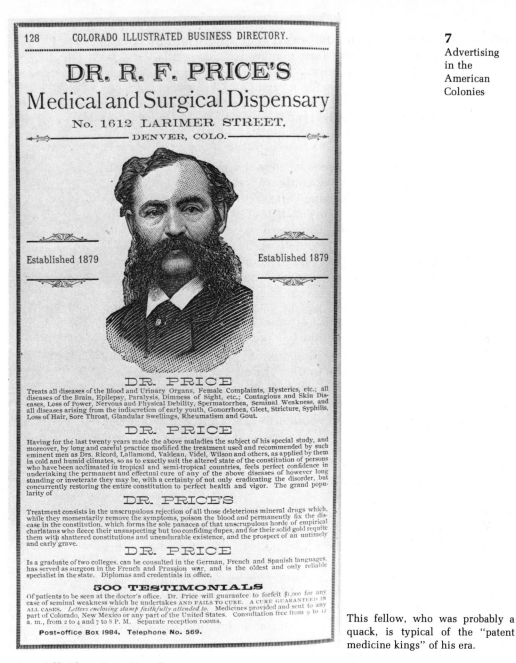

DR. R. F. PRICE'S
Medical and Surgical Dispensary
No. 1612 LARIMER STREET,
DENVER, COLO.

Established 1879   Established 1879

DR. PRICE

Treats all diseases of the Blood and Urinary Organs, Female Complaints, Hysterics, etc.; all diseases of the Brain, Epilepsy, Paralysis, Dimness of Sight, etc.; Contagious and Skin Diseases, Loss of Power, Nervous and Physical Debility, Spermatorrhea, Seminal Weakness, and all diseases arising from the indiscretion of early youth, Gonorrhoea, Gleet, Stricture, Syphilis, Loss of Hair, Sore Throat, Glandular Swellings, Rheumatism and Gout.

DR. PRICE

Having for the last twenty years made the above maladies the subject of his special study, and moreover, by long and careful practice modified the treatment used and recommended by such eminent men as Drs. Ricord, Lallamond, Valdeau, Videl, Wilson and others, as applied by them in cold and humid climates, so as to exactly suit the altered state of the constitution of persons who have been acclimated in tropical and semi-tropical countries, feels perfect confidence in undertaking the permanent and effectual cure of any of the above diseases of however long standing or inveterate they may be, with a certainty of not only eradicating the disorder, but concurrently restoring the entire constitution to perfect health and vigor. The grand popularity of

DR. PRICE'S

Treatment consists in the unscrupulous rejection of all those deleterious mineral drugs which, while they momentarily remove the symptoms, poison the blood and permanently fix the disease in the constitution. which forms the sole panacea of that unscrupulous horde of empirical charlatans who fleece their unsuspecting but too confiding dupes, and for their solid gold requite them with shattered constitutions and unendurable existence, and the prospect of an untimely and early grave.

DR. PRICE

Is a graduate of two colleges, can be consulted in the German, French and Spanish languages, has served as surgeon in the French and Prussion war, and is the oldest and only reliable specialist in the state. Diplomas and credentials in office.

500 TESTIMONIALS

Of patients to be seen at the doctor's office. Dr. Price will guarantee to forfeit $1,000 for any case of seminal weakness which he undertakes AND FAILS TO CURE. A CURE GUARANTEED IN ALL CASES. *Letters enclosing stamp faithfully attended to.* Medicines provided and sent to any part of Colorado, New Mexico or any part of the United States. Consultation free from 9 to 12 a. m., from 2 to 4 and 7 to 8 P. M. Separate reception rooms.

Post-office Box 1984. Telephone No. 569.

Denver Public Library, Western History Department.

This fellow, who was probably a quack, is typical of the "patent medicine kings" of his era.

strictures of laws, taxes, and boundaries that caused your future to appear to you very bleak. Although you and your friends did not use the term "marketing" when discussing your problems, this really was at the bottom of your troubles.

You lived, in mid-eighteenth century, in a "captive" market. Only British ships could bring goods to you, and only British ships could take

your products (mainly agricultural) away. Your ships were forbidden to
trade in foreign ports, but sometimes you evaded this regulation. John
Hancock, whose signature appears so large on the Declaration of Inde-
pendence, had a price on his head as a "smuggler." Prices of manufactured goods were three times those in Britain, and taxes were high. With
the failure of the tobacco crop in 1760, and the financial strain of the
Seven Years War, hard times were upon the land.

Colonial families tended to be large, and you may have had half a
dozen brothers and sisters whose ambitions were similar to your own.
From the rocky hillsides of the Berkshires in New England to tidewater
Virginia and the Carolinas, farmland was in short supply. The lands
beyond the mountains beckoned to you. In the fertile valleys of the Ohio,
of the Cumberland, and of the Tennessee, a person could carve for
himself/herself a new life. The trouble was that you and your friends
were forbidden by the Crown to cross those mountains.

Unknown to most young Americans, two powerful groups with important interests in the colonies were battling for ascendancy in London.
One represented the mercantile interests; the other, real estate. Powerful
mercantile houses, such as the Robert Hunter Company, Dyer, Allen and
Company, and others with great influence in Parliament, were contending with those who saw in the speculation of western land sales the
possibilities of untold millions in profits. The mercantile interests won.

In 1763 the Crown issued a proclamation demarking a line which
followed the mountains, ran down through central New York, Pennsylvania, and southern states to the border of East Florida. Beyond this
"Proclamation Line" no settler might pass, no trader without a proper
license might venture, and no purchase of Indian lands might be made.
An onerous tax on all imported goods was imposed to pay for the
support of the thousands of British troops needed to guard the Proclamation Line.

A few years later, you and your friends would take your squirrel rifles
from the mantelpiece. You would trudge down the dusty roads to Ben-
nington, and Princeton, and King's Mountain, to settle the whole thing
in your own way.

You not only helped to found a new nation; you opened up a conti-
nent. In the next 100 years, this mostly unknown land beyond the
mountains would enjoy a spectacular growth and development; and
advertising was to play a very important and significant role in the
development of America in the 19th century.

Advertising and the Growth of America

Come all ye Yankee farmers who wish to change your lot,

Who've spunk enough to travel beyond your native spot,

And leave behind the village where Ma and Pa do stay,

Come follow me and settle in Michigania,

Yea, yea, yea, in Michigania.

This was only one of the "singing commercials" that lured adventurous young Americans westward in the early years of the 19th century. There was much more advertising, in billboards and posters, in newspapers and brochures.

The Growth of the American Market

The development of the United States in the 19th century was marked by a series of constantly westward-moving frontiers. A "frontier" was defined by the Bureau of the Census as an area having not more than six or less than two individuals per square acre. New roads were cut through the mountains; canal systems brought western produce to eastern markets; and the steamboat and flatboat turned the rivers into highways. As the settlers poured in, new communities sprang up like mushrooms. Some of these "cities" never passed the planning stage; but by the 1830s, Vandalia, and Indianapolis, Louisville and Nashville were thriving communities. They had homes and schools and churches—but most significantly they had *consumers* who needed butter churns, plows, curtains for the windows, and a piano for the living room.

Manufacturers found themselves with an ever expanding "national" market. And in the nationally distributed periodicals of the day they found a very efficient way to tell consumers about products manufactured for mass consumption.

The need to maintain "standards," and to relieve the dreary monotony of frontier life, was answered in part by the 19th century's periodicals. By 1830, as many as 1,000 magazines were being published in the United States with a circulation of about one million.

One of the most popular of the early publications was *Graham's Magazine,* with a circulation of 35,000. The *Atlantic Register* of Charleston, the *Atlantic Magazine* published in New York, and the *Illinois Monthly Magazine* were also widely read. Publication put out by various church groups gained enormous popularity during this period. (The church-related magazines had a "built-in" distribution system that must have been the envy of every publisher.) The *Theological Magazine* was the first, published in 1796. The *Christian Examiner, Missionary Herald,* and *Methodist Magazine* were very popular throughout the country.

Unlike the periodicals of Colonial days, the 18th century weeklies and monthlies received considerably more advertising support; therefore they tended to be much longer-lived. Even in the early part of the century, advertising was noticeably on the increase in the weeklies and monthly publications that carried as much as 8 pages of advertising per issue.

Godey's Lady's Book, first published in Philadelphia in 1830, carried articles of particular interest to the homemaker. The magazines became popular with the manufacturers of dress patterns who offered their fashions via mail order.

The kids weren't neglected either. The *Youth's Companion* was very popular among teenagers from mid-nineteenth century on.

It is interesting to note, that way back in 1784 when the first successful daily newspaper was established, the word "advertiser" was in its masthead—the *Pennsylvania-Packet and Daily Advertiser.*

The 1830s saw the great giants of journalism stride onstage with papers whose names are familiar to us today: James Gordon Bennett with the New York *Herald*, Benjamin Day's New York *Sun*, and bewhiskered Horace Greely with his *Tribune* (1841) and his advice for all young men to head "west."

The Philadelphia *Public Ledger*, The Baltimore *Sun*, the Boston Evening *Transcript*, and the New Orleans *Times-Picayune* were all born about this time. And as the country spread west, few communities were long without a weekly or daily newspaper.

The *Western Sun* was published in Vincennes, Indiana, in 1808. The Missouri *Gazette* appeared in the same year. The Green Bay, Wisconsin, *Intelligencer* in 1837; the Dubuque, Iowa, *Visitor* in 1836; the Sioux Falls, South Dakota, *Diamond* in 1858; and the *Weekly Arizonian* in 1859 showed that newly established Americans were able to keep themselves informed on local happenings and merchants had a means of advertising their wares.

The papers of this era differed from the papers of an earlier day. For one thing, they were cheaper. Most of them cost but a penny. They were a lot less "intellectual" too. Rather than political debates or special party pleading, they carried articles and news of events of particular interest to the ordinary citizen. In doing so they vastly widened the base of their coverage, and thus became a more attractive buy for the advertiser of consumer goods.

Almanacs, such as the *Farmer's and Mechanic's Almanac*, became a productive vehicle for advertising during this period. The patent-medicine manufacturers found these an effective media and frequently bought multiple pages to promote their products. Almanacs had an advantage over the weekly and monthly publications in that, because of their editorial content, they would be kept on hand and referred to throughout the entire year. By the 1840s, manufacturers were creating their own almanacs and giving them nationwide distribution. Their coverage would boggle the mind of a modern media director. The biggest in the field was probably Ayer's *American Almanac*, which devoted itself to proclaiming the advantages of Ayer's Cherry Pectoral. By the end of the century Ayer was spending $125,000 on printing alone. It is estimated that in one year their circulation may have *exceeded 25 million*, including editions in 21 languages. In many early-American homes the almanac was the most popular reading matter around—except for the family Bible.

Early toothpaste ad.

Incidentally, almanacs are far from dead. The famous *Farmer's Almanac,* founded in 1818 and published in Dublin, New Hampshire, is still going strong and has a circulation that tops 5 million.

The Advertising Broker

It was in this time of the growing attractiveness of periodicals to the national advertiser that the modern advertising agency had its beginning. Brokers purchased space from publications at wholesale rates, and resold space to the advertisers at whatever markup they could demand.

History records that George P. Rowell was one of the first of these
"brokers" to buy publication space in wholesale lots. Volney Palmer, of
Philadelphia, who maintained offices in Boston and New York, was
probably the first of the "brokers" to not only purchase space but aid his
clients in filling it with proper copy. As a forerunner of the present "15
percent system" of reimbursing the agency, Volney charged the newspapers 25 percent of the cost of the ad; the remaining 75 percent was paid
for by the client. Ralph M. Hower, in his *History of an Advertising
Agency,* points out the significance of these embryonic agencies of the
1800s.

> In a larger sense, however, the agency's chief service in this early
> period was to promote the general use of advertising, and thus to aid
> in discovering cheaper and more effective ways of marketing goods.[1]

This shift from "advertising broker" to "advertising agent" was very
important; the emphasis had been changed from working for the interests of the publication to serving the interests of the advertiser. Thus
today *all* of an advertising agency's services are directed toward helping
the advertiser achieve his marketing goals.

How Advertising Helped to Build a Nation

If you will look about you in your classroom or office, it is almost certain
that your glance will fall on someone whose forebears came to this
country because of the promises it held for them. If your name is Kelly,
Schmidt, or Swenson, you might only have to look back to your grandfather or great-grandfather to find the young man who in the 1800s
braved the North Atlantic in an immigrant ship, and turned his face
toward the land of hope and adventure.

Quite probably those hopes of a new life in a new land had been
stirred in your forefather's breast *by advertising.*

> Both natives and foreigners who peopled the Great Plains were at-
> tracted by the most effective advertising campaign ever to influence
> world migration. Steamship companies, anxious to reap a harvest of
> passenger fares, invested heavily in European newspaper space, mar-
> red the walls of half the continent with their posters, and provided
> free transportation for immigrants wishing to revisit the Old Country,
> provided they urged others to return. Western states maintained
> Immigration Bureaus in the East and Europe, where hired agents

---

[1]Ralph M. Hower, *History of an Advertising Agency* (Rev. ed. Cambridge, Mass., Harvard
University Press, 1949), p. 27.

scattered propaganda and urged farmers to migrate to the land of plenty. . . . When compared with the Far West pictured by these expert boosters, even the Garden of Eden seemed unattractive.[2]

But the land agents and the steamship companies were not the only ones to use advertising methods to bring the new colonizers to the ever expanding West. The great land-grant railroads, stretching their rails across the unmarked prairies, had a tremendous stake in the colonization of the land by thrifty hard-working farmers and mechanics from Europe. They had vast acreage for sale—the alternate sections (one square mile) along the right-of-way "granted" to them as part of the deal with the United States government for undertaking to build the road. More important, they needed men who would raise wheat and corn, hogs and cattle, and establish the cities from which these products would be shipped back East to profit the road's stockholders.

The Burlington and Union Pacific each spent a million dollars in advertising.[3] This was a prodigious sum, when you realize that even as late as the 1920s only a handful of national advertisers even dreamed of an advertising budget of that size.

In Hamburg, Cobh, and Rotterdam, the railroads invested their advertising dollars in newspaper ads, posters, and brochures. They promised the prospective settler a land whose fields "*have yielded over 30 bushels of grain per acre, and many fields of corn over 70.*"[4]

Among the advertising techniques employed, at least one would be quite familiar to the modern copywriter. It was the "testimonial," in which immigrants told of their newfound wealth reaped from the fertile fields of the American West.

The railroads had something for the ladies too. A Burlington brochure promised: "*When a daughter of the East is once beyond the Missouri, she rarely recrosses it except on a bridal tour.*"[5]

Almost 14 million new Americans came to people the West in the years after the Civil War. Up to that time and well into the 20th century this combined promotional effort of land companies, steamship lines, and railroads, represented the greatest advertising effort the commercial world has ever known. As the historian, Billington, has pointed out: "No region in the history of the frontier benefited as did the Great Plains from induced colonization."[6]

---

[2]Ray Allen Billington, *Westward Expansion: A History of the American Frontier* (3rd ed. New York: The MacMillan Co., 1947), p. 706.

[3]Billington, *Westward Expansion*, p. 707.

[4]Billington, *Westward Expansion*, p. 707.

[5]Billington, *Westward Expansion*, p. 708.

[6]Billington, *Westward Expansion*, p. 708.

In the Days of "Anything Goes"

To understand what happened to advertising in the latter part of the 19th century, it is necessary for you to understand some things that were happening in America. By the 1880s, this country was bursting with strength and vitality. The last frontier had been breached. Great rail systems bound our country together from coast to coast. Cities flourished with successful mercantile operations. The ingenuity of our inventors seemed to know no end. In printing, communications, manufacturing processes, transportation, and agriculture, our "tinkerers" had far outstripped the rest of the world. In Bridgeport, Connecticut, a penniless mechanic named Elias Howe had discovered how to make a machine sew continuous stitches, and became a millionaire overnight.

Our natural resources in coal, oil, and timber had barely been tapped. In a day of untaxed profits, the new industrial millionaires could hardly discover new ways to spend their fortunes. They built town houses on Fifth Avenue in New York, and "cottages" at Newport, Rhode Island. They built yachts, and bought jewels and paintings. They also established libraries, founded universities, endowed hospitals, and built museums.

But it was also a time of terrible contrasts, when millions of American men, women, and children worked ten- and twelve-hour days for tragically low wages in mills, mines, and sweatshops. It was a time when hundreds of thousands of people went to bed each night literally "aching all over."

It was an age of innocence as well as of ignorance. Illiteracy handicapped up to 30 percent of the people. Many sizable communities had no high schools. If they went to school, most boys and girls received only the basics of "readin', writin', and 'rithmetic" before leaving for a farm or an apprenticeship. In many ways we were a very simple people. Getting a letter through the mail was an exciting event. A telegram could only mean a death in the family. Many people lifted a telephone receiver from its hook with fear and trembling (they were afraid of being electrocuted). The county fair and visiting tent show were exciting highlights of the year.

Into this predominantly rural, hard-working, unsophisticated America a new kind of millionaire was born—the "Patent Medicine King." The phenomenon of the success of patent medicines and the effectiveness of their advertising in the latter part of the 19th century defied belief. Great sums were spent in promoting medicines and devices. Even before mid-century, one advertiser was spending $100,000 a year. Toward the end of the century, million-dollar budgets were not uncommon to promote such famous nostrums as Lydia E. Pinkham's Vegetable Compound, Scott's Emulsion, and Pink Pills for Pale People. Just prior to the Civil War the value of proprietary medicine produced in this country was set at $3.5 million, according to the United States

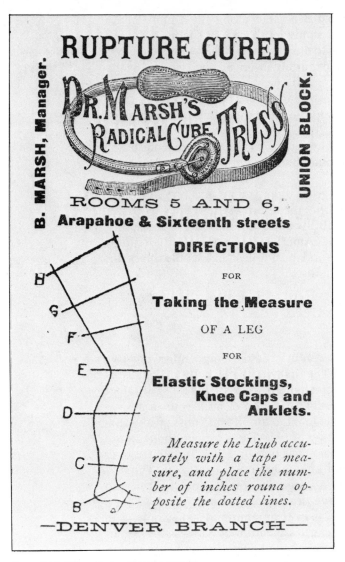

"Why Wear a Truss?" became one of the classic lines in early advertising. Selling trusses, like patent medicine, became big business. Apparently lots of people had ruptures but seldom had surgery.

Census figures. By the end of the century this amount had multiplied *twenty times.*

The industry, which had the largest advertising budgets of the day, left no stone unturned to find places to advertise its wares. In addition to newspapers, church publications, farm papers, almanacs, and periodicals, they brought a new dimension to outdoor advertising. If there was an empty space on a wall, fence, building, boat or a wagon, they filled it. There was hardly a barn or a barren hillside that remained unused. Men with paint, pots, and brushes, roamed the countryside. The Palisades above West Point, on the Hudson River, carried slogans for pills

and hair restorers, as did almost every cut along the Union Pacific
right-of-way. They mounted the sandwich board, put men on horses,
and hired sign carriers by squads to march single file down the avenues.
Handbills, song sheets, and theater curtains were utilized, as well as that
sensational crowd-gatherer, the "medicine show"—first used as a promotional device by the Kickapoo Indian Medicine Company.

Today's advertising men look at the patent-medicine advertising of
the 19th century and smile ruefully. Claims of cures for "insanity and
consumption," to say nothing of every other ache, pain, discomfort, or
mental disorder to which the human body might fall heir, were utterly
appalling.

The young giant—America—grew older, more sensible, and more
mature. The government, the public, the reformers, and the advertising
men fought to bring new responsibility and accountability to marketing.
New organizations, such as the American Advertising Federation,
shaped the ground rules and moral principles that would mark the
character of 20th century advertising.

Advertising Grows Up

In the first decades of the 20th century, advertising underwent two
marked and significant changes. The first was the recognition by advertising of its responsibilities to society and business. This recognition of
responsibility was evidenced by the formation of numerous organizations whose goals were the improvement in the effectiveness of advertising and control over its taste and honesty. What is known today as the
Association of National Advertisers, was born in 1910. Today its membership includes most of the well-known national advertisers. The Better Business Bureau stems from an organization originally formed to
guard against unfair and deceptive promotional efforts.

Some of the advertising agencies in your community may belong to
organizations such as the American Association of Advertising Agencies (the 4 A's) or the American Advertising Federation whose membership includes agencies in practically every city of any size in America.
Both organizations are dedicated to helping their members provide
better service for their clients, and greater efficiency for themselves.

Of great importance, too, was the development of a trade press within
the business. *Printer's Ink*, founded in 1911, and later *Advertising Age*,
for years kept advertisers aware of developments and changes in their
business. In addition, they lent their powerful voices in helping to
maintain standards of good taste and honesty. *Ad Age* continues to do
so.

The second significant development in the early 1900s was the
emergence of the national and regional advertising agency in much the
same form as we recognize it today. As you remember, very early in the
history of American advertising there came that memorable moment

when a manufacturer, having contracted for space from a "broker,"
asked for help in putting something effective in that space. Today
advertising agencies are tightly geared to do just that—to provide the
advertiser with all those services that will enable him to invest his
advertising dollars most effectively. In Chapter 4 we will examine the
modern advertising agency and see how it is departmentalized to
achieve this goal of maximum effectiveness in helping the client sell a
product.

The New Face of Advertising

The third development in modern advertising, and perhaps the most
interesting and significant of all, occurred in the first decades of the
century when a new *breed* of ad men emerged. Their ingenuity, imagination, and restless curiosity literally changed the face of advertising. It
changed from something that was basically a "notice" or a wild unsup-
portable boast, or simply an attention-caller, to a logical, carefully
thought-out *selling tool* fully integrated with the marketing strategy.

Edward Jordan, John Orr Young, Milton Feasley, Theodore Mc-
Manus, and a host of others dared to write well and differently, to test, to
prod, to examine, and to ask themselves time after time, "Why did it
work?" There is hardly a printed ad or television commercial you would
see today that does not bear the imprint of the work and the ideas of these
men. *This* was where advertising came of age, where it grew up from a
loudmouthed bumpkin to a serious, confident, well-informed young
"businessman." We are going to examine in detail just how the work of
those early ad men helped to make advertising an effective *selling
tool*—a hard-working partner in the "marketing mix."

"Marketing mix." That's what we come to next. . . .

WHERE YOU ARE

1. You have seen how advertising, much of it in forms we recognize
today, has been with us for many centuries.

2. You have learned how the advent of printing and the publication of
newspapers and periodicals gave important impetus to advertising.

3. You are familiar with the remarkable spread of journalism as part of
the growth of this country, and how advertising helped to make this
possible.

4. You have discovered the important role played by advertising in the westward expansion of America.

5. You have seen advertising in its "gaudy" era, and have identified some of the forces that brought it about.

6. You have made first acquaintance with the "new breed" of ad men and women who took the first steps in creating modern advertising.

QUESTIONS FOR CLASS DISCUSSION

1. What relationship do you see between today's so-called "drug culture" and the popularity of patent medicines in the 1800s?

2. As late as the 1870s there may have been *ten times* as many bootmakers and cobblers in your town as there are today. How do you account for this?

3. Many of the most popular products of the early 1900s are no longer with us; neither are some of the most popular publications. What is your explanation for this?

4. Government regulations, "consumerism," environmentalists, and modern "muckrackers"—are they good or bad for business? Take either side, and defend it.

5. In what ways would you say that advertising is a reflection of the society in which it exists, in the 1700s, the late 1800s, and today?

6. Can you cite an instance in modern times as to how advertising has helped to alter the course of history?

SOMETHING FOR YOU TO DO

Many people save copies of such magazines as *National Geographic.* Your public library also might have microfilmed material. See if you can find something from the pre-1925 period. Go through it carefully and see just how much advertising has changed in the past half-century.

Advertising Agent. Acts in behalf of advertiser, buying space and preparing advertising.

Advertising Broker. Buys up space from publications and resells it to advertisers.

Almanacs. Annual publications containing information on stars, weather, etc. Popular with farm families.

American Association of Advertising Agencies (4A's). Association of the biggest American advertising agencies. Many regional agencies belong to American Advertising Federation.

Association of National Advertisers. Trade group, leading national advertisers.

Bills and Posters. Originally printed forms pasted up on any available spot.

Broadcast Advertising. Radio and TV.

Church Publications. Magazines and papers published by church groups and distributed to their members. Important in early days of advertising.

Farm Papers. Publications edited for farmers and farm families.

Fifteen Percent System. Method of agency reimbursement. Agency retains 15 percent of media billing.

Handbills. Printed advertising material. Sometimes posted, sometimes given out by hand.

Marketing Mix. Combination of elements, common to the movement of goods, that affects their ultimate sales success.

Medicine Show. Traveling entertainment designed to draw a crowd to whom a product could be sold—usually a "cure-all," hence "medicine."

Outdoor Advertising. Generally used today to refer to billboards and spectaculars.

Point-of-Purchase Advertising. Advertising and promotion pieces in stores, often on shelves and counters.

Sandwich Board. Advertising posters suspended from the carrier's shoulders, front and back. A variation was a parade of posters carried on poles.

Siquis. Original name for posters. Now out of use.

Testimonial. A statement by someone attesting to the value or the efficiency of a product.

Trade Press. Publications edited for a particular business, profession, or trade.

SELECTED READINGS

Burchey, Stuart, (ed.). *The Colonial Merchant* (New York: Harcourt, Brace & World, Inc., 1966). This book will give you a good insight into Colonial Mercantilism. Ben Franklin's advice to a young tradesman (p. 113) is as applicable today as it was then.

Hindley, Diana and Geoffrey. *Advertising in Victorian England, 1837–1901* (London: Weyland Publishers, Ltd., 1972). This delightful book will give you a very good idea of what advertising looked like both in England and America at the end of the 19th century. I think you'll be amazed at how *pervasive* advertising was in those days. It was everywhere—including the sides of one of the pyramids!

Presbery, Frank. *History and Development of Advertising* (New York: Doubleday and Company, Inc., 1929). A standard and highly regarded work on the subject.

Rowsone, Frank. *They Laughed When I Sat Down* (New York: Mc-Graw-Hill Book Company, 1959). I hope you can locate this book in your college or public library because we will be referring to it again. Here you will discover some of the ads written by the men and women who have helped to usher in the era of modern advertising. Listerine, Jordon, and International Correspondence Schools—these are the old "classics" to which all ad people owe a debt. Later we'll be talking much, much more about them.

Sinclair, Upton. *The Jungle* (New York: Doubleday, Page, and Company, 1906). Journalists and novelists known as "Muckrakers"—the phrase was coined by Theodore Roosevelt—played an important part in the early 1900s in helping to bring about business reforms. Big mass circulation magazines such as McClure's and Collier's supported and encouraged them. Other writers in this category were Ida Tarbell, Ray Stannard Baker, and Samuel Hopkins Adams.

Sutphen, Dick. *The Mad Old Ads* (New York: McGraw-Hill Book Company, 1966). For a detailed look at some of the unrestrained advertising that ran in the latter part of the 19th century.

Young, James Harvey. *The Toadstool Millionaires* (Princeton, New Jersey: Princeton University Press, 1961). The story of the "Patent Medicine Era," and the men who made it.

Billington, Ray Allen. *Westward Expansion: A History of the American Frontier* (New York: The MacMillan Company, 1967). American history in terms of the men and women who opened the frontiers: The colonists, fur trappers, farmers, cattlemen, and all the rest. This is a fresh and exciting way to learn how the United States grew and developed. See also Bernard DeVoto's *The Course of Empire* and *Across the Wide Missouri.*

Hower, Ralph M. *History of an Advertising Agency (Rev. ed.* Cambridge, Mass., Harvard University Press, 1949). Fascinating story of N. W. Ayer & Sons, one of America's first and greatest advertising agencies.

chapter two

The Marketplace
and
What Happens in It

In this chapter we go into the marketplace itself. You will learn that all markets can be divided into "segments," and you will learn how to draw a profile of a marketing segment.

We will look at the major forces affecting a product on its journey from producer to consumer. And you will see how advertising always plays a role—major or minor—in the ultimate success or failure of the product. We'll conclude with two real-life stories of marketing ventures which show these forces in action.   **23**

There are as many definitions of marketing as there are authors of textbooks on the subject. Let us look at a couple of them:

Still and Cundiff call it "the business process by which products are matched with markets and through which transfers of ownership are affected."[1]

William J. Stanton has what he feels is a more precise definition than most. He calls marketing "a total system of interacting business activities designed to plan, price, promote, and distribute want-satisfying products and services to present and potential customers."[2] Note that he gives you a neat little handle in "plan, price, promote, and distribute."

The American Marketing Association defines marketing as being made up of "the performance of business activities that direct the flow of goods and services from producer to consumer or user."

This is a nice, simple explanation of what happens. Let us take a look at it to see if we can fix it in our minds in relation to the businesses that go on in your town. The key phrases are: "from producer to consumer," and "the flow of goods."

---

[1]Richard R. Still and Edward W. Cundiff, *Essentials of Marketing* (2nd ed. Englewood Cliffs, N.J.: Prentice-Hall, Inc. 1972), p. 3.

[2]William J. Stanton, *Fundamentals of Marketing* (4th ed. New York: McGraw-Hill, Inc., 1975), p. 5.

"From producer to consumer" means from the time the delivery express people pick up a carton of slacks from the manufacturer's warehouse loading platform, to the moment the salesclerk in your men's wear store hands you your wrapped slacks and your sales slip. At that moment, the product has completed its journey. (For simplicity's sake, we are going to leave "services" out of this discussion.)

You will notice that the second descriptive phrase speaks of the "flow"—the "flow of goods." It is as though someone had put your package in a fast-flowing stream that would carry it to the place where you were waiting. On the way a number of things might have happened to your package. It could have become snagged on a sandbar, or hung up on a dead branch. A rain could have swollen the stream and speeded up the trip of the package. A canal could have diverted it, or a waterfall destroyed it. A lot of things, both good and bad, could have happened as your package "flowed" along to you.

This is the fate of *every* product as it makes its way from the manufacturer's loading platform to its final destination—into your hands. A great many things *happen* to it.

I know a marketing person who sat down at lunch with some friends one day and listed some thirty-five "things that can happen." But for our purposes, we will examine only the major ones:

1. The quality, appearance, and performance of the product.
2. How much it costs.
3. Where you can buy it.
4. The promotional efforts, including advertising, that help to sell it.

Advertising, as you see, is one of the things that happen. These forces all work together. Sometimes some work harder than others. Advertising—and promotion—help them work a little *better*. And *always* these different factors in the "marketing mix" exert *different degrees of influence*. Sometimes advertising can be very important. For another product, distribution may be the vital force.

We will examine the four major factors in the marketing mix. But before we do, let's inspect the place where all these "happenings" go on—the market itself.

The Market and Its Parts

In the old days the "marketplace" was that part of the village where people came to make their purchases. Perhaps in your community, as in mine, there is a Farmers Market where the farmers come from miles around to rent display space for their products.

But as defined by the professional marketing person, a "market" is more than a place: it is also people—consumers with their particular needs, wants, and desires. You might say that the "market" for the person who sells fresh eggs in the Farmers Market is all the people who eat eggs and are within traveling distance of the sales booth.

In your town, the hardware-store's market is practically everyone (but particularly homeowners, and renters, who live closer to the store than they do to the hardware store in the next town).

On a national basis, the denture adhesive manufacturer has a market consisting of everyone who wears false teeth.

Market Segmentation

You should firmly fix in your mind the idea of "market segmentation." It is basic to all marketing plans, and therefore to all advertising plans. If you get it wrong, it can cost you a great deal of money. That is why we return to it time after time in this book.

In terms of what you have to sell, it means that some people in your area are much more likely to buy what you have for sale than certain other people. Obviously it is to your benefit to know who these people are, and where you can find them.

If you ask some of the merchants in your town to describe for you the kind of customers they wish all their customers were, they will happily tell you. The druggist, the butcher, the owner of a gift shop, all have their favorite customers. What emerges from their descriptions is a picture—a *profile* of an ideal customer.

The Consumer Profile

In describing a favorite customer, your storekeepers would describe a *segment* of your town's population. Quite likely these merchants would use some of the same measurements for picturing their favorite customers as are commonly used by marketing and advertising people.

In addition to their geographic location, consumers have the following characteristics which can be used to describe them: age, sex, income, education, ethnic background, marital status, religion, and occupation. Now let's take a look at these basic consumer characteristics; let's see how they might affect you as a young executive.

The Number of People

We have about 210 million people in the United States at the present time, and our population is still growing. It is also changing, shifting, and moving about. Some of our states, for example Florida and Arizona, have had dramatic increases in population in the last 10 years. In some areas there has been a marked movement from rural to city living.

These geographic shifts of people are important to you as a local merchant. Look at your own community. Perhaps the fine old houses of

50 and 70 years ago are now in the middle of the city, and great segments of your population reside in suburban communities 15 or 20 miles from the downtown shopping area.

The Money They Have to Spend

Of course one of the most important things for a merchant to know about his potential customers is the amount of money they can be expected to spend. We have statistical sources that will give you these figures on a statewide, county, and larger community basis. Money often moves with people. In my town, a series of high-priced condominiums were recently built and sold. This made it possible for one of the planners to build a small shopping center that features stores selling merchandise in high-price categories.

Men vs. Women

Probably there is no statistically significant difference between the number of men and women in your community. Yet at certain times of day, and in certain places, one group may far outnumber the other. For example, operators of fast-food takeout stores have discovered that one of their best locations is on the homeward route of working wives.

Young Folks and Old Folks

About 20 percent of our population is under 25 years of age, a fact the soft-drink manufacturers never miss. And our population of seniors over 65 is also increasing. You can't overlook this when you set up business. St. Petersburg, Florida, which has attracted many retired persons, boasts a population with the highest per capita ownership of common stocks in the United States. But I think you'd look very carefully before you opened a high-fashion dress shop in such a city.

Education and Occupation

Education and occupation usually go hand in hand, and may be recognized as the difference between the blue-collar worker and the white-collar worker. However, don't be misled into equating these two categories with high and low spendable income. Many blue-collar workers make more money than office workers; and there are certain kinds of products for which one class of workers will consistently outspend the other.

Ethnic Background

If you have something to sell that is more appealing to a Black than to a White, or to an Arabic-speaking person than to a Cajun from the bayou country of Louisiana, then race or place of national origin is important to you. As you have seen in Chapter 1, patterns of immigration have given many parts of our country a character of their own. I know a city where Majorcans (from the island of Majorca, off Spain, in the Mediterranean) represent an important segment of the population; and in another city the Lebanese are a well-defined minority. If you walk the streets of New Bedford, Massachusetts, you can hear Portuguese spoken by the descendants of men who once manned whaling ships and fishing trawlers.

Religion

Religion is a very easy segment to identify in your town. Simply look in the Yellow Pages of your phone book and count the number of churches belonging to the various denominations. Ordinarily this yardstick of profile measurement is not so important—unless you happen to operate a store selling books, films, and articles of a religious nature. It is also important if you are doing business with the Mormons in Salt Lake City, or with the Amish in southeastern Pennsylvania; then it can become very important.

Marital Status

Married vs. unmarrieds tends to even out nationally; but locally you can have wide variations. A college-dominated community, for example, would contain a high percentage of unmarrieds.

Taste and Style

Taste and style are factors that sometimes drive advertisers up a wall because they are so unpredictable. A few years ago no one dreamed that young men would be wearing the styles of shoes that they prefer today. Young women will tell you that the position of next year's hemline is anyone's guess. There are style "lags" too. What may be very popular in one city, won't catch on quite so soon in another city.

Don't Move Without a Profile

Whether you are a retailer or a manufacturer or someone about to embark on a business career, it is vital to firmly fix in mind the market profile of

your target customer *before any marketing move is made.* Later on in
this chapter we will examine a case history of some people who didn't do
this quite right, and what happened to them.

How to Get Market Information

There are a number of convenient places where you can get the information that will help you to draw a broad consumer profile. The most basic
of these is the reports published by the Bureau of Census of the United
States Department of Commerce. For a few dollars, you can buy the
reports on a state-wide basis. In "Numbers of Inhabitants," and "General
Social and Economic Characteristics," you can find the figures that will
help you draw a market profile.

The research director at your chamber of commerce can also be
helpful when you need facts not covered by the census figures, and
should be able to supply you with all kinds of facts related to your
community.

The person at the information desk at your public library is also a
good source. Most libraries have a business section in which a wide
variety of information is available.

Certain departments of City Hall can give you information on population trends, real estate purchases, automobile registration, and information from the tax rolls.

One of the very best places for market segmentation data is your local
media: newspapers, radio, and TV stations. These people are in the
business of selling market segments, and know their particular market
segment like the backs of their hands. When we come to the chapter on
"Media," we will go into some detail concerning the many interesting
facts compiled by publications and broadcasters about their audiences.

This is only the beginning. When we get to the important subject of
"Research," you will see many other ways you can measure the characteristics of a market.

The "Happenings"

We began this chapter by pointing out to you that some important things
can happen to a product as it "flows" from the maker to the buyer.

Because these "happenings" do not take place in a vacuum but in a
marketplace, we have defined that market and seen how it always
divides itself into segments with individual characteristics.

Now you are ready to get better acquainted with some of the things
that occur as the product flows along on its way to the consumer. Keep in

mind that this "stream" flows through a land peopled by buyers, some of **31**
whose faces are familiar to you.   The Life
and Liveliness
of the Product

The "Universality" of the Marketing Mix

Every product, no matter how popular or obscure, is affected by the
factors in the marketing mix; none is overlooked, and none is excused.
Whether it is a package of pins or an imported motor car, its destiny will
be governed by *the way it has been manufactured or designed, the price
tag it wears, the place where you can buy it, and the promotional efforts
put behind it.*

Although these marketing factors are always present, their strength
and direction are variable. For example, for years Hershey Chocolate got
along with practically no advertising at all. Sometimes there will be
powerful easy-to-identify factors, such as Polaroid's radical new design
and engineering. Very often a product will benefit from a combination
of factors, such as the Volkswagon whose price and design both appealed to the public. But in *every* case it is the marketer's job to make
sure that *all* the factors are just as right as they can possibly be.

As a businessperson, you are not always sure how the wind is
blowing—that is, which marketing factor is aiding the growth of your
product and which is impeding it. Sometimes it will seem to you as if
you were trying to solve an equation where all the factors are "x's." We
will observe, in fact, that manufacturers and their advertising agencies
spend great sums of money trying to discover what factors are exerting
which forces.

Now let's get to know these forces a little better so that you will be able
to look for them and identify them, and never make the dangerous error
of overlooking one when you prepare to go out and do battle in the
marketplace.

The Life and Liveliness of the Product

Every product has a "life." Some products, like some famous historical
figures, seem to go on forever. Others, like yesterday's rock 'n roll star,
have a meteoric rise to a brief period of fame and then disappear.

No one is more conscious of this "life" of a product than the people
who make it. They know that products are born, grow up, gain maturity,
and then die. Since neither the manufacturer nor the retailer is very
happy with an aging and feeble product, and since the consumer is
always attracted to the product that has life and liveliness, it is very
important for you to know just where *your* product stands.

There are two things that manufacturers can do to help themselves and their products: they can give birth to *new* products, and they can keep their old ones strong and healthy.

New Product Development

One way a manufacturer can protect himself is to introduce new and better products into his line. This is done in several ways. Major manufacturers, such as General Electric and DuPont, have special departments devoted only to research and development. Many marketing people today are of the opinion that not enough manufacturers rely on consistent, well-organized research and development. It is from these departments, where employees tinker, design, and make models every working day, that there may finally emerge a new product that will sweep the market.

You have seen many of these products born of the ingenuity of the research and development people: kitchen disposal units, television sets, office copying machines, electric blankets, home hair dryers, and many others.

You can imagine what a splash it makes in the marketing stream when suddenly someone comes up with a new product that brings forth fresh benefits to the consumer.

Of course not all new products are the result of efforts made by research and development. Employees often contribute new suggestions for new products. Inventions are continually being patented. Sometimes someone just has a crazy idea, such as the Hula Hoop, and a new product is born.

Product Improvement

Just look around you and see the changes and improvements that are continually taking place in the most commonplace articles. One of my favorites is the can opener. In the kitchen drawer at home you may find one of the old ones that cost but a few cents at the hardware store. It took considerable muscle to use, and left a very jagged edge around the top of the can. Then came the kind that operated with a turn-key. These were easier to work, and left a smoother edge. Later came the wall model with a handle to turn; it gave excellent leverage, and speeded up the cutting while making it easier to operate. Today, if you go to your appliance store, you will find beautiful electric models that require practically no effort on the part of the homemaker, and even hold the top of the can in their magnetized clutch after it has been cut. It's hard to imagine where the can opener can go from here. (But don't worry, someone may find a way to make it still better.)

Look at your refrigerator; it was born a completely new kind of product. No need to have an iceman come and fill it with ice twice a week. Since then, hardly a year has gone by without improvements: ice trays, meat and vegetable sections, defrosters, and decorator colors.

What you have seen is the first factor in the "marketing mix," the Product—when it is born, how it grows and improves, and what it will be able to do for people; all these things are going to influence it on its long journey from manufacturer to consumer.

How Much It Costs

If you were a seller of oriental rugs, hawking your wares on the streets of some Middle-East city, price would never be far from your mind. In fact, you and your brother rug salesmen have acquired the reputation of being among the finest price manipulators in the world. (A friend who has lived in Morocco once told me that the street vendors there have a different starting price based on whether you speak Arabic, French, or English.)

Price has sometimes been described as "what you can get for it," but it is not quite so simple. If you are a retailer or a manufacturer, you are sure to be faced with price decisions. In arriving at your price decision, you will have to take a number of things into consideration.

First, how shall you price the product in order to make a fair profit? Here you will have to think about your overhead, or your cost of doing business, or the wholesale price. What you finally decide will affect your *profit margin*, and it has to be big enough so that you will not be working for anyone but yourself.

In addition, you certainly will want to look around you to see what your competitors are doing. How do they price products similar to yours?

You may want to take into consideration the *amount* of this product you will sell, and the rate at which it will sell. As the volume goes up, you may be able to reduce your margin of profit.

You may wish to reflect on the *prestige* of your product by giving it an "uptown" price. To put it another way, prestige costs money. If we are looking for prestige in Scotch whiskey or in a car, then that's what we have to pay for.

Price can attract people to your product. By drastically lowering the price on a certain item, you may fill your store with happy shoppers.

You can use price to *segment* your market. Do you wish to deal only with the well-off, as in an exclusive women's dress shop? Or, are you after the mass market, as at Penney's or Sears? And by having products in several price lines, you can make sure that no one walks away from your store empty-handed.

You can put on promotions and special sales with price, and by setting prices at the right levels you can "skim the cream" off the market for a new and interesting product.

You must face the price decision. How you make this decision will certainly have much bearing on the success or failure of your product.

Earlier we spoke of a "stream" on which your product flowed from manufacturer or retailer, and how a number of things can "happen" along the way. But streams themselves can vary to a great degree. That is, the *methods employed* to get the product to market can differ—and this

Your choice of the right method of distribution will be very important, and to a great extent will be governed by what you sell and to whom you sell it. The people who make shaving cream have very different distribution problems from the people who grow tomatoes.

The manufacturer who is to get a product out into the "flow" of the marketplace must consider several factors:

Where he will build or lease storage facilities, and what capacity will be needed; the size of inventory that will be carried in each storage area; how the product will be transported, and the number of hours it will be on the road. A materials handling system will also have to be set up; for example, conveyor belts.

A policy regarding the size of orders must be determined—mail orders may have to be "handled" by hand, thus increasing costs.

Also a fast, efficient system for processing orders will have to be installed. Now, let's take a look at this from a practical standpoint to see how it works.

I know of a company here in Florida that deals in structural steel shapes, primarily sold to the construction industry. Most of their product is shipped to them from abroad—Japan and Belgium, and is unloaded at their docks at either Tampa or Port Everglades. This company has warehouses at these two ports, plus several others placed strategically around the state. The steel is transported to these warehouses by company truck. There is a great variety of steel forms in their inventory and it is carefully controlled by computer. The company is prepared to deliver steel shapes in its own trucks, but more frequently the customers' trucks pick up the shapes at the warehouse.

Probably the strongest selling point this company has is the completeness and availability of its inventory and the speed with which it can process an order and get the steel to the customers' construction site.

Look around you. There is a wholesale produce merchant in your town who receives fruits and vegetables via ship, train, and truck. He probably redistributes his products to local hotels, restaurants, and markets by means of his own trucks and those of his customers.

Middlemen. Throughout the country there is a vast number of other businesses essential in making goods flow from manufacturer to consumer. Generally they are termed "middlemen." There may be as many as 200 thousand merchant wholesalers in the United States making billions in sales each year, according to the 1967 *Census of Business.*

We must distinguish a *merchant wholesaler* from an *agent middleman.*

Merchant wholesalers. The merchant wholesaler takes title—that is, he buys the goods he sells to someone else; thus he has the full range of storing, handling, and inventory problems. Here are some *merchant wholesalers:*

General wholesaler—carries a wide variety of nonperishable merchandise. This is of less importance today.

Single-line wholesaler—carries products in a single line, such as foods or drug items.

Truck jobber—sells from a truck, and generally you can see him distributing dairy products or soft drinks.

Cash-and-carry wholesaler—you bring your own truck, pay for the goods and take them away. Your town probably has such a wholesaler who deals with the building trades.

Rack jobbers—usually these set up and serve a store within a store. The rack of newspapers and periodicals in your drugstore is very likely served by a rack jobber.

The agent middleman—on the other hand, does not take title to the goods. He usually represents either the buyer or the seller, sometimes both, and is paid a commission on the deal.

Here are some of the agent middlemen:

Brokers. Usually they don't actually handle the goods involved, but act as an intermediary in the transaction. So-called *desk jobbers* use their phones to shop around until they can put buyer and seller together for a deal.

Commission house. These exercise considerably more control over the merchandise than does the broker. Though they don't take title, they perform many functions of the merchant wholesaler.

Manufacturer's agent. Numerous smaller industrial firms use these agents. They represent a particular firm under contract in a specific territory. The manufacturer's agent will handle several "lines," but never competing ones. In effect they are free-lance salespersons paid a commission on sales, but representing a number of companies.

Resident buyers. You'll frequently hear of these in connection with the retail clothing trade. They often specialize. A department-store buyer might call on the services of a resident buyer who specializes in handbags, for instance. Be careful: a *resident buying office* is a store's own buying facility in the market. Chain stores often maintain *central buying offices.*

Export-import agents. If you live in a port city you will find plenty of agents who can help you sell your furniture in Guatemala, or aid you in establishing a market for Chilean wines in the United States.

These are but a few of the channels of distribution. Whether your product is to be sold in only one select expensive men's shop in major cities, or in every crossroad store, juke joint, pool hall and filling station in rural America, part of your market decision must be, "where will we sell it," and "how will we get it there?"

Promoting the Product

As a manufacturer you can take great pains designing a product, price it most attractively, deliver it to the right places most efficiently, and then sit back and forget about it.

As a retailer you can make careful selections to meet your customers' tastes, price them attractively, put them out on the counter and on the display racks, and forget about them.

You'd be surprised how often this occurs. As the old marketing slogan goes, "Nothing happens until someone sells something." Although you may have a very attractive product, properly distributed, priced and packaged right and on sale in all the right places, nothing really good happens till someone makes an effort to sell it.

That's what promotion is—an effort to sell—*any kind of effort.* It's the extra shove it takes to get things going. It's a full-page ad in your morning paper, or a cheery "hello" from a salesperson. It's a pyramid of bottles you nearly fall over as you enter the drugstore. It's the reminder that if you need a new shirt you probably need a new necktie to go with it. It's a chef in the kitchenwares department teaching you how to prepare an omelet. It's twelve 30-second spots a week on your TV station. It's a big tall guy signing a basketball for your kid in a sporting goods store. It's a billboard along the highway, a jingle sung on your radio, and a magazine ad that catches your eye. It's the extra shove that *makes things happen.*

And that's us—advertising. This is where we came in, remember? These are the main factors in the marketing mix. Advertising, as we shall see, is one, but they all work together. Sometimes some work harder than others. But advertising, and promotion, help them work a little better.

Two Case Histories

All the things we have been talking about happen every day out there in the marketplace. It's for real! So I thought that you might enjoy a couple of adventures in marketing. One is a sad story, and the other has a happy ending. Let's first take the happy one.

An automobile manufacturer had been caught in the squeeze of the
public's changing tastes in motor cars. The management had been forced to recognize that for a sizable segment of the market, the large-size luxury models were out—the kind they made.

They discovered—and it was a costly lesson—that the public was not ready to accept a car that was a stripped-down version of their large model. They simply hadn't paid enough attention to the public's true tastes.

Close investigation revealed that today's automobile buyer wants "class" in any size car. The buyer expects a *fine* car, even though it is small.

Armed with this information, the manufacturer went back to the drawing board and designed a smaller, economy-size car that was competitive in its price range. This model included many luxury touches that the public had come to associate with the name of this car maker. True, some of these touches had to be paid for as "extras" in the lowest-price line. But at least the customer had a chance to satisfy his taste for "class" in a small economy car. The line was a sales success.[3]

One of America's largest food manufacturers and distributors decided to start a new division that would deal in fine specialty foods. What statistics they could gather led them to believe that the country had the spendable income and had developed the tastes necessary to move gourmet-type foods in profitable volume.

Their decision to go ahead with the experiment in the new line was made despite certain warning signals: market estimates varied widely; many authoritative sources could not agree on basic facts; the business was so fragmented by small businesses that solid information was often difficult to come by.

Based on such information as they could gather, and probably indulging in some wishful thinking, the company arrived at a market profile of its primary potential customer: well-to-do, middle-aged, social, big entertainer, sophisticated.

The company's subsequent promotion, packaging, pricing, and distribution were all based on the assumption that now they had the right profile. They were wrong.

After about two years, the gourmet foods division was closed down at a tremendous loss to the company. All this happened some years ago. Maybe the country wasn't quite ready for gourmet foods that can be found in many supermarkets today. But today, as then, the profile is not what they thought it was. The country is full of young people, not particularly affluent, who have traveled or "eaten out" and are familiar with gourmet cooking. Many of them enjoy cooking and experimenting with new recipes. They find that serving a gourmet meal is an economical and enjoyable way to entertain another couple or two at home.

---

[3]Adapted from "The Problem of Evaluating Consumer Preference" in Edwin C. Greif, *Basic Problems in Marketing Management* (Belmont, Cal.: Wadsworth Publishing Company, Inc., 1968), p. 51.

Afterward, the chairman of the company was said to have remarked to a lady who stocked her yacht with his gourmet foods, "That was the trouble—not enough people with yachts!"[4]

So even these big boys had to discover, like the proprietor of the abandoned restaurant down the street, that you can't get your market profile wrong and survive. In the end it all comes down to people and how they feel about us, our product, and what we can do for them. *They are the buyers; it is for them that we design products, price them attractively, distribute them conveniently, and promote them aggressively.*

That is what we are going to talk about next—*Everybody*, the Consumer.

WHERE YOU ARE

---

1.   You can define marketing.

2.   You can recognize the eight major criteria we use in constructing a "market profile," and the sources you can consult for market information to be used in constructing the profile.

3.   You understand what a product's "market" is, and how that market can be segmented.

4.   You know what a "market mix" is, and can identify its four major components.

5.   You understand that advertising is a normal ingredient of the "marketing mix" and that it plays varying roles of importance in the mix, depending on the character of the product or service.

QUESTIONS FOR CLASS DISCUSSION

---

1.   Forty years ago marketing wasn't taught in most colleges, and few books existed on the subject. The French didn't have a word of their own

---

[4]Adapted from "Epicurian Delights" in Thomas L. Berg, *Mismarketing* (New York: Doubleday and Company, Inc., 1970), p. 46.

for it. But after the 1930s, businessmen became much more interested in marketing. Why do you think this happened?

2.   Although there are plenty of wealthy people in my community, there are few Rolls Royces. A few hundred miles away there is a community with lots of wealthy people and lots of Rolls Royces too. How do you explain this?

3.   Describe for the class a recent business success or failure in your neighborhood, and tell why you think it turned out as it did.

4.   Describe what business or service your immediate neighborhood or community is most in need of right now.

5.   If you could afford it, would you always go "first class"?

SOMETHING FOR YOU TO DO

Wherever you are sitting, right at this moment, reach out and touch something that is near you. Then trace exactly the commercial course by which it came to be where it is.

KEY WORDS AND PHRASES

Agent Middleman.   Go-between in completing a sale. Generally does not take title to the goods.

American Marketing Association.   Trade group of leading manufacturers and merchants.

Broker.   Brings buyer and seller together. Strictly an intermediary in most cases.

Commission House.   Business that takes a commission on all sales it makes.

Consumer.   The buying public.

Display Rack.   Arrangement for showing goods in stores.

Ethnic Background.   The broad group to which your forbears belonged, classified by trait, customs, etc.

Export-Import Agency. Agent involved in foreign trade.

General Wholesaler. Wholesaler who carries a wide variety of goods, often unrelated.

Inventory. Stock on hand in store, warehouse, or manufacturing plant.

Jingle. Song or ditty used to help sell a product on radio or TV.

Manufacturer's Agent. Selling agent for a manufacturer. May handle lines for more than one noncompeting company.

Materials Handling System. Mechanical means of moving goods quickly and efficiently.

Merchant Wholesaler. Agent who takes title to goods. May be general or specialty wholesaler.

Overhead. Cost of doing business (heat, light, rent) not chargeable to product.

Primary Potential Customers. The consumer who is the most immediate logical buyer of your product.

Product Life. Time-span in which a product is salable.

Profile. The "look" of a consumer or market group measured by certain definite criteria.

Profit Margin. Broadly, difference between wholesale and retail price.

R&D. Research and Development. That department of a business responsible for new product design and product improvement.

Rack Jobber. Wholesaler who stocks and maintains racks or display shelves and units.

Resident Buyer. Buying agent who maintains a permanent office near a particular market.

Single-line Wholesaler. Wholesaler specializing in one type of product, i.e., sporting goods.

Truck Jobber. Middleman who delivers and sells directly to retailer from truck.

Wholesale Price. Price set by wholesaler or manufacturer and charged to retail outlets.

SELECTED READINGS

Barnett, John, (ed.). *Paths to Profit. Case Histories in Marketing Success—And Failure*, (Princeton, New Jersey: Dow Jones Books, 1973). Marketing in action—a number of different views. If you are young, you'll especially enjoy the story on marketing to the "counter culture"—"Riches to Rags," p. 92.

Berg, Thomas L. *Mismarketing: Case Histories of Marketing Misfires,* (New York: Doubleday and Company, Inc., 1970). As Thomas J. Watson, Sr., of IBM, is quoted as saying on the dust jacket of this book, "You've got to put failure to work for you." It carries some lessons for the young businessman or woman: *Anyone* can make a marketing mistake. The bigger they are, the harder they fall.

Diamond, Jay, and Pintel, Gerald, Ph.D. *Principles of Marketing,* (Englewood Cliffs, New Jersey: Prentice-Hall, Inc., 1972). This is a good clean presentation of the complete marketing picture for students being introduced to the subject.

Dirksen, Charles J., Kroeger, Arthur, and Lockley, Lawrence C. *Readings in Marketing,* (Homewood, Illinois: Richard D. Irwin, Inc., 1968). Read this very comprehensive look at all phases of marketing through an extensive series of articles which originally appeared in a variety of business and professional publications.

Enis, Ben M., and Cox, Keith K. *Marketing Classics. A Selection of Influential Articles,* (Boston: Allyn and Bacon, Inc., 1969). The editors consider the articles contained in the book, "to be among the classics of marketing literature." Could well be. The article on page 365, "The Concept of the Marketing Mix," is by Neil Bordon, who invented the expression "marketing mix."

Kotler, Philip. *Marketing Management: Analysis, Planning and Control,* 3rd ed. (Englewood Cliffs, N.J.: Prentice-Hall, Inc., 1976). The emphasis of this comprehensive, up-to-date volume is on the discovery of market opportunities, innovation of new products, and management of products over the life cycle.

U. S. Department of Commerce. Social and Economic Statistics Administration. Bureau of the Census, *General Social and Economic Characteristics.* This is a basic source of demographic information. It is available at your local office of the United States Department of Commerce.

Still, Richard R., and Cundiff, Edward W. *Essentials of Marketing,* 2nd ed. (Englewood Cliffs, New Jersey: Prentice-Hall, Inc., 1972). This is a widely used and popular text which you may already have run into in a marketing class. Available in paperback. A very good basic book for you to have in your library.

chapter three

The Consumer and
Why He Acts
the Way He Does

In this chapter we will examine the target of our advertising efforts—the Consumer.

You will see that consumers are complex, and that their buying decisions are sometimes made for obscure reasons. The forces influencing buying behavior can come from a number of different directions, and are seldom based on economic reasoning alone.

This chapter will also give you an awareness of how the fields of Sociology, Anthropology, and Psychology contribute to our knowledge of why consumers act as they do.

Finally we will discuss some advertising of the past and present, and learn how a knowledge of consumer behavior can make advertising more effective.   **43**

A college student, working in a hat store, recently asked a number of customers why they were buying hats. The answers revealed considerable diversity of motives for the identical act: "I'm buying a hat to make me look older," said one. "My work requires the formality of a hat," said another, "it's as basic as a necktie." "My physician advised it," said a third, "because of my frequent colds." "My old hat is still in perfect condition," replied the fourth customer, "but styles have changed." "My fiancée prefers men who wear hats," answered the next customer, "and I'm not taking any chances." "I've always worn a hat," another man said, "I guess it's just a habit." "Why?" asked another customer. "Everyone in my group wears a hat, that's why." And still another explained, "My recent promotion has moved me into a neighborhood where people always appear to be expensively dressed, so I'm getting a new outfit."[1]

For a good many years, advertising people have been interested in the "psychology" of the sale. Why does one particular person buy a particular brand? What turns the buyer on, and what turns him off?

As early as the 1890s *Printer's Ink* remarked, "Probably when we are a

[1]John Douglas, George A. Field, and Laurence X. Tarpey, *Human Behavior in Marketing* (Columbus, Ohio: Charles E. Merrill Books, Inc., 1967), p. 50.

little more enlightened, the advertising writer, like the teacher, will study psychology." In fact it wouldn't be a bad idea at all if you, as a young marketing person, had a psychology course or two under your belt.

By the 1920s, when modern advertising was beginning to take form, consumers and what makes them tick had become of great interest to writers of advertising. Looking back at some of these ads of several generations ago, we can see that these old-timers did indeed have a pretty good handle on what motivates people to buy and they were not afraid to use it.

Since the 1920s, our knowledge has grown tremendously in fields involving "behavior"—psychology, psychiatry, anthropology, and sociology. All these have made a contribution to our understanding of why buyers act as they do. Much of what they have to say is difficult for the businessperson, who is untrained in these disciplines, to understand.

A note of caution: No one can provide you with a "hidden persuader" that will open the consumer's pocketbook to you. But through the work of the behaviorists, you can gain some insights to help you spend your advertising dollars more effectively.[2]

Consumers as Groups

You have already seen in Chapter 2 how we can divide a market into groups by segmenting it. We have "segmented" all people who wear dentures, or all people who can afford a Rolls Royce.

There are other ways to form consumer groups. I'm sure you have heard of people belonging to the "upper class," or the "lower middle class." Some years ago there was a motion picture called "Room at the Top," in which a young Englishman (Laurence Harvey) attempted to move out of his "class" by taking elocution lessons in order to acquire an "upper-class" accent. Much the same thing happened to "Liza Doolittle" in *My Fair Lady*.

Here in America we like to think that we have a "classless" society. It is difficult for us to set up arbitrary classes of people because the criteria keep changing and class lines become obscured. I'm sure you have someone in your town with an upper-class income and a middle-class mode of living.

The Social Research Institute of Chicago has conducted some of the most extensive studies into this matter of classes in America. Their figures show that we divide ourselves as follows: upper class, 3 percent; upper middle class, 12 percent; lower middle class, 30 percent; upper lower class, 35 percent; lower lower class, 20 percent. This is "probably the best estimate of the social class structure in America that presently

---

[2]William T. Ryan, *Principles of Marketing* (Homewood, Ill.: Richard D. Irwin, Inc., 1971).

exists, and is one that has been used extensively in the development of marketing strategy."[3]

There are other groupings with which you are familiar, such as "community college students," "the members of this class," or "the people who live on the west side of town."

Your social class ranking and the *prestige* accorded you may be two very different things. Hodge, Siegel, and Rossi have shown that college professors, most of whom would rank in the middle class socially, occupy eighth place in terms of prestige ahead of diplomats and lawyers, professions in which often there are found members of the upper class.[4]

How to Put the Group to Work for You

I'm sure you remember when you were a little kid, how important it was to be "one of the gang." If your particular bunch of friends were wearing corduroys that year, or bleaching streaks in their hair, you followed their example.

People don't outgrow this "gang" feeling very easily, and it is a good thing for you to remember as a marketer. Whether you call it "keeping up with the Joneses," or something else, it can be a very important factor in guiding buying behavior.

In York, Pennsylvania, I saw a smart young salesman for lawn-care products use this "gang feeling" to his profit. He selected a "group"—in this case middle-class homeowners. Then he picked out one of the homeowners, and offered to take care of his lawn *free* for a month just to show what he could do. The homeowner agreed, and in four weeks he had a lawn that was a beauty. It was as smooth as putting surface, emerald green, and there wasn't a weed in it. The homeowner was happy. But his neighbors *weren't* so happy.

Each night as they came home from work they had to pass that weedless, emerald-green lawn. Then they came to their own lawns and saw brown spots and crabgrass. The more they compared their lawns to that of their neighbor's lawn, the unhappier they were. They finally put their pride in their pockets and induced him to tell them the secret of his beautiful lawn. The good neighbor obliged them. By the next weekend, the lawn-care salesman had sold more bags of fertilizer, grass seed, and weed killer than had ever been sold within an area of three square blocks.

Go to certain bars in working-class neighborhoods and you'll see one brand of beer preferred to the exclusion of all other brands. In that neighborhood it's the *in* beer. That's all. Liquor salesmen will tell you that shifts in drinking tastes can first be detected in certain well-defined neighborhoods.

---

[3]James F. Engel, David T. Kollat, and Roger D. Blackwell, *Consumer Behavior* (New York: Holt, Rinehart, and Winston, Inc.,), p. 42.

[4]Engel, Kollat, and Blackwell, *Consumer Behavior*, p. 269.

This follow-the-leader principle has been used by apartment house owners and restaurant managers to their advantage. Realtors will "seed" a new property with prominent people—rent free. For a restaurant owner, the steady patronage of a star of screen, stage, or professional football is worth its weight in Kansas City sirloins.

Places are always being discovered, and abandoned when a new place takes the fancy of the group. Do you have someone in your town who always seems to be a step ahead of everyone else? "I discovered the greatest little shop yesterday!" If you know someone like that, get together and have a chat—let that person discover *you*.

Certain publications, such as the *Wall Street Journal*, *Time Magazine*, and *Scientific American*, call to the attention of advertisers that a high percentage of their readers are "opinion-makers" and "trend-setters."

I'm sure you recognize that snobbism and the use of status symbols sometimes play a major part in group-buying decisions. Among the young business executives in my town, the Mercedes-Benz 450 SL is very popular. There are other places where the restored Bugatti or Astin-Martin is the thing to be seen driving.

As you have noticed in advertising, some products frankly appeal to status or snobbism. It's the "if you've got it, flaunt it" idea. There are many ways to say it. "You've worked hard—you deserve one." "One of these tells the world you have arrived." "Use the brand the connoisseurs demand."

Sometimes the *association* of a product will give it attributes it may not have enjoyed before. Calvert ran a famous "Man of Distinction" campaign. It featured color photographs of distinguished-looking, successful businessmen. Calvert had no intention of being just another blended whiskey.

One of the first products to associate itself with famous beauties of stage and society was Pond's Hand Cream. Camel Cigarettes, in their advertising, have not only associated themselves with clean-cut rugged guys; they've *dissociated* from what they regard as the kooks and weirdos.

You can see this happening every day in your hometown. Restaurants, bars, schools, and even churches have an "association value." There are some golfers who love the game, but would rather be caught dead than play on a municipal course.

There's also another side to this "association" business. Some retail stores and restaurants keep people away because of the associations attributed to them in the public mind. Some "groups" feel much more comfortable shopping in certain stores than in others.

How Things "Look" to the Customer

Individual products and brands mean different things to different people. If I should say "Kelvinator" to you, it might trigger in your mind a reaction that would be quite different from that of your next-door neighbors. You should not be too surprised at this. It happens all the time. If someone mentions Ireland, your mind might react, "Strife, political trouble, IRA." Or you might think pleasurably of Guiness, St. Stephen's Green, and the library at Trinity College. You *see* Ireland, but in a quite different light.

This "image-making" is an inner psychological reaction, and it can have much to do with the product that the consumer ultimately chooses. Manufacturers spend a great deal of time and money establishing their images—corporate, brand, or product.

You Are More "Loyal" Than You Think

The consumer, for example, develops characteristic ways of evaluating products and services. He may highly prefer one brand, whereas he regards others as unacceptable. Truly, values and attitudes toward objects and persons represent an individual "map of the world." As such, they are a prime target for persuasive advertising, because of the assumption that behavior will change once an attitude is modified or redirected. The importance of this type of predisposition in understanding consumer motivation and behavior can scarcely be overemphasized.[5]

Every marketer attempts to create a "loyal following" for his product. To put it in another way, the marketer wishes to induce a favorable psychological reaction to the product each time you see it or hear about it.

This loyalty to a product or brand is not, as you have seen, the only factor that affects the buying decision. It is one of a number of factors, but plays a more important role in our buying choices than many manufacturers, retailers, and consumers realize.

One must remember that much of what the consumer purchases is not based solely on economic values, that is, values relating to price and utility of a product . . . motivation, perception, and learning, strongly influence the actual selection of products, and, when applicable, brands. A great many of the purchasing decisions made by consumers are strongly influenced by noneconomic factors.[6]

You see, many products in the marketplace are basically the same. Or, many products are of such nature that it is difficult for the consumer to distinguish them in use.

[5]Engel, Kollat, and Blackwell, *Consumer Behavior*, p. 42.

[6]David J. Rachman, *Marketing Strategy and Structure* (Englewood Cliffs, N.J.: Prentice-Hall, Inc., 1974), p. 188.

The well-known brands of gasoline vary only slightly in quality and price. You may be loyal to your brand of gasoline for reasons that have nothing to do with quality or price, but may have a great deal to do with the *image* you carry around with you of the service station and the people who operate it.

If you would like to conduct a "blindfold" test in your classroom or office, you can very quickly discover that "taste" has sometimes very little to do with brand preference. Whether it is a cola drink, beer, or cigarettes, or bourbon, even the most loyal advocates will have great difficulty in identifying their favorites.[7]

Images

The "image-makers" are all around us, and they are not confined to advertising. Publicists and press agents, retained by individuals, are paid to develop or change images. The Hollywood drum-beaters have in the past created "sex kittens" out of some very ordinary country girls.

Corporate Images

People, through their own efforts or the efforts of others, can reflect a certain image. Businesses can also fix a certain place for themselves in the public regard. To many large companies the "corporate image" is very important and carefully protected. In the next chapter we will talk about "institutional advertising." This is the kind of advertising designed to change or maintain corporate images. Most efforts of this kind take place over a long period.

Many years ago, the Metropolitan Insurance Company was generally regarded as a "poor man's insurance company" dealing mainly in 25¢-a-week "burial policies." Metropolitan set out to change this image. They did it by corporate advertising of an institutional nature. They did not argue that Metropolitan was *not* a company catering to poor people; rather they embarked on a series of "messages" in the public interest. They demonstrated, *by example,* that this company was progressive, brave, high-minded, and concerned with the welfare of the public. The messages, dealing with public health, were straightforward and interesting. It took great corporate courage to publish one of them, as it dealt with the dangers of venereal disease—a subject hardly mentioned in the press of those days.

Sometimes a company must fight to overcome an industry image. In the old days of unrestricted lumbering, hundreds of square miles of timberland were left ravaged and denuded. Today lumber companies

[7]M. H. Pronko, and J. W. Bowles, Jr., *Identification of Cola Beverages III: A Final Study,* Journal of Applied Psychology, Vol. 33, 1949, pp. 605–608.

such as Weyerhaeuser, and paper companies such as St. Regis, run ads
and commercials showing how by "tree farming" they are helping to preserve and enhance this important natural resource.

With the increased interest in ecology, many companies have called on their advertising agencies to protect their positions or to put them in a different light. Oil companies, in the wake of the oil spills, have gone to publications and television to show the relative cleanliness and safety of their operations.

We have been talking about corporate images for big companies. Does this apply to the smaller businessman? It certainly does. When a local retailer institutes a policy of "return the merchandise and your money refunded with no questions asked," the seller is saying to the customers, "I'm the kind of straight, honest guy you can trust."

We have a jeweler in my town who appears on TV every now and then and talks about his merchandise. There he is—a plain, middle-aged man, sitting behind a tray of engagement rings, or watches, and talking about them with pride and affection and knowledge. There is absolutely nothing professional about his accent or his delivery. He comes across as an utterly decent, honest jeweler with whom you'd like to do business.

Trade Marks, Labels, and Logotypes

To help you remember *who*'s doing the talking, companies and products have ways of branding themselves just as a rancher brands a calf so that he can distinguish it from other ranchers' calves.

Shell Oil Company's shell, the name Coke, the Campbell Soup red and white label, the Betty Crocker name and spoon, the Singer Company's "What's new for tomorrow is at Singer today," the round spot with the letters "GE" in script—all these are "brands" designed to help you identify the product.

The "brands" you see fall into different categories:

Brand names. Usually this is a made-up name which should be unique and memorable. Copywriters often spend hours thinking up new names for products. Some well-known trade names are Exxon, Teflon II, and Maybelline.

Symbols. These are literally "brands" which could be reproduced in iron and burned into a surface. The GE symbol or the Mazda "M" are good examples. Sunkist, and Chiquita Banana, put their symbols right on the fruit. Notice that whenever possible, your local car dealers put their "brand" on the cars they sell.

Names. To help keep its name memorable, Singer, for example, has been reproducing its name in the same script type for years, as have DuPont and Listerine.

By permission: Lippincott & Margulies, Inc.

A group of trademark designs from a leading industrial designer and industrial consultant.

Logotypes.   You will usually find these at the base of the ad, and often they are a combination of the company name, a symbol, and slogan if they have one.

Labels.   By means of color and design, labels brand a family of products, such as Campbell Soups, Maxwell House Coffee, or Green Giant canned vegetables.

Trade characters.   The symbol can be a human or a cartoon character. The Hathaway Shirt Man, Aunt Jemima, and Chef Boyardee, are some of the well-known ones.

Layout design.   Sometimes a brand will immediately identify itself by the design of its advertising layout. Brooks Brothers ads are immediately recognizable. Wallach's, another men's store, has for years used exactly the same all-type format. So familiar has it become, that the name "Wallach's" hardly has to be mentioned.

Slogans.   These are catchy, memorable lines that put a "handle" on the company. Coca Cola's "It's the real thing," "You can be sure if it's Westinghouse," and Honeywell's "The other computer company," are a few of them. Look for them just below the company's signature in an ad.

If you are ever in a position of thinking up a brand name for a product, be very careful. Many brand names have been thought up, registered, and never used. All slogans, symbols, names, and so on, must be "searched"—a legal process—to determine if someone has prior claim to them. Pamphlets and circulars on copyright are available free from the U.S. Copyright Office, Library of Congress, Washington, D.C. 20559. You can write for information.

You must also be very careful that your coined name does not have a connotation that you might not desire for it. This is particularly true if you are marketing abroad. Standard Oil Company dropped the "Enco" name when they found that in Japanese it means "stalled car." You will want to make sure that your trade name says something for you, if possible. "Gleem" is just great for a toothpaste. So is "Ultrabrite." And what could be better for a handy little tissue than "Kleenex"?

If you walk down the aisles of your supermarket you will see how important it is that you have a "brand" or design or label that quickly identifies you. Often in one supermarket alone, there are more than 1,500 brands or labels for you to choose from. This includes "private labels"—products packaged by the manufacturer and provided with the retailer's own label. Pantry Pride (Food Fair) sells a wide variety of products under its own label. There are about 400,000 trademarks registered in the United States at the present time.

Brands vary widely in their recognition, and, therefore, in their effectiveness. Some brands become so familiar to us that their names become "generic," that is, a brand name becomes the accepted name for *all* products in that category. Cut your finger, and what do you put on it—a band-aid. You patch a ripped page in your book with Scotch tape. With lower case initial letters they all are part of the American language, but they started as trade names.

Others are not so fortunate. Studies have shown that many people are unfamiliar with either the brand name or the manufacturer of a number of common household articles. Who made the bath towel you used this morning? Who manufactured the knives and forks you have on your table? What is the brand name on your kitchen pots and pans?

The Brand Name as a Handle

The "brand" or identifying mark on a product, whether it is a label or trademark or trade name, is a "handle." It is something for you to take hold of. In the case of canned goods on the supermarket shelf, you quite literally reach for it and then put it in your market basket. In every case, the label or trademark is a *device* put there to start a chain reaction in your mind. It can start a train of memories and learned facts, impressions, and wants and needs that will result in your reaching for brand "X" instead of brand "Y." It is like seeing the familiar face of an acquaintance coming down the street; you react, "Oh, here comes good old Don. I wonder what's new with him?" Or, "Gosh, here comes that awful bore Charlie—wonder how I can avoid him?"

Over the years, advertisers have spent millions of dollars so that when the consumer encounters particular brands on shelves or counters, he will greet them with shouts of recognition and delight. Advertisers certainly don't want you to cross over to the other side of the street. Whether you are General Motors or a guy selling ribs from a stand on the corner, you need not only an identity but something they can remember you by.

We have a fellow in our town who paints signs. He used to be known by something like "The Joe Smith Sign Company." He was in competition with a whole bunch of other "Smith," "Brown," and "Jones" sign companies. So he changed his corporate name. Now he advertises himself as "The Signman" and lets you know that if you dial the letters of the name, you get his shop. He has acquired a "handle" for himself.

The Folks Around Us

In the first chapter of this book we saw how the promotion money spent by railroads and land companies generated the waves of immigrants who populated the West in the 19th century. Our immigrant forefathers came from almost every country in Europe. We are proud of the American heritage of liberty and opportunity that brought these people to our country. They not only brought us their names, but also their habits and tastes and customs. We mentioned "ethnic groups," in the last chapter, and how there are pockets of "minorities" to be found everywhere in America. There still are many places in our country where English is the *second* language.

Because they are now so much a part of America, we tend to forget the contributions our forefathers have made to our lives today. Your favorite beer may come from a brewery started by a poor immigrant boy from Bavaria who escaped the repressions of 1849. The newspaper you read may have been first edited by a man who could not find freedom of speech in his own country. The very college you attend may be supported by a trust from the estate of a penniless young tailor who escaped from the Warsaw ghetto.

Otto Kleppner, in his great book on advertising, has pointed out how our ethnic backgrounds are revealed in the foods we eat.

Indeed, many dishes found in certain parts of the country are a direct identification of the people of that area with their cultural past. Pennsylvania Dutch cookery with its fastnachts and shoofly pie, has its roots mainly in the valley of the Rhine. In North Carolina, the serving of lovefeasts (sugar cakes, Christmas cookies, and large white mugs of coffee) is its Moravian (Czechoslovakian) heritage, while in Rhode Island, tourtiere (meat pie) reflects the French-Canadian influence. We have Cornish pasties (meat and vegetable pie) in Michigan, the Norwegian julekake in North Dakota. The heavy influence of

Mexico is revealed in the tamale pie and other Mexican-style foods of Southern California and the Southwest.[8]

From Polish wedding to Irish wake to Jewish bar mitzvah, we all differ from the folks around us in our inherited tastes and characteristics. This includes *every* facet of our lives. Ask any salesman who travels widely and he will tell you that the approach he makes to a customer in Oklahoma is far different from the one he makes in Boston. In Spanish Harlem, or Miami, there are certain products that simply don't move in the same way as they do in other parts of the country.

In no other part of the world are consumers and their behavior so complicated by the fact of national origin as they are in the United States. It is an important fact of marketing life that every person in business, and particularly in advertising, must keep in mind.

Consumer Motivation

In much the same way that six blind men would describe an elephant from whatever part their hands happened to touch, so the economist, the anthropologist, and the sociologist see the consumer reacting in their particular terms.

To the economist it is a matter of value and purchasing power. To the sociologist it is a matter of "groups" and "keeping up with the Joneses." To the anthropologist, tradition and national tastes play significant roles.

Now, in our effort to unlock the mystery of why consumers behave as they do, we are going to hear from another discipline—the psychologists. The area they and their friends in marketing have been exploring is vital to the understanding and creating of successful advertising: *what motivates the consumer to make the choice and make the purchase?*

What Motivation Is

"Properly translated, motivating human behavior means finding out the best method of convincing people rather than persuading them."[9]

First, let's make sure that we are clear in our minds as to just what "motivation" means. The word comes from a Latin stem—*motio* (a moving); also from our words such as motor, motion, and movement. So if we think of a word in terms of a motor, the modern phrase "it turns me

---

[8]Otto Kleppner, *Advertising Procedure* (Englewood Cliffs, N.J.: Prentice-Hall, Inc., 6th ed., 1973), p. 288.

[9]Ernest Dichter, *Motivating Human Behavior* (New York: McGraw-Hill Book Company, 1971), p. xiii.

on" makes some sense. Your motor gets turned on, and moves you to complete the act of buying.

If you will just think of yourself as a machine being driven along by a "turned-on" motor, you can readily see that this is just about what happens when you read an ad about a sale of slacks at a very attractive price. You "get turned on," go down to the store, and then purchase them.

Keep thinking of yourself as putt-putting along. That motor of yours can move either fast or slow. Sometimes it starts quickly; and sometimes, like a car on a cold morning, it starts sluggishly. Sometimes you rush down to the store to take advantage of the sale before everything is sold; and sometimes you consider long and carefully before making a purchase. Like a car, you can also head in different directions. When the bluefish are running in the surf, you can be strongly motivated in the direction of some new fishing tackle.

Just as you seldom find yourself driving along on a deserted highway, seldom do you find your motives operating alone. There may be a number of motives headed in different directions. But there will be a dominant direction that influenced your choice, just as there is a dominant direction to the flow of traffic morning and evening on a city's main arteries.

Goals and Needs

Our motives are also influenced by our goals and needs, and you should distinguish between the two. A *goal* is something you are trying to reach: an "A" in the course, or be elected class president. Usually goals are fixed and visible and lie in some direction. They are *exteriors*.

Needs, on the other hand, lie within us. Generally they are psychological in nature. Individuals may go to the hairdresser for a new styling, not because they need a new styling *but because they need to feel better*. They didn't need the new hair styling as a matter of physical necessity; they needed it as an emotional requirement. A hairdresser in my town told me that half the fun in his business is watching the customers come in with the blues and walk out with their new haircuts, ready to face the world again.

Day after day, teachers have to face the problem of the "unmotivated students" who drift along, goalless, and never achieve half what they might because nothing ever "turned them on." We are also familiar with the young people whose eyes are set on med school or a graduate degree. We see how motivation helps them to win credits.

The Buried Motives

As everyone who conducts a survey discovers, there are some very good reasons for people *not* to give you the true facts. Sometimes they feel that the facts might make them appear silly or inferior. Sometimes the truth makes them unhappy or uncomfortable. ("I don't know" is one of the most difficult things to say in any language.)

It's the same with motives. Sometimes our motives make us ashamed or fearful, so we deny them or bury them so deeply that we ourselves can't find them. But you can be just as strongly turned on by your hidden motives as by your more conscious ones. You just don't know from where motivating forces come.

Once I saw this happen to a friend of mine. See if you can figure out the "hidden motive." He was a short man, very quiet and conservative, and lived in a quiet suburban community with his wife and one daughter. His job was an important one, entailing the control and investment of the money in his company's employees' retirement fund.

All of us in the community commuted to work and many had second cars which we drove to and from the railroad station. My friend did not have a "station" car. Each night his wife met him with the family car. One day, as we waited on the station platform, my friend engaged me in a long and serious conversation. His wife caught too many colds. His daughter had to be driven to school every morning, and picked up late in the afternoon. He thought it was time for him to purchase a "station" car. What would I suggest?

I thought the question over carefully and told him that considering the snowy hills and cold mornings, a second-hand Volks might be just the thing. I also told him that I knew a man who had one for sale.

He thanked me, and abruptly walked away. I thought he seemed disappointed. A few days later he pulled into the station parking lot, gunned the motor a couple of times, and stepped out of a white Austin-Healy with red upholstery! Okay, doctor, what's your diagnosis?

How to Distinguish the Motives

Clinical psychologists spend a lot of time delving into people's personalities and trying to find out what makes them tick. To aid them in this, they have developed a number of "tools" which measure and reveal facts about ourselves. You have probably encountered some of these tests yourself, in the military service, in school, or in an office.

For the past 25 years, marketing experts and psychologists have been using these tests to help them understand consumer motivation. Here are some of the methods motivation researchers use to get at the facts.

The interview. This is something like the "couch" technique in which you talk freely, or an "encounter session" in which one gets right down to the true feelings. A session of this kind, led by an expert, might have a group of homemakers discussing their feelings about the chores of housekeeping. Much of interest might be revealed to an advertiser of a household product, such as furniture polish.

The TAT. This is the well-known Thematic Apperception Test. A *projective* technique is one in which you reveal certain facts by "projecting" yourself into a story or picture situation. An interviewer might show you a picture of a woman standing before a meat counter, and ask you, "What do you think is going through her mind?"

Word tests. Here we probe your feelings by asking you to complete a sentence such as, "I like Skippy Peanut Butter because. . . ." Or, you may be asked to associate one word with another, "Flour . . . Pillsbury; smooth . . . complexion."

Classification

Out of the tremendous amount of work that has been done there has emerged a classification of consumer wants, needs, and desires. There are many lists in existence. Psychologists and marketers do not agree on all of them by any means. Some are long, some are short. But roughly, here is what it all boils down to.

Physiological needs. These are the bodily needs; the instinctive animal reactions to hunger, sex, and cold.

The need to feel secure. The need for all of us to feel relatively safe. Freedom from fear. The need to be free from apprehension and worry.

The need for love. Not just romantic love, but the pervasive love the Greeks expressed as *agapé*. The need for acceptance and a sense of belonging.

The need for esteem and status. The need to be regarded with respect, to be somebody. The desire to have a recognized place in society.

The need to be your own person. The need to recognize and accept yourself as you are; to have your own standards, and live up to them. The "*I did it my way*" syndrome.[10]

The Use of Motives in Marketing

Because of what the marketers and psychologists have done in the areas of motivation, the word has gotten around that advertisers are out to take advantage of us by manipulating certain psychological forces against our will to their advantage. This is putting an age-old sales practice in a somber light.

What *is* true—and what has always been true—is that, *as salespersons,* we wish to present our merchandise so that it will best meet your

---

[10]This list closely follows Maslow, who is widely quoted in both Marketing and Management texts. See Engel, Kollat, and Blackwell, *Consumer Behavior op. cit.* p. 67.

needs and desires. This is what good salesmen have always done, often
instinctively. As Elmer Wheeler, whose bust has a place in the salesman's hall of fame, said, "You don't sell the steak, you sell the sizzle." The advice carries with it a whole basketful of psychological implications.

Back in the days when hardly anyone had heard of Jung, Adler, and Freud, and when the Thematic Apperception Test was as yet to be invented, salesmen prided themselves on being "psychologists." They may never have heard of "buyer motivation," but they were shrewd judges of human nature. They made it work for them.

It is interesting to note that long before most advertisers knew much about "consumer motivation" they were appealing to that same list of "needs, wants, and desires" that we recognize today. Many of the old ads which today we regard as great classics are, in fact, great classics in the use of consumer motivations, although they may not have been called that.

We have formalized our knowledge; we have given ourselves a new vocabulary, but basic selling psychology doesn't seem to have changed much over the years. As a result, it is possible to go right back to these old-time ads to show how a knowledge of man's basic motivating forces can help sell.

The Use of Physiological Needs

Let's start with hunger. We've already mentioned Mr. Elmer Wheeler and his admonition about "selling the sizzle and not the steak." What he was saying is that you sell the *anticipation of the pleasure* of eating the food itself. Look in any homemaking magazine today and you can see that dozens of ads, such as those for Kraft Foods, make a big effort to project "appetite appeal." Pictorially a Kraft salad is a work of mouth-watering art. Read the menu in your favorite restaurant. Few owners today would think of simply stating that the steak dinner costs $8.50. Rather they go into details about the well-aged, carefully selected U.S. prime sirloin, and the fluffy Idaho baked potatoes topped with crisp bacon bits and sour cream.

Security as a Psychological Need

Freedom from economic worries—indeed, from economic tragedy—was a far more pressing need in the early 1930s than it is today. In depression-ridden America there were few middle-class homes without economic worries. The International Correspondence Schools offered young businessmen a way to gain greater economic security for themselves and for their loved ones. Their ads showed their students bringing home the raise, being taken into the boss's confidence, and depositing money in the bank. "Like money in the bank," means being safe and secure. The ICS ads touched a real need, and were among the most successful ever written. In modern terms, you can hardly think of an insurance company that does not sell security and peace of mind.

The Need for Love and Acceptance

There is a great all-time classic that says it all in this category: "They laughed when I sat down at the piano." This world, as you know, is full of shy reticent people with a real need to be loved and accepted and looked up to. It hurts when you are the wallflower whom no one asks to dance, or when you are the kid who is left out when they are choosing up sides for a ball game. This great old ad is about one of these people, and how he wins his share of love and recognition and acceptance because he sent away for the piano lessons.

This recognition of the need for affection and acclaim is something that runs through much of today's advertising. What happens when Mrs. Jones quickly rubs down her furniture with a popular polish just before the garden club arrives? The friends come in and immediately ooh! and aah! over what a great little homemaker she is. The bride who finally gets it straight about how to make a cup of coffee is rewarded by a big hug and a kiss from her husband. In fact, the "reward" scene occurs over and over in our television commercials.

"Maybe Your Best Friend . . ."

Another great old campaign in this "need for love and acceptance" category is the one for Listerine Antiseptic. Originated by Milton Feasley, and for many years written by Gordon Seagrove, these ads played remorselessly on the danger of personal rejection due to unpleasant breath. Like the popular soap operas, they told the story of people who lost jobs and fiancées because they had a thing called "halitosis"—and no one had the nerve to tell them about it.

Today the theme of boy meets girl, boy loses girl, boy wins girl, and vice-versa, because of a shaving lotion or a deodorant or a toothpaste, is one you see constantly on TV.

Being Your Own Person

The psychological need for self-recognition and self-identity is last on some psychologist's lists, and seems to be less strong and more subtle than the others. An ancient ad that was years ahead of its time was one for the Jordan Motor Car entitled, "Somewhere West of Laramie." Advertising people generally regard it as one of the great ads of all time. It was *so* far ahead of its time, that only recently copywriters have begun to catch up with it. "Somewhere West . . ." was one of what might be called "the-wind-and-the-rain-in-your-hair" school of writing. Till

Somewhere West of Laramie

SOMEWHERE west of Laramie there's a broncho-busting, steer-roping girl who knows what I'm talking about. She can tell what a sassy pony, that's a cross between greased lightning and the place where it hits, can do with eleven hundred pounds of steel and action when he's going high, wide and handsome.

The truth is—the Playboy was built for her.

Built for the lass whose face is brown with the sun when the day is done of revel and romp and race.

She loves the cross of the wild and the tame.

There's a savor of links about that car—of laughter and lilt and light—a hint of old loves—and saddle and quirt. It's a brawny thing—yet a graceful thing for the sweep o' the Avenue.

Step into the Playboy when the hour grows dull with things gone dead and stale.

Then start for the land of real living with the spirit of the lass who rides, lean and rangy, into the red horizon of a Wyoming twilight.

JORDAN

JORDAN MOTOR CAR COMPANY, Inc., Cleveland, Ohio

This is one of the great ones. No one had ever written a piece of copy like this before. No one had ever taken this approach to selling cars. Compare it with today's motorcycle and sports car advertising.

then, no one had dreamed of writing an ad that way. The ad wasn't selling the Jordan car. It was selling something far more dear and precious to all of us—freedom. The chance to express ourselves. The chance to be individualists, different from the rest.

In recent times you have seen Honda and Yamaha ring exactly the same psychological bell as Jordan did so many years ago. When they show you roaring off into the sunset, up some lonely mountain trail, they are offering you the chance to buy a very precious commodity—freedom, getting away from it all, being your own person, and doing your own thing.

"I Was a Ninety-Eight-Pound Weakling"

There is one more ad in the psychological sweepstakes that I can't bear to overlook. More than fifty years ago, Charles Atlas first offered to put muscles on people. Mr. Atlas is no longer with us; but the ads go on, little changed from those that first appeared. They represent one of the great success stories of mail order selling.

What Charles Atlas is selling is *not* a set of barbells and the directions for using them. What he *is* offering has to do with one of our first category of motivations—the physiological one, sex; but it is sex with some interesting twists. True, there's always a girl around, whom the kid loses after the bully kicks sand in his face (or, in an earlier version, *winks* at the girl). After a few months on the bells, of course, he wins her back.

But there's a little more to it than that. Most adolescent kids *are* a scrawny lot. They equate muscles with manhood. At that age, if you men will recall, you worry a lot about being a man. That's one of the reasons why getting a driver's license is so important to most kids. It is an official document attesting that you are an adult. What Charles Atlas offered was a shortcut to manhood, with all the privileges and perquisites that go with it. The kids were grateful. They made him a millionaire.

The Sizzle—Not the Steak

Note carefully: In all the foregoing examples, the product—whether mouthwash, or barbell course, or music lesson—was *not* the thing being "sold." What was being offered to the consumer in each case was *the chance to satisfy a need or want or desire.*

This is a good bench mark against which to measure your advertising. Is your advertising directed to *what you want to sell,* or to *what the consumer wants to buy?*

It's worth looking for. It could make *you* a millionaire too.

1. You understand how consumers often function as groups, and how the pressure generated by the group can influence individual buying decisions.

2. You have learned the importance of "brands" and of "brand images." You are familiar with the various devices used to establish brand identity. You now know the role brand image or identity plays in affecting consumer choice.

3. You are aware of the unique character of the American market shaped by our growth as a nation. You know the marketing significance of ethnic traits, tastes, and habits, and how they can play a part in the buying decision.

4. You understand what "motivation" is, how it operates, and the different directions its forces can take in guiding consumer behavior.

5. You can define "goals" and "needs," and understand the difference between them.

6. You are aware that it is possible for people to have buying motives that are obvious and easily defined. You also understand that some of our motives are sometimes hidden from others as well as from ourselves.

7. You can list and define the basic kinds of physiological and psychological motives regarded as affecting consumer behavior.

8. You have seen how the forces affecting consumer behavior are applied to selling messages. You have acquired a yardstick that will help you to measure the effectiveness of your own company's advertising.

QUESTIONS FOR CLASS DISCUSSION

1. Defend or attack the following statement: "Without a detailed knowledge of consumer motivation we could not sell as effectively as we do today."

2. When, in your opinion, did psychology first play a part in selling?

3. It is said that America is a "melting pot." Does this mean that we are all in danger of being reduced to a "common denominator" of taste?

4. Vance Packard, in *The Hidden Persuaders*, says, "This book . . . is about the large-scale efforts being made, often with impressive success, to channel our unthinking habits, our purchasing decisions, and our thought processes by use of insights gleaned from psychiatry and the social scientists. . . . The result is that many of us are being influenced and manipulated, far more than we realize, in the patterns of our everyday lives." Attack or defend this point of view.

SOMETHING FOR YOU TO DO

You have learned how a number of factors motivate our buying decisions. Advertising, as you have seen, often appeals to these factors. Select ten printed ads and ten TV commercials and write the answer to the question, "What are they *really* selling?"

KEY WORDS AND PHRASES

Behavioral Sciences. Disciplines that examine man's behavior (Psychology, sociology).

Brand Name. The name the product carries on itself or its label (Mustang, Coke).

Buying Motive. The basic reason behind the buying decision.

Consumer Motivation. Forces that impel the consumer to act, or to act in a particular manner.

Image-Making. The building of an impression or reputation.

Label. Generally, the decorative cover on a can or jar bearing the brand name of the product and other information.

Layout Design. The manner in which the various elements of the ad are put together.

Logotype. Distinctively designed trademark or trade name. Sometimes refers to the whole signature at bottom of the ad.

Opinion-makers. People who set styles and whose tastes are imitated by other people.

Physiological Needs. A recognizable set of "wants and desires" present in all normal personalities.

Slogan. A catchy saying about a company or product.

Social Class Structure. The arbitrary division of people into social categories ("upper middle class").

Symbol. A picture or illustration associated with a particular product, e.g., the Texaco Star.

Trade Character. A character created in association with a product (the Hathaway Shirt Man, Chef Boyardee).

SELECTED READINGS

Britt, Steuart Henderson. (ed.). *Psychological Experiments in Consumer Behavior* (New York: John Wiley & Sons, Inc., 1970). This book consists of 32 reports of experimental projects in a wide variety of fields concerned with consumer behavior. It offers you a good, comprehensive look at how deeply the behavioral scientists have delved into the question of consumer behavior.

Clark, Lincoln H. (ed.). *Consumer Behavior: The Dynamics of Consumer Reaction* (New York: New York University Press, 1954). See particularly "The Anatomy of the Consumer" by Nelson N. Foote.

Dichter, Ernest. *Motivating Human Behavior* (New York: McGraw-Hill Book Company, 1971). Doctor Dichter is one of the great modern movers and shakers in the motivational field. Also see his famous *Handbook of Consumer Motivation* and any of his numerous articles in professional publications.

Douglas, John, Field, George A., and Tarpey, Lawrence X. *Human Behavior in Marketing* (Columbus, Ohio: Charles E. Merrill Books, Inc., 1967). Behaviorism as it applies to the whole marketing spectrum.

Engel, James F., Kollat, David T., Blackwell, Roger D. *Consumer Behavior* (New York: Holt, Rinehart, & Winston, Inc., 1968). A very detailed look at consumer behavior. The authors note how social and behavioral scientists are getting out into the "real world" with the growing recognition of the importance of the consumer in marketing.

Martineau, Pierre. *Motivation in Advertising* (New York: McGraw-Hill

Book Company, 1957). The author is one of the most prominent commentators on behaviorism in advertising. Also see his numerous articles in the trade publications.

Maslow, A. H. *Motivation and Personality* (New York: Harper and Row, Inc., 1954). The author is one of the more widely quoted psychologists in advertising and marketing texts.

Packard, Vance. *The Status Seekers* (New York: David McKay Company, Inc., 1959). Packard has raised the blood pressure of many an ad man. (But, many agree with much he says.) See also *The Hidden Persuaders* and other books of his on the American social scene.

Journal of Marketing Research, Journal of Marketing, and *Advertising Age,* regularly carry articles on consumer behavior and should be consulted.

chapter four

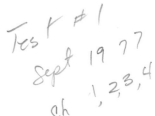

The Different Kinds of Advertising and the People Who Make It

In this chapter we learn to distinguish the basic forms advertising takes as it operates within the marketing mix.

You will then be introduced to all the people in advertising departments, in advertising agencies, and in collateral advertising services which contribute to the making of advertising and advertising programs.

You will begin to see, also, some of the differences between the agency business as most business executives in your community know it, and the agency business that is typically referred to as "Madison Avenue."

Advertising people recognize a number of different *kinds* or *forms* of advertising. They are differentiated from one another according to the different jobs they are designed to do.

As you have learned, a product "flows" along a route from producer to consumer. On its way, the product is either helped or impeded by certain forces: the quality of the product, its price, where it can be purchased, and the attitude of consumers. An integral part of this process is almost always advertising—"the push that makes things happen."

This "push that makes things happen" can occur any place along the route. Ideally it should occur *everywhere* along the route. Usually it does. That's why we can identify so many *kinds* of advertising by the way it applies its push all along the route of the "marketing mix."

This is very important for you, as a young business executive, to understand, for there are some marketers who feel that the only advertising that helps them very much is that which is beamed directly at the consumer.

Now let's take a look at these different kinds of advertising, and fix in our minds the *roles* they play in applying their push in the marketing process.

Institutional or Corporate Advertising

Institutional or corporate advertising often projects an *image* of the company. It is just as important for a company to have a good character and a good reputation as it is for an individual business person; and for exactly the same reasons. Your *name* has a great deal to do with the consumer-buying decision. Remember the local jeweler we mentioned, who projected such a good image of honesty and integrity while talking on TV about his products?

Copywriters have long known that a corporate name in the headline—*if the company's name inspires confidence*—helps to make a more effective ad.

Many companies carry this projection of a favorable corporate image right over into their general advertising. Westinghouse reminds us, "If it's Westinghouse, you can be sure." Texaco says, "We're working to keep your trust."

The fact is, *all* companies have characters and personalities of their own, and those characteristics affect their relationship with buyers and sellers alike.

Trade or Professional Advertising

Ordinarily you don't see trade or professional advertising unless you pick up a publication directed to a particular trade or profession. There are a great many of these publications, and manufacturers fill them with advertising addressed to retailers. The messages to the retailer are very different from those addressed to the consumers. In trade advertising, the manufacturer tells the retailer what he can do for him *in terms of the marketing mix*—new, attractive products, money-making volume, and profit spreads, ingenious distribution plans, and exciting promotional programs. Ads by drug manufacturers and equipment makers appear in *professional publications* such as *Journal of the American Medical Association*, and *Journal of the American Dental Association*; they are informative, and are beamed directly at particular professional groups.

Retail Advertising

You see and hear retail advertising every day. Without it, most newspapers and radio stations would not be able to exist. And your television station might find itself somewhat pressed. In most cities of any size, department store advertising represents an important source of income for newspapers. Retailers in your community advertise their goods in local media. If you have a Sears or a big discount center in your town,

This is a small version of the kind of retail ad you often see on Thursdays in your newspaper. Dozens of items, prices, and illustrations are often involved. They are usually prepared by the advertiser's own ad department, in this case Winn Dixie, Jacksonville, Florida.

you have received their brochures and newspaper inserts. Automobile dealers, tire dealers, food chains, and chain drugstores are other large users of retail advertising.

The merchant directs retail advertising to the consumer where he **71** lives and does his shopping. Often retail advertising is paid for in part or wholly by the manufacturer of a product, and is known as "co-op" advertising. Other retailers may receive "allowances" from the manufacturer for advertising their products.

Promotional Retail Advertising

At Christmastime, at back-to-school time, and at many other times during the year, you will see a special kind of retail advertising. This is advertising that does not directly advertise the product, but advertises the *promotion* of a product or group of products.

When a shopping center is going to put on its annual "Moonlight Madness Sale," in which merchandise is drastically reduced after 6:00 P.M. on a certain date, the center must announce the event. In order to insure the widest possible audience, the center will use all kinds of local media to announce the event days in advance of the sale.

If a famous author is going to sign autographs at the book store, or if a chef is going to give omelet cooking lessons in the kitchen-wares section of your department store, every effort must be made to let as many people as possible know about the event.

Often store promotions are sponsored by manufacturers. A cosmetic manufacturer may make a "beauty consultant" available. A manufacturer of women's sportswear may provide a traveling fashion show. If so, the supplier often pays for all or part of the promotion.

Industrial Advertising

Industrial advertising is simply advertising directed to a customer who happens to be an industry. Most people are not particularly conscious of industrial advertising because they have little occasion to see the publications in which it appears. But there is hardly an industry you might think of—from steel to coal, or from perfume to fishing—that does not have its own "trade book" devoted to the interests of the industry. As a young executive, you will read your industry's trade paper for both the editorial matter and the advertising. In our business we have some outstanding ones: *Advertising Age, Broadcasting, Art Direction,* are only a few of them.

Some of the businesses that advertise in a publication directed to the fishing industry are: boat builders, rope makers, engine manufacturers, makers of depth-sounding equipment, marine hardware manufacturers, paint manufacturers, and publishers of nautical charts and books.

OREGON BLUE LAKE GREEN BEANS

ITALIAN BUFFET SALAD—one of the new foodservice recipes.

Perfect in salads.

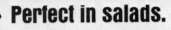

Salads worth their labor deserve greens and herbs that stand up and hold their flavor. You give them a crisp succulent flavor with Blue Lakes from Oregon, the one canned green bean that works wonders for menu planners. Blue Lakes grow best in Oregon. After all, it's their native state.

Dawson Incorporated, Portland, Oregon.

This is a typical association ad.

73

Trade Association Advertising

If you work for a manufacturer, the chances are very good that your company belongs to an association of manufacturers in its particular field. This association, to which your company pays annual dues, is devoted to your broad industrywide interests. Your association may maintain an office in Washington, D. C. in order to be close to political activity, and sponsor fairs and conventions. Whenever you see that a new Miss Cotton or Miss Washington State Apples was crowned, you can be sure that an association has been at work.

One of their most important tasks is to present your *industry's point of view* to the public. Advertising is often used to accomplish this. An industry may feel that its side of the story has not been adequately presented, or that its contribution to the economy is not appreciated. In such cases, association advertising and corporate advertising assume much the same appearance and work to much the same purpose. Sometimes you will see rivals contending within the same industry, such as Florida oranges vs. California oranges.

This kind of advertising, which encourages the consumption or use of cotton, leather, bananas, or milk, is known to marketing people as "primary advertising." It is differentiated from "selective advertising" that promotes a particular *brand* of cotton, leather, and so on.

Mail Order Advertising

Mail order ads are the couponed ads you see in magazines and newspapers, inviting you to send for a product that will be delivered to you by mail. Many famous successes have been scored by mail order advertisers, and much of what we have learned about advertising came from early ads with their measured coupon returns. Many publications devote special sections to mail order ads. Sometimes small shops venture into mail order and may find it a lucrative way to sell merchandise in addition to their regular retail business. *Warning:* In mail order advertising, many are called but few are chosen. You have to be very good to succeed.

National Consumer Advertising

National consumer advertising is the kind that makes up the bulk of the advertising you read in your magazines and see on TV. For the most part it is product advertising by the manufacturer, appealing directly to the person who will make the purchase at the store.

CORRECTION

Our ad that appeared in Friday's Times-Union featured Western Iceburg Cabbage at 35¢. This should have read as follows:

WESTERN ICEBERG

LETTUCE Lg. Head **29¢**

BANNER FOOD STORES

Putting together a chain store retail ad with dozens of items displayed is a difficult and exacting job. Inevitably, mistakes sneak in.

Fitting the Kinds of Advertising Together

Let us now see how the various *types* of advertising play their roles in the marketing mix. As an example, we'll use a paint manufacturer.

National consumer. The Smith Jones Paint Company will advertise its product in *House Beautiful* and in other publications that go to homeowners. Their objective is to convince the consumer of the high quality and economy of Smith and Jones paint, and to gain wide consumer acceptance for their product.

Trade advertising. Smith and Jones will advertise in such trade publications as *Hardware Age* to get hardware dealers interested in stocking Smith and Jones paints. They will mention high demand, good profit margins, and aggressive promotional support.

Retail advertisers. As an independent ad, or as part of a larger store ad, the Acme Hardware Company of Muncie, Indiana, will take space in the Muncie *Star Press* to promote its line of Smith and Jones paints.

Promotional-retail advertising. Acme Hardware will decide to put on a "Spring Spruce-Up Time" promotion. In the *Star Press*, and over station *WERK*, they will advertise the event and list as "special" the many products they have to aid the homeowner in fixing up his house. One of the items in the promotion will be Smith and Jones paints.

Mail order advertising. Acme Hardware gets a chance to buy, at a good price, books on home decoration. They decide to venture into the mail order business, and run couponed ads in the newspaper and in announcements over the radio. They hope to sell most of the books at a profit, and to get a good mailing list of people who are interested in home decoration and are therefore prime prospects for Smith and Jones paints.

Industrial advertising. Smith and Jones have a line of paints for use in industry and markets to users in industry. To promote this line, they take space in such industry-oriented publications as *Steel, Coal Age,* and *Fishing Gazette.*

Trade association advertising. Smith and Jones is a member of the National Paint and Varnish Manufacturers Association. This association is concerned about the use of outside building materials that do not require paint covering. They take space in publications directed to architects and builders, promoting the idea that "nothing protects and beautifies like paint."

Institutional or corporate advertising. The Smith and Jones Paint Company has a long-standing dispute with several unions affiliated with the AFL-CIO. The dispute is complicated and involves not only wages and fringe benefits, but safety and working conditions. To explain its position in the labor dispute, Smith and Jones takes full-page ads in the Canton, Ohio, *Respository,* and the Hammond, Louisiana, *Star,* where Smith and Jones have manufacturing plants.

The People Who Make Advertising

Now it is time, for you to meet the people who are responsible for this advertising which takes so many forms and appears in so many kinds of media. You will be surprised, when you reach the end of this chapter, to realize how many people in your hometown are concerned with the making and running of advertising. I suggest that you get to know as many of them as possible. They will welcome you into their shops and places of business, and be glad to explain how they do their work.

Not knowing who can do what, and for how much, can turn out to be expensive. The day may not be far off when you will be given the responsibility for producing a booklet for your company or getting a 30-second television commercial made. It is important to know the services that are available to you in your area, and to be acquainted with their individual capabilities.

The Four Advertising Departments

The Publication Advertising Department

When you call your newspaper to place a classified ad, you talk with the newspaper advertising department. A newspaper-space salesperson

who comes to see your advertising manager will be from that same
advertising department.

Publication advertising departments are different from all other advertising departments: their essential function is selling space. Because this is so, the advertising manager of your local newspaper has very different responsibilities from those of the advertising manager of a corporation. The newspaper advertising manager is essentially a sales manager, and his or her job is to oversee the placement of both retail and national advertising in the newspaper.

But note carefully: newspaper advertising departments also have a *creative capacity* of their own. There are many small advertisers in your town who do not have an advertising agency to do their work. For them, the newspaper advertising department is prepared to write copy and make layouts. Often the newspaper representative will write the ad for the retailer, and give it to one of the department's artists to lay out. Obviously it pays newspapers to provide this service; otherwise they might have to turn away potentially valuable clients.

Department Store Advertising Departments

The department store ad department differs radically from that of a publication. The department store has what amounts to an in-house agency that prepares advertising only for the store and its products, and is located in the store. Often it's a very exciting and hectic place. When buyers and department managers need advertising for a store item they usually need it in a hurry. Everything has to move like clockwork. Art work must be prepared, layouts designed, and copy written, often in a matter of hours so that the store's ad can reach the paper on time. Therefore it is essential for the department to be placed as conveniently as possible and be operated with tight, efficient control. Department stores have developed some very fine advertising people, and in our business it is said that "if you can survive and produce in a Macy's or Filene's, you can do it anywhere."

Department store advertising departments do not have to wait long to discover whether they have done a good job. When they run an ad for ladies' handbags, and the next morning have a mob waiting at the door, they *know* they've performed well. In *creative functions*—art and production—a department store ad department closely resembles that of an advertising agency.

Chain Store Advertising Departments

Very closely related to the department store ad department is the one found in your local food, drug, or general merchandise chain store. It differs mainly in the *type* of advertising it produces. The pages of food advertising in Thursday's paper, offering dozens of different items on "special," are produced in the chain store's own advertising department. The color brochures or inserts in your daily paper from Sears or Penney's, are usually made up in their own ad departments. Putting these ads and inserts together is a demanding and exacting job. Usually dozens of items are featured with illustrations and prices—and there's plenty of room for error. The job is not made any easier by the fact that store managers or buyers often do not decide on advertised prices until the last possible moment.

As with department store ad departments, sometimes they will produce their own radio and TV commercials. But it is more usual for stores to turn their TV production over to an advertising agency or a film production house, since TV requires a special kind of expertise generally not found in a chain store's ad department. These ad departments will often have a small printing press, and, using the skills of their art director, are prepared to provide collateral promotional material such as signs and posters.

The Corporate Advertising Department

A corporation's ad department has only a *limited* creative capacity. Primarily the corporate ad department's function is *supervisory;* it is the contact point between the company and its advertising agency. It is responsible for advertising budgets and for the general performance of the agency, though the final decision on retaining or firing an agency may be made on a higher level. The corporate ad department works closely with the marketing departments of the company, and is responsible for seeing that advertising efforts are completely integrated with the company's marketing strategy.

Just as most large corporations are departmentalized according to different plans—geographically, by brand, by customer, or by product—so are their ad departments. For example, several large food concerns market by brand, with brand managers and advertising departments concerned only with the marketing of that particular brand.

A large oil company may divide responsibilities in its ad department into consumer ads, institutional ads, and advertising directed to its industrial customers. Big manufacturers of electrical equipment and household appliances may have a different ad department *and* a different advertising agency to handle some of their wide variety of products sold to very different kinds of customers.

The position of advertising manager of a corporation is a very important one. Usually this individual is a vice-president of the company, and possesses the stature and background to deal with top-notch agency people, publishers, and suppliers. He must also have the management skills to keep the department completely in tune with top management, production, and sales.

Recap

Let's just review these four advertising departments so that you can keep them firmly in mind:

1. *Publication: A sales department* responsible for selling advertising space and serving advertisers.
2. *Department Store:* Primarily creative in function. It is geared to produce, quickly and efficiently, advertising for the store's merchandise.
3. *Chain Store:* Much like the department store's ad department, differing mainly in the type of advertising it produces. Usually it is limited to production of printed materials.
4. *Corporate:* Primarily *supervisory* and *coordinative* in function, works closely with advertising agencies, media, and suppliers. Coordinates with its own sales, production, and management departments.

The Advertising Agency

The modern advertising agency is the fountainhead from which flows most of the national and regional advertising you see in publications and broadcast media. Here originates the advertising for practically every famous brand you consume. Here also originate the orders to suppliers and media in which the advertisers' dollars are invested.

You will recall that in Chapter 1 we spoke of the development of the agency from space broker to the service that ordered space and prepared advertising for its clients. Basically this is what the advertising agency is today on a more elaborate scale. But the agencies also live in a changing world, and, as we shall see, the winds of change are blowing.

When most of us hear the words "advertising agency," we receive an image of "Madison Avenue" and the stereotypes we've encountered in novels and on TV. Actually the agency is a serious part of a very serious business—*marketing.* By its nature an ad agency contains more creative individuals than, say, an insurance company. You may find more beards and fewer neckties in an ad agency than at the Chase Manhatten Bank. But a TV director can be just as intense and professional over a camera angle as a banker over an international loan.

Have no illusions. The Madison Avenue version of the agency business is a tough man-killer. Accounts change hands with frightening regularity; sometimes for very capricious reasons. In a single year, millions in billing shift from one agency to another. Job security becomes a game of musical chairs. When an agency loses a multimillion-dollar account, it is a traumatic experience for everyone. Except in the very largest agencies, personnel adjustments must be made to withstand the sudden drop in income.

Personnel placement agencies, who cater to the ad business, estimate that the "life" of the average middle-income copywriter or art director in an agency is less than a year and a half. Little wonder that New York psychiatrists are struck by the number of their patients who work in advertising or related fields.

But there is a bright side too. To some, the business is so fascinating that they don't even imagine themselves anywhere else. It offers its people the satisfaction of seeing the tangible results of their talents and hard work. Monetarily it offers the young and gifted greater rewards than any other activity except perhaps show business. It is never dull; always exciting. There may be moments of dark despair, but these are always followed by moments of euphoria. Like show business, it has its glittering "stars." Like show business, too, it is kept functioning through the efforts of thousands of talented, hard-working, anonymous people who are the "supporting cast."

Strangely enough, few good books have been written about Madison Avenue. And it's a standing joke that the business seems to have done a better job for Smokey the Bear than it has for itself.

The large Madison Avenue agencies can be very fancy—with executive dining rooms, test kitchens, and TV viewing theaters. But, it has interested me to note, the average small-city insurance executive tends to have a far more magnificently decorated office than most big-agency executives.

Enough of Madison Avenue; it's a street on which you'll probably never walk. As a young business executive, working almost any place in America, the chances are about six hundred to one against your having anything to do with it. To understand why this is so, we will have to look at some statistics.

According to *Advertising Age*, quoting figures from the census bureau, in 1967 there were 5,618 advertising agencies in the United States, with a total billing of about $7.5 billion.[1] Today the figures for both are probably higher. It is interesting to note that the American Association of Advertising Agencies lists somewhat fewer agencies than the census. If you will look in the agency "Red Book," which is probably available in your library, you will find that the number of agencies for your city is lower than the number listed in your telephone directory Yellow Pages.

Providence, Rhode Island, shows 61 agencies listed in the Yellow Pages, and the Red Book has only 21. Charlotte, North Carolina, has 55 agencies in the phone book, but only 16 of these are listed in the registry. This great three-to-one divergence is indicative of the fact that *throughout most of the United States* the majority of "agencies" are one- and two-man shops, too small to be listed in the agency directory.

---

[1]*Advertising Age*, July 20, 1970, p. 10.

Available figures bear this out. In its "Compilation Advertising Statistics Since 1935," *Printer's Ink* showed that a relative handful—4 percent—of the agencies in the United States handle the bulk of the billing—70 percent; while a whopping 73 percent of the agencies must divide up only a mere slice of the pie—8 percent.

In other words, what we've come to regard as the advertising business is a relatively small group (perhaps 100 or so) of agencies handling a relatively small number of enormous accounts. According to *Advertising Age*, the top 100 agencies handle $5.68 billion in billings. To give you some idea of the size of their accounts, Procter and Gamble, the top spender, invests $310 million on its long list of products; General Motors is reported as spending $158.4 million.[2]

But for the great mass of American enterprises that spend advertising dollars the picture is different. About 4,000 agencies across the country have billings of less than $500,000 per year, and a great many of *these* do less than $150,000. For you and for the great majority of the business executives who spend promotional dollars on their products and services, *this* is the face of the advertising business as it is—and the one to which we direct most of our attention in this book.

As a young business executive, particularly a *local* business executive, the figures and the implications inherent in them are of great importance to you. What these mean, for one thing, is that the agency available to you in your hometown or in the nearest major city may not have the capabilities of those giants who produce a great deal of the advertising you are used to seeing in magazines and on TV. The big agencies with their enormous billings (J. Walter Thompson is one of the giants with over $700 million in United States and international billing) can afford to pay for the finest creative and executive ability.

From all over the country, ambitious and talented young producers, writers, artists, and account representatives flock to the "Madison Avenue" of a few big cities. It's the Big Apple—the place with the action and the money. One result has been a very serious drop-off in the quality of creative work available to the majority of advertisers in America. Advertising people themselves will be the first to point out to you that there still are cities in the United States of 500,000 and less, whose overall standards of advertising performance are pathetically low.

This cannot be laughed off with a shrug and the statement, "Well, you have to pay for what you get." The fact is that in advertising everyone *pays* the same. Whether you are an advertiser with a $10,000 yearly budget, or $10 million, the line and time rates are the same for *both* of you. As a small businessman, your advertising dollar is at least as important as that of some giant competitor; in fact, *more so*. (Fortunately this is a changing situation.)

---

[2]*Advertising Age*, August 26, 1974.

The Rise of the Regional Agency   **82**

The Different
Kinds of
Advertising and
the People Who
Make It

For some time now there has been a trend *away* from Madison Avenue and out into the rest of the country where most of the advertisers are. This trend can only be of benefit to every small or regional businessman. Even some of the Madison Avenue giants such as J. Walter Thompson, Young and Rubicam, and Wells, Rich, Greene have given some thought to the possibility of moving out of New York (*New York Times*, June 25, 1976).

As the economy has grown, and regional advertisers have had bigger budgets to spend on promotion, the health of the regional agency has improved. Added income has meant that they could compete with, if not match, the big agency's inflated salaries. Too, there has been a growing lack of enchantment with the Big City. Business publications report difficulty in inducing young business executives to make the move to the "main office." A number of corporations have opted for a smaller city or their own suburban "industrial park."

Many young people have become discouraged or disenchanted with the "rat race," and yearn for the less hectic pace of another city. To many, the lure of the trout stream or the ski lift only 15 minutes away from the office has proved irresistible. And the chance to raise the kids in a small-town atmosphere, without the drain of private schools and country clubs, has appealed to many others. The regional agencies haven't left a stone unturned.

Today, all across the country, there are ad agencies and peripheral services that do a perfectly magnificent job for their clients. It is too bad there are not more of them. Aggressive, "hot" regional agencies have long been aware that no one has a lock on talent; and if you went about it the right way, you could build a shop whose marketing know-how and creative ability did not have to take a back seat to anyone. Here is the way a regional agency goes after talent, in this case a copywriter. The ad appeared in *Advertising Age*:

We need an experienced writer who thrives on responsibility. One who isn't bashful when people (primarily AEs and clients) want to know the reasoning behind the writing. We need a writer who has the experience to help lead a young and aggressive creative group. A group that finds challenge in everything from 4-color bleed ads to $1,000 commercials. The writer we are looking for also believes living is more than an office 19 floors up. A person who'd be comfortable living on the other side of the fence where the grass truly grows. The writer we're looking for is looking for an agency that believes in new business, because that's what we're all about. If we're the agency you're searching for we'll show you our stuff—if you'll show us your stuff. But do it quickly. We needed you yesterday.

If you will look through the reference books in your library you will probably be able to find a chart depicting the departmentalization of an agency. You may study it with interest, but as we have said, it has very little to do with reality so far as you are concerned. Most of the agencies in your town are not like that. They *can't* be—not on a gross profit of $75,000 to $100,000 a year; and certainly not on a profit of less than $25,000 a year, a figure that would delight some "agencies" in your town.

But although many agencies in your town may not be as highly departmentalized as the Madison Avenue giants, they *are* prepared to deliver most of the services that a multimillion-dollar account expects from its agency. Let's take a look, then, and see what you, a business executive, can expect to get from your agency in your hometown.

Marketing Services

The principal of your agency should and probably will have a fairly good grasp of marketing theory. This person will undoubtedly have a good knowledge of the marketing situation in your community and in your region. He should be able to sit down with you and your sales manager and aid you in working out a sensible marketing plan for your product. He should know the *demographics* of the region, and the tastes and background of its people. And though knowledgeable about the other elements in the "marketing mix," it is in the area of people—customers—that this executive should be able to make the most valuable contribution to your marketing plans.

As you have already learned, promotion (advertising) is an integral part of the "marketing mix" so that you will *want* an agency person who can work closely with you in the marketing area.

A Creative Platform

Your agency people should be able to put together for you a "creative platform" or plan. It need not be a world-shaking document; the simpler it is, the better. A creative platform states for you, clearly and precisely, why your agency has prepared for you the *kind* of advertising it is presenting to you. What's the reasoning behind it; what is the philosophy? It should clearly state the goals of the advertising, and should rationalize the technique that has been used to reach those goals.

Copy

Your agency should be able to provide you with headlines and body text that are attractive, interesting, and hard-selling. Later on, we will provide you with the means of making a value judgment on copy.

Art

Attractive, clean, well-designed layouts should be presented to you for each ad your agency makes. In addition, your agency should have the capability of purchasing photographs, drawings, and other art work for you.

Research

The agency will have the means of setting up market research projects for you, and carrying them out for you on an acceptable basis. They should also be able to carry out some fairly simple forms of copy testing, and advise you on the "performance tests" that can be made on your advertising. They probably will not be able to help you very much in testing your TV commercials because of the expense and technical difficulties.

Media

You are going to need expert advice on the *amount* of advertising you will run, and where to run it. Your agency should know media (all the vehicles by which your advertising is brought to the consumer); have the means for placing orders for time and space, and promptly and accurately provide you with invoices and records.

Radio—TV

The agency will be able to have prepared and produced for you radio and television commercials of competitive creative ability and quality and in a wide price range.

Print Production

The agency will be responsible for the material necessary for the reproduction of your print advertising and will be able to order all type, engraving, mats, and so on.

As you have learned in the first chapter, one of the great watershed events in advertising was the installation of the "15 percent" system. Under this arrangement, the agency took a 15 percent cut on all space purchased from publications for its clients. It works this way: The agency places $1,000 worth of space and is billed $850.00 by the publication. The agency bills its client $1,000 and pays the publication $850.00—less a discount for prompt payment.

Newspapers have a special rate for retail advertisers and do not pay the 15 percent commission on this kind of business. Television and radio also pay the 15 percent (though this is sometimes negotiable). Outdoor pays 16 percent commission.

To receive commission on a national basis an agency must receive "recognition" from the publication association involved, such as the American Newspaper Publishers Association. This means that the association checks out the agency to see that it *is* an agency and a reasonable credit risk. On a local basis, the "recognition" is generally up to the medium being dealt with; some will ask for a credit statement, and others may not.

In addition, the agency derives an income from its markup of invoices for production items such as art, engravings, and type. The markup here is 17.65 percent or 15 percent of the gross. This is basically how it works. But the reality, particularly at the local level, is sometimes different.

Some years ago Ogilvy and Mather, today one of the great international agencies, shook up the advertising world by announcing that it had reached an agreement with one of its major clients to accept compensation on a fee rather than on a commission basis. The debate has been going on ever since. One argument presented by exponents of the fee system is that under the commission system the agency might be tempted to put more time and effort into commissionable work. Or, when an agency must put a lot of time and effort into noncommissionable work, there should be some fair method of compensation to the agency.

It used to be that the Advertising Trade Association forbade its members to rebate part of their commissions to their clients. But in 1956 the Department of Justice issued a consent decree and, as a result, today an agency is free to make any sort of deal it wishes to make with its clients.

Media Services and "Boutiques"

There have been other things stirring on Madison Avenue over the past few years. The advent of the independent media buying service was one. Specialists in this field handle the buying function for a number of advertisers or agencies as clients. Another change has been the more formalized use of outside creative talent through what is known as "boutiques."

For years top Madison Avenue art directors and copywriters have picked up an honest dollar on weekends by doing jobs for clients outside their own agencies, and even for other agencies. The moral line seems to be drawn at not working for an account *competitive* to the one in your own agency.

Lately very good creative talents have joined hands, formed their own shops (called boutiques) and sold their services to both agencies and advertisers on an independent fee basis.

So-called "house agencies" have always been with us, and are often frowned on by the rest of the business. In its purest form, a house agency is simply a corporate advertising department to which were added creative and media-buying capabilities. Commissions, of course, go into the parent company's treasury. Often house agencies fall somewhere in between. Lambert and Feasley, for example, was a house agency for Lambert Pharmaceutical Company products. But it also handled *outside* accounts, such as Phillips Petroleum Company, and made a healthy profit that was contributed to the corporate exchequer. Today there is a trend that seems to be completing the house agency circle and may revive its popularity. Corporate conglomerates are showing interest in absorbing profitable advertising agencies and letting them operate as independent entities within the corporate structure.[3]

The Agency Picture at Home

All that we have been saying about agency compensation and practice on Madison Avenue has long been familiar to your local advertising agency. Many of their accounts may be local retail enterprises, in which case there is no agency commission. To make a living, a fee *must* be charged. In many cases in which much of a client's business is non-commissionable, the agency will work on an agreed on monthly fee and commissions are charged off against it.

Rebating is nothing new either. Many local agencies, particularly when they have a large account, will find that they can get along quite well with it and themselves on less than the usual 15 percent.

In addition to commissions, fees, and the 17.65 percent markup on production invoices, many local agencies will bill their clients an *hourly rate* for the work of their art directors and copywriters. This rate is generally from $25.00 to $35.00 an hour.

The local and regional agency has long relied on outside media

---

[3]New York *Times*, October 23, 1974, p. 61.

buying services such as Blair Television, or companies representing groups of newspapers. These "representatives" perform an indispensable service for the small agency in which one or two persons may be responsible for all media purchases.

Though few cities under 500,000 will boast what Madison Avenue calls a boutique, the use of free-lance art and copy talent has long been a way of life with the smaller agencies. Independent "art studios" flourish in any city of size. When necessary they will retain a copywriter to perform special jobs; in effect, they become a boutique for the occasion.

The important thing for you to remember is this: Few of America's 4,000 local and regional agencies are "full service" in the way Madison Avenue understands the term. Few of them have under one roof all the departments representing client services, art, copy, print production, media, radio—TV production, research, and marketing. As has already been indicated (What Your Agency Can Do for You), the local agency is perfectly capable of delivering all these services by *retaining* them for you.

How the Work Is Done

If, as has been pointed out, most of the agencies in the United States aren't large or prosperous enough to afford the elaborate departmentalization of the large or medium-size full service agency, how do they get the work done?

Part of the answer has already been indicated to you: the smaller agency people put on different hats. A small-agency man may walk out of his shop as an account executive (the person in charge of the account and client services) and two hours later return to the office, take off his hat, and become what Madison Avenue recognizes as a copy chief. The person who does the billing may do all the media buying too. If there is a research project to perform, it is perfectly possible that everyone, including the receptionist, gets into the act. There's nothing wrong with this. It's the way thousands of American advertising agencies have been getting along for years. If they did not do it this way, they probably would not exist at all.

But these agencies in your community have other means of bringing you the total advertising package, and this is through the collateral advertising services that exist in most communities of any size. Remember, earlier in this chapter we said that you might be surprised at how *many* people are involved with advertising in your city? There are dozens of skilled people whose services are available to you and your agency. As a matter of simple economics, the agencies have discovered that it is much better for them, and for their clients, to retain these services rather than attempt to *staff* them.

Collateral Advertising Services

Art Services

In the Yellow Pages, under "Artists—Commercial," you will find listed the studios that specialize in doing graphics. Usually they will handle anything involving art or design from a business card or letterhead to an outdoor poster or color brochure. Some of these studios specialize in doing layouts for agencies. This arrangement is advantageous to the small advertiser as well as to his agency. Maybe the agency cannot afford to meet the salary of a full-time art director. It is far better, both from a financial and an artistic point of view, to retain the services of the best person possible, and the agency avoids the commitment to the overhead of salary.

In my town, which lists some 50 agencies, at the present time only three of these employ full-time art directors. If you are a small advertiser without an agency, you will find the commercial art studio most helpful.

Radio and Television Production

When television first came in, the big agencies toyed with the possibility of doing their own production. But they soon gave up the idea. Today most television commercials are produced by independent studios working in close cooperation with the agency television producer. Probably few of the agencies in your community have a television director; they go directly to the studio to get the job done.

You should distinguish between two sources for television commercials. If you have a television station in your town, you will find that it has the facilities for producing low-cost commercials. Many commercials for local retailers have been produced this way. You may also have a *motion picture production company* in your community or nearby in your state. These studios can handle any kind of a film job for you—from commercials to documentaries. They are prepared to supply all the creative talent—writers, artists, actors, producers, and so on, and will do "location" jobs when necessary. The costs are very difficult to "ball park," because so many variables are involved. Big-time national advertisers pay as much as $150,000 for a 30-second commercial. A rough estimate for a local advertiser might be from $2,000 to $3,000. If you do not have an agency you can go directly to these people for any film work, including slide film production.

The local radio stations themselves make a great many commercials. Often they are very good. The radio station representative who contacts you will gladly cooperate with you in seeing that you get a good commercial on the air.

Sound Studios

You'll find sound studios listed in the Yellow Pages under "Recording Service—Sound and Video." Often the small agency will go to them for help in making a radio commercial. They will make musical arrangements for you, hire bands and singers, and make a master recording with as many as eight sound tracks. If you want a jingle for your radio or TV commercial, this would be the place to go.

Printers

As a business executive it is important for you to be familiar with the printers in your community, and their capabilities. Be sure you distinguish between the small "job printers" who can handle the under $500.00 print order, and houses with four- or five-color presses who do the finer and more expensive kind of printing.

Outdoor Advertising

Your community has at least one company that handles outdoor posting. This is a "medium" through which your agency places orders for outdoor showings. Look for the company name on the board itself. They are also very knowledgeable about poster design; your agency may wish to go directly to them for the execution of your outdoor poster.

Car Card Advertising

Car card advertising is a "transportation medium." Car cards can be seen above the seats and at the ends of busses, subway cars, taxis, etc. Like the outdoor advertising firms, the car card people can be very helpful in giving you advice on dimensions and designs.

Direct Mail Houses

Direct mail houses will handle a "mailing" for you and your agency. A small city might not have this service. Look in the Yellow Pages under "Advertising—Direct Mail," or "Letter Shop Service." They will handle all phases of mailing, including the rental of mailing lists. Your local chain and discount houses are big users of the direct mailing companies.

Research

Research is an area that suffers badly when away from the big centers of advertising. Approach it with care. Your agency people may have had some experience in market, product, consumer, and advertising research. If not, there may be firms you can call on in your city. They will be listed in your Yellow Pages under "Market Research and Analysis." If none is available, try one of the marketing professors at the nearest university or community college; he ought to be able to handle the job for you with the aid of his students.

Writers

Free-lance copywriters are hard to come by in the smaller cities. Your agency, if it is on its toes, should know where to locate the best ones. You'll seldom find them in the Yellow Pages. We will suggest, under "Copy," several ways to solve this problem.

Artists and Commercial Photographers

Your art studio should be able to tell you immediately who are the good commercial artists in town. The curator at your local art museum or the head of the art department of your local college will know the gifted "semipros" and what they can do.

Almost every community has several commercial photographers. Often they are very good. The top-notch commercial photographers can be identified by the "ASMP" on business cards or letterheads. Today they are members of the Society of Photographers in Communications. ASMP refers to the old name of their organization, American Society of Magazine Photographers, whose initials they retain. You can get information on their members by writing to ASMP, 60 East 42nd Street, New York, N.Y., 10017. For less demanding and more economical jobs, agencies often use newspaper photographers on a free-lance basis.

People You Should Know

You should get to know the collateral advertising services. The quality of the services they can deliver and the prices they charge sometimes vary widely. Know their capabilities. You will find that most of them will welcome you into their shops, and will gladly explain how their operation works.

WHERE YOU ARE

1.   You can identify the various *types* of advertising, and you understand the part each one plays in the marketing process.

2. You can distinguish between the four different kinds of advertising departments in terms of the services each one provides.

3. You can define the basic functions of an advertising agency, and you understand the difference between most agencies in your community and the "Madison Avenue" type operation.

4. You understand the billing procedures followed by agencies which normally retain outside services to provide agency services.

5. You are familiar with the services available to agencies and their clients in most cities. Hopefully, you have visited some of them in your city.

QUESTIONS FOR CLASS DISCUSSION

1. Do you think it might be advisable to take all the small agencies in your community and make them into one large one?

2. If you had a $15,000 advertising budget, would you retain an advertising agency?

3. Under what circumstances do you think a regional advertiser should retain a large international agency?

4. Should the cost of "association" advertising be deductible as a business expense?

5. Where do you think the profit possibilities are greatest: in a one-man, medium, or large agency?

SOMETHING FOR YOU TO DO

You should, of course, visit a local advertising agency and get them to give you a guided tour. Many colleges arrange these trips for their students, and make them annual affairs.

You should also make it a point to visit all the collateral services listed in this chapter. Take your time, and spread out your visits. You will find that most people who run these businesses are very gracious about showing you around and explaining to you how they work. You'll get a lot more out of these personal visits than you ever could out of a textbook.

KEY WORDS AND PHRASES

Account Executive. Agency member responsible for one or more client accounts.

Advertising Age. Popular "trade" publication directed to interests of advertising people.

Advertising Agency. Organization that supplies its clients with advertising services.

Advertising Manager. Executive who is responsible for supervising the advertising efforts of the company.

Art. Refers, generally, to illustrative material used in advertising and promotion pieces.

Art Service. Organization that prepares and sells graphic work.

Boutique. Small shop that specializes in creative work.

Car Card Advertising. Posters that employ spaces in cars, busses, etc.

Chain Store Advertising Department. Department that prepares advertising for local use. (Distinguish from chain's central office ad department.)

Commercial Artist. One who produces art work for commercial use.

Copy. The words in an ad that carry the selling message.

Corporate Advertising Department. Responsible for company's advertising efforts. Headed by advertising manager.

Creative Platform. A formal statement of the basic philosophy and reasoning behind ad or campaign.

Demographics. Set of characteristics of a market or group. Used in drawing a profile.

Department Store Advertising Department. Creates the advertising for the store's merchandise.

Direct Mail House. Business that handles mailing of promotional pieces.

Freelance. Usually copy or art. Person who works independently or who takes on work outside his or her regular job.

Full Service Agency. Advertising agency that is staffed to offer the full range of advertising services to its clients. The majority of U.S. agencies do not fall into this category.

Hourly Rate. Rate that agency charges its clients for time creative people put on account.

House Agency. Agency set up by an advertiser to handle its own advertising, usually exclusively.

Industrial Advertising. Advertising directed to consumers of industrial products (coal mining equipment, for example).

In-house Agency. Similar to House Agency, except that advertiser buys most services outside from freelance operators, boutiques, etc. (much as smaller agencies buy from outside sources).

Institutional Advertising. Advertising that promotes the company as such, rather than one of its specific products. "ARMCO—Responsive People In Action."

Location Job. Filming outside studio, such as beach, street scene, etc.

Madison Avenue Street in New York City where many large agencies are located; used to designate world of "big" advertising.

Mail Order Advertising. Advertising, usually couponed, that uses the U.S. Mail to complete the transaction. Distinguish from *Direct Mail*, which sends the advertising itself through the mail.

Marketing Services. Those services that are available to help solve marketing problems.

Media. The vehicles by which advertising is brought to the attention of the public.

Media Service. A specialized business that selects and buys media for its clients.

Motion Picture Production Company (Film House). Organization that is staffed to produce film—motion and still.

National Consumer Advertising. Advertising to the consumer of nationally marketed products.

Newspaper Advertising Department. Newspaper sales organization that sells space to national and retail accounts. (Some creative capacity.)

Outdoor Advertising. Generally used to mean posters and spectaculars.

Primary Advertising. Promotion of a general concept, rather than a specific item ("Drink More Milk" as against "Drink Borden's Milk").

Print Production. The steps involved in preparing an ad, mechanically, for reproduction.

Promotional Retail Advertising. Advertising by a retail store publicizing a store promotion.

Radio-TV Production. The steps necessary to take a radio or TV script from written form to final broadcast form.

Rebating. The practice of returning a portion of the media commission to the client.

Recognition.   Refers to the acceptance of an agency or organization as a legitimate operation qualified to place business and receive commissions.

Regional Agency.   An off-Madison Avenue agency whose accounts come mostly from a particular area. Also, one of the larger agencies in a state or area.

Research.   The work done, by a variety of methods, in gaining advertising and marketing information.

Research firms.   Organizations that specialize in carrying out research projects for agencies, advertisers, and media.

Retail Advertising.   The kind of advertising done by local retail stores. Distinguished from *National Retail*, which is advertising prepared by the home office and distributed nationally.

Selective Advertising.   Often used in connection with "primary advertising." The advertising of a specific product or brand.

Trade Association Advertising.   Advertising sponsored by an association of marketers for the benefit of its members.

Trade and Professional Advertising.   Advertising directed toward specific types of business or professions.

SELECTED READINGS

Singer, Jules B. *Your Future in Advertising* (New York: Richard Rosen Press, Inc., 1960). On page 81 of this book, you will find an interesting chapter entitled, "Let's Discuss Advertising Opportunities Away from the Big Cities."

Obermeyer, Henry. *Successful Advertising Management* (New York: McGraw-Hill Book Company, 1969). A "how to" book for advertising managers, which also applies to business without ad managers. You'll find two excellent chapters on the subject, "Getting the most—and the best—from your advertising agency."

Mayer, Martin. *Madison Avenue, USA* (New York: Harper and Row, 1958). Read this for a good, hard, sober look at what Madison Avenue is and how it operates.

Lyon, David G. *Off Madison Avenue* (New York: G. P. Putnam's Sons, 1966). Amusing and informative account by an executive who got off the merry-go-round and started his own agency in his garage. You'll find some very good practical advice for the executive who is going to deal with a small agency.

Ogilvy, David. *Confessions of an Advertising Man* (New York:
Atheneum Publishers, 1963; London: Longmans, Green, & Company, Inc., 1963). When Ogilvy speaks of Winston Churchill and his character, it well may be that he is also speaking of D. Ogilvy. Like P. T. Barnum, in his wonderful series of "Memoirs," David is not adverse to a little playful distortion. You don't have to believe everything he says. But read the book if for no other reason than that it was written by the man who may have made a greater contribution to our business than anyone in the last 50 years.

Fitz-Gibbon, Bernice. *Macy's, Gimbels, and Me* (New York: Simon and Schuster, 1951). Life in the department store ad departments. If you are in the retail business, this book is required reading.

Advertising Management Development Committee, *Perspectives in Advertising Management* (New York: Association of National Advertisers, Inc., 1967). Nearly 150 presentations made at ANA conducted seminars. The big picture as seen by the big shots.

chapter five

Market Research—
The Need to Know

In this chapter, we talk about how important regular and dependable information is to the marketer. You will discover that a detailed knowledge of your particular segment of the market is essential to your success.

You will become familiar with some of the different kinds of market research and some of the methods by which this research is carried out. You will see how market information can help the small business as well as the large one.

You will be introduced to a kind of advertising research that is the essential first step in the creative advertising process.

If you had been a successful train robber in the West you would have done things in a certain way. You would have left very little to chance.

When it came time to stop the 5:03 from Laramie with the miners' payroll on board, you would have been prepared.

1. You would have chosen a bend in the track on an upgrade where the train would have to go slowly, and where the curve would conceal the torn up tracks until the last moment.

2. You would have known just about how big the payroll was, and which baggage car contained the safe in which the payroll was locked.

3. You would have been familiar with the type of safe, and the exact amount of dynamite necessary to blow it open.

4. Your gang would have the definite assignment of destroying the rails, overpowering the engineer, and opening the baggage-car door.

5. You would have provided an escape route—with plans for dispersing—making pursuit difficult.

6. You would have known the normal location at that time of day of all the sheriffs and sheriff's deputies.

7. You would have had an agreed-upon plan for the sharing of the loot.

If you and your partners had done your work well, you might have had a chance of pulling off a successful job and getting away to Mexico. Many of your fellow train robbers were not so fortunate. They did not do their homework as well as you did yours. Something unexpected went wrong, and they wound up swinging from a tree limb.

I'm pointing this out to you because, though it is important for you to do your homework if you are planning to hold up a train, it is even more important if you are planning to launch a new business or a new product. The chances of pulling off the train robbery are greater. Each year thousands of businesses that didn't do their homework die with their boots on.

Studying the Market

What we will talk about now is formally known as "marketing research." Mandell has a more meaningful phrase for it, "market intelligence."[1]

Gathering intelligence about the market is an absolute prerequisite to successful marketing. Since advertising is an integral part of marketing, market intelligence is also *first* required if intelligent and effective advertising is to be prepared.

The Need to Know What You're Getting Into

Before you can make any move in marketing—and this includes advertising—you have to know *what you are getting into*. Look around in your community and you will see the evidence of businesses that actually didn't know *what they were getting into*. The shuttered door and the "Closed for Repairs" sign hanging forlornly in a dusty window tell the sad story. The shores of every community are littered with the wrecks of business enterprises that started with high hopes, a great idea, and a hard-earned bankroll. If, before they opened their doors, someone could only have done them a favor and held before them a sign with that age-old piece of advice *"Look Before You Leap."*

Let me give you an example from our town of someone who didn't know what he was getting into.

On the banks of the river near the college where I teach, there is a beautiful little restaurant. It has been closed for some time now. The man who built it, did so with loving care. It had a Dutch windmill motif. I'm sure a great deal of his earnings went into it. His dining room was attractive, with glassware and silver sparkling in the candlelight, and he served interesting lunches and dinners at medium prices. But few people came to dine. After a while he had to close.

---

[1]Maurice I. Mandell, *Advertising* (Englewood Cliffs, N.J.: Prentice-Hall, 1974), p. 205.

Perhaps if he had looked before he planned and built the restaurant, he would have done it differently. He would have seen that businessmen in this part of town seldom go to a restaurant at lunch time. They take their lunch to work with them, or they go home for lunch.

He also would have noticed that in this part of town men don't generally take their wives or families out to dinner. They are good to their families, and they do lots of fun things together, but having dinner in a candlelit restaurant isn't one of them.

All that was easy enough to realize *afterwards*. You probably see what we're getting at because, in a sense, you have already been there.

The Profile of a Market

As you have just seen, our restaurant owner was blind to the *character* and *personality* of his market.

He didn't *see* which way the traffic flowed after 5:00 P.M.

He didn't *notice* all the hamburger palaces and the fried-chicken places.

He didn't *observe* the luncheon habits of the businessmen in his area.

He didn't *understand* the dining customs of the people who live in that part of town.

He was so unseeing because he didn't understand something you have already learned—that every market has a *profile* made up of its age, education, sex; income, religion, and some other factors.

You know, as he didn't, that people are social beings and react in groups (going home to lunch). You know that they have different psychological needs (barbecued ribs in the backyard versus candlelight dining).

By now you also probably realize that the restaurant failed because it was in the *wrong place* at the wrong time. There *is*, in our town, a *right place* for it.

A big part of the job of gathering market intelligence has to do with finding the *right place* for every store, every product, and every service that goes forth to do battle on its own.

Market Segmentation

You have already met the phrase *market segmentation* in Chapter 2. We said that some people in your area are much more likely to buy what you have to sell than are certain other people. We said that if you are going to be successful, you must find this segment. We also said that you can define your segment by drawing its *market profile*. Sometimes markets segment themselves; at other times the segmentation is deliberately created by the manufacturer.

The market segment for denture adhesive that keep false teeth from falling out was created by Mother Nature herself. It is defined by the number of people who have had the bad luck to lose their teeth and are forced to wear dentures.

Bath soap has a nice ready-made market segment—all the people who like to take a bath. But notice something: it is possible to break that big soap segment into other segments. We have perfumed soaps designed for ladies' baths. We have soaps that are meant for locker rooms, where sweaty athletes shower. We have soaps to improve the complexion. We have soaps for auto mechanics, and for homemakers who wash their own dishes.

Modern manufacturers have learned that a good way to create new business is to make a new segment for themselves. When your father first started smoking cigarettes, he didn't have too many brands to choose from. Lucky Strikes, Old Golds, Camels, and Chesterfields—they were the best known. Mostly they differed only in the appearance of the package. Today, if you do smoke, you have many brands from which to choose. You have a filter on your cigarette, or you have it flavored with menthol if desired. You can smoke one of a normal length, or a "king size" cigarette. You can choose a Camel, which hasn't changed an iota since it became so popular with the doughboys in World War I, or you can choose a Virginia Slim, a cigarette that was marketed especially to appeal to women.

Businesses often use price and "policy" to carve out their segment. A woman in your community may say to herself, "I am going to open a dress shop. *My* market segment is going to be well-to-do fashion-conscious women." Her *policy* will then be to design and furnish a store with an air of exclusiveness about it, and to stock it with the expensive clothes of top designers.

The big distillers have been very clever about market segmentation. Once upon a time, *one* whiskey distiller made *one* whiskey, just as *one* auto maker built *one* car. Today Seagrams has a brand and price for almost every taste and pocketbook. And think of all the different Fords you can buy.

I'm sure you can see the wisdom of this kind of segmentation. Why should I let you walk away from my store simply because I do not have the kind of product you want at the price you want to pay?

I hope you see now that as a business executive you can go either of two ways. Like the unfortunate builder of the abandoned restaurant, you can grope blindly ahead, not really knowing what you are getting into. You can *hope* that there is enough of a market segment for what you have to sell, and you can *pray* that enough of that segment will find you.

But faith alone is not always enough. A little good work helps too. So the wise merchant *knows* the town, *knows* the market segment, its dimensions, its characteristics. He also knows the customers—and if the town is small *all* about *them*, and the money in their pockets, their likes and dislikes, and their habits and styles.

Why is it so very important that you *know* the customer? That's easy. *If you don't know the customer, you can't talk to him.*

To Talk to Me, You've Got to Know Me

Wouldn't it have been awful if when Romeo made his impassioned plea to Juliet, she'd been on a balcony on the *other* side of the house? And suppose Mr. Lincoln had decided to stay home and issue the Gettysburg address as a press release?

Suppose, a few years from now, you have $150,000 of your company's money to spend but you don't *know* your potential customer. So you spend your money in the wrong place, at the wrong time, and talking to the wrong people. You waste it.

But as you have learned in Chapter 2, a marketplace consists of *more* than people. It's a place where all kinds of things are *happening*. It's a place where all kinds of things are going on that may be good for the sale of your product—or they may be bad.

Imagine yourself walking down the street of your hometown and stopping in at the big, well-kept home on the corner. You would meet the

Pantry Pride Supermarket, Jacksonville, Fla. Courtesy of Mr. Frank J. Thomas, Director of Advertising and Sales Promotion, Jacksonville Region, Food Fair Stores, Inc.

Soon customers will be filing past those modern check-out counters in this "marketplace." The more you know about these people, the more successful you will be.

Joneses, who live there. In addition to Mr. and Mrs. Jones, you'd get to know brother Bob, sister Jane, and young Ricky. Mrs. Jones is reading a book. Mr. Jones is trying to balance his checkbook, and is getting madder by the minute. Bob is in the garage tinkering with his car. Ricky is trying to do long-division problems in his homework and has forgotten to carry the "two." Jane is sitting in front of the television, seething because her boyfriend has failed to sympathize with her viewpoint on a matter important to her.

Before you leave the house you have become acquainted with the Joneses. You know much about them, and about what's going on in their house. Knowing about people and what is going on in the market is one of the most vital jobs of business. As you have seen, if you neglect to do it, or do it wrong, it can be fatal.

Let us see, then, how business goes about accomplishing this important task.

The Kinds of Marketing Research

A few years ago, the American Marketing Association did a survey of marketing research. They found the companies they questioned fell into five major classifications of research.[2]

1.   Market and Sales Research
2.   Market and Sales Research Functions
3.   Product Research
4.   Business Economics Research
5.   Advertising Research

Marketing and Sales Research

Probably more activity takes place in marketing and sales research than in any other. This is the "how are we doing" kind of research. One of the most common forms is the "Share of Market" study, which at regular intervals shows you just how you are doing in relation to your competitor. Sales research is also used to analyze sales results, to determine market characteristics, and to aid in the study of changing markets.

Market and Sales Research Function

The market and sales research function includes store audits, analysis of test market results, and studies of special tests and premium offers.

---

[2]James H. Myers, and Richard R. Mead, *The Management of Market Research* (New York: Intext Educational Publishers), p. 28.

Product Research

105
Types of
Research
at Work
in Your
Community

In product research you keep an eye on what your competitors are doing. What improvements have they made in their product? You also look into the opportunity for new products in your line, or a new use for your product. A good research and development department will carry on a continuing program of product testing.

Business Economics Research

Many business executives have a regular program of reading in order to keep themselves up to date on changes in the economic weather. Like the soothsayers of old, "forecasters" of business conditions over the long and short term are in great demand. Reading the *Wall Street Journal* every morning can be considered as business economics research.

Advertising Research

In addition to using and sometimes carrying out the above research, advertising research usually concerns itself with studying the various *media*. Thus advertising research uses are as follows: the cost of a particular medium, and the kind and number of people it reaches. Another kind of research is involved in looking into the psychological "needs, wants, and desires," that were discussed in the last chapter.

One of the most interesting aspects of advertising research is the study of the performance of advertising itself. Here we look at ads and commercials and try to either predetermine their performance, or analyze their performance after they have run. For the advertiser, this is an important kind of research and we will devote a chapter to it later in the book—after you have learned how to put together ads and TV and radio commercials.

Types of Research at Work in Your Community

The kinds of research we have reviewed may sound formal and theoretical to you. You may think that these are methods used only by the giants of industry and their agencies. This is not so. Every successful business uses them to some extent, although the user may not give them the same formal titles as we have.

I think you might like to meet a friend of mine, Mr. Deatry Lang, who runs a store in my town. He calls the store "The Movin' Dude"—a great name for a store, isn't it? He selected the name because he wanted to make clear that he was catering to young men who were "going places."

The Movin' Dude sells men's wear. The styles he features are very

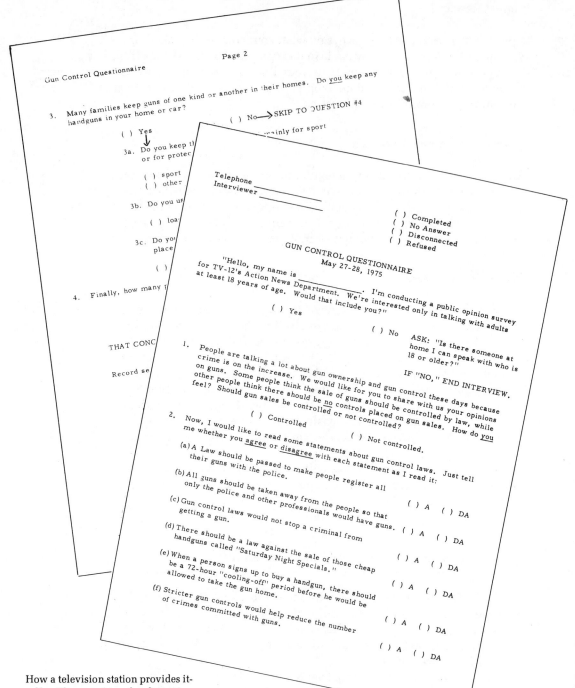

Page 2

Gun Control Questionnaire

3. Many families keep guns of one kind or another in their homes. Do you keep any handguns in your home or car?

( ) No →SKIP TO QUESTION #4

( ) Yes

mainly for sport

3a. Do you keep th... or for protec...

( ) sport
( ) other

3b. Do you us...

( ) loa...

3c. Do yo... place...

( )

4. Finally, how many...

THAT CONC...

Record se...

Telephone
Interviewer _____
_____

( ) Completed
( ) No Answer
( ) Disconnected
( ) Refused

GUN CONTROL QUESTIONNAIRE
May 27-28, 1975

"Hello, my name is _____. I'm conducting a public opinion survey for TV-12's Action News Department. We're interested only in talking with adults at least 18 years of age. Would that include you?"

( ) Yes

( ) No   ASK: "Is there someone at home I can speak with who is 18 or older?"

IF "NO," END INTERVIEW.

1. People are talking a lot about gun ownership and gun control these days because crime is on the increase. We would like for you to share with us your opinions on guns. Some people think the sale of guns should be controlled by law, while other people think there should be no controls placed on gun sales. How do you feel? Should gun sales be controlled or not controlled?

( ) Controlled

( ) Not controlled.

2. Now, I would like to read some statements about gun control laws. Just tell me whether you agree or disagree with each statement as I read it:

(a) A Law should be passed to make people register all their guns with the police.

( ) A   ( ) DA

(b) All guns should be taken away from the people so that only the police and other professionals would have guns.

( ) A   ( ) DA

(c) Gun control laws would not stop a criminal from getting a gun.

( ) A   ( ) DA

(d) There should be a law against the sale of those cheap handguns called "Saturday Night Specials."

( ) A   ( ) DA

(e) When a person signs up to buy a handgun, there should be a 72-hour "cooling-off" period before he would be allowed to take the gun home.

( ) A   ( ) DA

(f) Stricter gun controls would help reduce the number of crimes committed with guns.

( ) A   ( ) DA

How a television station provides itself with a variety of information about its market. These questionnaires were used by the Research Department of WTLV, Television 12, Jacksonville, Florida.

106

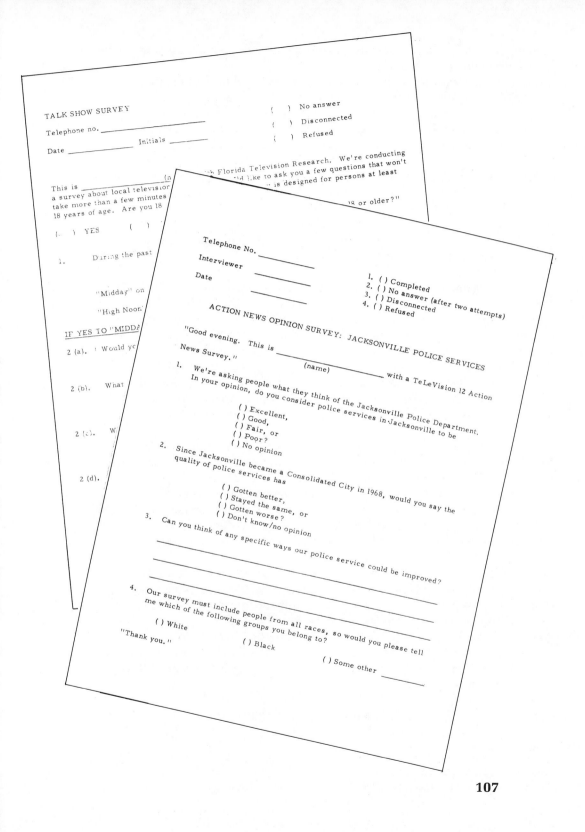

TALK SHOW SURVEY

Telephone no. _____

Date _____ Initials _____

( ) No answer

( ) Disconnected

( ) Refused

This is _____ (n
a survey about local television
take more than a few minutes
18 years of age. Are you 18

Florida Television Research. We're conducting
ld like to ask you a few questions that won't
is designed for persons at least

8 or older?"

( ) YES ( )

1. During the past

"Midday" on

"High Noon

IF YES TO "MIDD/

2 (a). Would yo

2 (b). What

2 (c). W

2 (d).

Telephone No. _____

Interviewer _____

Date _____

1. ( ) Completed
2. ( ) No answer (after two attempts)
3. ( ) Disconnected
4. ( ) Refused

ACTION NEWS OPINION SURVEY: JACKSONVILLE POLICE SERVICES

"Good evening. This is _____ with a TeLeVision 12 Action
News Survey."
(name)

1. We're asking people what they think of the Jacksonville Police Department.
   In your opinion, do you consider police services in Jacksonville to be

   ( ) Excellent,
   ( ) Good,
   ( ) Fair, or
   ( ) Poor?
   ( ) No opinion

2. Since Jacksonville became a Consolidated City in 1968, would you say the
   quality of police services has

   ( ) Gotten better,
   ( ) Stayed the same, or
   ( ) Gotten worse?
   ( ) Don't know/no opinion

3. Can you think of any specific ways our police service could be improved?

   _____

   _____

   _____

4. Our survey must include people from all races, so would you please tell
   me which of the following groups you belong to?

   ( ) White
   ( ) Black
   ( ) Some other _____

"Thank you."

107

modern. Mr. Lang runs a successful operation because he knows where he is going and what *he* is into.

I have talked with Mr. Lang about his business, and he told me that he, as a person who had been selling men's wear for some time, carefully considered the chances of selling his particular kind of far-out styles in this market. Before he even opened the doors of his store, he had a reasonably good idea of how many young men there were in town who would be interested in wearing the styles he was planning to feature.

What he carried out would be a type of market and sales research known as *development of market potential.*

The Movin' Dude also keeps its eye on its competition. There are only two other stores in town that carry about the same styles in the same price category. Mr. Lang also uses his eyes and ears to keep up to date on how their business is. More formally, you would call this a *share of market study.*

The management of The Movin' Dude goes in for a lot of *product research* too. Recently he had to make a decision as to whether his slacks would have belt loops, and whether the back pockets would have button-down flaps. Mr. Lang spent some time on the phone talking with knowledgeable men's clothing people in Atlanta and New York before he made his decision.

So far as *business economics research* is concerned, the proprietor of The Movin' Dude reads *Apparel Art* and *Men's Wear,* and makes a point of keeping himself thoroughly up to date on the economic trends in the market.

The Movin' Dude has done its own *advertising research* too. Although Mr. Lang's advertising budget is limited, he studied his market segment and the possibilities for reaching it. As a result, he hit on the distribution of leaflets at certain high-school football games as an effective and economical means of reaching his potential customers.

We have mentioned The Movin' Dude and its activities to show you that *any* business, large or small, can profitably use the tools of marketing research.

Marketing research, as practiced by leading corporations, can take some very sophisticated (and very expensive) forms. Companies such as General Foods, Bristol-Myers, and Kellogg spend hundreds of thousands of dollars each year on marketing research. But as you have seen, you don't have to be a multimillion-dollar corporation in order to justify marketing research. It is just as important for the smaller local and regional business to have access to all the "marketing intelligence" it can get its hands on.

Another way for you to look at this "marketing intelligence" is in terms of how the intelligence can be put to work for you. Myers and Mead have listed six questions that you might want to ask yourself about your business.[3]

---

[3]James H. Myers and Richard L. Mead, *The Management of Market Research op. cit.,* p. 28.

1. What are the basic trends in the domestic economy? How, specifically, will this affect the market for your product?
2. What changes can we expect in customer purchasing patterns? Will this be based on changes in real income, on changing tastes and values, or on changes in patterns of distribution?
3. What will our needs be over the next three years in terms of sales manpower? Branch offices? Distribution centers (warehouses)?
4. What new markets are likely to open up? What types of products or services will be needed to serve them? Are there promising markets we are not now serving?
5. Are there more efficient channels of distribution for our products? What new types of marketing institutions are likely to evolve?
6. What opportunities exist for our products or services in other countries? Are our international marketing efforts intensive enough?

109
Types of
Research
at Work
in Your
Community

How Can These Questions Affect Your Business?

What you have just read is not simply a list of offhand questions; they are questions that every business executive must continuously ask him- or herself. If you are to grow and prosper, you must get *most* of the answers *right* most of the time. To make sure you don't get the idea that only people listed on the New York Stock Exchange ask themselves these questions, let's try an experiment. I'm going to apply the following six questions to situations that I personally know about. You do the same.

1. Trends in domestic economy? In my area, high interest rates have cut way down on construction of condominiums and apartments. Many agencies and art services I know do ads and brochures for real estate developments. They all feel the financial pinch from the loss of this kind of business. Several have had to let their people go.
2. What changes can we expect in customer purchasing patterns? Several great names in hat manufacturing have suffered due to the change in customer purchasing habits. But hats, certain kinds of hats, are coming back big among certain kinds of purchasers. Look around your own campus, and you'll see what I mean.
3. Manpower needs? Despite a business recession, most of our local businesses are almost desperate for high-quality sales trainees and executives.
4. New markets likely to open up? The new styles in men's hats, replacing the old ones, is a classic example of a new market opening up. We have definite evidence in our town that, with increased prices, "farmers markets" are growing in popularity.
5. More efficient channels of distribution? L'eggs—the panty hose—discovered that they could depart from the usual channels

of distribution for women's hosiery. All kinds of stores, particularly food and drug outlets, carry L'eggs displays in our town.

6. Marketing opportunities in other countries? It has always seemed to me that Ireland does not develop its foreign markets aggressively enough. A friend of mine, an American, has helped to revive the Waterford glass industry of Ireland. Too few people know the beauty of Irish tweeds, lace, and linens. Maybe *your* foreign market is as near as the next county.

How to Get Market Intelligence

We have seen the importance of "knowing what you are getting into." We have seen how important it is to gather all kinds of intelligence about your marketplace and the people who live in it. We have also seen that market intelligence is no respecter of size, and that it is just as vital to the small business as it is to the large corporation.

Let us review, then, some of the methods used to gather market information.

Define the Problem

The people who carry out market studies like to define the problem. They want to know *exactly to what* you need the answers. What percentage of people prefer the taste of your ice cream to that of your competitor? How many people pass a given corner between 5:00 and 7:00 P.M.? *Not* zeroing in on your problem can cost you a lot of money and wasted time.

Background Information

Researchers sometimes call background information *secondary* information. You are already familiar with some of these sources from our discussion in a previous chapter.

Census reports. A basic source of statistical information. Information about income, number of people, education, and so on. See or write to your nearest Department of Commerce Office.

The public library. Contains all kinds of books and periodicals with information that may be of interest to you. This includes *historical* information about business in your community. Just tell the researcher behind the desk what you need, and you'll get lots of help.

City hall records. Tax rolls, automobile and business licenses, real estate records, and other information can be useful sometimes.

Chamber of commerce.   Most chambers of any size retain a research director. If not, someone will be glad to assist you. They usually have a finger on all kinds of information involving your local market.

National publications, local radio, TV, and newspapers.   The media are in the business of selling market segmentation. They carry on continuous research in order to reveal more and more facts about their readership. Simply write to the research director of the publication. They will gladly help you. This media is particularly useful when you are looking at specialized groups, such as fishermen or aircraft pilots. And your local TV and newspaper probably have someone doing research.

Trade associations.   As previously noted, trade associations exist to help the people in their particular fields. Even if you are not a member, they can be very helpful if you demonstrate a legitimate interest.

Syndicated research services.   These are in the business of providing regular survey information, and, in some cases, special studies. They are very much involved in media studies and in the reaction of people to ads and commercials. Among the more widely known are A. C. Nielson Company, Schwerin Research Corporation, and Daniel Starch and Staff.

Your own office.   Often your own office records contain information that can be of help to you. Sales records, price changes, customer complaints and comments, all can sometimes give you the facts you need. In many instances these will provide the *only* intelligence you need to make an accurate evaluation of your marketplace.

The trade press.   In Chapter 2 you learned the value of the trade press. Its publications are important not only for the advertising they carry, but also for the editorial information they contain. Clothing retailers, for example, read *Women's Wear Daily* to discover buying trends in other parts of the country.

Counts.   Just the simple act of *counting* things can be useful. Before a new poster location goes up, your outdoor company has performed a *traffic count.* Few franchise fried-chicken places are built until the company has an accurate reading on the flow and direction of traffic passing the store site.

Structured and Unstructured Research

Research professionals recognize two main types of research: *structured* and *unstructured.* If you sat down with a group, let them sample your new kind of yogurt, and recorded their comments, you would be doing *unstructured* research. The *depth interview* is a more sophisticated kind of unstructured research. Here a skilled interviewer asks questions designed to reveal your true thoughts and feelings. The interviewer must have professional skills because the techniques of psychological testing are then used. You may have had some experience with the projectional techniques in which the respondent is asked to complete a sentence or interpret a picture. As this type of unstructured research requires the services of a skilled interviewer, the average-size agency and small business firm have little opportunity to use it.

Structured research is the kind you can and should be using in your business all the time if you know what you are doing. The method, or methodology, as the pros love to call it, can be summed up in a rule that sounds like a newspaper reporter's description of the perfect lead—*who, how, what,* and *so*?

Whom Do You Want to Talk to?

The first vital step in the structured method is what is known in the trade as "selecting your sample." It is this clever sampling selection, for instance, that makes it possible for political pollsters to measure voting patterns so accurately in elections involving millions of people, although their samples are relatively small. The group *from which* the sample is taken, no matter what its size, is called a *universe.*

Research people recognize two kinds of samples: *probability* and *nonprobability.* You encountered a nonprobability sample when you got a group of pre-selected homemakers together in a room and asked them about your yogurt.

A probability sample is one in which members of your sample are selected at *random*—every tenth name in the phone book or every third house on Smith Avenue. In this random sample, everyone has an equal chance of being included, and of arriving in your sample by a random method that precludes any predictable chance of having been selected.

A simple mechanical method of compiling a random sample in your community would be to make a paper scale that marks off every tenth name in a phone book column. Then apply this to the third column in every page of the phone book.

A *stratified sample* is one in which you require your sample to meet a certain predetermined pattern of makeup; say, 50 percent Catholic, 25 percent Baptist, and 25 percent Episcopalians. These can be selected randomly.

How Do You Talk to Them?

The next important decision you will make is how you are going to communicate with the respondents in your sample. Probably the simplest way is to send out interviewers to ask the questions. Advertising copywriters often do this themselves on an informal basis. They'll spend some time in a supermarket questioning the persons in the checkout line, or they may talk to them in the parking lot.

One advantage of the *personal interview* is that you can cover a lot of ground and probe rather deeply. Generally speaking, people are more than willing to be questioned (it's a form of compliment) and they often show remarkable patience. The very fact that you are jotting down their answers or recording them seems to impress many persons.

There are, however, things to be careful of in this personal interview technique. The interviewer should be personable, objective, courteous, experienced in interviewing, and, above all, honest. There's always the chance that your *interviewer* may decide to fill in a few questionnaires (particularly when he is being paid per interview) and then go back to bed. And don't think that this won't throw your results for a loop! One way to protect yourself against this is to require names and phone numbers of those interviewed, and then run a validity check on, say, every tenth name.

Generally interviewers are paid by the hour (from the minimum hourly wage rate on up to $3.50 or $4.00, depending on the demands of the job and the skills of the interviewer) with a mileage allotment allowance if they must use a car. This is the most expensive method of interviewing, but you do get a lot for your money.

The *telephone* is a very handy gadget for interviewing. Maybe you've scrambled out of the shower, clutching a towel around you, to answer the ringing phone and you hear a voice ask you sweetly, "Would you please tell me what television show you are now watching?"

With a phone interview you can zero in exactly on the kind of people you want to question, all the ministers in town, all the plumbers, and so on. If the information you are seeking can be stated briefly (as above) then a phone interview is great. As many as 30 calls an hour can be made, and you can probably hire capable interviewers at the minimum wage. But for obvious reasons, it is very difficult to get any great depth of information this way.

The *United States mail* is often used to reach a sample of correspondents. The rate of return will vary widely, depending on how obligated your sample feels to give you the information. (There's always a handy wastebasket nearby.) This is very good for longer, detailed questionnaires requiring time and thought. You can cut out a fairly exact sample by using this method. Your local direct mailing house can supply you with suitable mailing lists, and also handle the envelope stuffing, addressing, stamping, and mailing for you.

The use of groups or *panels* has already been mentioned. All the big food packagers and processors keep a panel of homemakers on hand who can be called on to try a new soup or a slice of angel food cake. This method is particularly good when expert judgment is required. If six members of your town's scuba diving club pronounce your new wet suit superior to other suits, you can be quite sure you've got something.

Another thing, no matter how small your city, you can be almost certain

that it is possible to pull together a competent panel of experts in almost anything from birdwatching to brain surgery!

One of the simplest methods of collecting information for retail merchants is to put the questionnaires out on counters or tables where customers can get them. Retail salespeople, route men, and others in constant contact with the public, can also help you gain information if you will supply them with the proper questions. For example, the supermarket checkout girl is in contact with hundreds of customers per week. A simple question, calling for a "yes" or "no" answer, and a pocket-counting device, might uncover very interesting information at practically no cost. The small businessman has been overlooking some awfully good bets in gathering information.

What Shall You Ask Them?

We've already discussed some of the vagaries of human nature. So before we discuss the preparation of our questionnaire, here are a few basic facts about the human personality, stated in nonpsychological terms:

1. There are a great many people in this world who will guess, lie, claim, or swear (or, to put it more kindly, dissemble) rather than admit to you that they *don't know*.
2. Few of us ever give ourselves the worst of it. If I make $15,000 a year, I'll look you right in the eye and tell you its $20,000.
3. Most of us, being of a friendly nature, tend to tell people what we think they *want* to hear.
4. Most of us would rather *agree* than disagree.
5. We tend to frame our answers in the way that will reflect the most glory or prestige or credit on ourselves.

Now that you are aware of these horrid facts, I think you can see why it's not a good idea to ask in your questionnaire, "Like many people, do you enjoy vanilla ice cream?"

Suppose you were in the ice cream business, and wanted to find out how many people preferred vanilla. How would you ask the question? *You sneak up on it.*

First you might find out whether they eat ice cream by asking, "Of the following refreshments—cake, pie, ice cream, fruit, candy, or cookies, please indicate in the box beside each one whether you eat it often, occasionally, or never." Having in this manner established that you have an ice cream eater on the hook, you ask him to "Please indicate your first, second, and third choices among the following flavors—chocolate, raspberry, vanilla, tutti-frutti, or strawberry."

From this you would be able to tell not only the number of those who prefer vanilla, but also the relative preferences for all the other flavors.

I hope this clearly illustrates to you that one of the cardinal rules in making a survey is: never ask anyone to *tell* you anything. Let them *reveal* it to you.

So? What Did You Find Out?

If you have properly structured your questions, then, despite a relatively small sample, you will enjoy the thrill of having some real information revealed to you.

As in the ice cream survey, where you are dealing with numbers, you can't go wrong. If 55 demonstrated a preference for vanilla, 20 for strawberry, 16 for chocolate, and 9 for tutti-frutti, you can bet that you *are* in a vanilla market.

But be very, very careful. When a conclusion seems evident, don't jump at it. You can have the fact in your hand, and then blow the whole ball game by misinterpreting what that fact is telling you.

I know of one research organization that did a citywide study of supermarkets. The study was an expensive one, and, among other interesting facts, it showed that Store X's customers were *older* than the customers of the other supermarkets. The logical conclusion of the survey: store X had an attractiveness for the older customer.

It *was* a logical conclusion, except that the evaluator of the survey had jumped too soon. I was teaching a marketing class at the time, and we decided that the answer was too pat. We thought that maybe there was a different answer. So armed with *our* survey, we went out to store X, and began asking questions.

The older people existed in store X all right, and they had been doing business with store X consistently and for lengthy periods of time. In other words, you didn't just find more *older* people in store X; you found more *loyal* people. The other stores were getting a big turnover of young marrieds who were still experimenting around, trying this meat counter today, and that vegetable department tomorrow. But when they finally settled on a store, it was store X and they stuck with it. This was a very exciting piece of research information, and one that the survey people had completely missed because they had grabbed for the first brass ring that came along.

Structured Research—A Summary

Whom you question: It is necessary for you to get a random sample that reflects your universe. It should reflect the proportional makeup of your universe in demographic terms. You could not run an accurate bank survey by questioning only working mothers under age twenty-five.

How you question: There are four major ways in which interviews are carried out.

1. Telephone: It is inexpensive, gets many returns in short time, requires brevity, and sacrifices depth of inquiry.
2. Personal Interview: It is more expensive, slower, requires a certain amount of training and integrity on the part of the interviewer, affords good depth and detail, and has good returns. Few people turn down personable interviewers.
3. Mail: It can be very expensive per reply. Depending on the sample, a high percentage may go unanswered. Those who do answer are often willing to do so at length and express themselves fully. It is very good where expression of knowledgeable opinion is required.
4. Panels: The use of a panel can be both inexpensive and fairly fast. But remember—your panel must be made up of people knowledgeable in the area you are investigating.

What you ask: One of the most difficult aspects of structured research is this: Remember that people's personalities color their answers. Wherever possible, structure your questions so that the respondent *reveals* the answers to *you*.

What did you learn? There is no rule of thumb that can insure the accuracy of the interpretations of your results. Be careful of jumping to the obvious conclusion. There is always the chance that a deeper reason lurks beneath the apparent one. Be careful of those who find that the research confirms their preconceived notions. Don't throw out results that seem "impossible."

A Checklist for Good Research

The Advertising Research Foundation of New York has published a checklist you can use in evaluating your research project. You will find it useful. Here it is, in slightly modified form.

1. Under what conditions was the study made? Statement of methodology? Time covered? Organizations participating? Instructions to interviewers?
2. Has the questionnaire been well designed? Was it pretested? Does it contain danger of bias? Poor choice of answers? Too much demand on memory?
3. Has the interviewing been adequate and reliably done? Training, experience, and honesty of interviewers? Spot checks?
4. Has the best sampling been made and followed? Random sample is preferable.

5. Has the sampling plan been fully executed? Can variations impair validity?
6. Is the sample large enough?
7. Was there a systematic control of editing, coding, and tabulating?
8. Is the interpretation forthright and logical? All basic data that underlie interpretation should be shown. Analysis should be clear and simple.[4]

Research and Your Business

The nasty fact of the matter is that research is a tool that too many small businessmen use about as often as they use a laryngoscope. And it shouldn't be that way. Gathering information about your product and competitive products, and your customers and other people, should be as regular a part of your operation as sending out your invoices. Because what you don't know about your business *can* kill you—literally.

I do a little market-consulting on the side, and one of the tasks I'm often called on to perform is to determine what kind of market exists for a certain product. The trouble is that these people usually wait until they are in trouble before they call me.

What with the popularity of franchising, thousands of hard-working people are getting into businesses they know little about and are armed only with high hopes and dreams of financial security. I know a gentleman who has $15,000 worth of a certain kind of equipment that is just waiting in his storage area. At first glance, the item looks like a great buy for anyone who runs a service station, garage, or a wrecking service.

One of the first things I did was to call the president of the small firm that had manufactured this equipment. I said, "Hey, how did you come to design and build this thing, anyway?" He said, "Because it's a great idea, because it's needed. All my friends think it's a great idea, too. They told me so." "Tell me," I asked, "did you ever do a market study on this thing? You know, a feasibility study to determine if there was a real need for something like this?" There was a long, hurt pause. "Listen," he said, "I don't trust those market studies."

I could feel a chill creeping up my spine. It was then I knew that my client had just bought himself a $15,000 parking place on the boulevard of broken dreams.

Why is it so important for you, as a small businessman, to poke, probe, ask questions, wet your finger to see which way the wind is blowing, send out questionnaires, and conduct surveys? Because *the world changes*; sometimes it changes much faster than we realize. Life styles change, needs and desires change, fads come and go. *Life* and the *Saturday Evening Post* became one with Nineveh and Tyre. Something

---

[4]*Criteria For Marketing and Advertising Research* (New York: Advertising Research Foundation, 1953).

could be sneaking up on *you* while you are happily counting your profits.

Remember what happened to the hat industry. *Stetson*, for goodness sakes, is no more. The same thing almost happened to the shoe business. For years and years Jarman and Johnson, and Murphy, and all the others had been making the same beautiful shoes—in brown and black, in wing tip and plain. Year after year after year. And an awful lot of young fellows were beginning to go without shoes. All that was changed, however, in the nick of time. Today, for the first time since the Middle Ages, shoes are unblushingly wild. Men's shoes, for example: platforms, wild colors, box toes, and other designs. And they are selling like hotcakes. Fortunately someone had his finger up and discerned a change in the wind.

Something for You to Think About

Suppose people started going without the item you make or sell. How piteously you would cry, "Why didn't somebody warn me?" Consider yourself warned.

The Search for the Main Attraction

Early in this chapter we mentioned advertising research as one of the important factors in marketing research. Because much of this kind of research has to do with the *performance* of advertising, I think you will get more from studying it if we wait until later in the book to discuss it in detail.

After we see how advertisements and commercials are made, which we will be doing very shortly, we shall see how actual and potential performances can be tested.

There is, however, one kind of advertising research that is most important, and one that takes place logically as a part of marketing research. It is an important *first step* to the writing of any advertising platform or advertising copy. There are a number of terms for it, but we will call it "The Search for the Main Attraction."

What It Is

Whenever a circus comes to your town there is always the advance ballyhoo and publicity, and every spring the advance publicity features one *Main Attraction*. The circus never changes very much from season to season, but the *main attraction* always does. Sometimes it is a Hungarian with a company of waltzing horses; and one year, I remember, it was a living curtain of Dazzling Delightful Dancing Damsels. A circus

Sheraton...
Right on Waikiki Beach.

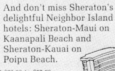

You're going too far to settle for less.

Waikiki Beach is the center of Hawaiian fun and excitement. And Sheraton has four luxury resort hotels right on Waikiki Beach. A fifth Sheraton is a half block away.

Sheraton offers a wide range of accommodations to suit your budget — from beautiful mountain-view rooms at the Princess Kaiulani for just $20.00* double occupancy, to sumptuous oceanfront Tower rooms at the Royal Hawaiian for $52.00.*

For reservations and complete information see your travel agent or call Sheraton at this toll-free number:

800-325-3535

And don't miss Sheraton's delightful Neighbor Island hotels: Sheraton-Maui on Kaanapali Beach and Sheraton-Kauai on Poipu Beach.

*$23.00 to $57.00 February-March

Princess Kaiulani
(a half block from the beach)

Moana
Surfrider

Royal
Hawaiian

Sheraton-Waikiki

Stay at one Sheraton, play and charge at all five.

Sheraton Hotels in Hawaii
SHERATON HOTELS & MOTOR INNS, WORLDWIDE
P.O. BOX 8559, HONOLULU, HAWAII 96815   808/922-4422

Fawcett-McDermott Cavanagh, Inc. Honolulu, Hawaii.

Here's an ad with a Main Attraction you could hardly overlook. The famous Waikiki Beach!

would no more dream of arriving in town without a main attraction than it would think of leaving the elephants home.

So now we shall talk about the *main attraction* for your advertising. How do we determine the feature your product has that makes it most attractive to the buyer? How do we develop that characteristic of your product or service which makes it possible for you to deliver the *benefit* that will satisfy the *need*?

Another way to look at it: The benefit is what the product will do for the customer. The *main attraction* is the quality you have *built into the product*. Sometimes your product may not already have a strong main attraction. Then it will be necessary to create a *main attraction* for it, particularly when there are many similar competing products on the market.

The discovery or creation of a *main attraction* is the most important and vital step *preliminary to the creation of the ads and commercials*. There are many ways to dig up a main attraction. Often, in the smaller agencies, it is the copywriter himself who does the job. Let's look at some main attractions—those characteristics that make a product different, and more desirable to a consumer than a similar product.

A nice simple one to start with is Sunbeam Bread. The main attraction about Sunbeam Bread is that it is Batter Whipped—which results in a finer-textured, more flavorful bread that stays fresh longer. Of course I very much suspect that *all* bread is batter whipped; but no matter, Sunbeam is Batter Whipped. Their agency was smart enough to *say* so.

By the same token, Lucky Strike cigarettes had for years a main attraction; they were *toasted,* a process not unknown in the tobacco industry. Very often a product will feature the commonplace, and, by featuring it, make it their exclusive property.

Sometimes your *main attraction* will fall into the "secret ingredient" category. Show me a manufacturer of barbeque sauce, and I'll show you a jealous possessor of a secret ingredient handed down from father to son to this very day.

Kentucky Fried Chicken's *main attraction* is "Finger Lickin' Good" because the batter in which the chicken is fried has a combination of herbs and spices known only to Colonel Sanders.

For years Colgate Toothpaste had a main attraction called MFP, which helped reduce tooth decay. Shell Gasoline contained *platformate*, which reduced engine wear and improved mileage.

Frequently main attractions emerge from the work of the research and development people, who labor all winter long with slide rules and sketch pads in order that next year's model may have a main attraction. Ford's Mustang was a spectacular example of a manufacturer-created main attraction; it is a reasonably priced, sporty-looking, hot-performing car that met the changing tastes of car drivers.

A refrigerator's main attraction may be decorator colors, or "no defrosting necessary," or ice-cube making and storing, or trays in the door. All are *ideas* from the drawing boards of research and development.

Sometimes your main attraction is neither a design, nor an ingredient, nor a process, but a concept. At a time when ocean travel was fast disappearing, the French Line told people, "Half the fun is getting there!" Their main attraction was this: the time to unwind and relax, the romance of shipboard travel, the wonderful food, the service, the companionship, and the time to enjoy it all.

The resort Virginia Beach says, "Don't run out of things to do before you run out of vacation." Their main attraction, as developed by the ad, is: "A million and one things for you to do and places for you to see around Virginia Beach."

Or take the History Book Club. Their main attraction is "Any three books 99¢"—though the headline on the ad says, "Vacation in the eighteenth century," and lures you on with promises of what a ball you're going to have reading about Napoleon, Jefferson, and the "enlightenment."

Or the Duff Gordon Sherries. It won't exactly bowl you over, but their main attraction is the fact that "the Duff Gordon name means great sherry . . . since 1768." In this case the headline sums it up "Six great sherries. One great name. Duff Gordon."

Here's one that ought to fascinate you, the Council for Financial Aid to Education, Incorporated. (All in favor, say "Aye!") This ad is asking for money. It winds up, "Give to the college of your choice." What's *their* main attraction? They come right out and tell you in the copy, "America needs these 'subsidies,' for we need more college-trained minds. *And that's the point of this appeal."* (Author's Ital.)

Here's an interesting ad by Hilton International for their hotel in Bogota, Columbia. It's all about what a great hotel it is, and in the very last line of the main copy block they give you *their* main attraction: "The Bogota Hilton. *It has everything."* (Author's Ital.)

You'll find it in almost every ad. The *main attraction* is the quality or characteristic about your product or service *that makes it especially attractive to the potential customer.* It's that something extra you and your product have going for you.

If you should open a restaurant next year, you're not going to open just a *restaurant,* but a place with that something *extra.* You're going to open a place with a *main attraction*—a place where people can eat all the fried chicken and shrimp they want for $2.00; where beer will be served with authentic North German cuisine; where everything on the menu is in French, or where the waiters come on between courses and do the quartette from *Rigoletto.* It's what makes your place different and attractive—*your main attraction.*

How Main Attractions Are Discovered

One of the interesting things that happen to advertising people is that they are forever sticking their noses into other people's business—literally. Very early you learn that it's a good idea to have strong legs and arches because you're going to spend a good many hours standing around in drugstores, or being conducted down lines of whirling machines, or peering into beer vats. If your instincts are right, you learn to talk to the right people and ask the right kinds of questions, and the particular kind of thing to look for. Most executives love their businesses and enjoy talking about them. They'll spend endless hours explaining to the uninitiated how one goes about getting that particular flavor in a beer, or how they achieved the beauty and utility of their newest refrigerator.

This business of "a walk through the plant," as it is known among ad people, is a ritual that must be repeated every time an account changes hands. One dutifully climbs into half-finished airplanes, or tries not to faint dead away at what goes on in a packing plant.

It can be dangerous, too, if you have a tendency toward daydreaming. I nearly got killed one time in a rod mill in Carnegie, Pennsylvania. The workers whip this white-hot stuff around as you'd twirl spaghetti on a fork. A snakelike piece of this lethal metal got loose and would have cut me off at the knees if someone hadn't kindly hauled me out of the way just in time.

But no matter how many steel rods you have to dodge, or how tired your feet happen to get, "a walk through the plant" is one of the most valuable ways to turn up those precious *main attractions* that are going to put you and your product an extra half step ahead of the opposition.

Often the people who run the plant are so close to it they can't see the woods for the trees. One time I was going through a cigarette factory with some people, when we came to a stainless steel drum in which tobacco and menthol were being blended. The plant manager didn't think it was such a great thing. Did anyone else have one? No, they had designed and built the drum themselves because they found it difficult to blend tobacco and menthol evenly. What did they call the machine? Why, they didn't call it *anything*, but it really worked. *Wow!* We could hardly wait to get back to our typewriters.

Very often the germ of a main attraction can be found buried in a dull, dusty, two-inch-thick research report full of graphs, pie charts, and statistics. Sometimes a report involving organic or inorganic chemistry, or physiology, will contain the seed from which a beautiful *main attraction* will grow.

Many of the *main attractions* found in gasolines, toothpastes, soaps, and polishes are based on facts disclosed in laboratory reports. Most cooking oils, for example, have a *main attraction*, which is "low cholesterol"—certainly a product of information produced by technical research.

At one time I worked in an agency that was desperate for a new theme for a breakfast cereal. The research director had for years possessed a tidbit of information tucked away in her files to which no one would pay any attention: A university research team (nice and independent) had been able to scientifically prove that when workers ate a nutritionally balanced breakfast, their production rate during the morning hours was superior to the rate of workers who had eaten an unbalanced breakfast or no breakfast at all. A copywriter discovered the tidbit, and was off and running. From it was born a campaign for the breakfast cereal that kept the account in the agency.

As you have learned under "unstructured research," one of the very best ways to turn up MA's is to *listen* to people. Let them chatter in an informal way about your product, and you will sometimes be amazed at the things they see in your product or in the things they like. And if you find certain words and phrases making a pattern throughout the interviews or conversations, note them well—because these are the very words you will later want to play back in copy to your potential customers.

A tape recorder is a very handy thing to have along on these sessions. An ad man was hunting for a main attraction for a beer account. He tucked his tape recorder under his arm, and started on a tour of bars and taverns. He'd step up to a bar, buy everyone a fresh round, flip on the machine, and start a discussion about beer. Of course the tape picked up all kinds of funny and outrageous remarks. But it turned up a gold mine of uninhibited information on beer, and beer drinkers, too.

Another variation of this, as you know, is the "panel discussion" in which a limited but representative group of people is asked to express its opinions. Panel discussions often turn up some surprising and valuable information. If you hear certain words or phrases repeated—even such as "scrumptious"—you'll know you are on to something.

WHERE YOU ARE

1. You understand the importance of the part played by research in marketing.

2. You have learned that if you are going to communicate with your market segment successfully, you must know all you can about those you wish to talk to.

3. You can define five kinds of basic marketing research. You understand how these can be used by the local marketer and small business.

4. You know a number of sources from which the marketer can obtain secondary information. You have identified these sources in your hometown.

5. You comprehend the difference between structured and unstructured research. You understand the basic steps in structured research.

6. You know four methods of carrying out a structured research program, and the advantages and disadvantages of each method.

7. You have learned the basic importance of advertising's *Main Attraction,* and the various kinds of research used to discover it.

QUESTIONS FOR CLASS DISCUSSION

1. Would you say that research is an exact science?

2. Some people feel that marketing research is an invasion of their privacy. Do you agree?

3. You have read that some companies sustained severe losses because they didn't do enough marketing research. Cite a case in which marketing research may have made your life better or more pleasant.

4. Five years ago, what was the *Main Attraction* of the car or toothpaste you know best?

5. If you wanted to find out how the adults in your community really feel about Women's Lib, how would you go about it?

SOMETHING FOR YOU TO DO

Design a market research project that will define and quantify the market for foreign sports cars in your community. On the basis of this study, you will make a recommendation as to whether it is feasible to establish an agency for foreign sports cars. If so, where in your community should it be located, and what potential sales level can be expected?

KEY WORDS AND PHRASES

Advertising Research. Studies that contribute to advertising.

Business or Economic Research. Studies of general business and economic conditions.

Census Reports. Studies of U.S. population made by Department of Commerce every ten years.

Coding. Giving systematic form to research.

Editing. Reviewing for errors.

Feasibility Study. To look into the possibilities of a market.

Franchising. The licensing of an operator—usually to run a retail outlet.

Interpretation. What do the facts really tell you?

Marketing Intelligence. Meaningful facts about a market.

Marketing Policy. The way you decide to go about marketing your product.

Market Potential. What the feasibility study shows you might be expected from the market.

Market Segmentation. The slices of a market according to certain criteria.

Methodology. The way you go about doing a job.

Panel. Group of consumers who can be asked for judgments and opinions.

Probability Sample. A sample in which we all have an equal chance of being included.

Product Research. Studies into the facts surrounding the goods themselves.

Questionnaire. A formal list of questions to be asked during a study.

Random Sample. A sample that is chosen according to a formula.

Secondary Research. Background information that contributes to over-all study.

Share of Market. That part of the market you possess as against your competitors'.

Stratified Sample. A sample that is divided in a manner that has been decided beforehand.

Structured Research. Studies in which a definite procedure is followed in gaining information.

Syndicated Research Service. Organization conducting regular research services that are sold to clients.

Tabulating. Putting the numbers together.

Unstructured Research. Informal studies that do not follow a predetermined form.

Walk Through the Plant. Traditional ritual that takes place when a new agency must be familiarized with all aspects of a client's business.

SELECTED READINGS

Davies, Anthony H. *The Practice of Marketing Research* (London: William Heinemann, Ltd., 1973). Marketing research from the British viewpoint. The British can't use the telephone for interviewing as we can, because of the weighing in favor of middle- and upper-class telephone-owning homes.

Green, Paul E., and Tull, Donald S. *Research for Marketing Decisions* (Englewood Cliffs, New Jersey: Prentice-Hall, Inc., 1970). University-level textbook. Chapter 1 will provide you with a good overview of marketing research.

Kleppner, Otto. *Advertising Procedure* (Englewood Cliffs, New Jersey: Prentice-Hall, Inc., 1973). See Chapter 14, p. 314, "The Search for the Appeal" for excellent treatment of the problem of discovering the Main Attraction.

Leonard, Dietz. *The Human Equation in Marketing Research* (New York: American Management Association, Inc., 1967). As the author says, "This book grew out of dissatisfaction with the results of traditional and conventional market research, which largely uses the *facts* as described through statistical tables but cannot begin to solve the human equation." Readable and practical.

Myers, James H., and Mead, Richard R. *The Management of Market Research* (New York, Intext Educational Publishers, 1969). See Chapter 2, p. 23, for an excellent exposition of the applications of market research. This would be a very good short book for you to read on the overall subject.

Uhl, Kenneth P., and Schoner, Bertram. *Marketing Research* (New York: John Wiley and Sons, Inc., 1969). Rather advanced stuff, theoretically, but contains a number of case histories that will be of practical interest to you.

Journal of Advertising Research, and *Journal of Marketing Research*. Files of these publications can be consulted for numerous articles of interest in the fields of marketing and advertising research.

chapter six

How Advertising Is Written

In this chapter we look at the copywriter.

You will become aware of some of the qualities a copywriter needs to have to perform well.

You'll see the steps the copywriter goes through before writing any copy.

You'll also learn the close relationship between the strategic steps taken in a sales presentation and those taken in preparing a piece of copy.

This chapter will show you, I think, how you can examine a piece of copy and form a reasonable judgment on its potential as a selling instrument.

You will, I hope, come away from this chapter with a new respect for the art of writing a successful selling message.

The Copywriter

The responsibility for writing ads and commercials rests with the copywriter. But as you have already learned, in smaller agencies this task is often performed by someone who might also be an account executive.

In fact, in times when agency profits are slimming, even the larger agencies begin to seek out people who can be both account executives and copywriters. A recent ad in *Advertising Age* placed by a well known New York agency says, in part, "You want to be a business person as well as a communications person. You like to get deeply involved with your clients' marketing problems, and feel at home with Capital Foods accounts. *You feel you get your best creative work done by doing it yourself.*" (Author's Ital.)

But whatever the title may be, there comes a moment when *someone* will have to sit down before a blank piece of paper and begin creating an ad.

What Does the Copywriter Do?

The term copywriter is not an exact job description. It could mean "the person who writes the words that go into the ad or commercial." But that **129** is not quite it. It's not as simple as that. The writer doesn't just write words. He or she creates selling ideas that are expressed in words and sounds and pictures.

Fortunately the copywriter doesn't have to work alone—at least not in the big agencies. Before and after the act of getting something down on paper, there are account executives, research directors, marketing directors, and art directors with solace, help, and advice. But after the captains and the kings have departed, and the cleaning crew has begun the evening round, if you look into an office where the lights are still burning and see someone sweating over a hot typewriter, chances are that you are looking at a copywriter.

What Is a Copywriter?

Writing advertising copy is hard work. It is hard work because (1) it is constantly demanding; (2) it calls for the command of a variety of writing styles; (3) it calls for a peculiar combination of natural talents and inclination that rarely occurs in one person.

Let's look at this in more detail.

Demand

A good copywriter seldom has to seek far for new worlds to conquer. Usually they are waiting for him on his desk when he arrives in the morning; or they may still be in his briefcase where he had placed them the night before. Aside from the "one-person" agencies, there are many of the over 4,000 smaller agencies dependent on one "creative director" to produce the bulk of their advertising.

Like the news reporter who must spring into action the moment the firebell rings, the "one-person" copy departments are constantly in demand to satisfy a client's unexpected needs. This leads to the next problem.

Variety

The average small-agency copy chief has to be a regular one-person band with words. He or she has to be a master of style—able to turn it off and on at will. Here are three paragraphs of copy taken from recent ads. Note the differences.

The BJM Mixer-Feeder will pay for itself year after year plus giving you additional profit in more weight gain on beef cattle and more milk production from dairy cows. (BJM Mfg. Co., Inc., Dodge City, Kansas.)

. . . . Settle in on Maui, where resorts range from casual to superific, then step back in time on Molokai and Lanai. Here, on the site of

Maui's new Kapalua Resort, nature fashioned a quiet cove to pic-
ture-postcard perfection. Warm crystal waters. Arching palms. And
distant Molokai, like a giant humpback whale on the horizon.
(*Maui—the most Hawaiian island of all*, Fawcett, McDermott,
Cavanagh, Inc., Honolulu, Hawaii.)

The important thing is that you try BEFORE you buy. You don't spend
a penny unless you decide to keep the luggage. And then you pay only
the low Fingerhut price of $29.99, plus shipping and handling, FOR
ALL THREE MATCHED PIECES. (Fingerhut Corp., St. Cloud, Minn.)

Different copywriters produced these particular pieces of copy. But in
the majority of America's agencies, the *same* copywriter must often do a
campaign for the local undertaking establishment before lunch, a TV
commercial for an auto dealer, and brochure for a farm equipment
company before closing time. While all *this* has been going on, she's had
an idea for her community United Fund on the "back burner."

Talents

If you could have arranged to inherit the traits of a mother who was a
successful novelist, and a father who was a great salesman, you'd probably make a good copywriter. Unfortunately the chromosomes don't
often fall that way. That's why good copywriters are so hard to find; and
why the really good ones are seldom out of a job for long.

The copywriter really has to have a broad spectrum of talents. On one
hand he's the brash, enthusiastic, ambitious salesman; on the other he's
the quiet, introspective, sensitive craftsman with words. No wonder the
combination is rare.

The Business of Words

Copywriting involves making words work for you. Words are the step-
ping-stones on which selling ideas are carried from you to your customer. This doesn't mean that you have to write brilliantly or beautifully. It *does* mean that you must write clearly and crisply. You cannot
afford the luxury of the 100-word paragraph. The 3-syllable words can
kill you.

Remember the dedication of the cemetery at the Gettysburg battle-
field. The "big" speech was made by Senator Everett. President Lincoln
offered a few "remarks" he had scribbled out on the way up from
Baltimore. Just a few common, simple words, arranged in his particular
fashion. Few Americans can ever forget them.

Somehow, it's the lines with the little words that seem to last the
longest:

"Give me liberty or give me death."
"Our Father, Who art in Heaven . . ."
"Let's win this one for the Gipper."
"We have met the enemy and they are ours."
"A good man is hard to find."
"Thou shalt not steal."
"Never look back; someone may be gaining on you."

Is Your Copy Understandable?

Advertising writing goes by a set of rules different from any other kind of writing. Sometimes people kid us about it. They point a finger and say, "Winston tastes good *as* a cigarette should." Or they look down their noses and say, "Your sentence doesn't have a verb."

I know. Because in copywriting, we have a rule that comes before all the other rules: *Make 'em read it!*

In the excitement of writing an ad, this is a basic rule we sometimes forget. If we can't get you to read our ad, to stay and listen to what we have to say, how can we sell you? Once we get you started reading our sales story, we're not going to let you go. And if some very simple basic rules of English construction happen to get busted in the process—why, that's too bad. We'd rather keep you reading!

We have to remember that we're not doing you a favor by writing this ad; you're doing *us* a favor by reading it. You didn't ask us to write the ad; you just happened to be there leafing through a magazine and stumbled on it.

So we make it just as easy as possible for you to read what we have written. If we think it will make it easier for you to get into the next paragraph, we'll end the first one with a leader, like this. . . .

And for the same reason we might even start the next paragraph with an uncapitalized initial word. We love leaders . . . they open up the copy . . . give it room to breathe . . . make it easy on the eye. And dashes—do we use dashes! They're like arrows. We also write nonsentence sentences like this. Short. Punchy. Most copywriters avoid the semicolon. (A review of the advertising in one of the largest circulation magazines uncovers *no ad copy* using the semicolon.)

A Readability Measurement

The grammar-rule breakers are useful on occasion. The very best way to keep your reader, though, is to make sure that your copy is simple, direct, and forceful.

Rudolph Flesch has given us a measurement by which we can judge

The only way to know which keyboard is best for your product is to feel our backside.

Gentlemen:

Feeling's believing. Show me a Bowmar Keyboard with the exclusive flat back, one-sided construction and wave solder capability. I want to see how thin this keyboard really is. All your words about Bowmar reliability won't convince me until I take a hard look at your design. So have your representative bring a sample keyboard to my office.

Name_____

Title_____

Company_____

Type of Application_____

City_____State_____Zip_____

Bowmar Instrument Corporation • Commercial Products Department
8000 Bluffton Road • Fort Wayne, Indiana • 747-3121

▋▋ Bowmar

Agency: Bonsib, Centlivre, Ferguson, Inc., Fort Wayne, Ind.

You can talk to the "trade" somewhat differently from the way you talk to the customer. The ad is unusual in that it is practically *all* coupon.

133

the readability of any piece of copy.[1] Using such factors as the length of sentences, number of sentences per paragraph, "personal" words, and the number of affixes per 100 words, he rates copy on a scale from "very easy" to "very difficult."

Here's the Flesch "quickie" yardstick: Take the average number of affixes per 100 words, (de-light-ed are affixes). Subtract the average number of personal references in 100 words, and divide by two. Then add the average number of words per sentence. Check the results against this scale:

Very easy	up to 13
Easy	13 to 20
Fairly easy	20 to 29
Standard	29 to 36
Fairly difficult	36 to 43
Difficult	43 to 52
Very difficult	52 or more

Not all copywriters carry the Flesch scale around with them. But I've seldom seen an effective piece of selling copy that didn't scale in the "Fairly Easy" or "Easy" category.

Maxwell C. Ross, a direct mail expert, has an interesting angle on this "simple copy" idea. He says (*Advertising Age*, November 11, 1974) that the following direct mail formula works like magic: "For every 100 words you write, make sure that 75 percent of them are words of five letters or less."

Ross further states, "Through the years I've tested [under exact-split conditions] direct mail letters which conformed to the formula against letters which did not. Every time—without a single exception—the simpler copy won!"

They will read you better . . . understand you more clearly . . . stay with you longer . . . and more often do what you want them to do. Besides, you'll be in pretty good company—company that includes Shakespeare, Lincoln's Gettysburg Address, and the Bible. I think you get the message; *plain talk sells.*

How an Ad Is Written

Before a copywriter gets to the point of actually putting on paper the words for the ad or commercial, he has gone through several steps.

1. He has taken a good look at the market segment, and knows the kind of people he will be talking to.

---

[1]Rudolph Flesch, *The Art of Plain Talk* (New York: Harper and Row, 1946), p. 65.

2. He has diligently searched for the *Main Attraction*, and has it firmly fixed in mind.

3. He has also sought out the *Subsidiary Main Attraction*—the other advantages that are built into the product.

4. He has determined the most important benefits that his product can offer the buyer.

5. In terms of psychological "needs and desires," he has calculated which of these benefits will have the greatest *appeal* to the consumer.

6. He has begun to turn over in his mind the ways in which this *appeal* may be expressed.

Now, maybe, is the time when he will sit and stare out of the window for a while, hoping to catch that flash of inspiration that will make the reader stay and read.

From this, I think, you can see why some copywriters say that the actual writing of the ad is the easy part. This is an exaggeration. But it is a fact that unless a writer has given serious consideration to the six points I have just listed, his chances of writing a good ad will be reduced. Most good copywriters think in these terms almost automatically.

You will note that most other salespeople do also.

Let's take a look at these six points in terms of a real product. You have been assigned to write a campaign for your client's new product—the Handy Dandy Electric Can Opener. The can opener is designed to retail for $9.95.

1. Your marketing people have informed you that their studies indicate a market segment consisting of middle class, homeowning suburbanites, usually identified as readers of the "Shelter Magazines" such as *House Beautiful, House and Garden,* and others.

2. The R and D people have come up with a complete new principle in can opening. Rather than the traditional circular cutting movement, they have devised an adjustable circular blade which severs and removes the can top in one instantaneous motion. You have decided to make this your *main attraction* and to tentatively call it "The Instant Electric Can Topper."

3. The research department informs you that their panel of homemakers have also found other attractive points. They liked the choices of ten decorator colors, and also the modern streamlined design of the can opener. They liked the safety feature, which prevents the opener from operating until the can has been fitted into its proper place. They were very enthusiastic about the speed with which it worked, and that they didn't have to "start" the can by giving it a twist when it wouldn't catch. Several also remarked that they liked it because it worked "without that horrid buzz-saw sound." You note these *subsidiary main attractions* for use in your copy.

4. It seems to you that the direct benefits are embodied in the machine's speed, infallibility, convenience, and safety.

5. The machine's very newness and originality present a natural built-in *appeal*. You know that, from a psychological point of view, the desire to be first, "out in front" with the latest, is a powerful motivator. You are also conscious of the psychological pull exerted by the homemaker's natural desire to be looked on as experienced, modern, and highly competent. Psychologists recognize it as the "nesting instinct."

6. You have begun to see this as a mail-order ad written in a straight-forward "hard-sell" fashion. The coupon appears to you as a means of testing the response to your copy.

```
                              Smith and Jones Elec. Co.
                              Handy Dandy Can Opener
                              Mag. ½ p.


              NEW--FROM HANDY-DANDY

          THE CAN OPENER THAT OPENS ANY CAN

                  IN AN INSTANT!

        Throw Away Your Old Can Opener--Every Modern
          Kitchen Should Have a Handy Dandy!  Can Topper
                                   new
        Here's the can opener that makes every other can opener
        old fashioned
        obsolete.  Be the first in your crowd to have one.  Works

        instantly and efficiently with the press of a button.  Ten

        decorator colors to choose from.  Safe.  There's never
                                         Instant
        been anything like the Handy Dandy Electric Can
        Topper
        Opener!


                      (coupon)


        Enclosed is my check for $10.99.  Rush me a Handy
                               Topper
        Dandy Electric Can Opener today.  (Name, Address,

        etc.)
                      (LOGO)
```

This is what my first rough draft looks like. I made a few changes as they occurred to me. I'll be making more later.

You go to work on your ancient machine (copywriters are always awarded the most battered typewriters in the office) and, several hours later, the first draft of your copy emerges.

You read the copy over a couple of times and stick it in your files. You'll see the art director about it in the morning.

These facts, this knowledge you have acquired about your product, comprise the *platform* on which you will build your ad. Often a copywriter will sit down and write out the platform in a formal way. In any case, the writer always has the basic platform facts in mind before he or she begins to write an ad.

The Salesperson's Side of Copywriting

Over the years, salespeople have arrived at certain conclusions about their business. We can't be sure exactly when a salesman first took apart a "sale" to see what made it tick. But we can be pretty well sure that the rug salesman we mentioned earlier, peddling his wares on the streets of some ancient city, had discovered a few things about what makes a successful sale happen.

Modern salespeople have made a science of their finds. Call it "the anatomy of a sale," if you will. Time after time they went back to a successful sale and replayed it the way a football coach will look at a game film.

Then they drew certain conclusions. If you come across some of the old inspirational salesmanship books by Napoleon Hill and Frank Bergson, you will find listed the principles of salesmanship. If you read any of the modern college texts on salesmanship, you will also find them listed there. Whether it's *How I Made a Million Selling,* or a recent college textbook, you'll find a surprising agreement among professional selling people as to just what takes place when a sale is successfully completed.

Here's what the authors of one of the most popular books on salesmanship have to say on this subject:[2]

What a Great Presentation Is Made of

A good presentation is a smooth and convincing salestalk that leads in a logical manner from its opening sentence to the close of the sale. It cannot be disjoined or confusing. It must be a well-forged unit. Even the smoothest salestalk has five definite parts, or steps. Each step must be accomplished before the presentation is complete. The five parts are these:

---

[2]Mark Jones, and James Healey, *Miracle Sales Guide* (Englewood Cliffs, N.J.: Prentice-Hall, Inc., 1973), p. 160.

1. Get the prospect's attention (immediately after introducing your-self).
2. Arouse his interest by describing benefits.
3. Stimulate his desire for these benefits.
4. Convince him that the benefits described are true, and that they can work for him.
5. Get him to take action and sign the order.

This, you understand, is from a book on salesmanship, not on adver-tising.

Here's another modern author on the same subject:[3]

> The selling process, that orderly progression that leads its prospect to make certain decisions, is the framework on which your sales presentation is built. . . . The knowledgeable salesman uses the various stages in the selling process to move the customer's mind to a favorable decision. This sequence of selling provides the framework within which you can make appeals to your customer's buying mo-tives. It is imperative for you to understand how to apply the basic principles of this selling process in the building of a sales presenta-tion that always places the emphasis upon the wants and needs in the mind of the prospect. There are five stages—*attention, interest, de-sire, conviction, and action.* . . .

Salesmanship in Print

The day we decided that "advertising is salesmanship in print" was the day modern advertising was born. It is hard to pick the exact date; but it is evident that by the 1920s there were many advertising writers around who realized that if an ad was going to be a salesperson, *it would have to act like a salesperson.*

Clyde Bedell, who had learned his lessons the hard way (through mail order advertising) says that even in the late 1920s and 1930s no one had compiled any copy principles and set them down in writing. Bedell himself was to help correct this situation with his great book on copy-writing. As he says, "What I would have given then for what this book details now!"[4]

As you will recall from Chapter 1, some very exciting things were happening to advertising in the 1920s. By means of coupon returns, ad people were finding out what worked and what didn't work. Whenever

---

[3]Edwin C. Greif, *Personal Salesmanship: New Concepts and Directions* (Reston, Virginia, Reston Publishing Company, Inc., 1974), p. 165.

[4]Clyde Bedell, *How to Write Advertising That Sells* (New York: McGraw-Hill Book Com-pany, 1940), p. 139.

an ad *did* work, the people who wrote it took it apart to see if they could determine just what it was that made it perform so well.

When a young man, Bedell relates how he went through this process as a mail order ad manager.

> After that came the time in Chicago when I spent close to two million dollars a year . . . in selling goods by mail. Any man who sends out mail order circulars or catalogues . . . waits anxiously for returns. It is natural for him to begin intently to study resultful advertising as against that which yields disappointing returns. *It is a matter of self-preservation.* (Author's ital.)

But Bedell, who had also been on the sales side, had seen something else:

> Selling orally has much in common with selling in print. As a sales manager, I found that the results produced by some two hundred salesmen were extremely spotty if the men were left to their own resources.[5]

As a result of his experience, Bedell set down what he termed his "Selling Strategies."[6] They are *exactly* the same as those you have already seen listed in the modern texts on salesmanship. They are:

Get attention
Arouse interest and create desire
Create conviction
Try for action

Victor Schwab, another highly regarded creative ad man, opens his book this way in Chapter 1:[7]

> There are five fundamentals in the writing of a good advertisement:
>
> 1. Get attention
> 2. Show people an advantage
> 3. Prove it
> 4. Persuade people to grasp this advantage
> 5. Ask for action

---

[5]Bedell, *How to Write Advertising That Sells*, p. 138.

[6]Bedell, *How to Write Advertising That Sells*, p. 139.

[7]Victor Schwab, *How to Write a Good Advertisement* (New York: Harper and Row Publishers, 1962), p. 1.

As you can see, salesmen and advertising copywriters agree. There *is* an anatomy to a successful sale, and it can be readily distinguished. This, they say, is what usually happens when a successful sale is completed:

1. You get the prospect's attention. You get him turned from whatever he is doing to what *you* are doing or saying.
2. You stir up the prospect's interest. You do or say or show something that moves polite attention up to a flicker of interest.
3. You create a desire on his part to possess what it is that you have for sale.
4. You convince him that you really *can* do for him what you claim. You overcome his natural hesitancy.
5. You ask for his buying decision. You make it just as easy as possible for the customer to say "yes."

In other words, a good salesperson acts like a good salesperson *anywhere;* whether his selling message is delivered across a desk or retail counter, or appears on a newspaper page, or comes out of a TV set or a car radio, it doesn't change the fact that *it is a selling message delivered by a salesman.* And if it is a *good* sales message, delivered by a good salesman, that's the way it's going to behave.

The good news for you is this: From now on you are going to look at any ad and make your own judgment as to whether it is delivering its selling message as a good salesperson should. You will see, to your surprise, that there is a certain amount of advertising that doesn't put on a very good sales performance. You will also determine, I hope, that if it is *your* advertisement—whether you write it or buy it—it is going to sell as a good salesperson should.

How Good Ads Act

We will now examine in detail the way advertising achieves the five basic steps of getting attention, creating interest, stimulating desire, imparting conviction, and asking for the order. It is not enough that an ad should take the required steps. The *real* test comes when we ask ourselves how well the steps were taken.

Getting Attention

In case there is any doubt in your mind about the importance of getting attention, think of it this way:

The beautiful maiden is tied to the railroad tracks, the 5:15 is due in two minutes, you've come to the last word on the page, and the story is continued on page 70. As you feverishly leaf to page 70, hoping against hope that the heroine will be rescued before the train arrives and cuts her in half, you come across an ad on page 61. There it is, full of vim, vigor, and sales ambition. Somehow it has got to reach out of the page, grab you, and say, "Just a moment, if you please, I have something here that I think will interest you very much." Quite a job.

But there *are* some headlines that reach right out of the page and grab you by the lapel. You've had it happen to you lots of times. You've read a lot of ads in your lifetime even when you were interested in something else. *Something* stopped you. Let's see what it might have been.

1. The headline talked directly to you. Chances are, it used the pronouns "you" or "your." But, it didn't leave any doubt that it was talking right at and to *you*—and not someone down the street. Like this:

    > YOU COULD BUY THIS PANASONIC
    > RADIO ON LOOKS ALONE—BUT WE
    > WON'T LET YOU

2. The headline said it was going to *do* something for you. Or, it was going to show you how you could do something for yourself. The world is full of people who want to know *how* to do things—*how* to be happier, *how* to have a clearer complexion, *how* to be more secure, *how* to play the piano. Years ago, the mail order people discovered that a *how* in the headline was a beautiful thing. Not because of the word itself, but because it is a very quick way of saying, "You can now have something you want." Here's a good "do something for you" headline from the Phoenix Mutual Life Insurance Company:

    > HOW WE RETIRED IN 15 YEARS
    > WITH $300 A MONTH

3. The headline made you wonder. "What's it all about?" Maybe it offered you something brand-new, different, better, or something you'd never been able to get your hands on before. Somehow the headline got across that "Maybe-I-ought-to-find-out-about-this" feeling. That's why you will so often see headline words such as "At last," "Now," "New," "Announcing," "Here's." Try this example from American Express:

    > NOW YOU HAVE A CHARGE ACCOUNT
    > AT MANY OF THE BEST STORES
    > IN NEW YORK

4. The headline gave you a promise of the good things to come. It was a can opener that opened a can better; a refrigerator that didn't need defrosting; or a soap that was kinder to your skin. You can see they didn't waste any time letting you know about it. Your copywriter probably has some very good and interesting things to

say about the product. He or she can grab your attention by introducing one of them in the headline. From Piedmont Airlines:

THE ONE AIRLINE WITH TWO WAYS
YOU CAN JET NONSTOP TO NORFOLK
AND ROANOKE

As we have mentioned, headlines will often use several combinations of these methods. There is one other way I can get your attention—by tricking you, by yelling "fire," or by being a phony. It's something no *good* salesperson would be caught dead doing. It doesn't pay in headline writing either.

Creating Interest

Sometimes people complain about ads and commercials that bore them stiff. They hate those ads for cold remedies where people are sniffling and sneezing all over the place. Those ads bore them *until they feel themselves coming down with a cold.* Then those boring ads interest them very much.

Let's take a look at what has happened in an ad that has caught your interest:

1. It told you it was going to do something for you. It began to reveal to you how, through what it had to sell, you would gain an advantage for yourself.
2. It went directly to a specific *need, want,* or *desire.* (Remember, you've already learned about the importance of this kind of motivation.)
3. The opening paragraph of the copy enlarges on its promise of good things to come for you that may have been started in the headline.

Here are two "interest arousers" from current advertisements.

It's a checking account that lets you write all the checks you want for just $1 a month. And a $500 savings account that pays you a full 5½ percent a year. (First National City Bank)

Every year, literally millions of men and women fail to take advantage of a legitimate tax break. They're people in business for themselves. Doctors, lawyers, shopkeepers, people who put in twelve to fourteen hours a day to make a success of something. If you run your own business, the Travelers can help you save some money. Money you might otherwise pay out in federal income taxes. (Travelers Insurance Company)

If you can hold out to people the hope of attaining something they would like to have, you almost automatically catch their interest. What you have to be careful of is that you offer your product in terms of what people really *want*. Both First National City and Travelers Insurance are on pretty safe ground. They know that a *real* interest exists in saving and making money.

Here are some other *interests* you should keep in mind. The interest in—

Making money
Being happy
Being proud of yourself
Making a good home
Having good health
Being looked up to
Gaining popularity
Improving yourself
Gaining social acceptance
Doing better for yourself
Being a leader, "up-to-date"
Being secure—"independent"
Being handsomer, or more beautiful

If you refer to what you have learned about "consumer motivation," I think you will recognize these "interests." What we have listed, in ordinary language, are the basic needs and desires most of us possess to a greater or lesser degree. Leaf through the handiest magazine; look at the ads. You will find that almost every one of the "interest arousers" (if they remembered to *use* an interest arouser) falls into one of the above listed categories.

Stimulating Desire

A good piece of copy makes you *want* what it has to sell. This, as every good salesperson knows, is the heart of the selling proposition. I have caught your attention, and excited your interest. Now I must take you one step further. The very best way I can get you to long for the product or service I have for sale is to make you see yourself *reaping the benefit* from the use of my product.

It is not enough to offer a furniture polish that will make tables glow more attractively; you must make the buyer see herself being complimented by her friends. It isn't enough to save money or invest it wisely; you must make the customers see themselves at the rail of a cruise ship, reaping the benefits of such a savings or investment program.

Time after time, all through the history of advertising, the most successful ads as measured by their couponed returns have made the prospect *see* himself. They make the prospect see himself, *in his mind's eye,* enjoying the benefits and reaping rewards of having bought the product or service.

Does the "health spa" in your community offer "a better figure?" Good. But it also had better offer admiring glances on the beach next summer.

Does the correspondence school offer courses of study that lead to new skills and self-improvement? Good. But it also had better show the student opening a paycheck with a raise in it, or receiving the boss' congratulations.

One of the great classics of copywriting, which you encountered in Chapter 3, is "They laughed when I sat down at the piano." That copy is *all* about the rewards and benefits enjoyed by someone who had been wise enough to send in the coupon and take the piano lessons by mail.

When the customer washed his mouth with Listerine, did he get better breath? Sure. *But he also got the girl.*

When the 98-pound weakling sent away for the barbells, did he seek bulging muscles? Sure. But more important, he sought the reward of social acceptance, self-confidence, admiration, and the reassurance of his manhood. If the ad can deliver *those things,* the barbells become a bargain at almost any price.

Imparting Conviction

Have you ever heard the Latin phrase *caveat emptor?* It means, "Let the buyer beware." There's a good bit of the *caveat emptor* in all of us. It's the natural instinct to pause before we make the final decision to buy and put our money on the counter. As a salesman you have to recognize this natural desire of the buyer to make *sure* he is doing the right thing. Because you do recognize this hesitance, you know that at this point in the selling process what is called for is reassurance.

The customer wants to be *reassured* that he is not making a mistake.

He wants to be *reassured* that you can do for him what you say you can do.

He wants to be *sure* you are on the level.

He wants to be *certain* he's going to get his money's worth.

It's up to you to supply the answers. You can be sure that a good ad does. Let's see how it does.

1. *With a testimonial.* A motion picture star says she uses it, and look at *her* skin. An ordinary citizen testifies that she just wouldn't use any other brand of coffee.
2. *With a money-back guarantee.* What have you got to worry about? If you don't like it, you can send it back and your money will be cheerfully refunded.
3. *A printed warranty.* This is usually printed with a fancy border that makes it look like a bond. Performance is guaranteed in black and white.

GUTS TO GO THE DISTANCE

THE PROOF IS INSIDE EVERY RED JACKET SUB.

It doesn't pay to cut corners on components. Because submersible pumps are tough to get at and take your valuable time to repair, you need a brand that's built for the long haul, through and through. Like Red Jacket subs.

Corrosion-resistant stainless steel cases surround impellers made of tough Noryl (In actual installation tests, Noryl Impellers showed virtually no wear after six years . . . pumping over 600,000 gallons).

And at Red Jacket **we make our own motors** to our own rigid specifications, so they'll go the distance. Windings are encapsulated in epoxy and sealed in stainless steel for long-haul performance. Red Jacket Submersible Pumps are easier to order, stock and service.

Available in 2 or 3-wire models. For complete information, talk to your Red Jacket distributor or write us.

Every Red Jacket submersible pump must pass a rigid final operating test before it leaves the factory.

RED JACKET PUMPS
DIVISION WEIL-McLAIN
BOX 3888 • DAVENPORT, IOWA

Agency: Creswell Munsell Schubert & Zirbel, Inc., Cedar Rapids, Iowa

Striking illustration, plus gutsy, factual copy, make this a handsome ad. Note the selling steps, from attention-getting to asking-for-order.

Before and after
copy and top photo
can be replaced
with local ones.

MY FORMER HUSBAND.

MY PRESENT HUSBAND.

There was more of my former husband to love, alright. But I still love my present husband even more. Of course, if you look closely you'll see that nothing has really changed but his physique. And his outlook on life. Mine, too. I guess you could say when the Weight Watchers® program made a new man out of my husband, it made a new woman out of me. At least, that's what my husband says.
— STAN WATIN

CLASS LISTING

Ad#194—220 lines

Agency: Ted Barash & Co., Inc., New York.

The "before and after" technique used as a convincer in this ad supplied to its franchisers by the parent organization.

4. *Scientific proof.* Independent testing laboratories are often called in to measure performance.
5. *Comparative performance.* The product is tested against other products. You've seen this in automobile advertising where comparative gas consumption figures are shown.
6. *Seals of approval.* Publications sometimes make tests of their advertisers' products and award the "Seal of Approval." The *Good Housekeeping* seal of approval is one of the better known.
7. *The reputation of your name.* You have already seen how companies strive to enhance their reputation for honesty and quality. Often the corporate name carries reassurance with it.
8. *Successful performance.* The fact that your product is "making thousands of new friends daily," carries a feeling of assurance with it.
9. *Demonstration.* The product is actually doing what you say it will do. Aspirin going to the center of pain faster. Tires running on spikes without blowing out.
10. *Free trial period.* Take it home and try it for ten days and if you aren't satisfied, send it back and no questions asked.
11. *Medals and awards.* Somewhat out of fashion today, but many wines and food products still carry in their advertising replicas of the awards they won at various "expositions." In England, the phrase "By Appointment to Her Majesty the Queen" is something like this.
12. *Craftsmen and designers.* You encounter this frequently in the retail clothing business.

Remember, the customer very naturally wants to be sure. It's up to you to supply the conviction.

Asking for the Order

No good salesperson ever lets a prospect get away without asking him or her for a buying decision. Here's what one of the top selling guides has to say:

Many salesmen do a good job with every step of the selling process till they get to the close, then they fail, and all their work is lost.

Because they don't know what to do in the all-important 5% of selling time that goes into the close, the 95% of their time that goes into the preliminary steps is utterly wasted.[8]

Any automobile salesman will tell you that the most alarming thing that can happen is to have the customer say, "I like the car, and I'm going to buy it. But first I'd like to talk it over with my wife."

---

[8]Jones and Healey, *Miracle Sales Guide*, p. 207.

Because you are writing copy, and not talking, you can't use the "multiple close" technique practiced by most salespeople. You can't keep your eyes open for the "buying signals," and then move in. As a copywriter you have to apply your close in orderly fashion: *after* you've gotten attention; *after* you've created interest; *after* you've stimulated desire, and *after* you've convinced the reader that you can do for him or her what you say you can. *Then* you are ready to ask for the order. Here's how it is done. Generally speaking, the cardinal rule is to make sure that you make it just as easy and convenient as possible for the reader to act.

1. Be sure the customer knows where he can find you. Tell him exactly where you are—name, address, telephone number, with a map if necessary.
2. Use a coupon. Put it in the bottom outside corner of your ad for convenience in clipping. Make it large enough so that it can be filled in easily.
3. Give the reader a free booklet, sample, or trial offer to send for.
4. Ask for action *now*. The quantity may be limited; the price may be going up.
5. In nationally advertised products or services, be sure to tell your reader where they can be obtained locally. "See your travel agent for details." "On sale beginning Monday at every Sears store."
6. Ask the reader to participate in doing something. "Compare our prices today." "Let us have your suggestions for a new flavor."
7. Give the reader a choice—and make the choice an easy one.
8. State the exact price and terms of purchase. Don't leave the reader wondering and therefore indecisive.

I'm sure that now you can pick up any newspaper or magazine and see dozens of ways the copywriters have "asked for the order."

Remember the ad we wrote earlier about the Handy Dandy Can Opener, and stuck it away in our desk drawer before telling the art director about it? Maybe we ought to go back and take another try at it. With our new perspectives, we might do it something like this:

(Attention)	**NOW—YOU CAN HAVE A KITCHEN "GADGET" WORTH ITS WEIGHT IN GOLD!**
(Interest)	Read How New Handy Dandy Electric Can Topper Makes Messy Can Opening as Old-Fashioned as the Icebox!
	If you've ever cut a finger, splashed a party dress, or wrestled with a stubborn, dull can opener—*forget it.*
(Desire)	Now you can top a can in an instant with a flick of your finger—even wearing your best party clothes—'cause there's no spurt or splash.

(Conviction)   You'll love it—quiet as a mouse, no buzz-saw noises. Comes in ten decorator colors. Rated "A+" by Consumer's Union and Good Housekeeping Test Kitchens.

(Order)   We're making you this special limited introductory offer because we know you'll tell your friends.

(Coupon)

(Order)   Yes, I want to be one of the first to use a Handy Dandy Electric Can Topper. Enclosed is my check for $9.95. Rush to . . .

Name: _____

Street: _____

City:_____ State:_____ Zip Code: _____

SMITH AND JONES ELECTRIC CO.
SYRACUSE, NEW YORK   13200

There Is No Magic Formula

Now you have seen how an ad is written. You have learned some of the major *techniques* and selling principles recognized by top salespeople and top advertising writers. But be warned—there is no magic formula by which a successful advertisement can be written every time. If there were, someone would bottle it and sell it.

In fact, some years ago, in one of the historical rip-offs in our business, a couple of guys *did* "bottle it and sell it." They claimed they had the secret formula for successful advertising and would gladly apply it to your advertising campaign—for a price. Some big national advertisers spent quite a few dollars on the "secret" formula before they discovered that the alchemists' age-old dream of turning dross into gold still hasn't come true.

A knowledge of the selling fundamentals is essential if you are going to write effective advertising, or if you are going to buy effective advertising. But the mere presence of those fundamentals in your ad doesn't guarantee you anything.

As Bedell has pointed out, "The unschooled or unskilled practitioner may believe that art is made by the rules. It isn't. . . . The unwary reader may also believe that on possession of the tools he becomes master of the art. He doesn't. Rules and tools in the hands of a carpenter don't make a Hepplewhite. Ten fingers and the mechanics of music don't make a Paderewski."[9]

---

[9]Bedell, *How to Write Advertising That Sells,* p. xviii.

Writing successful advertising copy is a tough and demanding job. It takes a knowledge of basic selling fundamentsls; a polished writing talent; the opportunity to have learned and absorbed and benefited from the coaching of the best of the business; and it takes experience—lots of experience.

There are people around, including *advertising* people, who feel that writing successful advertising copy is not so very difficult. Well, an appendectomy is really not a very difficult surgical procedure. I can tell you how to do it in less than one page of copy. Yet having read the procedure, I think you still might hesitate about taking up the scalpel and making an incision. I hope that you, or your copywriter, will pick up a pencil with the same seriousness.

Writing a successful ad is much more difficult than removing an appendix; and it takes *at least* as much skill, knowledge, and experience. Fortunately for you, bungling the copywriting job won't cost someone's life—just a few thousand dollars in lost sales, your job, or your business.

Awards

In our business, as you will discover, we are constantly giving awards, prizes, plaques, and also writing books and columns about the "best in advertising."

You will hardly enter a copywriter's office or an agency reception room, in which the walls are not lined with handsomely framed certificates for having been judged first, second, or third best in some kind of competition.

All this is quite harmless, unless you let it overimpress you. Rosser Reeves, who could be quite adamant about this sort of thing, once pointed out in an interview:

> When John Crighton was editor of *Advertising Age*, I said to him that somebody, someday, is going to put advertising awards on the proper basis. And, that basis is, does it work? The question has never been asked in any advertising award that has been given.

The trouble comes in the interpretation of the word "best." We don't mean "best selling," because the judges seldom have access to the sales figures. (There is the famous case of the TV commercial for a well-known upset stomach remedy. It was one of the most popular and widely acclaimed TV commercials of the day. It won a basketful of awards. But when a leading newspaper interviewed the sales director and asked him about the effect the commercial had on sales, he replied that there hadn't been *any* that he could detect.)

As someone has pointed out, if awards were given on sales success alone, our volumes of "best ads" would be filled with pages of nothing but those hard-boiled, hard-sell couponed mail order ads. But award giving isn't all footloose fun and games. It is a necessary and important part of the internal life of our business.

In making the awards, our fellow workers are recognizing and applauding a demonstration of professional skill. They are applauding a performance—a terrific layout, a great piece of copy, an exciting TV commercial. Yes, the name of the game is selling. But *part* of the name of the game is for advertising people to be able to do "their own thing" with skill and finesse and artistry.

When the home team scores the winning touchdown, half the stadium erupts with joy. Only a few people in the press box and along the sideline note that the block that had sprung the runner was of almost classic perfection.

WHERE YOU ARE

1. You understand the function of a copywriter in the process of helping to create advertising material.

2. You know how to get an estimate of the readability of a piece of copy.

3. You know the six preliminary steps to be taken before writing an ad.

4. You have learned the five basic steps that make up the anatomy of a selling message.

5. You have become familiar with most of the techniques used to apply these principles to advertising copy.

6. You now realize that this preparation of successful advertising is a difficult and exacting task.

7. You have acquired some bench marks by which you can measure the potential performance of your advertising.

QUESTIONS FOR CLASS DISCUSSION

1. Would a good salesperson make a good copywriter?

2. Would a good copywriter make a good salesperson?

3. Do you think Ernest Hemingway would have made a good advertising copywriter?

152

How
Advertising Is
Written

3. Do you think Ernest Hemingway would have made a good advertising copywriter?

4. What is the worst piece of copy you have ever seen? The best?

SOMETHING FOR YOU TO DO

Select a campaign or an ad from a current magazine that you feel does not exploit the five basic selling points to the extent that it might. Rewrite the ads completely and show how you, as a copywriter, would have handled the assignment if it had been given to you.

KEY WORDS AND PHRASES

Anatomy of a Sale. The identifiable steps leading up to a sale.

Appeal. Basic idea in copy designed to lead a buyer to action.

Art Director. Person who makes layouts. Head of art department.

Asking-for-the-Order. The part of the ad that asks the potential buyer to do something.

Attention-getter. The device or statement in the ad that grabs you.

Brochure. Small booklet or folder.

Benefits. What the product will do for you.

Conviction. Statements or devices that help you to believe what the ad has claimed.

Copy. The words in the ad or commercial.

Copywriter. Person who conceives and writes advertising.

Copy Chief (Copy Director). Supervisor of a group of copywriters.

Coupon Returns. The number of coupons you get back from an ad.

Desire-Stimulator. That which makes you want what the ad has to sell.

Interest-arouser. Those factors in the ad that appeal to your self-interest.

Salesmanship in Print. An early description of advertising.

Shelter Magazine. A publication whose editorial content is directed to home makers or home owners.

Terms of Purchase. Such as, "One free with every dozen."

Trial Offer. Send it back if you aren't satisfied.

SELECTED READINGS

Bedell, Clyde. *How to Write Advertising That Sells* (New York: McGraw-Hill Book Company, 2nd ed., 1952). One of the oldest and best texts in the field. Uses the scientific approach. Chapters 3 through 9, "A Method Approach to Copy," will be particularly interesting to you.

Burton, Phillip Ward, and Kreer, G. Bowman. *Advertising Copywriting*, 3rd ed. (Englewood Cliffs, New Jersey: Prentice-Hall, Inc., 1962). It examines the problems of writing copy for a variety of media, including mail order, outdoor, radio, and TV.

Greif, Edwin C. *Personal Salesmanship, New Concepts, and Directions* (Reston, Virginia: Reston Publishing Company, Inc., 1974). This book is an excellent modern treatment on the field of personal selling.

Schwab, Victor O. *How to Write a Good Advertisement* (New York: Harper and Row, 1962). A nice loose treatment of the subject by one of the "greats." It is a practical "how to" book by a master forged in the mail-order fires.

Jones, Mark, and Healey, James. *Miracle Sales Guide* (Englewood Cliffs, New Jersey: Prentice-Hall, Inc., 1973). An excellent text on salesmanship set up in an easy-to-absorb programmed learning technique.

Adams, Charles F. *Common Sense In Advertising* (New York: McGraw-Hill Book Company, 1965). It's just what the title says. A lot of good, commonsense advice on a number of problems faced by the copywriter. As the author says, he wrote it "for anyone who thinks that advertising is easy and that success in selling through mass communication can be achieved without real labor."

Rowsome, Frank, Jr. *Think Small: The Story of the Volkswagen Ads* (Brattleboro, Vermont: The Green Press, 1970). A beautifully put together little book detailing a successful campaign.

The Art of Writing Advertising (Chicago Advertising Publication, Inc., 1965). The title is somewhat misleading. This is not a "how to" book, but the report of a series of interviews with some prominent creative admen. Some of their observations are pertinent; some are not.

Advertising Age. See columns by William Tyler and Harry McMahon for commentary on current print advertising and television commercials.

Flesch, Rudolf. *The Art of Plain Talk* and *The Art of Readable Writing* (New York: Harper and Row, 1946). Mr. Flesch knows how to write, and he knows how to teach you to do the same. Both books get high praise from professionals in all communications fields.

Strunk, William, Jr., and White, E. B. *The Elements of Style* (New York: The Macmillan Company, 1959). This 95-cent paperback is in your bookstore, and ought to be on your desk.

chapter seven

Advertising Design,
Art, and Layout

In this chapter we outline the steps by which the physical appearance and design of an advertisement takes shape.

You will follow the stages a layout goes through, and you will become familiar with some of the basic art principles that apply to advertising layouts.

You will also become familiar with the art director's role in the purchase of advertising illustration.

You will complete this chapter, I hope, with a conviction of the importance of the close working relationship between art director and copywriter, if the best in advertising is to be achieved.

155

Nothing happens with a piece of copy until someone breathes life into it. Nothing happens with a radio commercial until sound technicians and musicians and actors do their work. A television script is just that—until a producer makes it come alive before the cameras. And the greatest piece of magazine or newspaper copy is lifeless until someone visualizes its appearance and arranges its parts in the most effective way possible.

That "someone" is called an *art director*. We are now going to talk about the way the art director does his or her job.

The Relationship Between Copywriter and Art Director

In a chapter titled, "How to Work with Copywriters—And Like Them Too," Stephen Baker (an art director) has his say:

> It is said of women that you can't get along with them, but you can't get along without them, either. This adage also applies to copywriters, according to many art directors.
>
> The fact is, however, that no two segments of an advertising agency have so much in common as art and copy—although this may come as news to some art directors and writers. The mode of expression is **157**

different (one uses a typewriter, the other a drawing pencil), but the goal is identical. Both are in the business of getting a message across with a fresh approach.[1]

It is possible to leave a piece of copy on an art director's table, go away, and hope that something good will come of it. Sometimes it does; more often it doesn't.

It is possible for a copywriter to sketch an ad *exactly* the way she wants it to appear. With the copy attached to the sketch, the copywriter hands it to the art director with the instruction, "Just clean this up a little for me, will you?" Something good may come of this. Usually it doesn't.

Of all the important moments in the birth of an ad, the one we arrive at now can be the *most* important: the moment when art director and copywriter sit down together to discuss what the ad is going to look like.

This is important for you to understand. Because if it does not happen, your chances of getting an attractive, hard-selling ad are going to be greatly reduced. The fact is that often this meeting of the minds does *not* take place. As we mentioned earlier, many of the smaller agencies in your city do not have art directors. By choice, they rely on an art service to make their layouts for them. The busy copywriter may find it inconvenient to drive across town to the studio, or he or she may feel that some scribbled instructions on the copy sheet are enough. Often it is not.

When you have something to say about your company's advertising, you will be doing everyone a favor if you insist that the art director and the copywriter get together—even if you have to take them to lunch. Here's why. . . .[2]

Visualization

The art director's most important job is not done with a drawing pencil; it is done with his brain—his imagination.

The art director has to see—to *visualize*—how the ad is going to appear. There is a headline with a basic idea in it; but how is that basic idea to be expressed in terms of what people will *see*?

An art director can readily do this alone, of course. But as the people who perfected the "brainstorming sessions" long ago discovered, some batting of ideas back and forth can be very productive. Major Madison Avenue agencies *expect* art director and copywriter to get together.

---

[1]Stephen Baker, *Advertising Layout and Art Direction* (New York: McGraw-Hill Book Company, 1959), p. 133.

[2]Stephen Baker actually put a tape recorder in an art director's office and recorded what went on between copywriter and art director in a visualization session. Baker, *Advertising Layout and Art Direction*, p. 135.

Some of the greatest campaigns of the past ten years have come from smooth, sensitive artist-writer *teams*. The outgrowth of the boutiques, already mentioned, stemmed from the close working relationship between writer and artist. For years at Young & Rubicam it was understood that the art director had not only the right, but the obligation to make comments and suggestions on the copy itself.

The Art of Seeing an Idea

The art director's visualization problem is like this: Suppose a piece of travel copy with the headline "Come to Paris in the Spring" must be

The style of this layout is the same for all ads done by this famous men's clothing store.

Courtesy of Brooks Brothers, New York, New York.

visualized. There is an almost infinite number of ways to visualize the idea of "Paris in the Spring"—everything from a simple chestnut blossom to a crowded street scene.

It is at this point that the art director begins to make *thumb nails*. These are small, rough sketches that portray the ideas as they come along—simply getting something down on paper—"noodling around."

These *thumb nails* provide the art director with something visual for discussion. "How about if we did it this way?" "Here's how I see it." "How about something like this?" The important thing is that the art director and the copywriter are beginning to *see*—to visualize—how the finished ad might look overall.

In the following pages you will see several ads with excellent visualization. But remember, what you are looking at represents only *one* possibility. You can leaf through a magazine, "second guess" the art director, and decide how *you* might have visualized the same ad. Remember that the basic idea is to come up with a visual presentation of your idea that is striking, eye-catching, and one that puts across your basic selling idea with impact.

Making Layouts

When art director and copywriter are satisfied that they have a good visualization for their ad, the art director proceeds to make a *layout*. The layout is drawn to the actual dimensions of the finished ad. It represents an arrangement of the parts or *elements* of the ad.

Art directors recognize a number of different elements that may play a part in the making of a layout. They are:

Headline	Picture captions
Subhead	Trademark
Main illustration	Slogan
Subsidiary illustrations	Logotype or signature
Body text	White space

Of course all these do not occur in every layout; but it is the art director's job to arrange the elements so that the design of the ad is eye-catching and attractive. Perhaps you have run across an ad that was so "busy" and confused that you instinctively refused to read it. In this case, the art director had not done his "arranging" well.

A layout has often been compared to the blueprint of a machine, or to an architect's drawing of a building. It shows you where things go. It also has other functions.

As a production guide.   In the next chapter, when we examine print production, you will see how many people are dependent on a layout in ordering and preparing art, engravings, and typography.

As an estimate guide. A number of printers, typographers, engravers, and so on, use the layout in giving the agency their cost estimates. It is important that they know *what kind of illustration, how much copy.*

161
Making
Layouts

Steps in Making Layouts

Roughs. Frequently an art director will take two or three *thumb nails* and make them into full-size *rough layouts.* In a *rough,* the illustration may be sketched in, the headline lettered in roughly but in a readable fashion. Copy is simply indicated by straight lines. The company's signature is roughly lettered in, and the slogan or trademark is indicated in pencil. In large companies, the art director may make up as many as a dozen *roughs* that will then be discussed with the copywriter and the account executive.

Comprehensives. When everyone is agreed on the rough layout, the next step is to prepare a *comprehensive.* A "comp" is a more refined version of the rough layout. In this, a photocopy or a photograph of the art work may be made and pasted in place. A copy of the logotype is cut from a proof of a previous ad and pasted in. The headline is carefully lettered in or pasted in from a typeset proof. The copy block is carefully lined in. If a type proof has been pulled (we'll talk more about this in the next chapter), the copy is cut out and pasted in. The entire layout is then placed on a "board"—a heavy cardboard sheet—or is mounted with the board used as a frame. The entire piece may then be covered with cellophane. The overall effect is sometimes more attractive than the finished ad itself.

As you have noticed, a lot of "pasting" went on in the above described process. This is why the juniors in the art department, who haven't as yet reached art director status, are known as "pasteup people."

You should understand that there is considerable variation in the use of *thumb nails, roughs,* and *comps.* On Madison Avenue, when a presentation is being made to a multimillion-dollar client, no expense is spared in preparing the "tightest" comps possible. Some agencies, however, rebel at incurring this expense—particularly if it is a *speculative presentation* and the agency is not yet in a position to know too much about the account and the product.

In your community, you will find agencies and art services following different practices. Sometimes the client does not expect to see a comprehensive, and is quite satisfied with a finished rough. Sometimes art service will dispense entirely with the thumb-nail stage and deliver a rough layout. Occasionally a client can simply be *told* what his ad is going to look like, or can be shown a *thumb nail.* Few small agencies and businesses can afford the cost of carefully finished comps—$75.00 to $150.00; neither can they afford the luxury of making copy changes on the type proofs—standard procedure in some of the larger agencies.

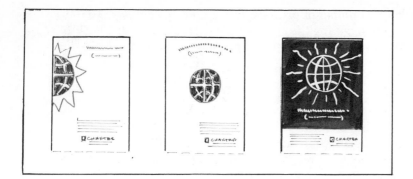

CHARTER
LAND/OIL/MONEY
COMMUNICATIONS/
INSURANCE

Charter -- Southern born and bred
(but now a citizen of the world)

From Corporate Headquarters in the Deep South (Jacksonville, Fla., where it was born), Charter now spreads across the entire business spectrum of the World. A conglomerate worth $141 million, it makes things happen in Land, Oil, Money, Insurance and Communications — anywhere in the world!

CHARTER
LAND / OIL / MONEY
COMMUNICATIONS / INSURANCE
P. O. Box 2017 Jacksonville, Florida 32203

Charter — Southern born and bred
(but now a citizen of the world)

Charter Advisory Company • Charter Mortgage Company • Charter Land & Housing Corporation • Charter Oil Company • Billups Western Petroleum Company • Charter International Oil Company • Charter (Iran) Petroleum Company • Charter Tire, Inc. • Charter Trading Company Manchester Terminal Company • Super Test Oil & Gas Company • Charter Sports, Inc. • Mason/Charter Publishers, Inc. • Dayton Press, Inc. Redbook Publishing Company • Downe Communications, Inc. (Ladies' Home Journal) • womenSports • Bartell Media Corporation • Louisiana and Southern Life Insurance Company

Courtesy of Ed Duckett, Art Director, Hubbard, Duckett, Mason, Don, Inc., Jacksonville, Fla.

The progression of a layout from "thumbnail" to "comp."

Agency: Spencer, Bennett, Nowak, Inc., Providence, R.I.

A nice example of a "balanced" layout. The product illustration is literally balanced.

How the Layout Person Works

As you have learned, the art director has to deal with different "elements" when designing the layout.

The art director thinks of each one of these elements, whether headline, illustration, or body text, as having a certain "weight." This is not weight in the "heavy" sense of the word, but rather weight in relation to the impact each element has on the reader's eye. It is governed by *size*, *shape*, and *intensity of color*.

This is where the "art" in art direction comes in. It now is the art director's artistic taste and feeling that come into play. In the arrangement of the different "weighted" elements he is dealing with certain long-established art *principles*. Leonardo da Vinci understood them well, and the youngest student at The Art Student's League soon learns them.

> If the layout man does not observe certain principles in designing the advertisement, he will fail in his efforts to present the selling message in the most effective manner.[3]

Let us now look at these principles, and see how the art director applies them in composing the layout. As you have read in the chapter on Copy, the mere inclusion of the 5 basic selling points in the copy is no ironbound guarantee that the ad will be successful. By the same token, you must realize that the adherence to the following basic principles of composition will not *necessarily* produce an effective layout. Taste, talent, and creative ability play a vital role in both copy and art.

The Principles of Composition

Balance. When the art director looks at an empty shape on the drawing pad his eye automatically goes to a point centered vertically, or a little to the left and somewhat higher than the middle of the ad. This is the spot that is referred to as the *optical center* of the layout—the first place your eye is most likely to go when you look at an ad. You can think of it as a *balancing point*, like the point from which hang the pans of an old-fashioned scale.

It is around this point that the art director will arrange the weighted elements. The two sides of the scale will be even and in balance, or uneven and out of balance. When the elements are in balance, the layout is said to have *formal balance*; when out of balance, it is called *informal balance*.

It is important to recognize this, because the balance of the layout has an effect on the viewer. If you look through *Fortune*, you will see a great many ads that are in *formal balance*. The *institutional* type of ad we have discussed is frequently in *formal balance*. With their large central illustration, carefully centered headline, and neatly balanced copy blocks, the ads give an impression of dignity and stability—just the image that

---

[3]Hugh G. Wales, Dwight L. Gentry, and Max Wales, *Advertising Copy, Layout, and Typography* (New York: The Ronald Press Company, 1958), p. 239.

Agency: Dawson, Inc., Portland, Oregon.

Note how the art director molds the layout to the line of the figure.

Take a yogourt to lunch today

brown bag it with Dr. Gaymont's

Delicious low-fat French style® yogourt— —a lunch in itself. Dr. Gaymont's yogourt satisfies your hunger 'til dinner; curbs your desire to eat.

9 fruit flavors—no mixing needed. Tasty chunks of fully ripened fruit are gently blended in the smooth, tangy Dr. Gaymont's yogourt: strawberry, pineapple, blueberry, red raspberry, spiced apple, peach, apricot, black cherry, mandarin orange PLUS vanilla and plain.

Dr. Gaymont's *yogourt* *french type®*

Where to buy it; call 234-7526

sunshine

SUNSHINE DAIRY

167

many banks, corporations, and insurance companies would like to project.

On the other hand, *informal balance* allows for much more freedom, dynamic movement, and excitement—all the things you want your layout to have when you are striving to make your voice heard above the others.

Eye direction. You will recall that when we were discussing copy, we said that the writer must use every device possible to *keep you reading.* He or she must hold your eye until the selling story is completed. The art director plays a major role in the selling-story effort. By applying some well known techniques of eye direction, the artist moves your attention from one place to another in the layout.

You have always read from left to right. So, on any page, your eye will naturally move in a diagonal left-right-downward direction. Probably the most obvious way to direct your attention is with a common attention-directing device such as an arrow. A pointing finger, a stop sign, decorative borders, and bull's eyes will often accomplish the same purpose. Frequently you will see these devices used in "buckeye" kinds of price newspaper ads.

Art directors also rely on more subtle techniques of eye direction long known and used by the great artists of history. Just as you can always gather some fellow gazers by standing and looking upward, so do eyes in the ad's illustration direct your gaze. The eyes usually look *into* the ad, or at the product, not away from it. *Physical movement* can also carry your gaze with it. The direction in which a thing or person is moving influences eye direction.

Illustrations. Illustrations are the ultimate in eye-catchers. It is important to remember that when there are several illustrations, the little one can dominate the big one if it is more interesting or attractive.

We are used to following things in *sequence,* so that the art director often uses this device too. A cartoon strip is a sequence of events. So is a TV story board. Frequently either sequence or repetition carries your eye from beginning to end.

Proportion. An important principle of composition has to do with the proportions of the sections of the ad. An advertisement with equal space given to headline, illustration, and body text can be very dull. *Unequal divisions* are usually more eye-catching than those with equal proportions. It is very easy for the art director to design a layout in which the parts are in almost equal proportion. As we have said, many of the more formal *institutional* ads are of this nature.

Many magazine ads are divided into parts approximately 2/10, 5/10, and 3/10 percent of the total.[4] In deciding on proportions, the art director

---

[4]Hugh G. Wales, *Advertising Copy, Layout and Typography,* p. 247.

is guided by the *importance* of the elements. A headline might be almost completely dominant. In another case, a striking illustration that "says it all" might be given the lion's share of the layout space.

Advertising Art Work

You've heard about one picture being worth a thousand words? Sometimes. And sometimes the illustration in an ad isn't worth *one* word—or a second glance.

EVERYONE WANTS TO BE WANTED, BUT NOT FOR THEFT.

Retail Bureau, Metropolitan Washington Board of Trade

Agency: Abramson/Himelfarb, Washington, D.C.

Simple typographic arrangement makes a striking page layout.

Making layouts is a *mechanically* artistic job. As you have learned, it is the task of arranging certain elements so that the results will be eye-catching and induce readership. You've also learned that there are certain principles of composition that apply, and of which the art director is fully aware as he or she designs the layout.

But when the time comes to select and buy this art work, the art director has few guideposts. Here, *in deciding what the picture should be*, the art director's taste and creative instincts come into full play. He or she can, at this juncture, play the key role in making a great ad or a hard-boiled egg.

There have been illustrations so meaningful that the ad didn't need any copy. Literally, the picture "said it all." Earlier we spoke of the art director as the person who "breathes life" into an ad. If it's going to happen, then this is where it happens—in the conceptualizing of the illustration itself.

How Advertising Art Is Purchased

All art directors and art services in your community know what art talents are available. They know their styles, their abilities, and their prices. When layout and copy have been approved by the client, it is then the art director's job to work with the artist who will do the finished art. Today, nine times out of ten, that means a photographer—for reasons that we will soon examine.

The art director picks up the phone and asks the photographer to come in to talk over the job. Again, as in dealing with the copywriter, this business of "talking things over" can be very important. You now understand why.

There is an exception to this procedure, particularly where the small advertiser with a limited budget is concerned. *Stock photo houses* have catalogues containing hundreds of photographs that are circulated to art directors and services. In these catalogues, the art director may find a satisfactory picture already in existence that can be bought inexpensively. Prices often vary according to where the illustration is to be used and how often it will appear. It may be that some of the photographers in your city have a file of stock photos the advertisers can buy at a nominal price. Public Relations departments of large companies can often supply you with good free art of subjects in their field.

There are two obvious drawbacks to purchasing "stock art." You and your competitor may come up with the same illustration in your ads. Choosing a ready-made picture, no matter how good it is, denies the art director and photographer the chance to create the shot that could make an ad take wings and fly.

Art director and photographer may discuss models, if the illustration calls for them. In the big cities there are *model agencies* that supply photographers' models of every type. These agencies distribute their catalogues to art directors and studios, and the art director may use the

Jan. 1974:   The end of the concrete foundation begins.

Read on ⟩⟩⟩ ------→

Startling photographic concept for the cover of a brochure for all-weather wood foundations (American Plywood Association).

Agency: Cole & Weber, Inc., Seattle, Wash.

catalogue in selecting the right model. Certain popular models, particularly fashion models and "cover girls," earn very high incomes.

If the "shot" is to be done outdoors, the photographer must arrange for a location. Most photographers have all kinds of information about locations tucked away, and they know the easiest and quickest place to go to get what they want. There's an abandoned surface-mining operation near our town that looks like the Sahara, sand dunes and all. When the cold winter winds blow down Fifth Avenue or State Street, you can find camera crews shooting "on location" in Florida and the islands.

If the shot is to be made indoors, *props* must be gathered and the set has to be "dressed." Exactly the same terms are used in the theater. *Props* stands for properties—chairs, beds, curtains, et cetera. *Dressing* means to arrange the *props* on the set. Large photographic studios retain a *prop manager* whose job it is to buy, rent, or borrow all the items that will go into the background of the picture or that the model will wear or hold. It's a demanding task. Today you may have to come up with a stuffed baby elephant, and tomorrow with an evening dress of the 1920s.

The art director may be present on the day of the shooting. Some photographers prefer to be on their own; others welcome the art director's presence on the set. But it is *now* that the miracle is going to happen. Maybe.

There are advertising photographers who make $5,000 with the click of a camera, and they earn every penny of it. When a magazine's circulation goes up 100,000 just because of a picture on the cover; when a quizzical glance pops out of a page and stops you cold; when you look at a photo and suddenly your eyes brim over with tears, then you can be sure that a good photographer has been at work.

Sometimes a photographer will take hundreds of shots before he is satisfied. Much of a model's value lies in having the ability to react, change expression, and move. The photographer shoots a variety of poses and expressions from a number of different angles. The results go on a *contact sheet*—a printout of many of the photos taken in a small size and unretouched. These an art director will examine under a reading glass in the hope of finding one that will do the job best.

Psychology of Pictures

A couple of chapters from now, when we discuss television, we will talk about something that is basically a psychological phenomenon: the *speed* with which pictures can evoke a mood, relate a situation, or tell a story. Sometimes a piece of television film is worth a thousand words *in just a few seconds*. This is the important thing about the single still photograph in an ad. It *evokes* something psychologically, sometimes very quickly and powerfully.

Stephen Baker lists some good reasons why photographs are here to

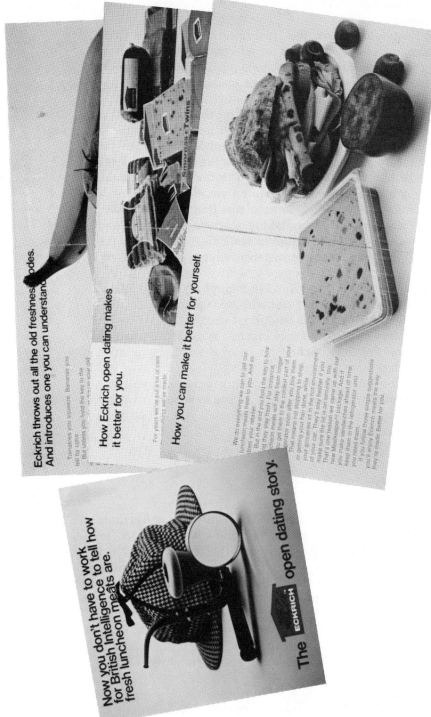

Agency: Bonsib, Centlivre, Ferguson, Inc., Fort Wayne, Ind.

Copywriter and art director worked closely together to produce this attractive trade brochure for a manufacturer of processed meats.

stay. There are also 6 kinds of contributions a good photograph can make. Note the following:[5]

1. *Realism:* People like to see the "real thing" in their ads. Good color photography does wonders for all kinds of products, from gleaming motor cars to steaming bowls of soup. Just look at the food photography in any homemaker's magazine!
2. *The feeling of "it's happening now":* Photographs—particularly news type photographs—put you right on the spot when it is happening. You are standing on the goal line when the touchdown is scored. You get involved. Remember, one of our big objectives in advertising is to put the reader "in the driver's seat" . . . to make him relate and see himself in that same situation. Photography goes a long way in helping you do that.
3. *Making the "cartoon effect" come alive:* Photographers have done some wonderful things in taking "cartoon situations" and giving them the added dimension of realism. A drawing of the eye-patched Hathaway man, for instance, simply wouldn't come off.
4. *The beauty and sensitivity of film:* Photographers are sometimes able to achieve a high artistic level with their pictures. A photograph can carry a tremendous emotional wallop.
5. *Photographs make excellent "convincers":* What better proof do you need than the unretouched photo of the weight reducer, before and after?
6. *Speed, flexibility, and economy:* A drawing or painting will take longer to complete than a photograph. As you have seen, a variety of shots can be taken at one session. If desirable, stock photos can be purchased inexpensively.

A Word for the Artist

All this may lead you to believe that a photo is the *only* way to illustrate an ad; obviously it isn't. If you look through *Business Week, Fortune,* or *Scientific American,* you will find many ads that could have been illustrated only by a painting or a drawing. With all its attributes, modern photography has pushed painted illustration somewhat into the background, both in advertising and editorially. But the pendulum may yet swing back again. If you are a young person, you should go to your library and study some issues of the *Saturday Evening Post* of the 1940s. You'll see the work of such great illustrators as Norman Rockwell, Al Dorne, Steve Dohanos, and a fellow who could paint freighters so well

[5]Stephen Baker, *Advertising Layout and Art Direction* (New York: McGraw-Hill Book Company, 1959).

you could almost taste the salt spray. These artists did things for a story that no photograph could have done.

But the reality of the situation is that great illustrators never come cheap. For most of America's regional advertisers, they would be quite out of the question. In fact for most of the advertising that you, as a young executive, will be doing, it might not even be suitable. There are exceptions, of course. I know of a bank in a small city in Georgia. They've done a campaign keyed to local history, illustrated the ads with paintings, and are hard-pressed to keep enough reprints of the illustrations on hand for those who want them.

WHERE YOU ARE

1. You understand the importance of a good working relationship between art director and copywriter.

2. You have learned what "visualization" is, and the part it plays in the creation of advertising.

3. You can recognize the various *elements* of a layout that the art director must take into consideration.

4. You can define the difference between "thumb nails," "roughs," and "comprehensive" layouts.

5. You are now familiar with some of the basic principles of composition governing the art director's work.

6. You know how art work is purchased, and some of the methods you can follow in your community in buying illustrations and photography.

7. You understand some of the psychological effects that may be achieved through the use of art work.

QUESTIONS FOR CLASS DISCUSSION

1. "One picture is worth a thousand words" has been around for a long time. What do you think about it?

2. It is said that many pictures have changed the course of history. Can you think of some?

3.   Which do you think portrays a person's character best—a caricature, or a photograph?

4.   You've seen how useful photographs are in portraying realism. How, then, did we portray realism *before* photography?

5.   Pick out an ad illustrated by a photograph. Present the class with an argument as to why the art director should have chosen and used a painting.

6.   Choose the most eye-repelling ad you can find, and explain to the class what went wrong with the layout.

7.   Who, in your opinion, has the most responsibility for an ad—the copywriter who must conceive the idea for the ad, or the art director who must execute it?

SOMETHING FOR YOU TO DO

You have been assigned to take a photograph to illustrate an ad for a motorcycle company. The headline for the ad is, "LIVE FREE!" Get a camera, then go out and take a picture that you think will make the most striking and meaningful illustration for the ad.

KEY WORDS AND PHRASES

Art Work.   Material used in illustrating and decorating an ad.

Body Text.   Main block of copy.

Buck-eye.   Corny, old-fashioned, standard.

Comp (Composition).   A highly finished form of layout.

Composition.   Arrangement of the elements of a layout.

Conceptualization.   How an art director "sees" a layout.

Contact Sheet.   Page of small, unretouched photographs.

Eye Direction.   Movement of eyes influenced by composition of layout.

Formal Balance.   Arrangement of a layout in which the elements balance one another.

Headline. Copy in prominent display. The words are an element of the layout.

Illustration. Picture featured in the ad (painting, drawing, or photo).

Informal Balance. Layout arrangement in which the parts do not balance one another.

Layout. The design of the structure of the ad.

Location. Place at which a picture is to be shot.

Main Illustration. Featured illustration in layout when there is more than one.

Model Agency. Organization that registers and supplies models for photographic and art purposes. Models of all types are pictured and described in model agency catalogues.

Picture Caption. Copy under an illustration referring to it.

Proportion. The arrangement of the elements of a layout so that they are in pleasing relation to one another.

Props (Properties). All the things that must be present in a scene before it is ready to be shot. The actor's cane is a "prop."

Roughs. Early form of the layout, very loosely done.

Shooting. Taking a picture—still or film.

Stock Art. Pictures on all kinds of subjects that can be purchased from a catalogue.

Stock Photo House. One who sells them.

Sub-head. Display copy subsidiary to headline.

Thumbnail. Small rough sketch of a layout idea made by the art director while "noodling around."

Trademark. A company's identifying sign.

Visual. Rough layouts made so that the artist can "visualize" the ad.

White Space. Unused part of the layout not occupied by copy, illustration, etc. It is a definite layout element.

SELECTED READINGS

Bockus, H. William, Jr. *Advertising Graphics* (New York: The Macmillan Company, 1969). Primarily for students of advertising art. The author calls it, "A workbook and reference for the advertising artist." Very good and complete.

Baker, Stephen. *Advertising Layout and Art Direction* (New York: McGraw-Hill Book Company, 1959). Like few other writers on advertising, this author stresses the importance of the working rapport between people: art directors and copywriters, account executives and clients, et cetera.

Visual Persuasion (New York: McGraw-Hill Book Company, Inc., 1961). Particularly good in examining the emotional impact of pictures.

Felten, Charles J. *Layout 4, Printing Design and Typography* (St. Petersburg, Florida: Charles J. Felten, 1970). Much of the material originally appeared in *Printing Magazine*. Very informative on the *readability* of advertising.

Wales, Hugh G., Gentry, Dwight L., and Wales, Max. *Advertising Copy, Layout, and Typography* (New York: The Ronald Press Company, 1958). One of the few books devoted to putting *all* the creative functions together in one place. You'll find Chapter 16, "Fundamentals of Advertising Layout" most helpful.

chapter eight

Printers, Engravers, and Typographers

In this chapter we follow the process by which an advertisement, brochure, or mailing piece achieves the form in which it finally appears.

The copywriter and art director have done their work. Now you will meet all the other people who must apply their skills so that an attractive, eye-appealing piece is produced.

You will learn about type and typefaces, and the different methods by which type can be set.

You will learn how different kinds of engravings are made, and the methods that may be used in printing the finished product.

And inspired by your curiosity, I hope you will visit some of the printers, engravers, and newspaper composing rooms in your hometown, and that you will see all these things firsthand.

179

A great deal has happened since the middle of the 15th century when a fellow by the name of Gutenberg carved out a letter from a block of wood, inked it, pressed it against a piece of paper, and thereby threw a lot of monks out of work. They had been busy, up to then, laboriously doing the whole thing by hand. The other thing this did was to cause an information explosion.

Within 50 years after Gutenberg had printed his Bible, there was scarcely a major city in Europe without a printer and publisher using the new idea of movable type. The ensuing flood of books, pamphlets, bills, and notices had an impact on the world that can scarcely be calculated. The advent of a *printed* Bible, in *English*—particularly the Tyndale edition—literally changed the world as very few single events had ever changed it before. Libraries moved out of monasteries and universities and into homes. "The library" became a reference to an important room in a well-to-do Englishman's house (a status his bathroom was not to attain for several more centuries).

Today, as I sit in my office, I am inundated by printed material—all of which I take much for granted. Beside me is an expensive machine that prints inked letters on a piece of paper at the mere pressing of a key. Gutenberg would have been delighted with this contraption, particularly with the feature that allows the writer to move from one line to the next simply by throwing a bar over. He would have been delighted by the typewriter, but not astonished. After all, the basic principle involved is quite similar to the one he invented some centuries ago.

Before me on my bulletin board are a dozen or so memos, reminders, and pleas, all printed and many out of date. The sheer volume of this printed material would have puzzled Gutenberg, who might have wonderingly asked himself if indeed there could be anything on my board of such vital importance that one was required to devote almost as much type to it as to Paul's letter to the Corinthians. The answer, of course, would have to be "no." But the very ease and speed we have given to the original process has now made it possible for certain people, who really have very little to say, to go on, and on, and on. . . .

I also have a couple of diplomas on my walls—the instructor's status symbols—and the Brothers in the monastery at Vence would find the lettering on them (a modern typeface called Ludlow Old English) not so different from the letters they used to make by hand. But I'm sure the Brothers would have exchanged some polite if not amused glances over the fact that my diplomas contain absolutely no color or decoration in the lettering—which results in a singularly dull-looking document.

Interior of a large supermarket. How many point-of-purchase display pieces can you count here?

Courtesy of Mr. Frank J. Thomas, Director of Advertising and Sales Promotion, Jacksonville Region, Food Fair Stores, Inc.

A lot of printing ink has gone under the dam since Gutenberg's day, and many wondrous developments have taken place in the art of transferring type and illustrations to paper. The culmination of all this is very important to you as an advertiser; for, willy-nilly, you will be involved in it whether you order a letterhead, a display piece, a package, or an ad.

Much that goes on in this field today is highly technical and involves electronics, optics, and computers. So to keep the subject within manageable limits let us go back to that moment when an account executive has hurried back from the client's office, clutching the new magazine campaign that, happily, has just been approved. After breaking the good news to all concerned at the agency, the account executive will drop the ads off at the production department, and the campaign will then be "put into production." It is this process of turning art, layout, and copy into a finished magazine or newspaper ad that we will now follow.

How Copy Is Printed

The first job the production manager has to undertake on the newly approved campaign is to get the copy transformed from typewritten copy on a piece of the agency's copypaper to the final form of typography in which it will appear in the printed ad. In larger agencies, this may be the sole responsibility of the production manager (though with the approval of the art director). In smaller agencies, the art director or art service usually assumes the responsibility for what is known as *type specifying.*

There are three basic kinds of specifications: the *size* of the type and the amount of space between the letters; the *identity* of the typeface itself; and the *width* and *spacing* of the lines.

Let it be said right here that type specification is in itself a subtle and demanding art. Much of the technique of advertising is involved with getting people to *read* your ad. The smart copywriter never forgets that it is the *writer's* job to carry your eye from word to word, from sentence to sentence, and from paragraph to paragraph, to the very end of the copy. If someplace along the line you, the reader, get tired, bored, or confused, the copywriter may have fallen down on the job and lost you. Once lost, it is very hard to get you back.

The copywriter has to keep this in mind, and, by the same token, so does the person who makes the type specification. It is possible to choose typefaces and type size and arrangements so badly that, before you know it, the poor reader is driven screaming out of the room. Usually, of course, it isn't quite as dramatic as that; but it can be just as fatal. The reader of badly set, hard-to-read copy becomes aware of a feeling of annoyance or impatience and quickly flips the page over.

On the other hand, well-set and thought-out type can add immeasurably to the attractiveness and sales power of an ad. And that's what you want in *your* ad.

Let us begin, then, by talking about the *looks* of the type—the typeface. Although there have been many designers and designs of type, perhaps the easiest way for you to begin to classify typefaces is to think of them in related sets as shown here:

Text and Display

Roman and *Italic*

Lightface and **Boldface**

Old Style and Modern

Serif and Sans Serif

With a little practice, you can look through a magazine and identify the letters that fall into the above categories. Certainly you always knew what *italic* looked like.

But in addition to the 5 sets of opposing features listed above, production people also have another way of identifying typefaces, usually by the name of the person who designed a particular style of lettering. Some of these famous names, which every production manager knows as well as his own, are: Claude Garamond, who lived in the 17th century; and William Caslon and John Baskerville who designed their typefaces in the 1700s. There are other well-known faces such as Bodoni, after an early Italian designer; and more modern faces such as Futura and Vogue. In addition, there are certain typefaces designed primarily as display type (for headlines, posters, and so on) with names such as Craw Modern, Brush, Deepdene, and Stymie.

Craw Modern

Brush

DEEPDENE

STYMIE Bold

Different "faces" have different looks.

There is one more element that enters into and makes your job more exciting. There are several firms in the business of manufacturing type. They are called typefounders, and sometimes they give a standard typeface an individual difference of their own. If you remember, I mentioned the fact that my diplomas had been set in Ludlow Old English. This face is very similar to Engravers Old English and Cloister Black manufactured by other typefoundries. The best known typefounders are Linotype, Intertype, Monotype, Ludlow, American Typefounders, and Bauer Typefoundry. When specifying type, the production manager will, if necessary, refer to a book supplied by a typefoundry. This book contains examples of all the typefaces that the foundry has available.

The Size of Type and Its Spacing

Another specification your typographer will need is the type size and the width of the lines. A piece of type is measured in *points*. There are 72 points to one inch. This measurement includes all the metal bearing the type and not just the letter itself. The most common sizes of *text type* are the 6, 8, 10, and 12 point. This book is set in 10-point type. Anything up to 18 points is considered *text type;* type from 14 points up may be considered *display type.*

Look at a letter on your typewriter. *Ascenders* are those parts of the type that extend above the basic top line of lower-case letters, as in small "d." The *descenders* reach below the base line as in small "p." A "d" and a "y" can therefore take up more vertical space than a capital "S." The width of the line of copy to be set is specified in *picas.* There are 6 picas to one inch. Another term you'll run into, particularly when buying space in a newspaper, is the *agate line.* This is the measurement of a column of type. There are 14 agate lines to one inch. Thus a 780-line newspaper ad could be 2 columns by 10 inches, or 4 columns by 5 inches.

To make a paragraph of type look readable it is sometimes necessary to get some *air* between the lines and the paragraph. This is done by *leading* or placing a thin sheet of metal between the lines of the set type. These come in 1-, 2-, and 3-point thicknesses. When the lines are unleaded, the paragraph is said to be set *solid.* This paragraph was set solid. The next paragraph is set with 2 points lead.

It usually takes about three days for a typographer to set the type to your specifications and get the printed type proof back to you. Many small communities do not have a typographer. In fact some large cities don't boast of one; it may be necessary for you to send out of town for your type needs.

The Methods of Typesetting

Hand composition. In the earliest days of printing, all type was set by hand. The individual letters, raised at the end of a piece of metal, were

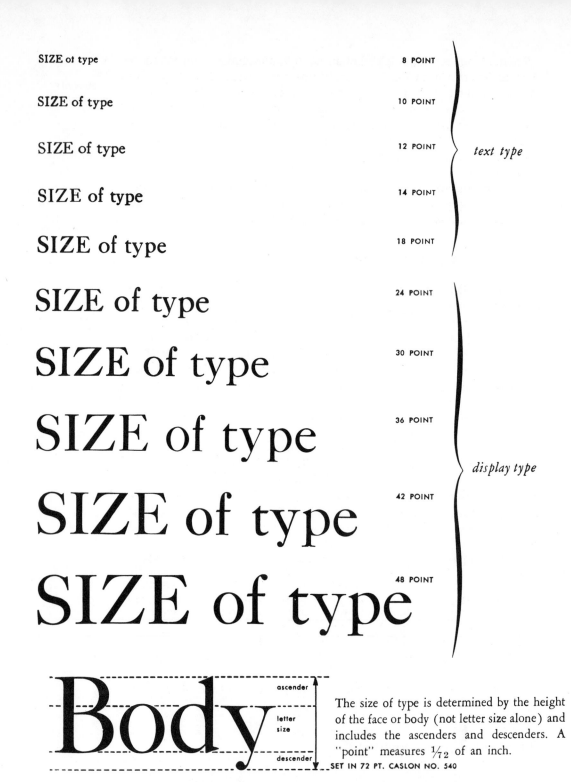

SIZE of type — 8 POINT
SIZE of type — 10 POINT
SIZE of type — 12 POINT — } text type
SIZE of type — 14 POINT
SIZE of type — 18 POINT

SIZE of type — 24 POINT
SIZE of type — 30 POINT
SIZE of type — 36 POINT — } display type
SIZE of type — 42 POINT
SIZE of type — 48 POINT

Body

ascender
letter size
descender

The size of type is determined by the height of the face or body (not letter size alone) and includes the ascenders and descenders. A "point" measures $\frac{1}{72}$ of an inch. SET IN 72 PT. CASLON NO. 540

Otto Kleppner, Advertising Procedure, 6th ed., © 1973, p. 396. Reprinted by permission of Prentice-Hall, Inc., Englewood Cliffs, New Jersey.

known as *foundry type*; they are so known today. All the metal pieces carrying the different letters were stocked in a drawer or a *case* into which the printer reached for the letters he wanted.

Originally all the capital letters were kept at the top of the *case*, and the small letters were kept in the lower part. Thus today we have the expressions "upper case" and "lower case," meaning capital and small letters.

Today the hand printer arranges his letters as he selects them on a *stick*. The *stick* has an adjustable slide on it by which the width of the line of type can be controlled. To make the line of type come out even at the right-hand margin, the printer inserts *spaces* between the words where necessary. The *spaces* are simply low blank pieces of metal. Printers become very good at estimating just how many spaces they may need.

When each line of type is completed, it is placed in a *galley tray*. When the printer has completed the *makeup* of the galley tray of copy, a proof is pulled and sent to the production manager.

Machine composition. The Linotype or Intertype machines, which you may have seen in the composing room of your newspaper, produce type in one-line *slugs*. An operator, seated at a keyboard, types out the needed letters. As the keys are hit, *matrixes* or molds of the letters are automatically produced. When a line of type in matrix has been completed, molten metal is forced into the molds, then quickly cooled, and a line of metal type has been produced—a slug.

Monotype involves two machines and two steps. It operates on the same basic principle as the Linotype and Intertype machines, but produces only one letter at a time. As with the Linotype and Intertype, the end product is a line of *justified type* (lined with an even margin).

Foundry or handset type is slow, expensive, and rarely used for body type.

Advantages and disadvantages of composition methods. Linotype and Intertype machines are widely used in the printing of books because of the speed with which they can produce copy. Since they produce one line at a time, there is no chance of scrambling letters as may occur with handsetting. But when a correction is necessary, it can be expensive because the entire line must be reset.

The Monotype machine is particularly well suited to tabular work where vertical rules are required; the slug-casting machines cannot do this so well. The Monotype spaces more perfectly, but, as noted, more errors can occur because of the single letter setting.

The Ludlow typograph. This method combines handsetting and machine casting. The *matrices* of the type are assembled by hand, and from this a line of type is cast in metal in a few seconds. A new line of type with fresh metal is produced each time with the Ludlow so that the letters are always sharp and clear. This method is very popular for setting newspaper and advertising headlines.

Photocomposition. This method would indeed have surprised brother Gutenberg. It is the most sophisticated of typesetting methods, and is becoming dominant in the setting of advertising text and in book production. It is also gaining popularity in advertising, since it is far more inexpensive than lino or Ludlow.

A compositor seated at a keyboard types out all the type to be set and the instructions as to typeface, size, line width, and so on. Then the computer tape, with this information on it, takes over. The letters of whatever face is demanded are all on film. A light source moves across the film and sends an electrical impulse into a cathode ray tube, which carries the image to a piece of photosensitive paper.

There are a number of advantages to photocomposition: its speed, the sharpness of the letters, and its economy over the casting of metal type. Because the photography is so flexible, type can be reproduced in any desired size. As Kleppner said, "You can do all kinds of tricks with the type—all from one little film. You can make it taller or shorter, wider or thinner; you can give it perspective; make it lean forward or backward; and do all the things for which, in the past, you had to have an artist hand-letter the effect you sought. It is indeed versatile."[1]

Typesetting typewriters. This is sometimes referred to as *cold type* or *cold-type composition.* It is *direct-impression* composition in which the lines may or may not be justified. The Varityper, IBM Selectric Composer, and Friden's Justomatic are examples of machines that use this method. And because correction tape can be used, this method is popular for updating catalogues and directories and thus avoiding expensive resetting.

A great many local retail merchants have their ads *pub set*—that is, the publication sets the type from its own *font* or supply of type. This is a great money- and time-saver, but you may find that your local newspaper has a very limited choice of type. If you live in a city of any size, however, you will find that your newspaper has sufficient typefaces and styles to meet the needs of most newspaper advertisers. Many magazines, particularly the trade publications, will *pub set* your ad for you. And many a deadline has been made because of it.

So now the production person has specified the copy and sent it off to the typographer, and in a few days receives a nice slick piece of paper with the copy printed to the stated specifications. It is up to the production person to read over this type proof most carefully to check for any errors, misspelling, badly set type, mispunctuation, or any of the million

---

[1]Otto Kleppner, *Advertising Procedure* (Englewood Cliffs, N.J.: Prentice-Hall, Inc., 1973), p. 409.

and one other mistakes that seem to creep into a piece of printed copy. Very often the copywriter will be asked to check the type proof. But most production people consider this as practically useless because they have learned, by long and bitter experience, that many copywriters get so carried away by the beauty of their own prose they could read k-a-t and never notice it.

The production person has a kind of shorthand that all printers and typographers understand, and these marks are the accepted way to call attention to typographical errors. Many printers employ a full-time *proofreader* who carefully checks everything the firm turns out. When you visit a printing plant, as you will, be sure to check with the proof-reader. This person can probably give you a booklet containing typographer's marks. Familiarize yourself with some of the common ones. In point of fact, it's quite possible that you already know some, since English composition teachers frequently use these marks when correcting papers—particularly the paragraphing marks (¶) and "SP" for spelling!

In print advertising there have been as many famous typographical

65   110   150

The higher the screen number, the more dots per square inch. But the higher the screen, the smoother the paper has to be so that all the dots will strike it.

boners as in, say, the well-known recording of bloopers made by TV and radio people over the years. The pages of your hometown newspaper are probably set by a Linotype machine, though a more modern form of photocomposition may be in use. In addition, as we have indicated above, your newspaper sets much of the type for its ads. You must visit the composing room of your newspaper, and let them explain the hot-type or cold-type methods they use in setting type. Again, these fellows in the composing room are real experts. They have spent years in their trade, and will be delighted to show you how a typesetting machine works.

Getting the Illustrations Ready for Printing

If you'll just go to your wastepaper basket, extract the morning newspaper and open it to the biggest ads for one of your department stores, we can start from there.

In one of the ads the illustration is probably a sketch of a young woman wearing a dress or suit. It is a simple drawing that consists of lines and shadings. Light and dark tonal effects are achieved by means of these shadings. Now get yourself a reading glass, and examine the shaded portions of the illustration. You will see that the shaded parts actually consist of one or more designs of dots or straight or crosshatch lines. This technique of shading is known as the *benday process*, after Benjamin Day, the American printer who invented it. It allows you to produce a more interesting and attractive picture than you might get if you used only unshaded lines. However, shaded effects can be achieved with lines alone by simply graduating the lines from thick and close together (dark) to thin and farther apart (white).

In looking through your reading glass, you may also notice some shaded areas that consist of tiny dots. This was achieved through *halftone screening*, with the sizes of the screen determining the darkness of the shading. The illustration is photographed with a screen containing a crosshatching of fine hairlines placed in front of the lens. The result is that the camera sees the picture through a series of tiny windows. You've probably seen something like this reproduced as "pop art." The smaller the dots, the closer to faithful reproduction. For fine screens, a smooth finish is required to reproduce all the dots. In newspapers, a 65 screen is used, and for magazines it is generally 120 (meaning 120 dots per square inch).

Color

The color you see reproduced in newspapers, and sometimes in magazines, is usually done by running the paper twice through the press—once for the black reproduction, and then a second time with a new plate that prints in the color portions. The magazine section of your Sunday paper may be printed this way. When the colors don't quite land where they obviously ought to, we say the reproduction is *out of register*.

If you are having a brochure produced in which there are some color photographs, you are in a far different ball game involving *color separation* and *four-color process plates*. Briefly, what is involved is making four separate pictures of your photograph using a filter to remove everything but yellow, red, and blue. Black, of course, is the fourth color. A separate plate is made for each of these colors, and with carefully mixed inks four runs are made through the press to combine them. The result is a full-color reproduction.

Three Different Ways of Printing

What happens next from the production person's point of view—the making of plates and engravings—depends on what kind of printing process will be used by the publication carrying your ad, or the printer who is going to make up your broadside or brochure. So let's examine these now.

The three major printing processes are: *letterpress, offset,* and *roto.* In letterpress, a raised surface is printed. In offset, a plain surface is used; and in roto, the printing is done from a depressed surface. Offset is also referred to as *photo-offset lithography,* and roto is sometimes called *intaglio* printing (pronounced in-tal-yoo). Each one of these has certain advantages related to pressrun (number of copies you are having printed) and the type of paper involved.

Letterpress. This is what happens when a key on your typewriter is pressed—a raised surface (the letter) is inked by a ribbon and pressed against the paper. A great deal of printing is done this way, and it gives good results. Probably most of the printers in your community have this kind of equipment. It is very good for color reproduction, and prints show sharp detail. In this case, the printer works from an engraved plate. Copy and art have been transferred photographically to the sensitive plate; acid is used to etch away the unwanted portions, and the remaining portions of the plate are printed.

Offset lithography. Offset lithography—often used for labels, posters, and point-of-purchase material—involves a photochemical process in which the ad or page of copy is photographed. The photo is transferred onto a sensitized plate by means of chemical action under strong light. Parts of the plate that are expected to print are receptive to and hold greasy ink, while the nonprinting portions are receptive only to water.

In this printing process a rubber roller gets into the act; this is why it is called "offset." The rubber roller picks up the impression from the inked plate, and in turn transfers it to the roller with the printing paper on it. When the roller is not used, it is called *direct litho.*

Offset has some advantages over *letterpress.* It can be used with either dull or slick paper, and the paper doesn't need to be glossy to reproduce halftones well. It's cheaper if you have a lot of illustrations to reproduce, as in a brochure. Since offset can print on low-grade paper and on large sheets of paper, it is generally the process used in preparing labels and large window-display pieces.

Rotogravure.   In a sense, rotogravure is the opposite of letterpress in that the printing surface is recessed rather than raised. The invitation for your wedding may have been printed this way. If you run your finger over the lettering you can feel it because the letter comes out slightly raised. In roto, the negative of your picture is transferred to a sensitized copper roller by means of photography and chemical action. The plate is inked, scraped clean of excess ink, and applied to the paper. In roto, the original copperplate or cylinder tends to be expensive. Rotogravure is used for long runs—75,000 to millions at low cost per unit.

Silk-screen printing.   There is another process—far less important than the three mentioned above, but very good for simple cards, posters, and display pieces. *Silk-screening* employs the stencil principle, in that black and colored inks are forced through the stenciled screen. A different screen is used for each color. Because you can *silk-screen* almost any kind of surface, this is the preferred method for preparing many point-of-purchase pieces.

Ordering Plates and Engravings

Now, back again to our agency production person. The decision of *how* the job is to be printed is an important one, for there are cost variables present involving cuts, plates, pressruns, and paper. There *is* a most satisfactory and economical method for printing the job. It is up to the production manager to choose the right one.

Thus if you decide that your job is to be printed by *letterpress,* the printer must be supplied with line plates, halftones, or color engravings as described above. If you decide on *offset printing* you send the shop a type proof of your copy and a *photonegative* of your art work, and the printer takes it from there and makes his own plate. In *rotogravure* work much the same thing takes place; reproduction is done from plates made from your negative, either by the printer or by a house that specializes in this kind of work.

Making Plates from Plates

There will be occasions when an ad is to run in several different publications at the same time, in which case *duplicate* plates have to be made.

There are available two ways of making duplicate plates: (1) *electrotypes* or (2) *mats* and *stereotypes*. Electrotypes are commonly known as *electros*, and you may be familiar with the method through that experiment in your physics class when you transferred positive ions to a negative surface by electrical current. Your original plate is pressed into wax, and the waxed surface is coated with graphite carbon particles. This is suspended in a solution with a copper bar, and the electrodes are hooked up. Soon there is a thin coating of copper over the graphite. Then the wax is removed, and hot metal is poured into the copper shell. You get an exact duplicate. This, with a proof of your ad, is sent to the publication.

For newspaper reproduction, *mats* are used. These are exact impressions of your plates in damp papier-maché. When dry, the material forms a hard matrix. At the newspaper they pour molten metal into the matrix and get a replica of the original plate called a *stereotype*, or commonly, a *stereo*.

Mats are inexpensive, lightweight for shipping, and are well suited to newspaper production. Sometimes they cause media people to worry because the mats have a tendency to shrink. You can order any quantity of mats from the same house that makes your engravings.

Paper

When submitting an estimate for a job, your printer will show you samples of the paper (*stock*) he intends to use. The inside pages are known as *book paper;* the outside, heavier paper, is *cover stock*. You should trust your printer's judgment on the page stock, since he knows his process and whether a *coated* (high gloss) paper or a *machine finish* (rougher) will handle the job best. On *cover stock* you have a far wider latitude. This can be very fancy—and very costly—too. The term-paper folders sold in your college bookstore are examples of cover stock.

Keeping It All Straight

As you have seen, the production manager has collected quite a pile of stuff along the way in getting ready for the final ad or brochure. There were carbon copies of the copy text, type proofs of the text, copies of art

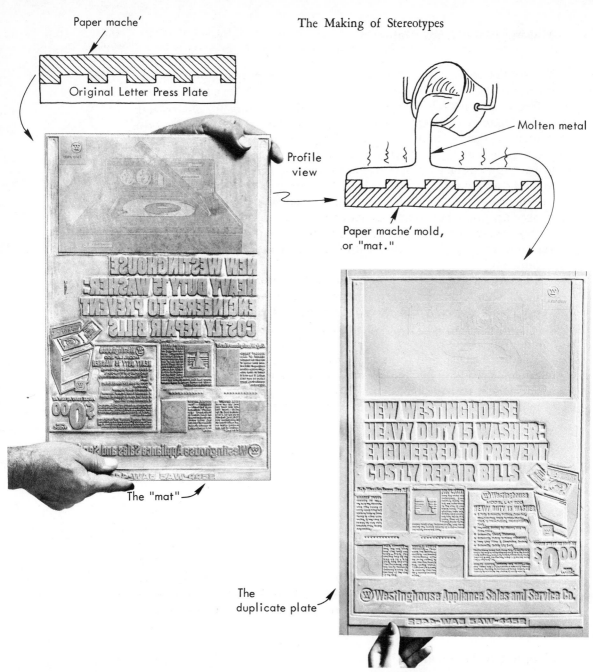

Paper mache'

Original Letter Press Plate

Profile view

Molten metal

Paper mache' mold, or "mat."

The "mat"

The duplicate plate

The mat. The least costly form of duplicate letterpress plate, and the one in widest use for newspaper advertising, is a *mat* or *matrix*. The mat, however, is only one half of a two-step operation. It is made by pressing a plate of the ad into dampened papier-mâché. When dried, the papier-mâché forms a hard matrix, from which it gets its name. When molten metal is poured into the mat and hardened, a metal replica of the original plate is formed, called a *stereotype* (or *stereo*).

Otto Kleppner, *Advertising Procedure,* 6th ed., © 1973, p. 421. Reprinted by permission of Prentice-Hall, Inc., Englewood Cliffs, New Jersey.

work, engraving proofs, color separations, to say nothing of the final page proofs or engraver's proofs of the finished ad. Your production manager has a very neat way of keeping all this straight—keeping track of all costs involved in the job, and seeing that it is completed on time. It's called a *job jacket.*

If you were to take a course in management from the American Management Association, somewhere along the line someone would mention a Gantt chart or a PERT system (Program Evaluation and Review Technique first developed by the U.S. Navy, and used in the planning and control of the Polaris Weapons System in 1958). These systems are basically time-event network analysis or "flow charts" in which an "event," or completed job, can be anticipated to take a certain amount of time.

The cover of the production manager's job jacket is, in effect, a flow chart on which every "event" leading up to the complete job can be recorded and assigned a completion date.

When our account executive came back from the client's office with the okayed campaign, one of the first things he did was to issue a *work order* on which was stated the publication date on which the first ad would run. Using this *closing date* of the publication (the last possible day they can accept copy for that particular issue—a deadline, fortunately, with a certain amount of built-in elasticity) the production manager works backward through engravings, type proofs, art work, layout, and the rest, to the copywriter—the ultimate "villain" in the plot. As can be seen, if the copywriter, after getting the work order, dawdles around too long getting into the mood, a drag can be imposed on the whole operation. The same with the others.

Some of the larger agencies, as mentioned earlier, often have *traffic* people who stick their heads into your office and ask, "Hey, where's that copy for Acme Nuts and Bolts? It was due three weeks ago!"

The job jacket also contains places in which to record all purchase orders to suppliers and the total production costs plus the 17.65 percent.

Controlling the Costs of Print Production

Each year a great deal of money flows through a print production department. Unless carefully controlled, leakage and inefficiencies can lead to considerable losses for both agency and advertiser.

As a young executive, one of the greatest contributions you can make is to exercise some form of control over your company's printing and production costs. The following words of wisdom are designed to help you do just that.

A typographic service has prepared a booklet for its customers that includes the following advice:

Make your instructions clear. Each job should be accompanied by instructions as clear and as comprehensible as it is possible to make them. Everything pertinent to the job should be included: the size, time wanted, number of proofs required, and kind of paper—if it is to be other than usual; instructions about cuts (where they are coming from and when) and whether you want complete or type proofs. Make your instructions clear, and you've already started to save time and money.

Send your typographer "clean" copy. Copy should be sent to the typographer in the most readable form in order to facilitate handling by the makeup people, machine operators, compositors, and proofreaders. Usually we are able to decipher a poorly written manuscript, but it takes time—and typography is billed on time.

Avoid complicated telephone alterations. Simple alterations by phone are always practical and actually save time. Lengthy corrections and copy additions should be picked up by messenger and executed, thus eliminating the possibility of misunderstanding and error that could result from phone conversations.

Get a "style" approved before setting large jobs. When starting to set a large booklet, or a series of ads, the approval of which may rest with many different people, we suggest that you first have a "style" page or ad set. Show it to everyone who must be pleased. When "style" has been approved, proceed with the rest of the job. It is easier to reset one page than forty-eight, if "Mr. Big" doesn't like the typeface.

Make your alterations on the manuscript. Alterations are an expensive factor of any advertising job and over which the customer can exercise considerable control. We would like to point out the obvious: If your copy chief, buyer, client, or any other interested person prefers to make copy changes in the job after it has been set, instead of on the manuscript, your typography bill is going to be higher!

Don't "makeup" a job when it is unnecessary. When you are going to pasteup a job and don't need it in the position of the layout, be sure to mark "galley proof" on your instruction sheet. Putting a form "in position" is exactly the same as putting a form in register. It takes time, and costs money.

Get layout approved before having the job set. Hastily executed tissue layouts are sometimes necessary, but usually they are costly. Any visual should be shown to the person or persons who will eventually O.K. the job. Maybe they can't be. Maybe it isn't possible to show the job until it is in proof form. We don't know. But this, too, comes high on the list of "How to cut your typographic costs."

Don't order more proofs than you need. Five proofs are included with hand composition and each alteration at no additional charge. All

extra hand proofs are billed on a "per each" basis. Typographers furnish
4 repro proofs. When time allows, they suggest that you see a rough proof before ordering the necessary repros.

Avoid switching cuts. Even though switching cuts from one job to another usually entails only minimal alteration, it is more economically feasible to order electrotypes of slugs, trademarks, and so on. Besides cutting costs, it speeds deliveries.

Quantity press proofs. Here's one case where ordering a larger quantity will bring down your "cost per proof." Take a two-color job. The forms must be locked for press, put into a register, and made ready in the same way for one proof as for a million. Therefore 50 or 100 proofs would cost only a few dollars more than 10 proofs. If you have use for them, it pays to order the larger quantity.

Grouping jobs for press proofs. There is a considerable saving over the standard scale where proofs can be grouped. Suppose you had four small ads and needed 1,000 press proofs of each. If you O.K. them all at one time, and the size of the form containing the four ads doesn't exceed 12½" x 19", we could run them "four up" and cut them apart after they were printed.

Avoid super-rush jobs. Printers are accustomed to fast work, but they can't go beyond a certain speed without spending extra money. For example, they often turn out a 10-hour job in 2 hours. To do this the printer puts 8 or more men on the job; comps wait around to hand other comps type and material the way a nurse waits to hand the surgeon scalpels and sutures. You get your job when you want it, but, from a cost angle, it's expensive. Of course, in many cases it's worth the extra money to you.

WHERE YOU ARE

---

1. You are familiar with some of the common typefaces and the categories into which they are placed.

2. You have learned how type is specified, and some of the terms used in doing so.

3. You are familiar with some of the marks used in correcting copy.

4. You are acquainted with the various methods of setting type.

5. You can define the difference between three common methods of printing.

6. You know how engraving plates are made.

7. You have learned the method by which the production manager keeps track of the jobs he or she is doing.

8. You have some good guidelines for keeping down production costs.

QUESTIONS FOR CLASS DISCUSSION

1. Would you consider the designing of a typeface an ''art''?

2. Would you say that the advent of color-print production was more important or less important than the introduction of color TV?

3. Why not simply mimeograph all books?

4. It is said that some color reproductions of famous paintings are better than the originals. Do you believe this?

5. It is said that some color photographs of food look tastier than the real thing. Could this be so?

SOMETHING FOR YOU TO DO

Visit the largest printing plant in your town, and ask them to show you how they work. Visit your newspaper to see how they prepare their pages for printing. Call on an advertising agency, if possible, and talk to their production manager.

KEY WORDS AND PHRASES

Agate Line. Unit of advertising space, 1 column wide, ¼ inch deep.

Air. When type or copy is "opened up" to give it more space.

Ascender. Part of the letter that arises above the main body of most lower-case letters, as in "b."

Benday. Engraving method by which shaded effects are gained with lines and dots. After Benjamin Day, the inventor.

Book Paper. Kind of paper used in printing books, brochures, etc. Lighter than cover stock.

Case. Holder for type faces.

Closing Date. Date by which plates must be received by the publication.

Cold Type Composition. Type setting done without casting metal.

Color Separation. Preparation of separate plates for primary colors in illustration.

Composition. Setting up the type for printing. Can be hand or machine.

Copy Reader. Person who checks over copy for errors.

Cut. Engraving or stereotype from which illustration is made.

Descenders. Parts of letters that descend below the main body of most lower-case letters, as in "p."

Direct Litho. Printing method by which treated surfaces of plate transfer ink to paper. Used for posters and packaging. Distinguished from *offset*.

Electrotype. Duplicate printing surface made by electrodepositing metal on a plastic mold.

Engraving. Preparing a printing surface by making impressions or marks on a metal plate.

Foundry Type. Type held in a case, to be removed and set by hand.

Four Color Process. Means by which color reproductions are made with separate printings of four different color plates—yellow, red, blue, and black.

Galley Tray. Tray designed to hold type.

Gutenberg. German monk who invented hand setting of type in 12th century.

Halftone. Reproduction made from a plate that has been photographed through a screen which breaks the picture into dots.

Hot Type. Type cast from molten metal.

Job Jacket. Folder or envelope in which stages of production work are filed and recorded.

Justified Lines. Lines of type that are spaced out so they are all the same width.

Leading. Spacing type by means of thin lead strips.

Letterpress. Printing done from a raised surface.

Lower Case. Small letters.

Machine Composition. Setting of type mechanically, as with linotype.

Machine Finish. Moderately slick paper that will take a halftone.

Make-up. Arranging elements on page before reproduction.

Matrix. A mold of pulp paper from which a metal plate can be made.

Offset Lithography. Printing process in which impression is transferred from a metal sheet to a rubber blanket, which contacts the paper.

Photo Negative. Negative from which plates are made.

Pica. Unit of width in printing. There are six picas to an inch.

Plate. Metal used in reproduction in printing process.

Proof. Sample of the reproduction. Proofs are "pulled" for inspection.

Pub Set. Printing set at publication from the publication's own type.

Register. Getting lines and colors to match evenly. Color sections that overlap are "out of register."

Rotogravure (Intaglio). Printing from chemically-etched roller plates on a rotary press.

Silkscreen. Method of reproduction by which ink is forced through a stenciled screen.

Slug. A line of type.

Specify. To indicate type sizes, faces, etc.

Stick. Instrument on which hand-set type is composed.

Text Type. Kind of type usually used in body of copy, usually under 18-point size.

Traffic Manager. Person who is responsible for supervising flow of work through various departments.

Typeface. The distinguishing design of letters.

Type Foundry. Place where type is manufactured.

Upper Case. Capital letters.

Work Order. Order that formally specifies the particulars of a job, including closing dates.

SELECTED READINGS

Cardamone, Tom. *Advertising Agency & Studio Skills: A Guide to the Preparation of Art and Mechanicals for Reproduction* (New York: Watson-Guptill Publications, 1959.)

Eckman, James Russell. *The Heritage of the Printer* (Philadelphia, Pa.: North American Publishing Co., 1765.)

Jackson, Hartley Everett. *Printing, a Practical Introduction to the Graphic Arts* (New York: McGraw-Hill Book Co., 1957.) Just what the title says for "the beginning student in the graphic arts."

Schlemmer, R. *Handbook of Advertising Art Production* (Englewood Cliffs, N.J.: Prentice-Hall, Inc., 1966).

Strauss, Victor. *The Printing Industry, an Introduction to Its Many Branches, Processes, and Products* (Washington, D.C.: Printing Industries of America, 1967.) This one has it all. May be in the reference section of your library.

chapter nine

How TV Commercials
Are Written
and Produced

In this chapter we look at the television commercial.

You will see why a television selling message differs so much from print.

You will learn why television, when properly used, can be such an effective medium.

You will meet many of the people who are involved in making commercials.

You will see how a television script is prepared, and you will become familiar with the wide range of costs in making a commercial.

Television brought a whole new exciting dimension to advertising. It wasn't only that we had a new media; it was the fact that we had a whole new set of techniques for reaching out to people and getting a message across to them.

Advertising was not unfamiliar with the theater and its disciplines. Many radio directors had a background in stock and on Broadway before settling down to a steady livelihood with an agency. But with TV we suddenly had at our disposal all the magic of the living theater itself, to use or misuse: lighting, directing, set design, makeup, music, and acting.

We woke up one morning, and *Variety*—the gospel according to Broadway—was being delivered to every agency in town. So that's what this chapter is all about—The Theater.

What happens in the theater is this: You are sitting in a big room with about 500 other people. Then the lights go down, and, at the end of the room you are all facing, a curtain is drawn back to reveal someone's apartment (not a very well-kept apartment at that). Of course you know this couldn't be so because who has ever heard of an apartment with one wall missing?

You can also see people strolling past outside, and hear the sounds of street vendors, and people talking, and the sound of an old-fashioned trolley bell; and you know this could not be so either, because all there is back there is the brick wall of the theater and a lot of ropes.

So the play goes on, and you get caught up in the story of a mixed-up dame who comes to visit her sister and brother-in-law in New Orleans. The brother-in-law is a fellow named Stanley. Blanche really gets hurt when her brother-in-law's friend decides that maybe she isn't all she says she is, and knocks the rose-colored lamp shade off her light bulb. In the third act you see her as she begins to sink slowly to her knees from all the blows life has given her. They have to send for a doctor and a nurse to come and take her away and, as she straightens herself up and walks through the room where her brother-in-law and a bunch of his crummy friends are playing poker, she says to them, "Don't bother getting up. I'm only passing through."

That's when you and a couple of hundred other people want to stand up and call out to her, "You're going to be all right, Blanche. They'll take good care of you. You're going to be all right, Blanche. We understand you, and we love you." But you don't, because in a minute the curtain comes down and then goes up again, and all the actors and actresses are taking bows and smiling at your applause, and you remember now it wasn't real at all. It was just an illusion.

Just an illusion. . . .

I sincerely hope that you will pay very close attention to the next few pages because although it is true that a great deal of money is wastefully spent in advertising, the degree of misspending increases in reverse proportion to the size of the advertising appropriation (Norris' First Law). I believe that more money is being wasted in television than in any other advertising medium (Norris' Second Law).

Now just in case your uncle happens to be a charter member of The National Association of Broadcasters, and tells you "Don't you believe it!" you might ask him this: While driving down the highway, how many times has he heard someone remark what a lousy billboard he had just seen? How many times has he observed someone look up from his magazine or newspaper and moan about an ad he'd just read? Very seldom, I imagine. But how many times have he and his friends snapped the switch while muttering, "Hooo boy—was *that* a terrible commercial!" At least once a night. That's how often. And you know, they are *right*. They may not know exactly why, but they *are* right. In many cases those commercials are awful and they not only don't sell anything but repel potential buyers.

As you've probably suspected, that spectacle of the local used-car dealer, using gestures he could have learned only in a high-school elocution class, inviting you in for a good old-tire-kicking deal, is neither television nor advertising nor selling. It's an ego trip—and an expensive one.

It also happens, I suspect, because some people who write TV commercials really don't like *people* too much. When people—which means *us*—become stereotypes, such as the bumbling inept husband, or the dopey suburban housewife, or the illiterate longshoreman, or the garrulous cab driver, it makes us all a little uncomfortable. One of the most embarrassing things I know is watching an actor playing a longshoreman in a commercial, and delivering lines written by someone who had never been on a pier and wouldn't know a baling hook, hand truck, or a longshoreman if he sat down on one. Count and treasure the number of times you could like and relate to someone in a TV commercial.

Why does this happen? It happens because television is a tricky and difficult medium, not always appreciated, often misunderstood, and very often not exploited to its full potential.

Let me sound another word of warning. The eye of the television camera is a discerning one. Under the strong studio lights it reveals wrinkles, sags, and blemishes you didn't know you had. It also reveals the wrinkles in your personality. Many a politician has been destroyed because, under the probing eye of the camera, it became evident that his veneer of sincerity only partially cloaked the soul of a highwayman. So you'd better know what you are up to before you expose your product to a television camera—which, of course, is why we have professionals who *do* know what they are doing.

Who Is Involved in Making a Commercial?

As you have seen, when a print ad is to be produced, there is a lot of preplanning involved. Main selling points must be decided on; psychological needs and desires defined; and the demographics of the market understood. All this must also take place before a television commercial is written.

Usually the account executive will get together with the writer and discuss what is needed. As the person in closest contact with the client, the account executive will be able to convey any market or product information it is important for the copywriter to know.

As with the print ad, the account executive will alert the production department and a *job jacket* will be opened for the new television project. If this is a new venture for the client, it may also be necessary to alert the media department so that they can begin buying the *time spots* in which the commercial will run.

When the account executive has delivered all instructions and orders, the copywriter goes to work on the *TV script*. In the big agencies there are many writers who do practically nothing *but* TV scripts. Their particular talents are well suited to the creation of an advertising message that uses motion pictures, sounds, and spoken words. Some of the younger TV commercial writers have seldom been called on to write a print ad. They get lost in the medium. There are some very fine print copywriters, too, who simply don't "see" a selling message in terms of the theater.

This is one of the reasons why good TV commercials are so hard to write. Primarily they are selling messages, and all the rules of selling apply; but they are not *illustrated* selling messages. They are something quite different; they are selling messages related in terms of performers and sound and audible words.

Usually the copywriter on a TV script works alone, more so than the print copywriter. Many a TV script writer will close the office door and actually act out the various scenes in the script till he is "seeing" them.

When his rough script is completed, the copywriter takes it to the art director who will make a *story board*. In some agencies that have small-budget clients, the story-board step will be omitted because of cost. If so, the script alone is discussed with the client. Again, the copywriter may attend the meeting and demonstrate the script by "acting out" the parts for the client. The story board is a series of sketches in sequence. With accompanying copy, the sketches show the action that will take place as the sounds and words are being heard. Usually the pictures are sketched, but some of the fancier story boards are in color photos and closely follow the action that will take place in the final commercial.

Writing a Commercial

Everyone should write his own television commercial at least once. So this is where you are, and you are about to write a 30-second television commercial.

The first thing you do is get an ordinary piece of copy paper and draw a vertical line down the middle. This is very important, as we shall see, and maybe you ought to borrow the art director's T-square and triangle for the occasion. The reason this line is important is that it divides the page into a right side and a left side.

On the right side you are going to note all the sounds in your commercial—music, thuds, squeaks, words, and the like. On the left side you will note how the pictures, those that appear on the screen during your commercial, will look. For reasons I don't understand, and which are probably very deep in the mythology of television, we don't call it the "sound side" and the "picture side." We label the right side *Audio,* and the left side *Video.*

Another reason for dividing the page in half is that by putting your audio and video notations in juxtaposition, you can show exactly what you want the viewer to see and hear simultaneously.

One more thing before we start. There are certain words used in the trade to describe the movement of the camera. To give your work a professional flair, you may want to use some of them.

A *close-up* and an extreme *close-up* picture are labeled a CU and an ECU. To *pan* is to sweep the camera across the scene. *Long shots* and *medium shots* (LS and MS) are self-explanatory. To *dolly* is to move the camera in or out of a scene. This can also be done by adjusting the camera lens. *Fades* and *cuts* you've seen lots of times in the movies. A fade can give an impression of time passing. The abrupt cut can quickly take you from one place to another. A *dissolve* is when you fade out one scene while fading in another scene. A *super* is when you superimpose something on the picture. This is the way they show you the down and yardage in a football game without interrupting the play.

There are numerous other tricks they do on the screen that you probably have noticed: stopping motion in mid-flight, dividing the screen in quarters, or dissolving a scene with a diamond pattern. Some of these are made by "optical houses," and many TV stations now have their own optical equipment by means of which the producer can sit in his control booth and produce the effects manually. When you visit your local TV station, as, of course, you are going to do, be sure to ask them to show you any optical equipment they have. Not all stations have optical equipment, and those that do will be enchanted if you ask them to show you theirs.

On the sound side you may see notations such as *VO*, which means that you see the action and hear the "voice over" but you don't see the speaker. *ANN* means the announcer or straightman who is delivering the message; otherwise you indicate the speaker by "Voice number one," "Girl," or "First gravedigger," just as in a play script. Sound directions are sometimes given, such as *music up and out*, which means that you give it a final blare and stop; or *music under*, which means that you are able to hear music in the background but "under" the dialogue.

Having told you about these nice professional-sounding words, let me tell you something else. For years advertising copywriters and TV producers have been playing a little straight-faced game in which the copywriter, having just been taken off a posthole-digger account (quarter pages in 42 farm papers) and given a shot at a dog food commercial, is positively giddy. He lards his script with all kinds of cuts, dissolves, fades, ECU's, and dollies. The producer gravely accepts this script, reads it over, and then goes ahead and shoots the thing as he pleases—which is probably just as well.

The Rough Script

Before we go further along the route of TV script to finished commercial, let us now write a rough script of our own.

You will recall that in our discussion of copy we did an ad for the Handy Dandy Electric Can Topper. Since we have already done our homework on that product—main selling points, psychological appeals, market situation, and so on—let us use that one.

But what *kind* of commercial do you want to do? As you have learned long ago, TV commercials come in all shapes, sizes, and personalities. We could try to do a commercial with a humorous situation, or one with cartoon animation; we could use a testimonial, or an old-fashioned, straight "stand-up" pitch. We could also write a catchy jingle, and have a choral group sing the praises of the Handy Dandy Can Topper.

Remember, we had already defined our market segmentation for our

Agency: Radcliffe Advertising, Inc., Jacksonville, Fla.

This 14-panel story board was originally done as a continuous accordion fold. It has been separated for the purposes of illustration. Note that the video direction has also been included in the small type lettering. This is a particularly complete board for the director to follow.

210

can topper: the semiaffluent young homemakers who take pride in the manner in which they run their homes and kitchens. Knowing this, I am going to write my commercial in a style to which they can easily relate. There won't be anything very fancy or tricky about it. I am simply going to set up a *bad* situation they can recognize, and then show how it can be turned into a *good* situation to which they can relate.

I have to keep in mind, also, that this is a *sales* message. So, if possible, all the basic selling steps must be present: attention, interest, desire, conviction, and action.

Now I must tell you that as a copywriter, long before I take a piece of paper, draw a vertical line down the middle, and slip it into my typewriter, I know pretty well where I am going with the script. After thinking about it for some time, I *see* the commercial this way:

A young woman who is giving a party comes into the kitchen to check the dinner that is about to be served. She fumbles around in the kitchen drawer and finds an old-fashioned can opener, and struggles with it to open a can. The can slips, and splashes beet juice all over the front of her dress. She is horrified and exasperated. I'm going to come in close on that expression with the camera and freeze it (make a still picture of it). Then, using her face and her expression in *rear screen projection* (in effect, using the still picture of her face as a background) I'll bring on a straight announcer to demonstrate the can topper and make the sales pitch. Then I will go back to the kitchen and show the hostess using the can topper under happier circumstances.

As in so many other commercials you have seen, I have set up a problem showing that my product has a unique ability to solve that problem; and I have also offered you the benefits you will enjoy as a result of solving the problem with my product. In show business, they say that the most basic plot of them all, from Shakespeare to Arthur Miller, is "boy meets girl, boy loses girl, boy gets girl."

On page 212 you will see illustrated just how my first rough draft of this 30-second commercial came out. I have indicated the selling steps for your information. Ordinarily this would not be done on the usual script.

There are several important things in this rough draft for you to note. The actress' movements and expressions have enabled me to set up a mood and a situation in just a few seconds. I have not had to jump around but have confined the action to two basic sets. The camera has given me the flexibility to get in very close to the subject. The medium has given me the opportunity to *demonstrate* how my machine works. These are some of the basics that, when properly handled, make television such an effective selling medium.

My commercial may not win any blue ribbons or awards, but I do think it would sell some can toppers. Perhaps you can write a better one. Knowing all the facts about the Handy Dandy Electric Can Topper, how would *you* go about selling it via the television medium?

You could start with a different situation: she scratches her finger, or

VIDEO	AUDIO

```
               VIDEO                                    AUDIO

ATTRACTIVELY DRESSED YOUNG WOMAN         (SOUND:  PARTY NOISES AS DOOR
COMES THROUGH KITCHEN SWINGING DOOR,     OPENS, THEN UNDER.)
LAUGHING AND REPLYING TO SOMETHING
OVER HER SHOULDER.  _ _ _ _ _ _ _ _ _ _ _ (attention) [1]

CU AS SHE PULLS OPEN DRAWER OF TABLE.

ECU HAND PICKING UP OLD-FASHIONED CAN
OPENER.

CUT TO WAIST SHOT AS SHE STRUGGLES                             5 sec.
WITH CAN.

CUT TO CU OF HER FACE AS SHE GASPS.      WOMAN: (GASP) Oh, good grief!
       _ _ _ _ _ _ _ _ _ _ _ _ _ _ _ _ _ (interest) [2]
PAN DOWN TO STAINED DRESS AND UPSET
CAN.

CUT BACK TO HER FACE AND ZOOM IN TO
ECU OF HER HORRIFIED EXPRESSION.

FREEZE THIS SHOT.
                       OR
THEN FADE TO DEMONSTRATR WITH CAN-       DEMO.:  I hope you never get
TOPPER ON TABLE IN FRONT OF HIM.         caught in a situation like that!
BLOW-UP OF WOMAN'S FACE IS BACK-         No experienced homemaker uses that
DROP. DOLLY IN SLOWLY AS DEMO.           kind of a can opener anymore. She
TALKS.                                   takes the mess and struggle out of
        [3] (desire)- - - - - - - -      can opening with this Handy Dandy
                                         Electric Can Topper.

DOLLY IN TO ECU AS SLIPS CAN IN,         Look how quickly and easily it works.
PRESSES BUTTON, AND CUTS CAN TOP.        Slip the can in and ZIP--off the top
                                         (comes) No mess, no struggle, no
       [4] (conviction)- - - - - -       jagged edges.  So easy.
CUT TO HOSTESS IN DIFFERENT DRESS, AS    Good Housekeeping Approved. Only
SHE PUTS PLASTIC COVER OVER HER CAN      $10.99 wherever appliances are sold.
TOPPER AND PATS IT LOVINGLY. SHE             Your Handy Dandy Elec Can Topper
SWINGS AROUND, PUSHES KITCHEN DOOR,      Order now and get your free plastic
THEN TURNS AND WINKS KNOWINGLY AT        protective cover.
CAMERA.  FADE.                               (Ask for order.) [5]
```

Rough draft of Handy Dandy Can Opener Commercial.

she can't find the can opener in the drawer. You could start on a positive note: one of her guests comes into the kitchen with her and admires her new can opener, and the hostess explains how it works. Maybe we should not have a female demonstrator, or maybe we should have a home-economics type to make it more believable. Perhaps you have a better idea.

213

How Can
You Sell
Anyone
Anything
in Thirty
Seconds?

How Can You Sell Anyone Anything in Thirty Seconds?

The other day I read a very good book on store display (*Create Distinctive Displays*, by Kenneth Mills and Judith E. Paul; Prentice-Hall, Inc., Englewood Cliffs, N.J.). One of the very first things the authors had to say about the function of a store window is that it should never be forgotten that *the window is a "salesman"*; and being a salesman it should *act* like a salesman. It should attract attention, create interest, stimulate desire, impart conviction, and get action (ask for the order).

Now all this has a very familiar ring to you, I am sure, because in our chapter on copy we went to some lengths to explore the parallels between the anatomy of a sale as carried to successful conclusion by a salesperson and the anatomy of a written selling message. This, however, was the first time I have ever known anyone to think about something as inanimate as a store-window display in these terms. But when you *do* think about it, it's completely logical. A store-window display *is* a salesman. That's what it's there for. So the authors of *Create Distinctive Displays* proceeded to demonstrate to their students the techniques in decorating a window to make it accomplish the 5 basic selling steps.

I find this very interesting because a window display is a big still picture. Just one. And, if it is there, it can gain attention, create interest, stimulate desire, impart conviction, and influence people to buy—what *you* should be able to do with a whole series of moving pictures, enhanced by sounds and words, and music, *even though you are up there for only 30 seconds*.

I mention this only because there are still a lot of people around who think it's impossible to sell anyone anything in 30 seconds, so they buy television time and accept television commercials "that keep their name in front of the public." I can't think of a more expensive calling card! Don't *you* ever fall into that trap. When you look at your proposed television commercial, look it in the eye like a salesperson; if it doesn't look right back, send it back to the drawing board until they bring you one that does!

By this time, I think, you have recognized the very sobering corner into which we have painted ourselves. If a television commercial is to be a selling tool (and anything less can be as costly as paying alimony to three spouses) then everything we have said about advertising as a selling tool must apply to it too—the appeal to key needs, wants, and desires; the determination of the most appealing main attraction; the

Producer: Communications 21, Jacksonville, Fla., for Pantry Pride.

A television production crew working late at night, shooting in a food store interior.

presentation of the selling story in a way that commands attention, creates interest, stimulates desire, imparts conviction, and asks for the order. *All in thirty seconds!*

Quite an order, you say? You're right. It's quite an order. And that is why television is a tricky and difficult medium not always appreciated, frequently misunderstood, and very often not exploited to its fullest potential. It is why, on this very night in Peoria, Illinois, Norris' Second Law is working overtime. And, by the same token, it is why the 30-second television commercial is one of the most potent and most explosively effective selling devices we have in all marketing. To make this so—we have a problem.

Is It One of Theirs, or One of Ours?

There is a little psychological phenomenon that you probably recognize but have never thought too much about it. If you happen to be a bird-watcher you'll know that it takes but a split-second glance for you to identify a Belted Kingfisher sitting all hunched up on a limb over the pond, waiting for a minnow to make a wrong move. I know guys who can

214

spot a Red-Shinned Hawk at 1,500 feet. During World War II, armies
developed an identification technique that enabled troops on the ground
to distinguish, at a glance, a Messerschmitt from a P46. *A glance*, it
should be noted, takes but *a fraction of a second.*

But that isn't all. You don't just identify the Messerschmitt. Your
brain instantaneously plays back to you a whole complex of fears,
memories, emotions, facts, or attitudes about Messerschmitts.

This phenomenon, known to psychologists as the "phenomenal logical recall effect," is one of the factors that makes the television commercial such a potent selling tool. For it means that with properly handled
sound and images I can evoke *in you, in a relatively brief span of time,*
emotions, and reactions that would take far longer if it were necessary
for me to develop them in words.

The key word is "evoke." I sometimes ask my class how, in less than
two seconds, they would evoke "Paris" to a television viewer. "Easy,"
they'll say. "A quick flash of the Eiffel Tower, a couple of toots on a
French taxicab horn, and the first couple of bars of the *Marseillaise*
played on a concertina—*Violà!*"

In less than two seconds they have opened up a very floodgate of
emotions and memories for many people. For some it's the smell of
chestnut blossoms after a spring rain, a crowded sidewalk café on the
Champs Elysée, the reflections at night on the River Seine, eating an
omelet in a little restaurant, shopping in a flowermarket, or the little
plaques that mark the fallen resistance fighters—all these and much,
much more. They have quickly *evoked* Paris for me, but it would take me
many words to tell you just how I *feel* about Paris. See if you can pick out
the places, often near the beginning of commercials, where in just a few
seconds a mood or concept is *evoked.*

A few years ago, an automobile tire manufacturer ran a series of
commercials. The psychological thrust was our anxiety for the safety of
our loved ones while driving. To set up this situation, for which they had
the answer, they needed to portray situations in which young women
were trapped and terror-stricken because of a faulty tire.

Let me see if I can portray the scene to you in words.

"As the tire blew, Dorothy slammed her foot on the brake. For a
moment she just sat there, still convulsively grasping the wheel. Then
she opened the door, and stepped out on the gravel road to look. The tire
was quite a flat, all right. The right rear. She stamped her foot in
annoyance. But she had never *changed* a tire. She wasn't even sure
where the tools were. Some small animal rustled in the bushes beside the
roadway and startled her. She looked around her. Not a gleam of light
relieved the gloom. Could she walk back to the nearest town—in the
dark? Somewhere an owl hooted mournfully. Maybe someone would
come along soon. But who? Maybe a nice man with his wife and kids,
driving home. Or maybe . . . ? A cold terror began to grip her. Despite
herself, she wept."

That's about thirty seconds of copy read silently or spoken. Now look at what the TV commercial did. They showed the girl beside the flat tire; the gloom-enshrouded road; you heard an owl hoot; and the camera came in close to catch the growing expression of fright on the girl's face. *TV made its point in about three seconds.*

What did they do? It seems simple enough. They just took a picture of a girl standing on a dark road beside a flat tire and looking scared. *Don't kid yourself.*

They created an illusion, *evoked* a mood, and started a psychological flash about "what if it was *my* wife and she was stuck out there in the dark alone, and some rapist came along and talked her into the car with him, and . . . and. . . ." And it took about 30 skilled people to do it, in addition to a well-trained young actress who is in the *business* of creating illusions or evoking emotions simply by the movement of an eyebrow or the motion of a hand. Remember, way back in the beginning of this chapter, we said something about TV being show business? This is what we were talking about; for all the skills and disciplines necessary to produce a play or a motion picture are also needed to produce a 30-second TV commercial.

The People Who Make Commercials

Next time you watch one of the network "spectaculars" or "documentaries," notice the credits flashed on at the end. Count 'em. Usually I get

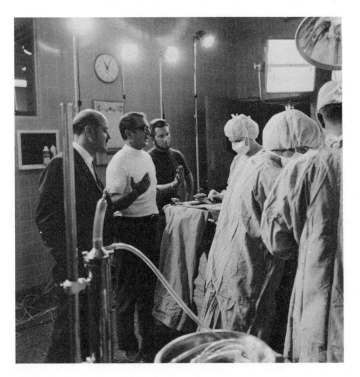

Operating room, preparing to shoot a commercial for Blue Cross/Blue Shield of Florida.

Production: Lawrence E. Smith Associates. Agency: Bunker and Bell Advertising, Jacksonville, Fla.

between 20 and 30. Script people, artists, cameramen, assistant directors, makeup people, costume designers, assistants to the producer, sound engineers—and they are only the *important* people.

They don't always have so big a crowd around when the majority of commercials are made, especially Off-Broadway commercials. But a big-time, big-budget soap or soft-drink shooting can attract quite a mob. The important thing for you to know is that all the professionals listed above don't necessarily have to be present when your commercial is being shot; but their *skills* have to be present, or you and your commercial are likely to be in trouble. Let your makeup person do a sloppy job, and that $2,500-for-two-days' actress will look awful. A cinematographer who gets careless with the lighting can wind up with a commercial that looks as if it had been shot in someone's cellar.

We mention these possibilities to you because there are a number of clients around who have no conception of the time, talent, effort, and money it takes to make a good commercial. There is hardly an agency person now alive who has not endured, at least once in his career, the client who airily said, "Oh, just give us something like those Alka Seltzer commercials. You know, to the point, product identification, a few laughs. . . ." *All on a $500.00 budget!* He should—as they say in the subjunctive—live so long.

Something for you to remember: Have the courage to tailor your TV production to the realities of your budget. A TV studio can bring in a good 30-second commercial for you for $500.00, but you will have to do without the camels and the dancing girls.

Actors

Sometimes it's difficult to find the right talent for locally produced TV commercials. New York, Chicago, and Los Angeles are full of actors and agents, casting directors, and TV production houses doing big-budget commercials for multimillion-dollar advertising accounts. But you're in Des Moines, Iowa, and you have a prosperous business, with distribution mostly west of the Mississippi, and an advertising budget of about $300,000. *You* are the one who has to be careful, especially if your agency brings you a commercial that depends on dialogue and action by people (actors).

As we have already pointed out, that nice young man who comes out of his front door, picks up the morning newspaper, and amiably discusses with you his recent experience with the nicest insurance agent in the world, is *not* the kid next door. He is a paid professional performer, who is doing things with his body and his voice that are deliberately conceived to evoke a response.

A great many local TV producers, you will notice, avoid the actor difficulty by shooting *voice over,* or by establishing their characters as speaking with a couple of words and then taking the camera off them and putting it some other place. This is often done when you do have a sports or singing star who has a nice personality but doesn't pitch particularly well. There have been some notable exceptions—Tom Harmon and Joe Garagiola come to mind. And all Bill Russell has to do is giggle—and I'm *sold!*

Because the actor's speaking *in sync* (the sound of his words synchronized with the movements of his lips) presents certain difficulties, TV producers have gone to other techniques such as those just mentioned. Another good way, and one that TV producers find *very* comfortable, is to let your selling message be carried by a jingle or musical theme while the camera is free to roam. The producers love this because it gives them a chance to improvise. You'll often see this technique used with beer and soft-drink commercials—the gang on the beach, with the cameras slowed down to ¾ speed.

The cinematographers have come up with some striking and beautiful pictures using this technique because their innovative inclinations are given free rein. But there are limitations, too. This kind of commercial lends itself much more to the mood-setting or theme-stating technique than it does to hard, direct-product sell.

The Sound of Music

You can, of course, hire one of the local barber-shop quartets to wail a few bars for you, or get someone you know who plays a guitar to riffle through a couple of chords, and the results won't necessarily be bad. But for a real professional job of instrumentation or voice recording, you should go to a *sound studio.* You'll find these listed in the Yellow Pages under "Recording Services—Sound and Video." Some of these, you'll find, are primarily interested in pop recordings; but you'll probably discover at least one studio that is definitely interested in working with agencies and TV producers.

The right sound studio will know every voice and instrumentalist in town. They should be able to put together any kind of combo you need, from symphony to rock; and they probably have the skills to write and arrange a singing commercial or jingle.

Their studios are packed with electronic sound-recording equipment, and part of their professional skill involves the mixing and blending of sounds from 6 to 8 different tracks. Call on the studio nearest you, and let them show you their equipment and how they use it.

Casting the Commercial

Many larger agencies and TV production houses have either a professional casting director, or someone who acts as a casting director. At the local level, the TV director usually fulfills this function. The big-city casting director knows all the agents and model agencies in town. When the commercial is ready for production, it is the casting director who alerts the agents to what is needed. And one morning when you come in, the reception room will be filled with sixteen-year-old ingenues or middle-aged ladies who can speak authoritatively about cake mixes.

Good actors don't come cheap. The minimum (scale) for a AFRA or Screen Actors Guild member is $158.00 a day plus travel expenses. This wage, whether scale or not, is then repaid every 13 weeks while a commercial is running. The top performers, many of whose faces have become familiar to you in a variety of commercials, receive much more for their performances—$1,500 to $2,500 is not uncommon. These fees are negotiated by the TV producer directly with the actor's agent.

That's Madison Avenue and the big budget. But what about the smaller advertiser in Racine, Wisconsin, or Scranton, Pennsylvania? His agency—or his writer—has come up with a commercial idea he's crazy about, but it calls for a performer who can do it *right* if the thing is to come across. Can he do something about casting the part without going way over budget? He can.

Fortunately, the good Lord in His wisdom has endowed many of us with a pure undiluted strain of Smithfield Ham. Let the houselights go down, and the curtain go up, and we're off and running. If there's a college in your town, chances are it has a drama department. This means a whole bunch of kids, and their instructors, who have ambition, enthusiasm, and sometimes remarkable skills. Do a part for you in your commercial? They might even pay you for the privilege!

Chances are, too, that there is at least one "Little Theater" in your town. That means another source of talent and not all of it as amateurish as you might think—particularly on the distaff side, where you're likely to discover a woman who has given up the boards for a life of suburban domesticity but still retains much of her old magic. It would be worth your while to attend some of these Little Theater productions. Meet the director, who'll be only too happy to steer you onto some talent if you'll explain what you are looking for.

The growing popularity of that institution known as the Dinner Theater is another interesting source of acting talent. There are now some 50 Equity dinner theaters as distinguished from summer theaters—the "Straw-Hat Circuit"—around the country. This means a continual flow of talent of very high quality; and it may well be that you might get some of these people (particularly in the supporting cast) to work on a regional commercial for a reasonable fee. Talk to the theater's resident manager about this.

Sometimes it's a very good idea to reverse the process and write the commercial to fit the actor. Writers often do this, and quite successfully. They discover that a particular character is going to be available, and they build the whole commercial message around him. We had an actor come through our town, one time, who did a very good Bogart. For the next six months, there was this guy representing drugstores, car dealers, appliance stores, and whistling through his teeth about the charms of their products while a piano played background that was almost "As Time Goes By," though not quite.

Probably the most simple and least expensive way for you to have a TV commercial made is to use your local TV station's facilities and let them do it on tape in their studio. Simplicity is the key, though being simple is not always easy. If you have a demonstrable product, keep it close and let a pair of hands do the manipulating. Otherwise keep the product still, and let the camera move around it. You'll use a *voice over*. Using their equipment, their writer, and their director, if you plan things carefully you can often bring the commercial in for as little as $100 including a couple of tapes.

The other side of the coin is the *location shot*, and this can sometimes run into real money because costs are not as strictly controllable as in a studio job.

TV producers are full of horror stories about things going haywire on location, and part of the producer's expertise is knowing where he can go to find a location that looks like a Peruvian jungle or the Sahara within five minutes' driving time of the studio. In the past this business of location shooting has been known to get out of hand among the big spenders, with production crews happily taking off to the Bahamas or Antigua for a couple of weeks for something that could just as easily have been shot in the local zoo.

It takes 18 feet of film for a 30-second commercial, and a cinematographer will often take as many as 4,500 feet to get what he wants. Cinematographers often "see" a better shot while they're shooting the planned one, and shoot the same scene two or three different ways. This consumes time and film, but they often luck into some very good footage.

The vagaries of Nature also play a major role in location shooting; the sun always goes under a cloud at the wrong time, and the vagaries of human beings can play more havoc. The people who have rented you a team of sky divers, or a herd of Herefords, are often blithely unaware of the problems facing a production crew.

But don't let *location* scare you. By the use of *voice over* and careful preplanning, you can often come up with an effective commercial shot on a fishing trawler or at a ski resort. I have seen some good ones done in the $2,000 and $3,000 range.

Processing

When the producer has finished shooting, the film is processed in the film laboratory as an *uncorrected print*. These are called *rushes*. It is from this mass of film (there may be several hours' worth) that the producer selects and edits the shots into a *rough cut*. You may have heard of the Hollywood actor who complained that all his best scenes "wound up on the cutting-room floor." This is when it happens. When the producer is satisfied that he or she has the best possible sequence to tell the story, the rough cut goes to the *optical house* where such optical effects as *fades* and *supers* are put in.

The sound track that has been recorded at the sound studio is now added, and when it is all put together you have a nearly completed job—the *answer print*.

Laboratory technicians correct this answer print for color, light density, sound synchronization, and photographic quality. This final product is called the *master print*. If the commercial is to be shown by a number of stations around the country, copies are made from this master print in whatever quantity is necessary. The job is finished.

WHERE YOU ARE

1. You know how a television commercial is written, and you can write one yourself.

2. You understand the relationship between a TV commercial and all the factors involved in creating an effective selling message.

3. You are familiar with the various people who are involved in making a television commercial, and the tasks they perform.

4. You know how to go about getting a television commercial produced, and you have some idea of the costs involved; you have learned some of the ways in which these costs can be held down.

5. You have looked around your town (it is hoped) and discovered the people who can be of help to you in producing and writing a television commercial.

QUESTIONS FOR CLASS DISCUSSION

1. What is your favorite television commercial? Why?

2. What is the worst television commercial you have ever seen? Describe it in detail.

3. Do you think it is right to come into anyone's home and call attention

to such unpleasant subjects as hemorrhoids, underarm odor, and scalp itch? As an advertiser, defend yourself.

4. Some people say that commercials that make you laugh don't sell anything. What do you think?

5. How many commercials would you say you saw last week? Describe the opening scene in three of them.

SOMETHING FOR YOU TO DO

Rewrite the Handy Dandy Can Topper commercial *your* way.

KEY WORDS AND PHRASES

Agent.   Usually an actor's representative.

Ann.   Abbreviation for "announcer."

Answer Print.   Commercial at the stage before final corrections when pictures, opticals, and sound are put together.

Audio.   The sound part of a commercial.

Casting Director.   Person responsible for choosing and hiring acting talent for a commercial.

Cinematographer.   Operator who shoots the film.

C.U.   Close-up.

Cut.   Abrupt transition from one scene to another.

Dinner Theater.   Restaurant in which plays are put on. Price of admission covers both food and play.

Dissolve.   See "fade."

Dolly.   To move the camera around.

E.C.U.   Extreme close-up.

Fade.   Picture gradually grows dim and disappears. When another comes in the same way it is a "dissolve."

Little Theater.   Groups of amateurs who do theatrical productions.

Live.   Not on film. The performer is "on camera."

Master Print.   Final version of film from which duplicate prints are made.

Optical House.   Place where optical changes are added to film.

Pan.   To sweep camera across scene.

Processing.   Work on an original film to bring it to stage of final "master print."

Producer.   Person responsible for the shooting of a commercial.

Rear Screen Projection.   Where a second image is projected on a screen behind the one being photographed.

Rough Cut.   Stage after first filming has been edited.

Rushes.   The results of the first filming.

Scale.   Basic wage for union actors. Some receive payments each time the commercial is run. These are called "residuals."

Script.   Written dialogue and camera directions.

Show Business.   All theatrical presentations, from vaudeville to Shakespeare.

Sound Studio.   People who specialize in making recordings.

Stand Up.   When message is delivered by person simply standing before camera.

Stock.   Also "summer stock." Touring theatrical companies.

Story Board.   Series of pictures mounted on a board with captions below; used to present an approximation of the commercial.

Straw Hat Circuit.   Professional summertime theater.

Super.   Words or picture placed over another picture on TV films.

Sync.   Where sound and movement coincide. When they don't it's "out of sync."

Tape.   Videotape. Newer than film. Picture and sound are recorded together on magnetic tape. Fast, convenient.

Time Spots.   Sometimes just "spots." Time purchased from local stations. "National spots" are network purchases.

Uncorrected Print.   Rough film before corrections for color, sound, opticals.

V.O.   Abbreviation for "voice over." Speaker is not seen on camera.

Video.   The filmed part of the commercial that is seen on the screen.

SELECTED READINGS

Diament, Lincoln, (ed.). *The Anatomy of a Television Commercial* (New York: Hastings House Publishers, 1970). This fascinating book will take you step by step through the creation of an award-winning commercial by a big Madison Avenue agency and its production house. It's all there; from the moment the copywriter slips the first yellow sheet of paper into the typewriter, to the finished product. All involved tell what they did and how they felt about it. Read this, by all means, if you are really interested in making television commercials.

————. *Television's Classic Commercials* (New York: Hastings House Publishers, 1971). For the television script writer, a number of samples of excellent commercials written for a variety of products in 1948–1958. The author calls it television's "golden age."

McMahan, Harry Wayne. *McMahan On Television Commercials* (*Advertising Age* column). See the back issues of *Ad Age* for comments by this long-time observer of the TV commercial scene.

Riso, Ovid. *Advertising Cost Control Handbook* (New York: Van Nostrand Reinhold Company, 1973). See Chapter 12, "Television—The Mass Medium," for an excellent exposition on the costs involved in all phases of commercial television. Incidentally, this chapter is headed by a quote worth keeping in mind: "The agency man on the job may know copy, art, and layout, but he may not know theater. TV is theater. (Signed) A Production Manager."

Wainwright, Charles Anthony. *Television Commercials* (New York: Hastings House Publishers, 1970). Discussions with some thirty television specialists about their craft. Much of it is very personal. Good in explaining working relationships.

chapter ten

Radio Commercials

In this chapter, we will explore the background of radio—how it developed, almost died, and was born again in its present form.

You will see why radio makes such an interesting medium, particularly for the local advertiser.

You will learn how to go about getting a radio commercial prepared, and who can help you in your hometown.

You will see a radio commercial written in the form of a rough script, and you will know how to go about writing one yourself.

When your dad was a little kid, the chances are he got hold of one of those round Quaker Oat boxes, a coil of copper wire, a crystal, and a couple of other esoteric objects including "binding posts," and made himself a Radio.

He and his pal next door would rig up an aerial between the houses, clamp on headsets, and then fiddle with the crystal until, wonder of wonders, KDKA or WFIL came in ever so faintly with a dance band or someone delivering a lecture on the care and raising of chrysanthemums.

It was the beginning of a remarkable era whose social and psychological implications the Ph.D's can tall you about, but whose impact, in terms of entertainment and marketing, hit this country in the 1930s, 1940s, and 1950s with the force of a West Indian hurricane.

The "console" became a part of the furniture in everyone's living room; and an Atwater Kent became a status symbol only slightly less potent than a Rolls in the driveway. From a generation where "live entertainment" meant an occasional appearance by a touring stock company, or a couple of turns of vaudeville at the local movie house, we became a generation that at the drop of a baton could tell the difference between the A&P Gypsies and Paul Whiteman's band, and who would no more have thought of missing any of the latest Amos and Andy episodes than of going without our supper.

227

Names like Graham MacNamee, Gabriel Heatter, and (at least to the fight fans) Sam Taub, became as familiar to us as our own. We heard the roar of the crowd as heavyweight champion, Jimmy Braddock, rewrote the Cinderella story with a Jersey City accent; or as Light Horse Harry Wilson swept down Franklin Field against Navy. And we anguished at the unfair predicaments a generation of soap-opera heroines endured.

In short, a lot of people came into our homes who had never been there before. And many of them had something to sell. We listened avidly to a banjo-dominated band called the Cliquot Club Eskimos, who were plugging ginger ale. And we hummed along with a bass baritone known as "Singing Sam, the Barbasol Man." His jingle about the charms of Barbasol Shave Cream is forever planted in the minds of literally millions of middle-aged men.

There was a woman "talk" show by Mary Margaret McBride, and was such a potent marketing tool that *Printer's Ink,* the ad trade bible, called her impact on her audience, "Perhaps the most outstanding reliance upon the word of a human being in the commercial field."

I think you know what comes next. A villain named Television ties Radio to the trestle just before the 5:15 is due to come thundering down the tracks, and that's the end of good old Radio—almost, but not quite.

Before we come to radio's big resurrection scene and the new giant that lives in your hometown, let's talk about the old radio, the one we left for dead in the 1950s, and about some of the things it taught us.

Radio was America's first mass home-entertainment form and, as such, it demonstrated that America could be entertained *en masse* any time. This may seem obvious to you. But remember that prior to World War I, despite movies, vaudeville, circuses, band concerts, minstrel shows, touring repertory groups, and "artistic concerts," the greatest part of American entertainment was pick-up style. It was the gang on the porch with a ukulele, or around the stand-up piano in the living room, or down at the depot with a barber-shop quartet plus five friends from the fire department.

Suddenly now, with the advent of radio, it was possible to flip a switch anywhere and hear the great bands, the great singers, comedians, speakers, weather prognosticators, and people who knew the price of hogs in Iowa City that day. We discovered that people were receptive to all kinds of entertainment and that, if you were good, they would attach themselves to you and avidly and loyally listen to you week after week.

But the sponsor found out something, too. He discovered that with the flip of *his* switch, every evening at 7:30, he could have a couple of million customers right in the palm of his hand—ready, eager, and willing to hear what he had to say about *his* product. It was a very heady discovery.

Another thing we found out was that people have imagination —wonderful, receptive, and creative imagination. Once this was discovered, there emerged one of the great folk heroes of the radio era—the Sound Man.

The sound man was just as surely an artist in his own right as, say, Rubinoff and his Magic Violin. These sound men were the blood relatives of that later group who discovered that while a plate of vanilla ice cream does not look like a plate of vanilla ice cream very long under the studio lights, a plate of mashed potatoes does—particularly if you pour something over it which may or may not be chocolate syrup. These were the same artisans who wanted to know, and with justifiable outrage, *why,* if it was O.K. to put makeup on the President of the United States when he appeared before the camera, it wasn't just as O.K. to touch up the bottle of soft drink with droplets of condensation before making a commercial.

In the days of the sound men there were no FTC types around to point accusing fingers and cry out that they really *didn't* have a horse in the studio, but just a couple of coconut-shell halves they were slapping on the table; that the door hinge wasn't rusty—in fact there *wasn't* any door—but just a couple of dry sticks being rubbed together. The sound men were wonderful. With almost limitless ingenuity they created out of paper clips, washboards, tin cans, paper, and you name it, the sound of almost anything. Their excruciatingly drawn-out door squeaks and hair-standing-on-end screams froze millions of listeners to their chairs each night. One of the great virtuoso performances of the craft was the creation of Jack Benny's "dying Maxwell." This wheezing, sputtering, emphysemic automobile became one of Benny's standard sound gags. The sound of the last gasp, slightly offbeat, convulsed everyone who heard it.

The Rebirth of Radio

There's another thing you want to know that you might not be aware of if you are still on the sunny side of thirty. In much the same way that, with the advent of TV, people left radio for dead, so radio ostensibly killed the record business. Probably this sounds fantastic to you today—what with young recording millionaires springing up all over the place. There was a time when the record shops were closing up as if a plague had just passed by. Everyone figured: Why spend 75¢ for a record, when you can twist a dial and get Phil Spitalney and his All Girl Orchestra for free?

Television knocked radio down, but it didn't finish it. Before long, radio rose again—somewhat altered in appearance, but bigger (though not necessarily better) than ever before.

After the first glamor of TV wore off, and people began to settle down a little bit, it became apparent that lots of times you couldn't watch TV. You couldn't watch it while shaving, or driving a car, or doing housework, or studying your homework, or walking on the beach, or even when milking a cow. But you *could* listen to radio. So radios again began to appear everywhere, even in kitchens. Then came bedroom clock-

radios, pocket transistors, car radios, and today the somewhat unbeliev-
able figure you hear bandied about is *four* radios to every household!

TV was great in the prime hours from 6:30 P.M. to 10:00 P.M.; but the
rest of the time was radio's, with millions of listeners at all odd hours.
The programming, of course, was completely altered. The great "Hours"
of old, and the "Big Shows," all a-glitter with stars, were no more. In
their place appeared the fast-talking, jiving "DJ" and his endless assort-
ment of recorded tunes. In turn this led to a very interesting development for every marketer: a far more neatly divided segmentation of the
market than had ever been possible with the old-style radio or modern
network TV.

As more and more radio stations were licensed around the country,
competition, particularly in the cities, became more fierce for a slice of
the market. Fortunately there was a slice of the market available for
almost everyone, what with our wide-ranging taste in popular music.
From the wildest far out modern jazz idioms to country western, gospel,
sweet, the Spanish beat, long-haired, and anything else you could think
of, it was possible to sweep the dial and discover the sound of your
choice. This is exactly what people did.

In more sophisticated centers, certain departures were made from this
format. A few went to the all-talk, and on a number of stations the get-
it-off-your-chest-with-a-phone-call format became popular. These featured MC's who were either wise and glib or rude and glib; but whether
wise or dumb or rude or courteous, they usually could present an answer
to almost any question besetting mankind without ever drawing a deep
breath.

Another aspect of this closely divided segmentation, derived not from
programming but from electronic engineering is the FM station. You
should be familiar with the terms FM and AM. They stand for *frequency
modulation* and *amplitude modulation*. The two terms describe the
sound waves broadcast by the stations.

Amplitude modulation refers to the varying sizes of the waves. Their
frequency remains constant. With *frequency modulation* it's the other
way around. Here the size remains constant, and the frequency is the
variable. When you see a station listed as a 1,500 kilocycle station, that
means 1,500 of its sound waves pass a particular point each second.

The two kinds of waves present certain advantages. AM waves travel
primarily along the ground and are deflected by the earth's curvature.
They gradually lose energy and fade. AM waves also shoot into the sky.
At night we have over us an electronic ceiling of particles called the
ionosphere, and AM waves ricochet off this and come back down some
distance away outside the normal 200-mile limit for AM waves. That is
why sometimes at night you can be driving along, and suddenly discover yourself listening to a high-school basketball game in Fort Wayne,
Indiana.

FM waves don't have the normal reach of AM waves; they are limited
by the horizon which, if I remember my seamanship correctly, is about

12 miles. However, booster stations can extend their coverage. The interesting thing about FM is that it allows for a more faithful reproduction of sound without outside interference. In turn this has resulted in a kind of programming that caters to an audience of music lovers, whether they happen to love Beethoven, Hector Berlioz, or Joan Baez. Programming on FM stations seems to be more flexible, too, since being sure of the intellectual capacity of their audience they can go for such features as repeats of BBC programs and even more esoteric fare.

The important point for you to remember is that both FM and AM stations give you a remarkable choice of audiences. Which brings us back to our old friend, *market segmentation* discussed in an earlier chapter. We'll talk about this considerably more in the chapter on media, but I'm sure you get the point. *The audience pie-slicing of local radio stations through the medium of their programming policies presents local and regional marketers with some very, very interesting advertising opportunities.*

How many radio stations in your town? Listen carefully to each one and categorize it—country, western, modern ballad, gospel, and so on. Now see if you can picture the person, *everything about him,* who listens to that station.

How to Write a Radio Commercial

We will write a radio commercial together; but before we begin this task, perhaps we should look up the possibilities inherent in this form of selling.

The Radio Advertising Bureau, a "spokesman" for the industry, has compiled a list of some 17 classifications for radio commercials based on an examination of their library of over 10,000 commercials. In the list you will find such categories as "product demo," which communicates "how a product is used, or what purposes a product serves"; or "customer interview," in which a "spokesman" for the product and a customer discuss the merits and advantages of the product. Then there is "product song," in which "music and words combine to create musical logo as well as sell products."

Kleppner adds still another interesting category that may be the most fun of all—"ad lib from fact sheet," which is where you put down all the salient facts about your product and let the announcer take it from there.[1]

But although compiling a list of identifiable types of radio commercials is interesting, I wonder if it isn't a little like identifying snow crystals—when what you are really interested in is how the skiing at Stowe, Vermont is this weekend.

---

[1]You'll find all seventeen listed in Otto Kleppner's great text, *Advertising Procedure* (Englewood Cliffs, N.J.: Prentice-Hall, Inc., 6th ed.), p. 447.

The point is that when it comes to radio commercials, any number can play.

Why There Are So Many Good Radio Commercials

If you could talk to some of the agency people from New York and Chicago who are invited around the country to judge advertising (the high point of the season for most ad clubs is the annual awards dinner) you would find that most often they are impressed by the quality of the radio commercials being turned out on the local scene.

It might be a little too much to expect that a five-man shop in Albuquerque, New Mexico, would be able to hit the standard of creative quality in all media of, say, Doyle, Dane, Bernbach. But in radio, day after day, local stations are broadcasting for local advertisers commercials whose creative qualities and selling performance are quite as good as anything being produced by the most prestigious advertisers in the country.

The reason for this phenomenon can be traced to the nature of selling radio time. Although in network radio and big-city radio it's often a matter of satisfying availabilities for advertisers, in the rest of the country, sometimes with as many as 25 stations fighting for a piece of the same market, you get a very different and a much more competitive situation. In Jacksonville, Florida, for example, a city of 500,000, there are 15 radio stations. Lansing, Michigan, has 9; Youngstown, Ohio, boasts of 11; and San Francisco, California, has no less than 34 radio stations.

The result has been that for most radio station reps, selling time has become a very exciting and competitive game. Quite some time ago these reps discovered that the most effective way to sell a local account was to create a program for the client and let him listen to it. They discovered that they could talk coverage and cost per thousand all day and get nothing in return but a glazed stare. But let the client hear his very own quartet belting out the charms of Smith's Bathroom Fixtures—and whamo! He was *sold*.

Moreover, the rep had a very real vested interest in the selling effectiveness of such a commercial; because, though after a while Mr. Smith might tire of the jingle, so long as people kept knocking down the doors to buy his bathroom fixtures, the rep had a very dependable piece of business.

Today, all over the country, there are hundreds of radio station reps who have risen to the top of the competitive heap because of their creative abilities as well as their selling styles. Working closely with sound studios and their sophisticated electronic equipment, they are bringing the glad tidings to a lot of hometown advertisers.

So when you start thinking about writing your own radio commercial, look out—you're going to be in very fast company.

From now on be a student of radio commercials. Your own car or bedroom radio is your classroom. Listen intently to *every* commercial. See if you can pick out the winners. Listen carefully for the way they handle sound effects. When you hear one you really like, call up the station and ask who did it. If it was one of their boys, they'll probably take you out to lunch.

233
Why There
Are So
Many Good
Radio
Commercials

There's one thing about writing a radio commercial: you don't have to face, as you do in TV, drawing a line down the middle of the page. This means that instead of facing two empty halves staring back at you from the page in your typewriter, you now have a single expanse that can sometimes look as flat and as empty as the Sahara south of Timbuktu —especially when there is a deadline peering over your shoulder.

Radio doesn't have so many of those delicious terms such as "fade" and "pan" and "ECU" for you to be concerned with, but it does have a little dandy all its own of which you may wish to avail yourself—"SFX." Everyone *I* know just writes "sound" and lets it go at that. But don't let that discourage you if you feel like using it.

Remember, the same basic rules apply in writing a commercial for radio as for the TV commercial you wrote in the last chapter. But in radio, since the market segmentation is likely to be much narrower, you've got to *see* the person you're talking to. Be sure you know your *main attraction*, and be very sure you know the psychological need or desire you will try to reach out and touch with your appeal. And, of course, the rules of selling apply just as surely to a radio commercial as they do to any other piece of copy: *get attention, create interest, stimulate desire, impart conviction,* and *ask for the order.*

This time we are writing for a medium very different from television. For example, we don't have the wonderful *demonstration* quality inherent in television, nor the attention-getting abilities of a picture. But we do have *sound*, and we will be able to use more words than we did in the TV script.

I've had my feet up on my desk all morning thinking up a radio commercial for our Handy Dandy Electric Can Opener, and, the way I *hear*, it goes like this: Because I'm working with sound I'm going to exploit it to the fullest by introducing my commercial message with a high-pitched buzzing sound. It also gives me a chance to take a crack at the popular electrically driven can openers with the whine familiar to every homemaker. It's a sound most of them don't like, as our research shows.

Then, also, because I'm working with sound, I'm going to introduce an actress with a Zsa Zsa Gabor accent to make the sell. Why Zsa Zsa Gabor? Because she is sophisticated and the *last* person you'd expect to be selling can openers. A good attention holder. It gives us a chance to get in a little humor too. I'll finish off with a straight announcer asking for the order.

You'll see the first rough draft of this treatment illustrated as follows:

(Sound: High whine like sawing.)

Voice #1: Somebody's cutting down a tree!

Voice #2: Wrong!

Voice #1: It's someone in a dentist's chair.

Voice #2: Wrong again!

Voice #1: I give up. What *is* that terrible sound?

Voice #2: It's the hostess in the kitchen trying to get the top off a can with one of those noisy openers that go 'round and 'round and 'round.

Zsa Zsa: (Party noise up and under.) What a lovely party, darling. I've just met this charming fellow—he makes battleships or something. But I couldn't help noticing, darling, *vy* do you use this old-fashioned can opener? *Such* a bore. Haven't you heard about zose Handy Dandy Electric Can Toppers? Fantaztic! Everybody's mad about them. You simply press a button and POP—the top comes off! It's so easy. Promise me you'll get one, darling. You know—my grandfather Boris could open a can of caviar with his teeth!

Voice #2: Thanks for the good advice, darling! Ladies, be sure to see the Handy Dandy Electric Can Topper tomorrow! No mess, no stress, so easy to use! You'll find it wherever good electrical appliances are sold. Only $10.99. Buy it this week and get a free plastic protective cover!

Produce your own commercial. Get hold of some of your friends to do the various voices, sounds, musical effects, and so on, put your script on tape, then play it back. You may be surprised and pleased at what you have accomplished.

WHERE YOU ARE

1. You have a grasp of the history and background of one of the important mediums of advertising.

2. You have discovered how the nature of the medium lends itself to market segmentation. You have defined, in your community, the segments reached by your radio stations.

3. You are aware of the phenomenon of the high quality of locally produced and written radio commercials and the reasons for it.

4. You have seen how a radio script is constructed, and you can write an acceptable radio commercial for yourself.

QUESTIONS FOR CLASS DISCUSSION

1. How many radios do you own? How many hours a day is a radio turned on where you are?

2. Why don't we have radio "stars" the way we have famous TV personalities?

3. Who do you consider as the best DJ in your town? Do you have any idea what his pay is?

4. Some DJ's are highly paid. Putting records on turntables sounds like easy work. Why the high salaries?

5. If you were going to own and manage your own radio station, what would your program policy be?

SOMETHING FOR YOU TO DO

Select a retailer or a small manufacturer in your community. Learn as much about the business as you can, then prepare a series of radio commercials for him—either on paper or on tape. Submit them to him for his use. (Sell them to him, if you can.)

KEY WORDS AND PHRASES

Ad Lib. To talk freely without following script.

Amplitude Modulation (AM). Transmission in which the size (amplitude) of the electromagnetic wave is varied.

Availability.   Time spots that are unsold and available for purchases.

Frequency Modulation (FM).   Transmission in which the frequency of the wave varies.

Ionosphere.   Layer in the upper atmosphere. AM waves bounce off it, FM waves don't.

Prime Time.   Broadcast time that commands particularly good audiences.

Product Demo.   Technique by which a product's use is demonstrated on camera.

Sound.   The audible part of a commercial.

Sound Man.   Sometimes "Sound Effects Man." Creates, in studio, all kinds of sounds by artificial means.

SFX.   Script designation for "sound."

SELECTED READINGS

Barnouw, Erik. *A Tower in Babel: A History of Broadcasting in the U. S.* (New York: Oxford University Press, 1966). Read this for background.

Chester, Giraud, Garrison, Garnet R., and Willis, Edgar E. *Television and Radio* (New York: Appleton-Century-Crofts, 1971). See Chapters 17 and 18 for technical aspects, and Chapter 21 for commercials.

The Best of Old-Time Radio (Columbia Musical Treasures, four sides, 33⅓ rpm, 1969). More fun. You can have your parents join you.

Settel, Irving. *A Pictorial History of Radio* (New York: Grosset and Dunlap, 1960). Even more fun. You'll meet some old friends looking a lot younger.

Willis, Edgar E. *A Radio Director's Manual* (Ann Arbor, Michigan: Campus Publishers, 1961). This is a good college textbook concerned with principles and techniques.

chapter eleven

Selecting and Buying Advertising Media

*In this chapter we examine the selection and buying
of advertising media. In other words, the spending
of our advertising dollars.*

*We will review some of the things you must know
about yourself and your product before you begin to
make your media plans.*

*You will become familiar with the procedure for
buying space and time, and with some of the
specialized terms used in media buying.*

*We examine the major media available to the
advertiser, and some of the advantages and
disadvantages of each.*

*You will be offered a technique you can apply to
solving your own media problems, in an effort to spend
your own advertising dollars wisely.*

Some of the nicest people I know are media directors, and I suggest that they are also among the most unsung. Whoever heard of anyone getting an award for the best insertion order of the year?

Yet it is possible to make a case for your media director being the key person in the whole advertising setup. Though your product may be outstanding, and your creative people may have outdone themselves, if your media director falls down on the job—you're *in trouble.*

We've used the salesperson analogy before. Let's use it again. If you supply your salespeople with the wrong leads or no leads at all, they find it very tough to sell your product. If you send your advertising to people who have neither the inclination nor the money to buy your product, you are wasting what may be very good advertising.

So now we have arrived back in Chapter 4, in which we examined profiles and market segmentation. As we said then, emphatically, if you don't know who your potential customers are and where you can find them—*you are no place!*

If you are to stay in business you must know your potential customers and where to find them, and *at the lowest possible cost.* It is the media director's job to discover for you the answer to this riddle. To put it another way, *media selection is the art and science of putting your advertising dollars to work for you where they will do the most good.* We have no way of knowing, but probably there have never been a great **239** many perfect media plans. One thing you can be sure of is that your town is full of people who are spending their advertising dollars in the wrong (for them) places, and for all kinds of reasons, few of them having anything to do with scientific media selection.

To prove to yourself the inherent dangers as well as the opportunities in this situation, I suggest you do this: Approach some of your local advertisers and ask them questions such as, "Why don't you ever use radio?" Or, "Have you ever thought of using outdoor?" If the answers come back, "Oh, I don't know—we've just never used radio, that's all." Or, "Because my wife doesn't *like* posters, that's why!" Then I'm sure you'll begin to see what I mean.

Now before we pull the curtain back and reveal to you why good media directors die young, or at least get frosty around the sideburns at an early age, and why it is so easy for your ad dollars to get lost out there someplace, let's go back to this business of . . .

Customers and Where You Find Them

Earlier we said that one of the most important keys to marketing success is not only knowing *who* your customer is, *but what he is like.* Advertising dollars, however you spend them, don't just deliver to you bodies; they deliver people . . . personalities . . . with hangups, fears, prejudices, likes and dislikes, and a lot of other things.

I sometimes put this question to my classes: "If you could have a Rolls Royce dealership here in Florida, where would you locate it?" Usually they don't have too much trouble with that one—Boca, Palm Beach, Naples. But then I say, "Yeah, but what's wrong with our town? Half a million people, quite a few of them making more than $75,000 a year, according to 1970 census figures. Plenty of rich doctors, real estate tycoons, bankers, and insurance men. Why not here?"

That bothers them a little. "Well," they say, "there just are no Rolls here. It's not a good Rolls Royce town, *for some reason.*" (My ital.)

That *"for some reason"* is what you want to look out for, because my students are right. This has been a poor Rolls market, *for some reason.* One of my students, who is a part-time mechanic at the Porsche dealership, tells me there are about 30 Rolls Royces and a couple of restored Bentleys.

Remember the retailer's "perfect customer" we mentioned? I hope you checked out that one with some of the storekeepers you know, because it's true; and it is a principle that also applies equally well for you. No matter what you sell, there exists for you a market of perfect customers—the kind it is more profitable for you to deal with than any others. It is advertising's job to search out those perfect customers in as undiluted a concentration as possible, and to deliver your selling message to them. And it isn't easy.

Recently I watched another of those fried-chicken places open on what seemed to me to be the wrong side of a main artery—the other side

from the home-going traffic. What I didn't know was that the side street outside the door led directly down from a vast middle-class residential area, and customers liked the convenience of not having to get mixed up in the main street traffic. That franchiser *knew* where the customers were.

What if you were selling marine hardware? Easy, you might say. Concentrate on the yachting centers on the West and East coasts. But you had better remember that all the dam-building that has been going on across the country has resulted in some big boating centers in such places as Oklahoma, Arkansas, and Tennessee.

Whole communities change entirely with the seasons. Newport, Rhode Island is a far different place in August than it is in December. And though Miami Beach and Palm Beach are nice winter resorts on the South Florida Coast, the similarity ends there.

Fortunately for you, you now have help in finding out what your customer looks like and where he can be found. The media themselves are ready to deliver into your hands the information they have compiled, at great expense and effort, about *people*.

The media game is played two ways. You want to find your customers and discover how you can reach them most efficiently and economically. The media people want *you* to know how many of your customers *they* talk to, where they are to be found, and how economically they can aid you in reaching them.

Media representatives can be very, very helpful. It's their *business*, literally.

Your agency media director spends a great deal of time with *media representatives*. Media reps arrive with facts and figures, graphs and charts, and surveys and studies, all designed to impress the prospective advertiser and his agency with just how big a slice of what kind of market they can deliver most effectively.

Recently, for a class demonstration, I wrote to *Ebony Magazine* (Johnson Publishing Company) for some of their demographic studies. I received a ton of material. Let's see some of the facts about its readership that *Ebony* can share with us:

There's a fourteen-page, illustrated, two-color study revealing the drinking habits of black Americans in the 15 leading metropolitan markets—by brand label and type of drink. Another compares preferences in food products between *Ebony* homemakers and total U. S. homemakers. There's a profile of the "Ebony Woman," delineating her in 13 different categories. There's one on the "Ebony Man." There's a breakdown of how *Ebony* householders spend their vacations. And that's just the beginning. If you are interested in selling cosmetics, or furniture, or fashions, they've got some interesting facts for you gathered by reputable research firms.

Get the idea? The information is there, ready for you if you want to use it. And this same kind of market information is available to you through any medium you might consider using, including your hometown newspapers, radio stations, TV stations, or outdoor people.

What Can You Afford?

One of the things you will have to think about very seriously is how much money you can—or should—earmark for advertising. All big companies have budgets, or *appropriations*, which are part of each year's marketing-promotional budget. Procter and Gamble, for example, finds that they can spend about $190 million to promote their products in a variety of media. Coca-Cola spends about $50 million; Eastman-Kodak spends about half of that. These are the big boys.

But what about the regional and local advertiser? There is no handy rule of thumb to tell you quickly what percentage of your marketing dollar should be promotional. But there are certain guidelines available to you. If you are a bank, insurance company, hardware dealer, or the like, you can get the figures that will show you how much is being invested in your particular field as a percentage of gross profits or annual sales. These figures are most readily available to you through your trade association, or through the leading trade publications in your field. In this area, *Advertising Age* is also an excellent source of information.

Even the big spenders don't throw their money around as though it was going out of style. Quite the opposite. They can afford and demand the very best media services. But whether you are big or little, the problem always boils down to: here's how much money we can afford to put in this particular market. Now *where* will we put it so that it will do us the most good?

How Often Should You Advertise?

How often should you advertise—*when* and for what *length of time*? This question involves *frequency* and *continuity*. The chain food stores in your town are nice examples of people who get an "A" for both. Just as surely as the sun rises in the East and sets in the West, there they are every Thursday morning with double-page spreads advertising the weekend specials. They've always done it that way, and, unless food goes out of style, they probably always will.

For the rest of us, the answers may not be so pat. Is your product *seasonal?* Maybe you will want to come on big with the bikini promotion in April or May? Or, how about all those weekend plumbers, who turn up in your hardware store on Saturday mornings? You're going to have something for them in the Friday paper, aren't you? On the other hand, you may be a car dealer or an insurance agency and you will want to keep your name up there in front *all* the time.

What Is the Competition Doing?

There's a lot of follow-the-leader being played in media selection, and it is something to look out for. Just because the dominant company or product in your field is putting most of its weight in a particular medium, there's no reason why you should have to follow its lead. In fact, maybe it's a good reason why you ought *not* be where he is—particularly if he can outspend you.

There's a thing in baseball called the "let-up pitch." This works also in advertising, both in copy and media. Just when the opposition is digging in its heels and waiting for the high hard one, *that's* when you throw that big slow one up there that looks as big as an August moon. Media people have endless stories of folk heroes who, when their Big Competitor was spending all his dollars in network television, bought 100 percent showings on golf-course trash receptacles and within a few months had gained a dominant share of the market for their product.

What Does Your Product Look Like or Do?

If you have a good-looking (particularly a mouth-watering) product, such as one of those Kraft dishes, or a steaming bowl of vegetable soup, or a Persian rug, or furniture polish, your media-buying decision is going to be influenced by that too. Slick-paper magazines can make your product look really good. Newsprint can't do it so well. And radio, of course, not at all. On the other hand, you might have a new kind of potato peeler that is just crying for demonstration, and spot TV *would* be your medium. That's *another variable*.

We now have mentioned 5 balls you will have to juggle before you can sensibly begin to zero in on the *kind* of media mix or the one medium that holds the most promise for you. And all this before you ever begin to make the decision on *which* radio station, or newspaper.

1. Who are your customers? What do your customers look like? Where do you find them concentrated?
2. How much money can you afford to spend?
3. How often should you advertise, and how much? Is your product seasonal?
4. What kinds of media are your competitors using? Are you in danger of being forced into a "second-class" position in certain media because they can outspend you?
5. What kind of product or service do you have for sale? Is it something that looks good? Does it lend itself to demonstration?

However, even if you are not in a position to retain one of those new Madison Avenue media services that have lately found much favor, don't be discouraged. If you remember the 5 foundation stones, you will not get off to a bad start. If you know who your customers are, then you can be sure there is *one most economical way* of getting the word to them. You just have to keep looking until you find it.

I know of two educational institutions, both of which are greatly interested in enrolling persons from the poverty areas to be trained in the industrial arts. One of the schools went about soliciting them in the traditional way many schools still use. They ran ads in the morning newspaper, offering courses in welding, carpentry, brick laying, and the like. The ad stated the number of months the course took to complete, the tuition, and the starting date. That was about it. (I'm sure you have seen similar ads every fall in your hometown paper.) But nothing happened. You see, the students they were after *don't read the paper.*

The other educational institution went about it differently. They got in touch with the pastors of every ghetto church, and asked for ten minutes on Sunday morning to tell the congregations what they were prepared to do for their neighborhood and for their kids. I don't say that they took any twelve-string guitars with them; but before the selling team was through, the congregations were talking back to them. And in the following days the school had more applications than it could handle.

Where to Find Out About Media

Before we begin to examine the various media available to you, and the advantages and disadvantages inherent in each, let's look at some of the tools and some of the technical language involved in media buying.

The first thing you should examine closely is a copy of *Standard Rate and Data.* These volumes, published by Standard Rate and Data Inc., of Skokie, Illinois, are the basic books of reference to be found in every media department. In every major field of the media—newspaper, magazine, farm paper, business paper, radio, T.V., direct-mail, transit—they list *all* the media in each category, together with all the pertinent information of interest to the media buyer. *Space* or *time cost, circulation, audience, closing dates,* all are of principal interest. Your public library may have some back issues of the *Standard Rate and Data* on its reference shelves; if not, any one of the ad agencies in your town will have one and would probably let you inspect it. The marketing department of a nearby college or university might be another source. Look up your hometown newspaper, or radio station, and note the standardized manner in which the necessary information is set forth.

In addition to these thick-as-telephone-books volumes, the media issue *rate cards.* These can be simply one-page affairs, or elaborate brochures basically setting forth the same information that is contained in SRD, but with a little more sell. These cards are always carried by sales reps and left with their accounts. And since these cards are published more frequently than SRD, they carry the more recent changes in rates.

Buying Representation

You will note, too, that *buying representative offices* are listed in the radio, TV, and newspaper sections of SRD. These exist as a convenience for the media buyer, who may wish to buy space or time, with a long list of publications or stations. Blair Television, for example, has affiliations with a wide list of radio and TV stations. Mathews, Shannon & Cullen, Inc., represents several hundred newspapers. A marketing student would recognize these offices as "desk jobbers"; they remove from the media director the burden of having to contact a large number of publications or stations individually, and they perform the service of searching out *availabilities* and placing the *orders* on a commission basis. (*Availabilities*—those time slots radio and TV stations have available for sale to advertisers at any given time.)

Costs. When looking at your copy of SRD, you were probably struck with the *variety* of charges made by the medium for its time or space. This medium is simply saying to you, "Some places and some times are more valuable than others." In newspapers, you can specify ROP (run of paper) in which case the makeup man puts your ad where he thinks it will best fit. You may specify the sports page, or woman's page, for which you may have to pay a higher rate. You already know that papers have different rate structures for *national* and *local retail* advertisers.

Radio stations will charge you more for spots during *drive time* (the hours when people are in their cars, going to or coming from work) or for time next to popular news broadcasts or features. Same with TV. The *prime time* viewing hours (6:30 P.M. to 10:00 P.M.) are recognized as being more valuable than, say, something next to the early morning funnies.

Position. There are also discounts and special treatments available to you. If you are a new and potentially valuable account, most publications will start you off by giving you an excellent *position* in their book. Old and valued advertisers, of course, get the more favored positions *up front* (Facing *inside front cover* is a particularly choice one) or next to a popular editorial feature.

If you are a local advertiser, it will pay you to give some attention to this matter of position. If you find your ad buried at the bottom of the page by an avalanche of other advertisements, you have a right to call the newspaper rep or their advertising department. You can tell them that next time you would like to have your ad placed next to some interesting reading matter. If you are selling automobile tires, you may want to specify the sports page. But note: If you are selling condominiums, *everyone* goes in the real-estate section. Maybe you ought to ask for the woman's page for your ad. You can also get discounts on *frequency* and volume deals, and most stations have neat little packages of *time combinations* they will sell you at a discount.

TV has another thing called a *preemptible rate* which means you get a break on the price if you agree to let the station take back the spot if they get a chance to sell it to an advertiser at a higher price or as part of the package deal.

As with ROP (above) you can often get a lower rate by allowing the station to use their discretion in scheduling your spot. (*ROS*—run of schedule.)

With all these variables there is considerable room for negotiation, particularly in highly competitive radio.

Sizes.   Magazines generally sell themselves in sizes ranging from ¹/₆ of a page to a *full bleed page* (in which the illustration "runs off" the page); or *spreads* (2 facing pages) and charge more for the *inside cover* or *inside back* positions. *Closing dates* (the date when your plates must be in the hands of the publisher) are generally 60 days prior to publication. And note: the *publication date* and *cover date* are two different things. *Outdoor boards* as well as *car cards* are offered in ¼, ½, and *full showings* with a variety of shapes, and, as in the case of car cards, positions from which to choose.

The outdoor company in your town may offer a #25, #50, and #100 showing. This means that, using figures arrived at by the Traffic Audit Bureau, they are prepared to offer you a mix of illuminated and nonilluminated boards that will generate an audience equal (in the case of #50) to 50 percent of the population in your community. It does *not* mean 50 percent of the available boards. *Outdoor* is also bought in time segments, usually in units of 30 days. Your outdoor posting company will probably be able to offer you, in addition to the *24-sheet*—the most common size of billboard—*30-sheet, painted boards*; some odd sizes, such as *parallelogram plus square*, and possibly a *spectacular*.

Bus or *car cards* are an interesting medium with their low costs, captive audience, repeat riders, and on-the-way-to-shop customers. But you have to be careful. The Lexington Avenue Express (subway) carries many a Wall Streeter on his way to work; but in quite a few southern cities it's mostly low-income persons who ride public transportation.

Direct Mail can be a tricky and yet often rewarding medium. Services of direct-mail houses are used by supermarkets and other retailers to bring their message to specific *kinds* of people or to specific neighborhoods. We have already suggested that you visit your nearest direct mail house and learn how it operates. You may be surprised at how skilled they have become in unerringly putting your message into the hands of those you want to reach. If they lease a mailing list for you, it will run about $25.00 per thousand names. They will probably not charge you a "list price" when they put a mailing into specific neighborhoods or towns for you. The costs run about 8¢ per piece for third class, to 25¢ per piece for a first-class mailing, but inevitably this is subject to change. We will devote a chapter to direct mail and mail order.

We have not yet exhausted the media possibilities, and it will pay you
to look around in your town to see what else is going on. It has been said that if there is an empty space, someone will come along and want to put an ad in it. Maybe so. People stick them on top of taxicabs, trail them from airplanes, print them on matchbook covers, paint them on park benches, paste them on trashbaskets and even on sidewalks.

But don't get the idea that advertising can be thrown around indiscriminately the way it used to be in the old days. There are plenty of controls over the indiscriminate uses of advertising. City councils, garden clubs, environmentalists and others all make their voices heard. Recently, in our town, the subject of using bus stop benches for advertising purposes was the subject of hot debate.

Specialties. There's a whole great industry involved in *advertising specialties,* and you'll find them so listed in your Yellow Pages. These people sell gadgets designed to keep your name and selling message before the public—pens, pencils, address books, rulers, billfolds, memo pads—and you've seen and used these time after time. We'll have more to say about them under "Sales Promotion."

The Numbers Game

Through the services of private and industry-supported groups we are able to ascertain circulation with great accuracy. One of these is the Audit Bureau of Circulation, whose ABC insignia you saw directly under the title of the publication in the SRD. There are others, such as the Traffic Audit Bureau we mentioned. The important thing for you to remember is that *every* medium, no matter what it is, should be able to tell you *exactly* the number of people they can deliver at any given time. In addition to their own counts, they should have figures from reputable independent sources. Call the advertising department of your paper and ask, "Would you please tell me what your circulation is, and what percentage of the homes in our town you reach?" When they tell you, you then ask gently, "How did you get those figures?" They should be able to reassure you that their figures are statistically valid. You can do the same thing, with variations, for any other medium. "That billboard, there on the corner. How many people pass it each day? How do you know?"

The Money Game

As you already have seen, each medium states very clearly how much you're going to have to pay it to carry your advertising message. You've also seen that this figure is subject to numerous variations involving *time, space, frequency, purchases, position,* and *color* and *shape,* and how hungry they are for new business.

Our problem now becomes related to one faced by the shopper who stands in the supermarket trying to figure, without the aid of a computer, whether it would be better to buy the 2 for 29¢ 16-ounce cans of peaches, or the 32-ounce giant economy size at 86¢ with an 8-ounce can free with every purchase of the giant economy size—one to a customer, minimum grocery order of $5.00.

What you *really* want to know is not how much the ad or commercial will cost, but *how much will I have to pay for the opportunity of putting my sales story before one potential customer?*

You can get this figure by dividing the cost of your ad or commercial into the total circulation or audience. Media people do this to get a handy figure that is referred to as CPM, *or cost per thousand.* The amount of money involved is divided by the number of people reached in thousands. This, of course, is a very simple yardstick. You have already seen that a number of other factors must play a part in your media decision.

The newspapers have a *milline rate* that gives you a figure of cost per line per circulation. It is arrived at by multiplying the paper's line rate by one million and dividing by the circulation. But in making this kind of a decision, here's what you are much more likely to be up against: Would I be better off buying one 600-line newspaper ad per week at a cost of $435.00, or buying 6 30-second radio commercials per week on four different radio stations, here in town, at a cost of $360.00?

If you've done your homework, you shouldn't have too much trouble arriving at a figure you can work with: the cost of reaching one potential customer under the alternative plans. But, please, note again: this cost per potential customer figure is but *one* of the criteria you will want to use in arriving at a sensible media buying decision. Early in this chapter we mentioned a number of others: customer profile, customer location, size of ad budget, frequency, seasonal implications, type of product, and so on.

All these have to be accounted for, and at the end of this chapter we will take a dry run through a media problem to see exactly how you would do it.

But first we must examine another set of variables: the differences in media *as media.*

The Guessing Game

As a means of bringing your selling story to people, an outdoor board is as different from a radio commercial as a matchbook cover is from a magazine. You need not be too concerned about this. Very early in this book, if you recall, it was pointed out that the brain—where the buying decisions are made—is not concerned about the *sources* of the information fed to it through our aural and optical senses.

What you *do* need to recognize is that each medium functions particularly well in certain areas, and does less than well in other areas. Take warning: there are those who make a profession of marching up and down the land proclaiming the superiority of this or that medium over everything else. There are even some agency people who out of faith or prejudice or inclination habitually guide their clients' dollars into a particular medium.

There is no such thing as a medium superior to other media. What there is, is a *medium whose characteristics are best suited to your product and your sales story.* Let's look at some of these characteristics.

Newspapers. The newspaper is the traditional medium for the local retailer, particularly department stores, real estate agents, and automobile dealers. A "quick read" through an evening paper probably gets more time than a morning edition. Usually it gives excellent coverage, especially in the growing number of one-paper communities. But be careful: coverage varies widely and can fall as low as 65 percent in some cities. But coverage is *well defined.* It's flexible; you can move quickly in and out of newspapers as market conditions warrant. Newsprint (paper) quality makes good reproduction, particularly color, difficult. Art work for newspapers should be tailored for that medium.

Outdoor. Outdoor advertising certainly is seen by a wide variety of people. It's a highly flexible medium, purchasable in specific localities. Higher traffic speeds make many boards difficult to read. Creatively a *very special case.* The illustration and 4 or 5 words have to sock the message home immediately. It takes quite a bit of time to get a poster designed, printed, and up. It can't move as fast as with radio and newspapers. It has always seemed to me the perfect political campaign medium: big splash for a little money, controlled circulation, limited time span, candidate's name and face up there big, and room for short simplistic emotional appeal. Good as "reminder" support for multimedia campaigns.

Spot radio. It's difficult to reach a *wide* audience with this medium, even with multiple buys; but it's a beautiful *segmenter* of markets, and particularly attractive to local advertisers. It often has loyal, habitual followers. Spot radio ads offer a chance to get inexpensive, highly creative commercials. You can't *show* your product on radio, but don't forget what we have said about the sound man's magic.

Local TV. Local TV ads are great for mass coverage, with some segmentation possible due to differences between daytime and nighttime viewers. It's superb, if you have a product that lends itself to demonstration. But—creatively—you are up against the biggies. You're only up there for 30 seconds, so your commercial had *better* be good.

Magazines. Magazines can be highly selective (*Yachting, Mademoiselle, Georgia Farmer*). They have a long life and multiple

The window on his world.

The oil man.
The decision maker.
In exploration. In production.
Drilling. Pipelining. Refining.
Gas processing. Petrochemicals.

This year, this man will find
more late news, more new technology,
and more than 3500 pages of advertising
in fifty-two issues of the
Oil & Gas Journal.

If you are an advertiser
with something to say to
any phase of the petroleum industry,
say it where the oil man
will see it first.
Every week.

OIL & GAS
JOURNAL

The Leader.

THE JOURNAL IS ONE OF FIVE OIL INDUSTRY MAGAZINES
FROM THE PETROLEUM PUBLISHING COMPANY.

Agency: Ackerman Incorporated, Oklahoma City, Okla.

Another interesting ad by a famous and long-lived industry magazine. Note the clean, attractive layout, and striking illustration.

250

readership in barber shops, dentists' waiting rooms, and the like. They're often read at a leisurely pace. Better paper stock makes for good color reproduction. The regional issues for regional advertisers may offer fair coverage and high prestige value. But general magazines may have much waste circulation (like newspapers) depending on your product. Even with general magazines, readership may vary widely with geographical location. Nationally distributed magazines and newspapers will sell you space on a limited geographic basis. For details see your copy of SRD.

Direct mail. Direct mail is excellent as a thorough mass-medium coverage for selected audiences. It enables you to zero in on all the dentists in town, or on all the stores selling lawn and garden supplies. You can pick up people newspapers miss. It's great for chain stores or for multiproduct brochures, but care must be taken with the covering letter. It's a job for a real expert. There's much waste circulation sometimes; low returns are normal, cost per reader high.

The Media Mix

If you will now run through some of the other advertising media we mentioned earlier, I think you can pretty well figure out for yourself what the advantages and limitations of each one might be. Often a special situation will make a medium particularly effective. A case in point: Matchbook covers have proved particularly successful in selling home-study courses in mechanics, air conditioning, and the like.

Do you see what we are up against? A set of variables (but not complete unknowns) that we must juggle properly in order to find the correct answers to the riddle, "Am I getting to tell my story to the *most potential buyers in the most economical way?*"

Making the Media Decision

Now I'd like to show you how you can approach a sensible media decision. I don't guarantee that this method will make you rich and famous, but you may sleep a little better tonight. Since I'm sure that the boys in the media department at Kenyon and Eckhardt don't need any help from me, I'll slip down to the local level where most of us operate and we'll do a run-through with a store I know about here in our town.

"The Movin' Dude"

This store is in a low-rent area of the inner city. The Movin' Dude sells men's clothes. Very up-to-date, flashy men's clothes. So let's see what you'd do if you were in the business of selling clothes to a clientele that doesn't walk but moves.

First take two pieces of paper. Headline one "The Circumstances," and the other, "The Possibilities." On the first one list the following categories, leaving a few lines between for notes.

1. What does my customer look like?
2. Where is he?
3. How much can I spend?
4. How often should I advertise?
5. What's the competition doing?
6. What does my product look like?

On the second piece of paper list the following:

1. T.V.
2. Newspaper
3. Radio
4. Outdoor
5. Direct Mail
6. Magazines
7. Other

Now let's take Page One, and fill in the answers from what we know (or what we can go and find out from The Movin' Dude).

1. *What does my customer look like?*

   He's black; but maybe 15 percent are white customers. Age 16 to 30. Definitely far out in taste. Doesn't mind spending for what he wants. Wants to be there *first.*

2. *Where is he?*

   All around me, this part of the city gets a big play from black trade. No problems. Six buses stop at the corner.

3. *How much can I spend?*

   I've got a good profit margin on these clothes, low overhead; but I'm not always sure about taste swings. For the short term, let's say $300.00 per week.

4. *How often should I advertise?*

   Don't know about that, but I do know that when I have it, they've got to know about it—*now.*

5. *What's the competition doing?*

   Don't think you'd call Sears Men's Store real competition; too

conservative. But there are one or two other guys here in town
with a policy like mine; they're running 400-line ads in the newspapers fairly often. Feature black models.

6. *What does my product look like?*

Look around—mod, up to date, flash.

Now with that page beside you for ready reference, let's go down Page Two.

1. *TV.* Tempting. I've got a product that cries out to be seen. If I could get one of the local DJ's to model and make the pitch, this might be a good bet. Inexpensive commercial, but programming a problem. I'd have to buy spots near pro football or basketball. But this is a definite possibility. We have a blaxploitation movie house here in town, too. Maybe could run the one-minute spot there cheaply.
2. *Newspaper.* The competition is already there, and I'd only wind up in a space war. Besides, I want to show *color* and *fabric.* Hard to do with newspaper reproduction.
3. *Radio.* Well, I know what my guys listen to. *All* of 'em. The small stations. Might even do a trade-off for time. I can easily afford 20 to 25 one-minute spots a week. I'll let the DJ do his own pitch from a fact sheet.
4. *Outdoor.* Can't see it in my situation.
5. *Direct Mail.* Most of my customers don't get letters, and they are not enthusiastic about reading a whole bunch of stuff.
6. *Magazines.* Nothing here. Sports programs might be a good bet, if the price is right.
7. *Other.* There's an African jeweler in town. I might get him to make me a "Movin' Dude" bracelet or neck chain.

I didn't just make this up. It's real. And I think you can see that if the Movin' Dude could put together a media package such as the above —consistent radio to his market segment, plus TV one-minute spots in special situations, plus programs (football and basketball, high-school and college) and promotion where the black audiences are strong, he'd have a reasonably solid program.

WHERE YOU ARE

---

1. Now you know why it is so important to understand the segmentation and demographics of your market.

2. You know how space and time are purchased in various media, and you are familiar with some of the terms used by media people.

3. You are familiar with the major factors influencing the choice of media.

4. You have learned what the major vehicles for the advertising message are and some of the advantages and disadvantages of each one.

5. You have the tools to construct a sensible media plan of your own.

QUESTIONS FOR CLASSROOM DISCUSSION

1. Of all the different media in your city, which *one* would be most likely to reach the people in your classroom most effectively?

2. There may be a way to advertise in your community that has been overlooked. Can you think of one?

3. Which of these two publications do you think would deliver more of the same *kind* of potential customer—*The Christian Science Monitor*, or *Field and Stream?* Explain your reasoning.

4. Do you think the "late night movie" is a good place to advertise on TV? Defend or attack the position.

5. If you wanted to reach the people in your particular part of town most effectively with advertising, how would you go about it?

SOMETHING FOR YOU TO DO

Pick your business or product, preferably a local one, since you'll be more familiar with the local scene. Using the two-list system, work out what seems to you to be a defensible media plan for them.

Appropriation.   Money designated for advertising purposes.

Audience.   Readers, listeners, or viewers who receive your message.

Audit Bureau of Circulation (ABC).   Industry-supported organization that oversees and accredits circulation figures.

Bleed Page.   Page on which printing is carried to the very edge of the sheet.

Buying Representative.   Organization that handles the buying of space and time for clients.

Car Cards.   Display cards carrying advertising messages, used in cars and buses.

Circulation.   Number of people reached by a publication. Radio and TV call this "audience."

Closing Date.   Date on which material must reach publication in order to appear in a certain issue.

Continuity.   Material in script that is followed in radio or TV.

Cover Date.   Date printed on the cover of the publication.

CPM.   Abbreviation for "cost per thousand."

Frequency.   Waves per second transmitted by a station. They are measured in kilocycles or megacycles.

Full Showing.   In outdoor, a #100 intensity showing (but not every board in market). In car cards, a space in every car.

Line Rate.   Cost per line of newspaper space.

Media.   Vehicles (in newspapers, radio, TV) over which advertising messages are carried.

Media Director.   Person who is responsible for the selecting and buying of media.

Milline Rate.   Measurement of the cost of one line of space per million readers. Formula: 1 million × the line rate, divided by the circulation.

National Rate.   Rates charged national advertisers by media. It is more than local retail rate.

Newsprint.   The paper on which your newspaper is printed.

Painted Board.   Outdoor display that is painted, as opposed to one that consists of printed sheets of paper.

Preemptible Rate.   Reduced rate for time that may be taken back by station for special events, news, etc.

Publication Date.   Date on which a publication appears on the stands.

Rate Card. Brochure on which rates for time and space are published.

Readership. Number of people who get to read a publication during its life.

Retail Rate. Space and time rates charged to local retail advertisers.

R.O.P. Run-of-paper position. You'll accept any position in which the publication wishes to place you.

R.O.S. Run-of-schedule. Same as above for commercials within a specific time period. (6:00 P.M. to 10:00 P.M., M, W, F.)

Seasonal. Advertising and marketing policies that are affected by the changes in the seasons.

Space. The number of lines and columns occupied by an ad.

Specialties. Items available as gifts and reminders on which a company name or advertising message is printed.

Spread. An advertisement occupying two facing pages.

Standard Rate and Data (SRD). A series of publications giving pertinent information (costs, circulation, etc.) about various media.

Thirty Sheet. Same board as twenty-four sheet with copy carried out to the edge. In effect a "bleed" board.

Time Costs. Prices charged for spots on TV and radio.

Twenty-four Sheet. From days when printers used to deliver paper in 24 separate sheets. Today it indicates the normal 12' x 25' board with about a 6" border of white space.

SELECTED READINGS

Barton, Roger. *Media In Advertising* (New York: McGraw-Hill Book Company, 1964.) Very comprehensive. Good reference book on the subject.

Brown, Lyndon O., Lessler, Richard S., and Weilbacher, William M. *Advertising Media: Creative Planning In Media Selection* (New York: The Ronald Press Company, 1957.) Another good basic book.

McNiven, Malcolm A. (ed.). *How Much to Spend on Advertising* (New York: National Association of Advertiser, Inc., 1969.) This highly authoritative book, produced under the auspices of the AMA's Advertising, Planning, and Evaluation Committee, contains 10 articles by executives responsible for the allocation of advertising budgets.

Riso, Ovid. *Advertising Cost Control Handbook* (New York: Van Nostrand Reinhold Company, 1973.) See Part 3, "The Media," for excellent coverage of media costs.

Media/Scope. This professional publication contains many articles that will be of interest to you.

chapter twelve

Copy Testing

In this chapter we take up the important and often neglected area of copy testing.

You will see how you may test advertising copy before it is written, after it is written, and after it has been published or broadcast.

You will be introduced to some of the testing procedures now commonly used. You will observe what they can do and what they cannot do for you.

You will become familiar with the important DAGMAR principle. You will see how you yourself can apply tests that will help you judge how hard your advertising is working for you.

You will become convinced, I hope, that copy testing is one of the most important jobs in advertising. **259**

"What did my advertising dollars do for me, and what can I expect them to do for me next time?" This question should be on the tip of every marketer's tongue; and every advertising agency should be prepared to search objectively for the answer to so serious a question. Although they have not always been willing to do so, today more and more agencies are investing a portion of the budget in advertising research. The comment of D. R. Lucas and S. N. Britt is apt here:

> True, most advertisers give lip service and their hearty "amens" to the statement that more money should be invested in advertising research. But most stop short with the "amens." They have been agreeing with each other, especially in public addresses, for the past thirty years or more that advertising research is desirable, but very few really carry out advertising research on any significant scale. Too many prefer to rely entirely on their own personal judgment of advertising effectiveness, while at the same time they may pay many thousands of dollars a year for rating services which are circulation figures rather than measures of advertising impact.[1]

---

[1]D. R. Lucas, and S. N. Britt, *Measuring Advertising Effectiveness* (New York: McGraw-Hill, Inc., 1963), p. 6.

If you have taken considerable time and trouble to evolve the very best
ways to spend your promotional dollars in a particular market, then you
deserve to know the outcome of that investment. There is no point in
flying blind if you can avoid it. Also, you have the responsibility of
insuring success in every way you can.

We will now examine some of the methods that are used in calculat-
ing the impact—past, present, and future—of your advertising effort;
and I will suggest to you some relatively easy and inexpensive ways you
can wet a finger and tell which way the wind is blowing.

The Mixing Bowl

You will recall that way back in the second chapter we talked about a
thing called a "marketing mix," and about some of its major elements,
such as research, development, distribution, pricing, promotion, packaging, and retailing. We stressed that the *degree of importance* of each of
these factors tends to vary from product to product. We mentioned a
cigar company that does comparatively little formal advertising, but has
a fantastic distribution setup. You also saw how research and development, by coming up with new and startling product improvements, can
upset the whole market.

It is because of this marketing mix and its ever-varying components
that often it is so difficult to point to an advertising campaign and say,
"That one was great, it worked." Or, "That one was lousy." It is as
though you were being asked to solve an equation that is all X's, and the
power of the X's is unknown.

Advertising people tend to be paranoid about this fact, and with
reason. It is not at all uncommon for some manufacturer with a shoddy
product, spotty distribution, vile packaging, practically no markup, and
a reputation for not paying his bills on time, to glower around furiously
as the disappointing year-end sales figures come in, spot the agency
cowering in the corner and scream, "Off with their heads!"

And, of course, it works the other way. If the product is a wild success,
the agency won't hesitate to bask in the happy glow of prosperity even
though the sales department secretly suspects that it was *their* efforts
that prevailed despite all those expensive commercials. The rule seems
to be this: If it's an Edsel, stand in the back row and contrive to be
blowing your nose at the moment the shutter clicks; if it's a Mustang,
insert yourself in the first row between the president and sales manager
with your arms draped over their shoulders.

The reason we are pointing out what should be obvious to
everyone—that an equation with 6 unknowns is tougher to solve than an
equation with 2—is that it is *not* obvious to everyone, and the woods are
full of advertisers who blithely blame the advertising agency when the
product doesn't sell, and just as blithely assume that the agency must be
good when the product moves well.

When Research Can Help You

Testing Before the Ad is Written

In the chapter on copy you encountered some research methods used *before* the ad is written.

When you walk through the factory, look at the machinery and ask questions about it, that is research.

When you stop shoppers in supermarket parking lots and engage them in conversation about a product, *that* is research. The agency person who took a tape recorder into bars and talked to beer drinkers was gathering information. He was helping to build a better advertising campaign. Certainly the person who asked the women to taste the yogurt and listened for word patterns in their replies was performing research *prior to the writing of the ad.*

Testing While the Ad Is Being Written

Testing while the ad is being written is something many copywriters indulge in. It may be as simple as showing a headline or copy idea to several people in the office. Sometimes the writer will prepare several headlines or pieces of copy and ask her friends to give her their opinion.

The conferences between art director and copywriter are a kind of testing period. Here ideas are tried, kept, altered, or rejected.

You can perform a more elaborate kind of pretesting by subjecting your copy or selling idea to a panel of consumers, or by showing them to people on the street.

Testing Before Publication

Some of the larger agencies have taken elaborate and costly steps in order to get some line on the effectiveness of their ads before they commit their plates to final publication. Several agencies publish actual magazines in which their test ads appear. Copies of the magazine are sent to a list of "subscribers" who are later questioned about their reactions.

For the average agency, this technique is out of the question. But you can test ideas and techniques if you are willing to go to the expense of extra comprehensive layouts. In this way, ads that are very close in appearance to the final published version can be paired and reacted to by your respondents.

In any of this kind of testing it is wise to be wary. Unless you get a dramatically different reaction to one ad as opposed to another, you might better follow your own instincts. At best this is a quick, inexpensive way to settle differences of opinion about a campaign or selling idea.

You must remember that catch-as-catch-can opinions asked of the person in the street are frequently unreliable. In opinion tests of this kind, often the ad with the biggest illustration or blackest headline will get the nod. You also have to face the possibility that all the ads you are testing might be ineffective, and what you end up with is simply the best of a bad lot—unknown to you.

Testing After the Ad or Commercial Has Run

Testing after the ad has run is the important measurement of the ad or commercial's effect. How many sales are the result of this particular ad? How deeply did you penetrate the consciousness of the public with your selling ideas? How much *better* are you recognized now than you were before the campaign ran? These are some of the questions copy testing seeks to answer *after* the ad or commercial has appeared.

The Rules of Research

Perhaps you should now turn back to Chapter 5 on market research, and review the principles you have learned there. These same basic principles apply to copy testing.

The sample.   You must be sure that you question the right *kind* of people. Your sample must be a reflection of your market or potential market. Remember that an out-of-balance sample will give you out-of-balance answers.

The questions.   In copy testing, as in market research, it is important that you ask your questions in such a way as not to influence the answers. Sometimes, as you will see, we deliberately try to influence the answers. When this method is followed, we call it *aided recall.*

The questioners.   There are many kinds of copy testing that require nothing more than a good supply of common sense and the ability to add and subtract. Other forms require the services of a well-trained professional. If you should get into the area of copy tests that use techniques adapted from psychological testing, this would be particularly true.

The results.   Just as many market tests have been wrecked on this rock, so copy testers must be most careful in evaluating the results of their inquiries. Sometimes you just don't want to *believe* what people tell you. Sometimes, by a queer subconscious twist, you read into the results what you hoped would be there in the first place. I know of an agency for a major cigarette account whose copy testers worked out a unique way of pretesting their commercials against the competition's. For some reason, they practically never came in second.

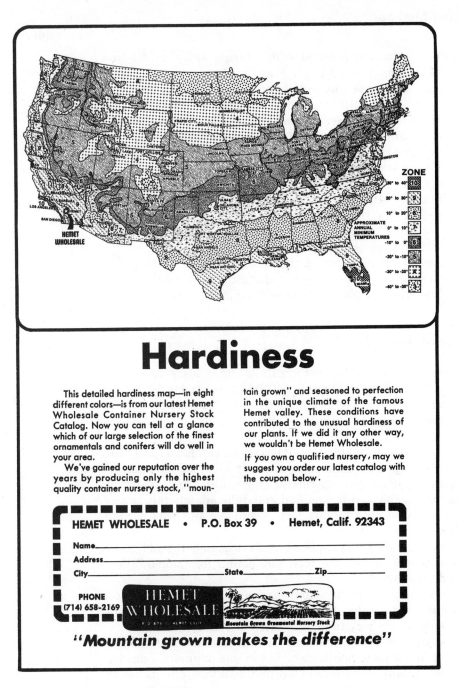

Hardiness

This detailed hardiness map—in eight different colors—is from our latest Hemet Wholesale Container Nursery Stock Catalog. Now you can tell at a glance which of our large selection of the finest ornamentals and conifers will do well in your area.

We've gained our reputation over the years by producing only the highest quality container nursery stock, "mountain grown" and seasoned to perfection in the unique climate of the famous Hemet valley. These conditions have contributed to the unusual hardiness of our plants. If we did it any other way, we wouldn't be Hemet Wholesale.

If you own a qualified nursery, may we suggest you order our latest catalog with the coupon below.

HEMET WHOLESALE • P.O. Box 39 • Hemet, Calif. 92343

Name_____

Address_____

City_____State_____Zip_____

PHONE
(714) 658-2169

HEMET WHOLESALE
P.O. BOX 39 HEMET CALIF.
Mountain Grown Ornamental Nursery Stock

"Mountain grown makes the difference"

Agency: Pettler Advertising, Inc., Oakland, Calif.

This advertiser digs up new prospects ("If you own a qualified nursery . . .") with an attention-getting illustration and catalogue offer in his couponed ad. He got measurable results.

The methods by which copy is tested before, during, and after, fall into well-defined categories. We shall now examine them.

Some methods are beloved by professional organizations that have been in the copy-testing field for years. They have developed highly trained staffs to perform the research, and have perfected sampling and inquiry methods that they believe give them valid answers.

As with *all* testing methods, there is no universal agreement on the efficiency of these methods and the validity of the results. Researchers are continually rewriting and revising their methods in an effort to make them more efficient. In the past, researchers and copy testers with new claims have had an inclination to claim a little too much for their techniques. Every so often, the world of advertising is shaken by revolts or charges against one researcher or the other.[2]

Fortunately an industry-supported organization, the Advertising Research Foundation, tries to keep an eye on things. They not only police but often confirm widely used methods with studies of their own.

Seen, Associated, Read Most

One of the most widely known copy tests is the *readership survey* perfected by Dr. Daniel Starch. The *Starch Surveys* are used to determine the readership of a particular ad in a particular publication a short time after it has appeared.

Unaided recall. In the unaided recall test the researcher approaches the person in the sample, determines if he has actually read the publication, and displays certain ads. By careful questioning, the researcher then determines whether the person had noted the ad; whether it was associated in his mind with the product advertised; and whether the person had read most of the copy.

From these facts, the Starch people are able to assign to the ad figures representing a percentage of the total circulation for "noted," "associated," and "read most."

The technique followed by the Starch surveyers is known as *unaided recall*. The questioners are always careful not to drop any hint or prompt their respondents in any way in getting their answers.

These scores are a lot of fun, especially if your ad rates higher than a competitor's ad in the same publication. When this happens, agencies have been known to wave the superior figures under their clients' noses

---

[2]See "Variance on New Simmons Data Have Magazines Baffled and Angry." *Advertising Age*, November 18, 1974.

and shout in triumph. However, *all* readership figures have to be re-

garded with some reservation. After all, the only thing they claim to
show you is *readership*. They can't tell you *who* read your ad, and they
never said they could.

For almost any product, as you know, the market is always fractional.
For soap the fraction is big. For antique cars the fraction is small. A
publication can deliver only a fraction of its readership who are my
potential *customers* (the segment). If I got a small fraction of your
readership to read my ad, did I get a fraction of the fraction? Did my
fraction of your readership include *any* of the fraction of my potential
customers? Speak up, my boy.

Unfortunately, one of the statistics our readership studies can't provide is "Slammed down magazine, jumped into car, flew into store, and
bought one."

Aided recall. The research firm of Gallup and Robinson is usually
associated with another form of readership survey that seeks to probe
deeper into the reader's knowledge of and reaction to an ad. In this
survey, the reader is prodded a little (*aided recall*) to give the answers.
"Did you see the Buick commercial last night?" "What features of the car
did it mention?" "How would you sum up your impression of this car?"
As you can see, you can go quite deeply with this, especially in discovering the effect of certain claims.

This technique is very popular for testing television commercials.
Burke Television Day-After Recall is one outfit doing this. It lends itself
well to telephone interviews, and can be used in a limited market. You
have to be careful, though. It takes an experienced interviewer to steer
clear of the point when the "aid" becomes a little too "aided" and
distorts the results.

There are other methods of testing commercials, such as springing
them on movie audiences, or showing a series to a captive audience and
letting them make a selection of advertised and unadvertised goods
immediately afterward, or getting them to answer a questionnaire regarding what they have seen and the message they have retained.

Opinion tests. Another way to find out something about your advertising is to ask people what they think about it. It's a very inexpensive
way, too. You've seen a lot of these *opinion tests* in the form of television
commercials—those in which the hidden camera makes a shopper sip
one coffee while she tells someone off camera how good it is. The
headache remedy people have also done some very effective commercials using "live" interviews with people telling how quickly their
headaches have disappeared.

Opinions are most valuable *before* the ad runs. They can help you,
particularly when you are undecided about several appeals or illustrations. You could show an accordion folder with 6 ads in it and ask,
"Which one of these do you find most attractive?" Or let a respondent

read two pieces of copy and ask, "Which of these two sounds most convincing to you?"

Panels. In our discussion of market testing, I think we mentioned that some of the big advertisers have groups of users whose opinion they can call on. This is a technique that can also be used for copy. You might term it "group opinion."

Psychological tests. Copy testers have adopted some of the instruments developed by psychologists. Instead of delving into your psyche, they delve into your consumer attitudes. If you've ever visited a clinical psychologist, or applied for a job with a big corporation, you may have taken one of these tests.

Some tests are what the psychologists term *projective technique;* that is, you *project* yourself or your opinion with a given situation. Sometimes you are asked to simply complete a sentence. "I like . . .'s coffee because. . . ."

Or you may be shown a picture and asked to describe what is going on in it. The interviewer may give you a word, then ask you to give him the first word that pops into your mind. Or you might be asked to fill in an empty cartoon balloon.

These tests, adopted from the psychologists, take quite a bit of expertise. I don't advise you to get into them unless you feel that you are quite capable of handling them properly. But they could turn up pure gold. If you could discover a deep-seated psychological feeling about your product, you might develop the basis for a strong selling-appeal.

Depth interviews. Psychologists sometimes find it helpful to let us lie on the couch and ramble on. This technique has also been tried in copy testing. But as in analysis, it takes a real pro to quietly lead the conversation in the right direction.

Coupons and hidden offers. One of the earliest forms of copy testing used the coupon. You've seen some of these ads in the chapter on copy. This is a particularly handy technique for an advertiser who has something to sell by direct mail and who does consistent advertising, such as book publishers and record clubs. *Naturally* they use the coupons. But it is the copywriter, as you have discovered, who should look at the returns and ask himself, "Why did it work?"

A close associate of couponed ads is the hidden offer. If an offer of a free booklet is contained near the end of the copy, you will at least know how many people read far enough to be attracted by your offer.

Both the couponed ad and the hidden offer can be used in matching one ad or one appeal against the other in a *split-run* test. Many newspapers will have split runs available to you. A random 50 percent of the issue runs one of the ads, and in the same issue the other 50 percent sees your other ad.

Test markets. A number of smaller cities across the country are traditional test markets. The idea here is to take an inventory count (the bench mark) and then introduce the promotional package into the market for a given length of time, and then reinventory to measure the impact of your promotion. By using several cities with different promotional packages in each one, a comparison of sales impacts can be made. The well known Nielson Studies are the inventorying side of this technique.

Awards. Award-winning commercials, ads, and campaigns sometimes get a lot of attention when people are trying to judge the effectiveness of advertising. Sooner or later an executive will escort you through an agency, modestly indicating the walls covered by awards, framed and neatly arranged. Or you will meet a copywriter with a proof book full of them. The implications, of course, are clear.

When Les Pearl was creative director at BBD&O (Batten, Barton, Durstine and Osborn) a young writer approached him and asked how he could gain fame and success in the ad game. Les told him to go forth and edit a book to be called something like *The One Hundred Best Ads of All Times.* He would then automatically become an authority on copy. When the word got around about what the young copywriter was doing, he was snowed under by 5,000 entries from guys who wanted to be forever enshrined as writers of "one of the one hundred best ads of all times."

But the whole thing backfired. He made a hundred new friends and 4,900 new enemies.

Getting the Message

One of the things that has long piqued the curiosity of advertisers is, "Just how loud and clear *are* people getting my message?" Another good question they sometimes had to ask themselves is, "Do they understand what I am saying?" Because the human animal, being the complex creature that he is, often sees something red where you have carefully painted it blue.

So advertisers will run an ad (or better yet, a series of ads using varying techniques and appeals). After a period of exposure they will send forth their teams of researchers to determine, via detailed questionnaires, just what points were made most effectively. Results of these tests are often surprising, and always interesting. However, there are some drawbacks that may have already occurred to you.

For one thing, no one can assure you that you are testing the *best* appeals. It's like watching the first claiming race at Hialeah, which no one in his right mind would bet on. You could get a winner, and still have a dog. Also—and you may question the researchers closely on this one—just because the reader *got* your message doesn't mean that he

bought it. Oh no it doesn't! Which Ad Pulled the Best offers some
fascinating results on readership tests.[3] The title is slightly misleading.
It depends on how you interpret the word "pull." It doesn't mean which
ad *sold* best, or which ad *worked* best. All it really means is which ad got
the highest scores according to the research firm that did the job. But I
think you'll enjoy the book. It will introduce to you some of the top
people of copy research. Note too that there is, even today, a tendency to
promise that just beyond the distant hills there is a city called Quivira
where the streets are paved with gold and emeralds.

The Possible

Now for the good news. For the great number of America's advertisers
who have never heard of Starch, or Gallup, or Robinson, and couldn't
afford them if they had, there are still sound reasons for getting a fix on
just exactly what it was they got for their advertising money. As previously stated, this happens much less often than it should. But it is
certainly better for you to ask the question of yourself, than to have some
troublemaker ask it of you at a stockholders' meeting.

DAGMAR

When a few years ago the Association of National Advertisers sponsored
a study entitled *Defining Advertising Goals,* they turned the thinking of
a lot of people around about 180 degrees on this whole matter of copy
testing.

What the author, Russell H. Calley, had to say was this:

Advertising's job, purely and simply, is to communicate to a defined
audience information and a frame of mind that stimulates action.
Advertising succeeds or fails, depending on how well it communicates the desired information and attitudes to the right people at the
right time and at the right cost.[4]

This concept has become known as DAGMAR—*Defining Advertising
Goals, Measuring Advertising Results.*

When I write an ad or a commercial, I'm trying to tell you something;
I'm trying to inform you; I'm trying to alter the direction of your thought,

---

[3]Carroll J. Swan, *Which Ad Pulled the Best* (New York: Funk & Wagnall, in cooperation
with *Printer's Ink,* 1951).

[4]Russell H. Calley, ed. *Defining Advertising Goals* (New York: Association of National
Advertising, Inc., 1961).

make you aware of something, get you interested in something, get you excited about something, get something fixed in your mind, help you to recall something. Those are my *goals*. My success or failure in achieving those goals, I can measure with great accuracy. This is good news for every advertiser who has ever wondered where the dollars went.

There's nothing so new about goal setting and goal achieving; but what shook up a lot of people about Calley's book was that he came right out and said that except in certain cases—such as couponed ads—it is very chancey to try to measure an ad's effectiveness in terms of sales results alone. You've already learned that the marketing mix contains a lot of "X" factors. What makes it exciting, of course, is that what we can measure is the *anatomy of a sale:* how *well* did I get your attention; how *great* did I make your desire; to what an *extent* did I convince you; what amount of action did I get?

Many instructors set up a series of learning goals—what they want to *get across* to their students in that particular lesson or series of lessons. Then they test and measure the *degree* to which that goal has been attained. The teacher is really testing himself—how well did *he* succeed in *communicating* the knowledge to the students? If he succeeded measurably well, they got their money's worth. If he failed, they didn't get their money's worth. (When I explain to my classes that it's really *me* who is being tested by their exam, they sneer.) But it's so.

Surprisingly, although it's often difficult to trace the effect of advertising on sales—for the reasons we have already examined—it is fairly easy to trace the effect of advertising on *ideas*. I can *tell* whether I have impressed you, or gotten across to you, or convinced you, or interested you, or fixed something in your mind. And what is even more interesting, I can *tell to what extent* my advertising has done these things in comparison to my competitors' advertising.

How You Can Do It

Let us now run through some not-so-hypothetical cases to show you how it's possible to discover what kind of a job you are doing in getting across to the public. That isn't an especially eloquent way of putting it, I know—"getting across"—but it is really what this is all about.

How many banks are there in your town? It's an old cliché in the trade that all banks are the same: they save money, lend money, invest money, store valuables, run Christmas Clubs, and perform a number of other functions. All with money. True, these functions are the same; but the banks aren't the same—not by a country mile. That's why bank presidents keep getting fired; why some banks grow and expand, and others just putter along; and why banks have a person they often call "Vice-President, Client Relations." That person is a *salesmanager!*

Most of the banks in your town are struggling to gain distinction, to have a personality, and to be *outstanding* in some way—all to the end that they may sell more of their banking services. How well are they

doing this job? It's not too difficult for you to find out. We might start by trying to discover just how effective they have been in buying recognition for themselves with their advertising dollars.

Clip out the ads for your local banks till you have a sample from each one of them. Note that each has a slogan or catch line that is often part of the logotype or an integral part of their signature, such as "The Bank of Friendly People"; or, "Where Your Money Works Harder"; or, "Ask and Ye Shall Be Given." List these slogans, and, applying any of the techniques you have learned, ask a random sample of newspaper readers, "With which of our banks do you associate the following slogan?" A 200-person random sample should quickly show you which bank has made the most impact on the public with its slogan.

Let's take a look at another group of merchants in your town, those who are big and consistent users of local advertising media: the automobile dealers. Here, again, they sell the "same thing"—cars and service; but they sell different cars at different prices, all backed by massive national advertising.

Each one of these dealers is a distinct personality. Most of them are prominent in your community, and, for the most part, long-established and exceedingly proud of their reputation. And that "reputation" can usually be categorized as one of "fair dealing and good service." Through advertising and through sound business practices, basically this is what the dealer has been trying to establish with the public.

Using the techniques you have acquired, prepare a sample and questionnaire that will reveal the relative standing of car dealers in your town as measured by their reputation for fair dealing and service. Remember, you never come right out and ask people if they like chocolate ice cream. You let them *reveal* their feelings. "I am a foreigner, and not used to American ways of doing business. I wish to buy a car. Will you recommend three or four dealerships I might consult?"

Let us peel off another layer of advertising sophistication. As you have noticed, in the above test we have sought to reveal degrees of recognition and degrees of acceptance. Now go back to all the car dealership ads and examine them again. You will find that each has an appeal about the dealership. You will recognize that quite aside from the autos, they are selling either our old friend the main event or the psychological need.

Usually you can condense the thought into a few words. Here's a man who says he'll stand on his head to make a deal with you. Another "in the suburbs" advises you to "travel a little farther, and save a lot." Another offers a "buyer protection plan." Which of these appeals, *as an appeal*, impresses the public most? Can you find out? You certainly can.

Now here's the payoff for you. Once you've established your position in relation to your competitor's, you have established a *bench mark* and can proceed to set goals for yourself—which is where we came in with Mr. Calley and his book.

If you are the third best-recognized bank in town you can say, "I want

the kind of advertising that, in six months, is going to make me the
second best-known bank in town." You've established a goal, and you
have a bench mark; and in six months, after your advertising has run,
you can conduct your survey again to see for yourself exactly how much
relative recognition your advertising dollar has bought you.

The same can be done for the degree to which your story has been put
across, and the relative effectiveness of the message you have been
using. The good news is: *bench marks can be established and progress
toward communication goals measured.*

How About the Future?

If you can use goal-setting and establishment of bench-marks to measure
communication effectiveness, can you use the same techniques to get
some sort of a fix on *future* effectiveness? Yes, you can—if you will
recognize that in an ad or commercial there are also variables that can
alter results. Don't be disturbed by this, because all we are really saying
is "Watch it. The effectiveness of an ad can be altered by how you say it."
And you already know this. So you have to say, "For the moment I'm
going to eliminate the *how* and stick to the *what*." Let's go back to our
copy lesson again.

You'll recognize that getting attention, creating interest, stimulating
desire, imparting conviction, and asking for the order are all "how"
things. In fact, you have learned many of the techniques for doing each
one. But your main event—your basic selling approach, psychological
or not—is a "what" thing. It isn't a technique, such as getting a doctor to
endorse your product (imparting conviction); or offering your product
for a limited time only at a reduced price (asking for the order). It is a
communicable concept . . . a selling idea . . . an action-impelling
thought; and, by itself, it can be quite accurately measured for effectiveness.

Remember, we have already gone out and measured the relative
impact of a few *main events* for the car dealers. Now suppose you should
completely change your approach to selling cars or bank services or
something else. This is what actually goes on all the time in your town.
Accounts switch agencies, or new advertising managers come in, or
clients get tired of their advertising and demand something fresh. Suddenly you not only have a lot of new "hows" (techniques) but you often
have new "whats" (appeals). Wouldn't it be nice if you could measure it
all beforehand? You could, if you had established a *bench mark.*

The person who went out and asked certain questions about the *main
event* is now in the enviable position of simply slipping a new appeal
into the questionnaire in place of the old one, and seeing how that
serves. (Remember: Here we're not testing for impact, which would be
affected by time or exposure; we're testing for believability and acceptance.)

Remember when you got your new glasses, and the optometrist kept
trying different lenses until he found the perfect combination for you? Same thing. And if, by some great stroke of good fortune, you come up with an appeal that tests out head and shoulders above all the rest—grab it and run!

Testing the "How's"

If you will recall, back in the chapter on copy, we talked about how, by counting coupon returns, the old-timers discovered a great deal about the *techniques* of advertising. You'll remember how they watched with fascination as the coupon returns were radically altered just by saying something in a slightly different way.

The split-run couponed or hidden-offer ad is made to order for testing *techniques*. Keep your previous selling approach the same, but alter the *techniques* and *devices* you use to present your story. If you had a chance to look at *Which Ad Pulled the Best?* you saw opposing techniques matched against one another to discover which would pull the most readership. With the split run, you'd be doing the same thing with coupons or hidden offers.

Today a great many papers in the U.S. offer split runs. If your hometown paper doesn't, I'd suggest that you try running your ads two or three weeks apart.

What has been suggested to you in this chapter is that if you are willing to accept the impact of ideas as a measure of the effectiveness of your advertising, you can have it relatively easily and inexpensively. And by judicious testing you can get more for your advertising dollar, year after year. A *bench mark*, a *goal*, and some simple but carefully constructed *research studies* are all you need.

You'd think that everyone would do it, wouldn't you? But they don't. Even though promotional dollars are usually an important cost of selling, you'd be appalled at how many advertisers don't know the answer to "What is my advertising doing for me, and how can I get it to do more in the future?"

I know of few other areas where business people have a chance to improve performance so dramatically and make their dollars work so much more efficiently.

Despite the reservations with which all research methods must be regarded, I hope you will adapt what you can for your own use. If you discipline yourself to adhere to basic research principles, you can make copy testing—before, during and after—pay off for you. Remember that many advertising people, particularly advertising research people, regard the lack of copy testing as scandalous. You can serve your agency or your company well if you help to fill this void.

WHERE YOU ARE

1.   You now understand the trap that awaits those who equate advertising performance with sales success, and vice-versa.

2.   You are aware of certain research techniques, such as readership surveys, reader recall studies, TV commercial product performance tests, and inventory counts.

3.   You understand the use of coupons or hidden offers in split runs of newspapers as a testing device.

4.   You comprehend the philosophy of testing the *communicative* effectiveness of advertising, and the use of bench marks and goals —DAGMAR.

5.   You have the knowledge and the skills to conduct tests that will reveal to you the believability of sales appeals, psychological approaches, or main attractions; you have the skills that will allow you to test the relative effectiveness of various advertising techniques.

QUESTIONS FOR CLASS DISCUSSION

1.   If copy testing can give you a good idea of what you are getting for your advertising dollar, why don't more people do it?

2.   If consumers have reasonably definite ideas about advertising, as most of them seem to, how do you think this affects copy testing?

3.   How would you go about discovering how many people in your town listened to a certain TV program?

4.   Not everyone agrees with Calley's DAGMAR principle. What do you think their objections might be?

5.   If you were a business executive, and your sales were holding up well, would you ask your agency to do copy testing for you?

SOMETHING FOR YOU TO DO

From among your classmates, select a "research team." Assign a task to each one: building the questionnaire, selecting the sample, keeping the records, and so on.

When you have your team completed, go to an advertising agency, or a broadcast station, or a manufacturer, and offer them your services. Ask them to let you carry out for them a copy-testing procedure at no cost to them. You must assure them of complete confidentiality and that the results will be theirs exclusively.

KEY WORDS AND PHRASES

Advertising Research Foundation.   Industry-supported organization that oversees research activities in advertising.

Aided Recall.   A method of determining how much of an advertising message a person has absorbed. Respondent's memory may be "jogged" slightly.

Bench mark.   A fixed position from which it is possible to make a measurement.

Burke Television Day-after Recall.   Popular television research organization.

DAGMAR.   A system for measuring advertising effectiveness.

Depth Interview.   Questioning that probes deeper than the factual interview.

Exposure.   The extent to which people had an opportunity to see an ad.

Gallup and Robinson.   Long-established advertising research firm known for readership studies.

Goal Setting.   A management technique for directing and controlling an enterprise or program.

Hidden Offer.   An offer that is "buried" in the text of the ad.

Interviewer.   Person who does the questioning.

Opinion Test.   One in which people are asked to render a judgement.

Projective Technique.   A method of psychological testing.

Readership Survey.   A study to determine the number of people who have noticed and read all or part of an ad.

Respondent. Person being questioned or interviewed.

Sample. A group chosen for questioning.

Split Run. When the circulation of a publication is made available to an advertiser in two random halves.

Starch Survey. Well-known firm specializing in research studies.

Test Market. A city in which an advertising campaign or marketing plan is tried out.

Unaided Recall. A method of interviewing in which no attempt is made to "jog" the respondent's memory.

SELECTED READINGS

Rober, Burton (ed). *Advertising Handbook* (Englewood Cliffs, New Jersey: Prentice-Hall, Inc., 1950). This book has a good, concise chapter on copy testing by a widely respected expert, John Caples, pp. 369–402.

Lucas, D. R., and Britt, S. N. *Measuring Advertising Effectiveness* (New York: McGraw-Hill, Inc., 1963). A complete work on the subject.

Mayer, Martin. *The Intelligent Man's Guide to Sales Measures of Advertising* (New York: Advertising Research Foundation, 1965). An interesting book by a well-known writer in the advertising field.

McNiven, Malcolm A. (ed). *How Much to Spend for Advertising* (New York: Association of National Advertisers, Inc., 1969). A series of nine articles by experts, under the sponsorship of ANA's Advertising and Evaluation Committee. Broader than just copy testing itself. Will be of interest to any business executive.

Caples, John. *Tested Advertising Methods* (New York: Harper & Row, Publishers, Inc., 1961). This is probably the classic in the field. It has been around since 1932, so be sure to get one of the newer editions.

Swan, Carroll J. *Which Ad Pulled the Best?* (New York: Funk & Wagnall, in cooperation with Printer's Ink, 1951). Which ad got the highest score, according to the research firm that did the job. An enjoyable book with information by top people in copy research.

chapter thirteen

Direct Mail

In this chapter we examine the fascinating world of "mail order." Most ad agencies and letter houses are now using the term "Direct Response" in place of "Direct Mail." However, for our discussion, we'll refer to it by its original name, "Direct Mail."

You will become familiar with the different techniques used by people who sell directly through the U.S. Mail.

We will look at the content of the mail solicitation and see the job each part does.

You will also learn something about the art of writing a mail order selling message.

You are going to see how "lists" are prepared, and how you can go about getting a mailing list of prospective customers.

You will be introduced to the "letter house" and see how it operates.

By the end of this chapter, you should have an awareness of the many ways "direct mail" can be used to help a business grow and prosper. **279**

There is a kind of advertising that for years has used the United States Post Office to help accomplish its purpose. The people who use the U.S. Mails to help them sell things, have two distinct methods of operation:

1. The marketer who uses the mail to *solicit* your order, and also uses the mail to *return* your order.
2. The marketer who primarily uses magazines, newspapers, and catalogues (but, also a variety of other media, as we shall see) to solicit your patronage, and uses the U.S. Mail to deliver your order.

The first method is usually referred to as *direct-by-mail;* the other is more properly called *mail order selling*. Both methods involve the *direct* response of the buyer to the seller, and represent a form of marketing in which the retail store is bypassed.

The Importance of Direct Mail

Before we discuss the various forms of selling through the mail, let's talk about the implication this kind of advertising has for a young business executive. **281**

Probably there isn't a car dealership, insurance agency, or hardware store in your hometown that doesn't get down on its knees each night and pray for someone who is able to write a letter or design a mailing piece so good that an instant response of orders and inquiries would pour in.

Any sales manager of a car dealership in your town would love to be able to send out a letter to 100 persons, and get 5 of them to come in and look at the new models. The manager knows that if only 1 of these 5 mail-solicited prospects actually buys a car, the mailing would pay for itself and also show a handsome profit.

But how to write a letter that will gain a response from those 5 prospects? That's the problem. A letter—the simplest kind of mail advertising—is well within the budget of even the smallest business operating in the most limited market. The trouble is: what is well within the budget of the small business is usually well outside its capacity.

Here is a letter I have recently received from a hotel in our city.

> Dear Mr. Norris:
>
> Why not hold your next affair at our hotel? We have a number of rooms available, and will provide excellent food and service. We hope you will give us every consideration, and we will do our best to work with you.
>
> If interested, will you please call me at the office any day between nine and five.
>
> Sincerely,
>
>
> Banquet Manager

That, my friends, is a letter such as a great many business executives receive. But it isn't a letter that *sells*.[1] You will see why. Toward the end of this chapter we'll try to help the banquet manager write a more effective sales letter.

How You Can Use the U. S. Mail

No matter what kind of business you are in, it is almost *inevitable* that you will ask "Uncle Sam" to help you sell. No matter whether you are a manufacturer or wholesaler or retailer, whether what you sell is expensive or cheap, whether your market segment is large or limited, you can and should use the U. S. Post Office to help you promote your business.

For one week I saved all the mail we received at our house. It turned out to be quite a stack. After I had eliminated a few personal letters and a few bills, it was *still* quite a stack.

---

[1] It is estimated by the Direct Mail Advertising Association that less than 7 percent of direct mail is prepared by professionals.

25 Sylvan Rd. South / Westport, Conn. 06880

Dear Friend:

    Two years ago, I wrote a letter telling the story of how on a trip to Japan I was invited to a Japanese businessman's house and saw something that made my eyes pop! It was a new fangled kind of knife.

    This knife cut through roast beef as if it were so much pudding. I saw it core an apple in one continuous stroke. I saw it slice bread a sixteenth of an inch thin!

    This knife looked different than any I had ever seen and as it turns out it is made differently (and better) than any other knife the world has ever seen. (I'll give you all the details about how it is made a little later.)

    Well, I'll admit I was really impressed with those knives. But if I had known the difference they would make in my life I would have jumped up and down and yelled "Whoopee!"

    You see, I prevailed upon my host to give me some of these incredible knives. I took them home. I got a kick out of demonstrating them, I can tell you.

    A friend of mine watched me carve a turkey and had to be convinced that the knife was not some sort of ingenious electric instrument with hidden wires or something!

    Only trouble was that whenever I demonstrated one of these amazing new knives I would have to give it up. Everyone who saw it wanted it - in fact they wouldn't take "no" for an answer.

    By the time my own mother saw me use the knife I was out of extra sets. When she heard that I had given a set to my mother-in-law and not to her - things got a little sticky!

    It was obvious to me that there was a real need for a superior knife. Why ... my friends had stripped me clean of these knives in a matter of days!

    So I got up some money and with the kind help of my friends in Japan arranged so that the knives could be purchased by mail in America exclusively through me!

    Then, I wrote my letter and hoped for the best.

Written for Discovery House, Inc., Westport, Conn., by Bob Jones of Westport, Conn.

The opening page of a 4-page letter from Ross MacKenzie of "Discovery House," Westport, Conn. This is mail order copy at its best. Note how the writer has achieved a note of sincerity, honesty, and ingenuousness. Note particularly paragraph 4—also the last line on the page. This writer knows what he is doing.

There were letters from two alumni associations asking me to help

support certain programs. There was another inviting me to join (at
$65.00 per year) a certain educational body. There was an offer of an
interesting gadget designed to open almost any kind of bottle, can, or jar;
to pry, to lift, to twist, and to do many other things. I was invited to take
advantage of special offers to subscribe to three different magazines. I
was given a chance to buy a new edition of a dictionary that is reduced
way down from the original in size but comes with a magnifying reading
glass. I was asked to help disadvantaged children—African, Asian, and
American Indian. My congressman, it turns out, could use a couple of
dollars to help him clean up some old campaign debts. That was just the
beginning.

Hardly a day goes by in my office here at school that I do not receive
information or solicitation from one of the textbook publishers.

After you have finished this chapter, I want you to save one week's
mail that comes to your home. By then, I hope, you will be able to
recognize most of the devices and techniques. Actually *examine* the
individual pieces for yourself. See what they have done. The variety is
great. You may learn techniques the textbooks haven't even mentioned.

Some Basic Facts About Mail Order

There are things you ought to keep in mind about selling that uses the
U. S. Mails.

1. It's a tough and demanding way to sell. You either make it, or you
    don't. There's none of this business of "the operation was a
    success, but the patient died." In this end of the business you
    produce—or get out.
2. It's a job for specialists. This type of selling presents many prob-
    lems ordinarily not found in preparing print or broadcast adver-
    tising. The best people in the business have devoted themselves
    to it. More important—they've proved they know what they're
    talking about. As I may have mentioned, there is many a high-
    priced Madison Avenue copywriter who wouldn't dare touch a
    mail order ad with a stick.
3. Successful mail order can make you rich and famous overnight.
    There were a couple of nice middle-aged ladies who ran a typical
    "Gift Shoppe" in a small New England town. One day they
    scraped the week's profits together and invested in a 2-inch ad in
    one of the "Shelter" magazines. They offered an old-fashioned
    pewter cream pitcher. A couple of days later, they were national
    marketers.
    There was a backwoods shop in Maine that used to sell to the
    lumbermen and fishermen. Sometimes, when they got back
    home, the visiting sportsmen would write and ask for an item.

The store got the idea, and began sending out a little catalogue. Today there are tiger hunters climbing Kilimanjaro who wouldn't walk a step without a pair of pack boots from L. L. Bean's.

285

Different
Ways of
Selling with
the Help
of the
Post Office

4. It requires as much, and probably more, insight into the human condition than any other form of advertising. A message in the mail from me to you is an intimate thing. Once you start reading, it's just you and me—my style and personality appealing to your style and personality. A great deal of mail order copy, you'll find, is quite intimate and down-homey. The writer may be the president of a multimillion-dollar mail order operation, but in his letter he'll come across like your old friend from next door. Often he'll even make himself out to be a little stupid—
"I was dumb enough to buy all these transistor radios. Won't you please help me get rid of them?"

5. Mail order writing is a *different* kind of copywriting. For one thing, the copywriter is *out there* longer. The copy in a circular, brochure, or catalogue will run far longer than most print publication copy. The customers want it longer. If they are going to read it at all, they want all the details. Another point: not every writer can command that "Gee, shucks, ma'am" style that is often demanded. Farther along in this chapter you'll see how the really great mail order writers did it.

Different Ways of Selling with the Help of the Post Office

Couponed ads. Let's start with some old friends of yours, the ads with coupons in them. This, as you will recall, is one of the oldest forms of direct response advertising. Many of the finest old ads, much like those mentioned in Chapter 1, made use of coupons.

In a previous chapter we discussed *split runs* in copy testing. You can see how well couponed ads would lend themselves to this. Couponed ads also gave the early copywriters a chance to study technique. There are advertisers who sell their products only by couponed order, who have been at it for 50 years or more. Imagine what they must have learned about advertising their products.

You have seen this same thing in the "Which Ad Pulled Best?" feature. I must admit I don't always do well at this "which ad pulled best" business when the answer is printed upside down on another page. The *wrong* ad often looks best to me for a number of sound, logical reasons that I'd be glad to explain to anyone who cares to listen.

The tough trick in taking advantage of what the coupons show was most effective, is to repeat the lesson you have apparently learned. Okay. Ad "B" pulled better than "A"; but can I, as a copywriter, reproduce exactly the same set of techniques and appeals that made "B" work better?

Couponed ads are a tougher breed of salesmen than most print ads.

They are doing a different job. Many magazines and newspaper ads are designed to inform, to enhance the prestige of a product, to announce new features in a product, or to convince you that it is superior to a competitive product. These are all perfectly legitimate aims for which advertisers gladly spend their money.

Not so the couponed ads; these are interested in only *one* thing—to take the order for the product. Success or failure has but one measurement: how many coupons get cut out and sent back with accompanying check or money order. That's *all* that counts.

It's like the salesman who spends a couple of hours convincing a reluctant customer that Chevrolet makes the best car in the world. After two hours he returns to his office with the empty order blank in his hand. "Well," he says, glowing with pride, "I really convinced *that* guy!" Sure.

You probably have already discovered some print ads that violate our basic salesmanship principles—get attention, create interest, stimulate desire, impart conviction, and ask for the order. But in a couponed ad you will *never* see the salesmanship principles neglected for one instant.

The reason is obvious. Everything in the ad is directed to just one purpose—to get the reader to act, to cut out the coupon, and to make the purchase. Couponed ads can't indulge in the luxuries many other ads afford themselves, such as the beautiful art work, the humor, the understated subtleties. The couponed ad must work as hard as a door-to-door salesman.

Catalogues.   With the advent of free rural delivery of the U. S. Mail in 1876, and parcel post in 1913, it became possible for millions of homebound families to make their purchases in a new and convenient way from an illustrated book that gave a description of each item and its price.

If you have seen that reproduction of the old Sears-Roebuck catalogue, you can just imagine a farm family seated around the Franklin stove on a winter evening and carefully debating their choices. Each book contained order blanks (as they do today); and it was possible to buy just about everything conceivable from the great "Mail Order Houses," Sears Roebuck and Montgomery Ward.

In a day when well-stocked department stores were limited to the larger cities, and a journey of only 20 miles in a horse-drawn wagon was a long and arduous trip, you can see how popular the catalogues were with the farm families.

Catalogues are still popular. Sears prints about half a million each year. Many other enterprises have found the direct-order catalogue a great selling device: discount stores, specialty shops, and hobby and craft material manufacturers.

The single-order mail proposition.   You've seen many of these. Unlike the mail order house that supplies you with a catalogue from which you may order items over a long period of time, the single-order mailing presents you with one proposition on which it asks you to act immediately. All its eggs are in one basket—or in one envelope. Often the envelope itself is cleverly designed to lure you on to open and examine the contents. Inside you will usually find:

287

Different
Ways of
Selling with
the Help
of the
Post Office

1. A covering sales letter
2. A brochure describing the merchandise
3. A return order blank with postpaid envelope
4. Swatches of material or samples where possible
5. Certificates of guarantee or money-off coupons

Putting this package together is a demanding job. As postal rates go up, these mailing pieces become ever more elaborate in their efforts to promote the sales of big-volume and big-profit items.

Direct mail advertisers. Here we use the U. S. Post Office to help us place an advertisement in a potential customer's house. We may or may not provide the means for a potential customer to make an immediate order from the advertised items.

Every week chain food markets will send out weekend "specials," which may be two-page folders on newspaper stock. These will be mailed to every home within a certain area.

The inserts you often find in your daily newspaper are also used as mailers. Drug, clothing, tire, jewelry, and home-furnishings dealers are big users of these elaborate color brochures you find in your mailbox. Here, of course, since they are local merchants, the main purpose is to get you to come in and buy rather than order directly from the brochure.

Letters. Probably the most simple form of direct-order solicitation through the mails is the letter itself. As we have indicated, it is also one of the most difficult. Millions of such letters are written each year; letters asking you to contribute, asking you to join, asking you to send for something. Next to face-to-face retail, there probably is no purer form of selling. The recipient reads what you have to say and either throws the letter into a wastebasket, or responds to your appeal.

Lately, direct response to mail solicitation has gained tremendous importance in politics.[2] With new laws limiting the size of potential contributions, suddenly it has become necessary for the candidate to appeal to the broad base of the electorate for cash donations in relatively small amounts. Mail solicitation is the quickest and most inexpensive way—if it's done right—to do this. Suddenly the person who can write a strong-pulling sales letter is in great demand.

Maybe you can write that kind of letter. If you think so, you can go to

---

[2]See "The Master of Campaigning by Direct Mail," *New York Times,* January 24, 1975.

Over 1½ million families travel with Fingerhut® "Lightweight" Luggage, Mrs. Norris ...

... and when that many people buy our luggage, you know it has to be an exceptional value ... because all 1½ million tried the luggage FREE for a full month <u>before</u> they bought!

NOW YOU CAN TRAVEL-TEST IT ABSOLUTELY <u>FREE</u> FOR 30 DAYS!

Find out firsthand why so many people prefer our luggage and give it as gifts for graduations, anniversaries and birthdays. Use it as your very own for a full month FREE! Compare it to luggage sold in stores in Ponte Vedra.

Just check (✓) the luggage color you like (Avocado Green, Riviera Blue or Charcoal Gray) on the attached Free Trial card and drop it in the mail. I'll send you:

24" PULLMAN   21" WEEKENDER   17" VANITY

That gives you the right size suitcase for every travel need ... whether you're going by car or public transportation ... whether you're taking a long vacation or a short weekend trip around Florida.

The important thing is that <u>you try BEFORE you buy</u>. You don't spend a penny unless you decide to keep the luggage. And then you pay only the low Fingerhut price of $29.99 plus shipping and handling*. FOR ALL THREE <u>MATCHED</u> PIECES.

And just for travel-testing this fashionable 3-Pc. Luggage Trio at my expense ...

... I'LL SEND YOU FREE GIFT MERCHANDISE!

(over)

You risk nothi[ng] ... you decide to [...]

And the[n ...] handli[ng ...] that i[s ...] each, [...]

If you de[cide ...] back. [...] andise [...]

Start [...] don't [...] have [...]

Che[...] fica[...] -- the so[...] will be on its [...]

<u>BUT PLEASE ACT NOW!</u> [...] we may soon have to limit first-[...] orders on a first-come, first-[...] chance by waiting too long.

Sincerely yours,

M. Fingerhut
President

MF:eb

P.S. Fingerhut "Lightweight" Luggage is an ideal gift for all gift-giving occasions

*Fingerhut terms: NO DOWN PAYMENT REQUIRED. Cash price of $29.99 plus shipping and handling. Total deferred payment price of $37.53 includes a FINANCE CHARGE of $2.95 at the ANNUAL PERCENTAGE RATE of 20%. On your purchase of $29.99 paid on Fingerhut terms of $4.17 per month for 9 months, total FINANCE CHARGE is only 32.8¢ per month.

FINGERHUT CORPORATION
11 McLELAND ROAD, ST. CLOUD, MINNESOTA 56372

Now get beautiful luggage at a down-to-earth price!

This new molded, vinyl-covered luggage looks just as expensive as luggage you'll find in department stores for $30.00 per piece!

Yet, here is a 3-Piece Set for the unbelievably low price of only $29.99 plus shipping and handling!* That's for all three — 24" Pullman, 21" Weekender, and 17" Vanity! And that's for all the features you'll find in luggage costing much more!

All vinyl-covered. Rich, leather-look grain that's scratch, scuff, stain, weather-resistant. No trouble to keep new-looking.

SURPRISE BONUS GIFT!

We have purchased an inventory of first quality liquidated and distress merchandise and we're going to give it all away to our customers as BONUS GIFTS.

Just try our Fingerhut® "Lightweight" Luggage, and I'll see that you get one of these gifts with the regular gift merchandise described in my letter.

This warehouse clearance merchandise is in perfect condition, undamaged in original cartons and except for our special purchase we could never afford to send you this Bonus Gift.

I think you'll be pleasantly surprised, so I hope you'll send your Free Trial Card as soon as you can, while we still have a good selection of Bonus Gifts.

M.F.

5-010116-0008

Your Free gift!

Go in high fashion and style with this matching Pull Purse

Fingerhut Corporation, St. Cloud, Minn.

A classic example of the direct mail offer. Illustration of merchandise, free offers, and a highly professional 4-page letter. Note little touches such as "Intended for the Norris family only." Pieces like this should be closely studied.

289

Agency: Adtron, Inc., Bloomington, Ill.

Mail order newspaper supplement of 6 pages by a nursery man. The supplement includes an order blank on the last page.

the state legislature and see your representative before the next election. Say to him, "Let me have five hundred dollars to cover the mailing, and I will write a letter that will bring you five thousand dollars in contributions." If you pull it off, he'll put his arms around you, hug you, and promise you the next available ambassadorship. (This is not quite such a remote possibility as you may think. We had a young man in our town, who since high-school days had been a nut on research. He figured out some ways to predict in advance how the vote would go. His system turned out to be amazingly accurate. Today, politicians on the national scene are fighting for his services. And a fella from Georgia got him!)

Stuffers. Many businesses that normally use the mails to send out their monthly invoices take advantage of this to enclose "stuffers"—pieces of selling material that get a free ride. Your phone bill, for example, almost always contains some material either selling a phone company service, or telling you something that the company wants you to know. Department and drugstores, in fact any business, can use its customer's invoice to include an added plug for its goods or services at a very nominal cost. Often suppliers themselves will provide the store with this printed material for free to help promote the sales of their products.

290

Who Gets Your Mail?

One of the most interesting facets of direct mail advertising is its ability—*through selective mailings*—to get your sales story into the hands of the specific customers whom you wish to reach. This is the direct-mail specialty—the ability to zero in on *exactly* the kind of customer you wish to sell.

Remember our earlier talk about market segmentation, and market profiles and their importance to your business? Well, no one is able to cut the slice any more accurately or thinner than the direct mail executive. Although costs are higher per customer reached than the costs of the newspaper and television advertiser, that differential is made up by direct mail's ability to get the advertiser's story into the hands of the people who are most likely to buy. A good "clean" list (as free as possible of persons who are deceased or have changed their address) is a valuable item. It is something that its possessor guards fearlessly, and something you will have to pay for if you want to use it.

How Mailing Lists Are Compiled

One of the most simple ways to compile a mailing list is to use the list of charge customers at your store. Manufacturers simply use the list of customers with whom they ordinarily do business. Note that, in this instance, you are not soliciting new customers but selling to already established customers. This makes your job a lot easier.

House list. If you should receive a letter from your department store advising you of a special "preview sale"—the store's established mailing list is being used. Often this is called a *house list.* The *stuffers* that come with your invoices are the same thing.

Response list. Another means of compiling lists is through response. If you enter a contest, sponsored by a local store, to win a 24" TV set, your name, taken from the entry blank, goes on the list. If you fill in one of the coupons often found on college bulletin boards, you can be sure you will wind up on someone's mailing list. If you've ever had the experience of getting a direct mail piece from someone and wondered, "How in the world did they ever get *my* name?" this is what happened: you put your name and address down someplace.

Credit cards. If recently you've been caused to wonder what your friendly Gulf dealer was doing peddling coin collections or something else by mail, you have to look only as far as the credit card in your wallet.

The tremendous growth during the last ten years of the use of credit cards has caused a revolution in the mail order business. Just look at the figures: BankAmericard and Master Charge have a list in excess of 60 million card holders. That's 60 million good credit people who can be induced to buy by mail. Sales through bank credit in 1969 accounted for $5 billion dollars. It is estimated that by 1976 this amount will have reached the staggering total of *$75 billion dollars.* In addition, it is estimated there are 200 million oil-company cards in circulation.

The great growth in the use of credit cards has not only provided mailing lists; the availability of guaranteed consumer credit has made it possible for the mail order merchant to really raise his sights considerably. Prior to credit cards, it was difficult to sell an item for more than $10.00 by mail order. (In fact that was one of the "rules" of mail order.) Today, as you may have noticed, it has become common to offer items for $100.00 or more by mail, *on credit.*[3]

List brokers. If you were able to find and inspect a copy of *Standard Rate and Data* for newspapers or TV, you saw the kind of book that exists for those who wish to lease mailing lists rather than use newspaper space or TV time. You may find a copy of this SRD book for mailing lists harder to locate than the one for publication and broadcast media. Not all agencies in your community will subscribe to this one, since they have limited use for it. Other means of leasing lists are also available to them, as we shall see.

If you come across the SRD directory for direct mail lists, inspect it. You will be astonished. Listed in it you will find brokers who rent mailing lists. The usual price is about $25.00 per 1,000 names. You can specify that you want to reach stamp collectors, or proprietors of pro-golf shops, or managers of restaurants with tablecloths, or people who make models from hobby kits. You name 'em, they've got 'em.

Part of the trick in selecting a productive list for your mailing lies in the creative imagination you use in the process of selection. For example, if you are selling a special water-resistant varnish for use on a boat, it is not too hard to see that a list of sailboat owners might be a very rich vein for you to tap. But what if you are selling subscriptions to a magazine such as *Natural History,* or *Scientific American?* What kind of list would you select to reach the most potential subscribers? Again, the lessons we have learned about market segmentation come in handy here. We must be able to *see* and *describe* our best potential customers.

---

[3]Quoted from "Direct Marketing: The Unknown Giant" by Robert Stone, Chairman of the Board, Rapp, Collin, Stone and Adler, Inc., Chicago, Illinois, and reproduced in the Direct Mail Advertising Association Manual.

Mail Order Testing

In a previous chapter we talked about testing and how few advertisers really use it as much as they should. Not so the mail order person. He *lives* by testing!

Louis E. Rudin, an authority in the field, said, "People ask me, 'How can I avoid mistakes and insure success in mail order selling?' My answer is simple. 'Go ahead and make mistakes. *But never make the same mistake twice.'* "

Mr. Rudin has a few words of wisdom for all who would enter this exciting business:

> If you're looking for a magic formula, some sacred incantation that will make failure disappear or will make success certain, I have news for you. There isn't any magic wand you can wave. Success in mail order is not done with mirrors. The truth is, it requires infinite attention to detail, practice and more practice, a constant seeking after perfection to be a success at magic or mail order.[4]

The fact of the matter is that the successful mail order specialists never stop trying, testing, experimenting, and correcting mistakes. They use many of the testing techniques you have already learned about in the last chapter. They keep careful and detailed accounts of their costs and their returns. Mail order merchants are continually examining their lines to determine if there is something else they can sell profitably. Experience has shown that *anything* can be sold by direct mail, from clothespins to cemetery plots—and successfully.

I once knew a couple of agency executives who decided to take a flyer in mail order sales. The product they chose was a rabbit's foot. That's right, that good-luck charm people carry around. They were smart enough to choose, as advertising media, publications read mostly by poor people. In other words, people who were down on their luck and could use a little help.

For a while their mail order rabbit's-foot business went along all right. They were doing a little better than breaking even. As you would expect, they tinkered with the copy and experimented with the media. Nothing they did seemed to increase their returns very much. But like good mail order people, they kept searching for the key that would unlock the door to significant returns. They finally found it.

One day, in looking over the letters that often came in with the dollar

---

[4]From "Never Make the Same Mistake Twice," by Louis E. Rudin, of Louis E. Rudin and Associates, quoted in DMA Manual.

they charged for the rabbit's foot, one partner noticed a curious thing. Many of the letters from these poor, worried people told how they prayed that their luck would be changed by the rabbit's foot. *Prayer*—that was it!

The two entrepreneurs made a slight change in their offer at no extra cost. From then on, in addition to the rabbit's foot, they offered a prayer (it was the Lord's Prayer printed on a small piece of paper). The mail orders increased significantly. Perhaps this operation was not as callous as you may have labeled it. Perhaps, for one dollar, the buyers also received a little hope in the package; a powerful weapon in the fight against despair.

Choose I   write on Paper Turn In

What Direct Mail Can Do for You

Most of us think of direct mail as something that arrives at our house asking us to join a record club, or offering shoes or neckties for sale. Not so. There are many uses to which you, as a business executive, can put direct mail. It can work for you as an *integrated* part of your marketing effort. The Direct Mail Association lists no less than 48 ways to use direct mail. Here are some that can help you:

Securing inquiries for salesmen. A letter offering a booklet or information can often pinpoint prospective customers by the response. Schools and insurance companies often use this technique to provide "leads."

Keeping contact with customers after salesmen call. For years smart salespeople have written a "thank you" note after making a call or completing a sale. It's a quick and easy way to reinforce the sales pitch or to encourage goodwill. Frequently used by car dealers.

Collecting accounts. Writing a letter of this kind is an art in itself. Never lose your sense of humor. Give the customer the benefit of the doubt—right up to the moment you hand the account over to your lawyers.

Winning back inactive accounts. A little time spent in composing a "Hey, we haven't heard from you lately, and we *miss* you," can often be very profitable. Everyone wants to be wanted.

Driving home sales arguments. Frequently a sales approach will include material of a technical or scientific nature that cannot be properly covered in a face-to-face encounter. A follow-up letter, listing additional facts, often helps.

Developing sales in territories not covered by salesmen.   Often used

by manufacturers searching for out-of-state distributors.

Educating dealers about your product.   Salesmen can do just so much with dealers and clients. This is a good way to put helpful printed reminders into the hands of people at the retail level.

Selling other items in line.   This is something no good direct mail person or retail merchant ever neglects. It lends itself nicely to stuffers in invoices.

open house   Register for Free 8×10 color portrait

Bringing customers back into the store.   This falls into the category of invitations to style showings or "preview sales" already mentioned.

Increasing consumption among present users.   A booklet of recipes is a good example of this.

Opening new charge accounts.   You'll have to construct your mailing list very carefully for this one.

wedding

Capitalizing on special events.   The birth of a baby is certainly a "special event"; and don't be surprised if the mother gets letters from a number of merchants offering diaper services, baby books, and baby cribs. Insurance salespersons also use this technique successfully by writing to recently promoted executives.

Building goodwill.   Such a simple thing as dropping a letter of congratulation on the anniversary of a customer's business can make very good medicine for you.

Capitalizing on other forms of advertising.   You can get a lot more mileage out of your current print or TV campaign by sending out tear sheets or pictures with a covering letter.

Research for new ideas.   Simply asking your customers for their ideas can bring more than goodwill.

Raising funds.   There probably are at least 20 organizations in your hometown that depend on letters to solicit funds. This is in addition to all the national organizations. Productive fund-raising letters are among the very toughest to do. They demand the services of a real pro. As has been mentioned, this kind of letter has become particularly important in political campaigns.

Announcing change of address.   Lets people know when you have moved, or changed your phone number, and at the same time it does a little selling for your product or service.

Stimulating interest in upcoming events. If you are having a sale, an opening, a "day," or any other happening, including the arrival of "Miss Cotton" at your store, you can let your customers know by mail.

Keeping yourself in the customer's mind. Letters of this kind are particularly useful for organizations that cannot afford to do a great deal of advertising, and whose services are often a one-shot deal. A firm of office decorators can be an example. Office redecoration is something most executives do only occasionally, and the decorator has no way of knowing just when the decision to redecorate will take place. An occasional mailing to a list of executives may put the decorating firm in the forefront of their minds when the day of decision comes.

Getting the "full story" to the customer. You may have a product or service with a fairly complicated sales story. What can't be completely reviewed in print or in broadcast advertising can be written in detail in a brochure with covering letters. This technique is often used by industrial advertisers.

Distribution of samples. If your product will fit into an envelope, this is a very effective way to get it into the customers' hands and create new users.

Securing names for lists. You can enlarge your mailing list by writing to distributors and retailers for names of prospective clients.

Costs of Direct Mail

Don't kid yourself. Direct mail is expensive. That is, compared to other types of media. It is expensive in reaching potential customers. It costs far more to reach 1,000 customers with a mail-order piece than it does to reach the same number of people with a newspaper ad.

But direct mail people don't figure that way. Their calculations are made in terms of *cost per inquiry* or *order*. The mail order advertiser keeps careful records of the number of sales produced by each mailing.

It is estimated that over 50 percent of the people who go into the mail order business fail because they fail to take into account all the costs of doing business. The experienced mail order executive calculates *every* possible cost before launching her prospect. Before she even licks a stamp, she knows exactly what percentage of returns she is going to achieve in order to break even.

Mail order people have a rule of thumb on returns related to costs (though these can sometimes vary widely).

- For items costing $3.00 to $5.00 the usual return is 2 to 3 percent.
- For $11.00 to $15.00 items, 1 percent to 2 percent.

- For $25.00 to $30.00 items, ½ percent to 1 percent.
- Inquiry producing letters usually bring a response of 10 percent to 20 percent.
- Questionnaires produce a response of 10 percent to 20 percent (Again, it depends on whom you're questioning. I've gotten 90 percent returns.)[5]

But note: As we have said before, the widespread use of credit cards has upped this figure considerably.

Writing Mail Order Copy

All the lessons you have learned about writing advertising in the chapter on copy apply here, and then some. Mail order copy really is most difficult to write. It doesn't ask you to believe something, try something, change your mind about something, or think about getting something. It asks you to *do* something—and *right now*.

The whole thrust of mail order copy is to bring you right up to the point where you will clip the coupon, or write your order and send it in.

As you know, successful mail order merchants are great testers. They never stop testing. That certainly goes for the copy they write. So, as might be expected, over the years they've uncovered quite a few basic mail order copy principles they live by and that take some of the chance out of their chancey business. Here they are. Some you'll recognize from the chapter on copy.

Talk about "you."   Mail order people never for a moment forget that they are talking to you; and that *you* are what you're interested in *right now*. "The minute you use it, you feel like a new person!"

Put captions under your pictures.   The space under a picture is a good place to drive home a point. We almost automatically look at picture captions. Notice that in this book I use picture captions to say something more than "this is an illustration of a retail ad."

Don't write over anyone's head.   Time after time, humans have demonstrated their ability to grasp *ideas*. It's the *words* that sometimes give them trouble. Nobody is asking you to "write funny." Just deliver all the facts in the clearest, simplest way you can. Keep the sentences brief, keep the words short (less than seven letters if possible).

Use subheads.   Go to your library and look at a copy of an old-time newspaper. The copy editors on these old papers weren't afraid of

---

[5]Russel Barton, (ed.). *Advertising Handbook* (Englewood Cliffs, N.J.: Prentice-Hall, Inc., 1950), p. 579.

subheads. They used as many as 10 of them. They told you what they
were going to tell you in the story, and then they told you. Be sure to get
as many of the important points of your story as you can up there in the
big type, where people can't miss them.

Offer something for nothing.   Years ago the mail order writers discovered that the words "Free" or "Free Offer" worked like magic. Even if
it's only free advice you are giving, or a free trial offer.

Don't be afraid of long copy.   Copywriters for nationally advertised
products are often limited by design layout or the client's belief in
"short, punchy, copy." Not so, the mail order writers would tell you;
they could go on for as long as they have something important to say.

*Make clear in the headline and subhead what your proposition
is.*   This is probably the most striking and interesting thing you have to
say. If you've got a product, and are confident enough to go into direct
mail with it, you shouldn't be shy about mentioning it. "Here's a tool that
will do 16 different jobs for you in your kitchen. For only 98¢ you can put
this 'Homemaker's Helper' to work for you."

Describe your offer in loving detail.   You don't just stop with saying
you have a "Homemaker's Helper" for 98¢. You describe, in minute
detail, *everything* about it from its superchromed tungsten steel to its
ingenious feature that removes the tops from jars with a twist of the
wrist.

Keep right on selling in the coupon.   Don't waste the space or hesitate
to give the final push. "Yes, I'd like to try, absolutely free for one month,
your new easy way of learning French. My name is. . . ."

Sales Letters

I'd like to quote to you what an expert, Earle A. Buckley, has to say about
sales letters:

"You *must* create interest, or your reader won't even finish the letter."

"You *must* create a desire for whatever you're selling, or obviously
you can't hope ultimately to consummate a sale."

"You *must* make your reasons for buying convincing, or the prospect
won't feel that it is to his advantage to buy."

"And you must lead him into some kind of action; otherwise his
enthusiasm will cool off before you have a chance to cash in."[6]

---

[6]Earle A. Buckley, *How to Increase Sales With Letters* (New York: McGraw-Hill, Inc.,
1961), p. 14.

Sound familiar?

Mr. Buckley leaves off the "attract attention" step, since by opening the letter you have already accomplished this one. His advice is the same "anatomy of a sale" that we talked about in our Copy chapter.

In a letter you have an added advantage—space. Many sales letters will run up to 250 words or more, and may be carried on a four-page folded piece of paper.

Buckley lists 17 points that he evaluates in estimating the effectiveness of a letter. They are very good check points for you to have in front of you when you are preparing a letter. Here they are:

1. *The appearance of the envelope:* If it is your business, you should already have a smart, good looking envelope. Note what other direct mailers are doing to grab and hold your attention with the design and the copy on their envelopes.

2. *The appearance of the letterhead:* Same comment as above; this, of course, is your calling card.

3. *Does the opening sentence create immediate interest?* Step 2 in the anatomy of a sale.

4. *Do you arouse desire in the following sentence by picturing benefits and advantages to the customer?* Step 3.

5. *Is your reasoning convincing? Do you impart believability?* Step 4.

6. *Do you have a worthwhile proposition to offer?* You shouldn't be writing the letter if you haven't.

7. *Does each sentence and paragraph lead into the next?* Are you writing the way a good copywriter should?

8. *Are you writing in the language of the prospect?* Again, as a good copywriter, you must write to the level of comprehension of your audience.

9. *Have you used a psychological appeal to a need, want, or desire?* You know all about them.

10. *Have you given the prospect enough information to act on?* This, of course, is a basic mail order principle. Give your present prospect the full story.

11. *Have you used a testimonial?* Not always possible. You recognize this as part of the "conviction" process.

12. *Does your letter contain a guarantee of satisfaction?* This is not always possible either, but include one if you can.

13. *Have you asked for some definite action?* Step 5 in the anatomy of a sale.

14. *Have you made it easy for the prospect to act?* This is the same principle as putting the coupon in the lower outside of the ad. The more convenient, the better.

15. *Have you given a good reason to act now?* This is part of a salesman's close, as you will recall.

16. *Have you read the letter aloud, given it to someone for criticism, slept on it, and taken a fresh look at it?* This comes under the heading of editorial discipline.

17. *Have you enclosed a folder, circular, or other brochure with your letter? Always try to leave them with something to remember you by.*[7]

These 17 guidelines of Mr. Buckley's are very good ones. If you can manage to meet most of them, you should wind up with a very effective letter.

Remember the letter from the banquet manager of the hotel that I quoted in this chapter? I said it was *not* a sales letter? Let's see if we can't rewrite that letter the way the banquet manager should have done.

> Dear Mr. Norris:
>
> They say that back in the '90s no one who was there ever forgot one of Diamond Jim Brady's parties. I'd like to make a "Diamond Jim" of you!
>
> The right kind of affair, properly run, can enhance your reputation and that of your organization.
>
> It's a grand feeling to have your guests come up to you, slap you on the back, and say, "Brother, you people really know how to put on an affair."
>
> We're experts in the art of running dinners, luncheons, and meetings smoothly and efficiently. We handle more of this business than any other hotel in town.
>
> I'll gladly sit down with you and plan for your bar and menu—all within your budget. You'll find us very flexible.
>
> A supplier has been good enough to present us with a case (sample) of imported champagne, which has been chilling for the past several days. I plan to have a few friends and customers in on this Friday afternoon, around five o'clock, to taste it. Won't you join us? No need to acknowledge. I'll have my secretary call your office in a couple of days to remind you.
>
> Looking forward to meeting you.
>
> > Sincerely,
> >
> > Ralph Jones
> > Banquet Manager

(margin notes: Interest; Bennefits; Action; Reason for Action)

WHERE YOU ARE

1. You are aware that "direct mail" or "mail order" isn't the quick and easy road to riches that some people seem to think it is.

---

[7]Earle A. Buckley, *How to Increase Sales*, p. 25.

2. You can differentiate between the various kinds of direct selling techniques that use the U. S. Mails.

3. You recognize the physical elements that go into the usual mailing piece.

4. You know what a "list" is, and how to go about getting one.

5. You are familiar with the "letter house" and the services it can perform for you.

6. You have learned the basic rules of writing effective mail order copy, and you should be able to write a result-getting sales or solicitation letter.

QUESTIONS FOR CLASS DISCUSSION

1. If you were going to choose a product to sell by direct mail, what would it be?

2. What do you think the political effects are likely to be of increased individual solicitation of campaign funds through the mail?

3. What, in your opinion, is the biggest problem facing direct mail sellers today?

4. Present to the class the most impressive mailing idea piece you have received lately, and describe in detail what the mailer has done to make his piece effective.

SOMETHING FOR YOU TO DO

You and your classmates are now in the mail order business. Get everyone in the class to buy equal shares, select your product, go through the whole process that you have learned in this chapter. See how far over the break-even point you can get. You'll be surprised how much using your own money will do for you.

Catalogue. Printed material containing descriptions, prices, and illustrations of merchandise.

Clean List. Mailing list that is free of addresses of persons who have moved, died, etc.

Cost of Inquiry. The total cost involved in inducing one reply.

DMA. Direct Mail Association—the trade body.

Direct Mail. Proposition that comes to you through the mail, and to which you reply through the mail.

House List. List of names compiled by a store or a company; usually composed of its customers.

Inquiries. Replies to offers.

Inserts. Material inserted between pages of a publication.

List Broker. Business that sells or rents names and addresses for direct mail use.

Mail Order. The purchase of an item by ordering it through the mail.

Response List. List of active customers.

Returns. Number of replies to an offer. Usually "coupon returns."

Selective Mailing. Mailing to a restricted list of persons, e.g., "Orthopedic Surgeons."

Single Order Mail Proposition. Offer that contains the entire deal in one envelope.

Stuffers. Extra advertising material that is added to a mailing of invoices, or the like.

Swatches. Small samples of material usually included in *Single Order Mail Proposition.*

SELECTED READINGS

Buckley, Earle A. *How to Increase Sales with Letters* (New York: McGraw-Hill Book Company, Inc., 1961). This is a practical and concise "how to" book.

Caples, John. *Tested Advertising Methods* (New York: Harper & Row Publishers, 1932). Old but good, by a master in the art of writing mail order copy.

Nauheim, Ferd. *Business Letters That Turn Inquiries Into Sales* (Englewood Cliffs, N.J.: Prentice-Hall, Inc., 1959). A very good book in that it will give you many examples of result-getting sales letters.

Direct Mail Manual (New York Direct Mail Advertising Association). This is a loose-leaf binder consisting of "Manual Releases" sent out to members. It's all pure gold. Written by pros for pros. Obtainable only through members, though I'm sure the Association (230 Park Avenue, New York, New York, 10017) will put your school library on their mailing list for these releases when requested.

Crown, Paul. *Building Your Mailing Lists* (Dobbs Ferry, N.Y.: Oceona Publication, Inc., 1973). Good little book for anyone who is thinking of getting into the mail order field.

Graham, Irvin. *How to Sell Through Mail Order* (New York: McGraw-Hill Book Company, Inc., 1949). A very complete textbook on the subject. By now it may be slightly out of date in some areas.

chapter fourteen

Retail Advertising

In this chapter we are going to look at a very different world of advertising. Retail.

You will learn of the special problems that must be met by retail advertisers.

You will see how, in many ways, retail advertising differs from the advertising of national manufacturers.

We will look at that unique "house agency," the department store advertising department, and at how it operates.

Some steps will be suggested by which the small local retailer can approach his or her advertising program and help make it operate most economically.

The various media used by retailers will be examined, and you will see what advantages exist for the retailer in each one.

When you walk down the main street of your town you are walking past America's big advertisers—the retailers.

Taken in total, retail advertising represents billions of dollars in promotional effort each year. Individually, compared to Standard Brands or National Distillers, they are not much; but in terms of impact within their market they are far more important—many of them—than the most promotionally minded national advertisers.

You need look no farther than your hometown newspaper. I think it will be quite obvious to you that if it were not for the advertising by the stores in your town, there wouldn't be any paper. The same thing applies to the radio stations in your city. Network TV, of course, is heavily used by national advertisers. But you can bet that hometown stations like to get all the retail advertising they can. Every day their salespeople are out pounding the pavement, fighting the other media for the local merchant's patronage.

This chapter will be important to you because the chances are very good that you may wind up in a retail job. For every job of a marketing nature in manufacturing or distribution firms, there must be 100 openings in retail selling. The farther away you live from the great centers of manufacturing, the truer this becomes. In fact, I'm not sure it isn't just as true for the big centers. Look at it this way: To support just one manufacturer's representative—say, of cosmetics—takes the efforts of **307** hundreds of retail salespeople, display people, buyers, and promotion and advertising people. Without them the line doesn't move; and if the line doesn't move, the manufacturer's representative is out of a job.

Moreover, as a knowledgeable advertising person, you have a greater opportunity to make a contribution than you would have almost anywhere else. As you will see, retailing has many problems, and retailers are not always as well equipped to cope with their advertising and promotional problems as they might be. There's a real chance for you to shine.

As you have learned in an earlier chapter, there is a separate kind of advertising that can be identified as "retail." You have seen an example of it pictured, and you have learned to distinguish it from "trade" and from "institutional" and from several other kinds of advertising. You have also discovered, in a later chapter, that there are several different kinds of operations called "advertising departments." Among these are the advertising departments found in department stores, and those found in chain stores.

So now you are already aware of some special differences between the way a retailer advertises and the way someone like Coca Cola goes about it. But there are a great many more factors that make retail advertising special, and we will now examine some of them.

Special Considerations in Retail Advertising

The Variety of Retail Outlets

If you will look in your morning newspaper you will see a great variety of retail advertising. Some of it will be in the form of full-page ads featuring women's dresses for a large department store. One ad might be quite small—a one column by 2-inch ad for a tailor who does alterations. You may also see an ad featuring a dozen or more items, with prices listed for each one. This carries the signature of a well known chain department store. Still another ad, near the "society page," may feature a new style available at one of the most exclusive women's dress shops in town.

As you see, there is not just *one* kind of "retail advertising," but *several* kinds of retail advertising. These *kinds* of retail advertising vary with the kinds of stores that run them. Look at the advertising again. In a number of ways, the biggest department store in your town is quite different from the biggest discount operation in town. You'd say, too, that the problems encountered by the tailor who does alterations are considerably different from the problems encountered by an exclusive dress shop that features high-style women's clothes.

Because each one of these stores is different, and because each has distinct and different marketing problems of its own, it follows that each has different advertising problems. And it also has different approaches to solving these problems.

As we have mentioned, the traditional city department store has its own advertising department. This separate department draws its character from the type of business done by this kind of store.

Department stores are concerned with selling a wide variety of products for which there is a continuing demand. Among them are housewares, clothes, furniture, sporting goods, jewelry, books, and a great number of other items. These are always competitively priced. Their styling is always up to date, and they are designed to meet the broad popular taste. Everything about department store merchandise lends itself to being sold *now* and in as great a volume as possible. Tomorrow may be too late. Tomorrow the styles may change, or the public taste may shift. When a store has 12 dozen of something in stock, those 12 dozen must be *moved out* to make room for the next 12 dozen.

Immediacy

The first thing you will notice about department store advertising is its immediacy. The product is on sale *now*—and you should come downtown first thing tomorrow morning to buy it. There is always an air of something special about department store ads, an element of news.

As a matter of fact, there are many shoppers, and not just *women* shoppers, who look carefully through their newspapers each day to see what is "new" in the stores.

Department Store Advertising Shows You the Product

This is not the glamorized photo or illustration you may see in *national* advertising but a factual, down-to-earth picture of the product *as it looks*. If a department store ad is showing you a woman's suit, the illustration is intent on showing each detail of the construction of the garment, the way it fits, and the way the designer planned it to look on the human figure. Of course the store wants the picture to look nice, but they are also aware that the practiced eye of the buyer will be looking for just such details and expect to find them.

Fashion illustration for department store advertising is an interesting field all its own. The young person who can illustrate clothes with a flair, and can give the illustrations a distinctive, immediately recognizable quality is always in great demand by department stores. For setting the "tone" of the store (something we will talk about a little later) the illustration plays an important part.

Department Store Copy Is Usually Brief and Factual

Department store copywriters seldom follow the "anatomy of a sale" points that you have learned; rather they place much faith in the attractiveness, need, demand, uniqueness, popularity and price of their product to make the sale for them. The department store copywriter concentrates on giving you the *facts*—all the facts—about the store's products. The copy wastes no time in getting down to the nuts and bolts of who made it, what it's made of, what its features are, what colors and sizes it comes in, and what it will do for you. But don't think that department store copywriters can't be just as clever, amusing, startling, inventive, and hard-selling as any of the Madison Avenue pros. (See Bernice Fitz-Gibbon's *Macy's, Gimbels and Me*, listed in the reading suggestions at the end of this chapter.)

Department Store Layouts Are Clean, Simple

No one I can think of uses newspaper space in such a prodigious way as does the department store. If you live in a city of any size, about one-fourth of all the advertising in your newspapers is represented by the big department stores. That's quite a slice. Department stores think nothing of devoting a whole page to the promotion of a single item (particularly a *style item*). This means that the department store art director is freed from some of the limitations imposed on the layout artist who is designing a magazine ad or a limited-space.ad in the newspaper.

The result of abundant space, big, simply done illustrations, short copy, and short to-the-point headlines, is usually an attractive and easy-to-read ad with plenty of white space.

The Department Store Advertising Budget Must Be Flexible and Productive

National advertisers, at the beginning of the fiscal year, usually set aside a definite amount to be spent on advertising. Their agency is informed of this figure, and this is what they plan to spend for their client.

Department stores, too, have budgets. But because their whole business is highly promotional in nature, they must be prepared to be much more flexible in the investment of their dollars. Special situations and special opportunities often arise in department store retailing, and sometimes the store must move fast to take advantage of these situations. As a result, department store budgets are continually under review.

Department stores anticipate various "events" during the year, and allocate their budgets to meet the needs of each event. Each year they know there will be a "back-to-school" sale, and a "white sale," and a special "late summer" clearance. So the department stores "calendar" their selling year.

The production of ads occurs at a far faster pace in the department store than it does in the more leisurely paced agency. Many department stores operate on a three-week advertising production schedule—that is, three weeks from the initial order to the appearance of an ad in the paper. I've known department store advertising departments where three weeks would be considered sheer luxury. There is a good reason for this limitation on the time to produce a department store ad: merchandise managers and department buyers want the ad to run at *exactly* the right time. They keep a wary eye on competition, and don't want to commit themselves too soon. Department heads also want to be sure of shipments. One of the most excruciating things that can happen to a buyer is to run a successful ad that brings the customers flocking into the department—and then find a shortage of merchandise.

Department Store Ads Tell You "How Much"

As you have noticed, nationally advertised products seldom have a price tag on them *when advertised by the manufacturer*; sometimes, though, you'll find a "suggested retail price." But department store ads seldom leave off the price. It's part of their promotional game. After all they are dealing with *shoppers*, and that means people who are looking not only at quality and availability but also the comparative costs.

Retail Ad Departments

The retail store advertising department is a unique development in advertising. It is an expression of the fact that retailing itself is different. Although many of the advertising problems that face retailers are the same as those of anyone else, there are a few that are peculiarly their own.

Timing

As we shall see, timing is one problem. This doesn't mean just getting the ad out fast; it means bringing the right item before the public at just the right time. If you can break your ads for lawn products on the famous "first day of spring" when suddenly the air is soft, and the sun is warm on your shoulders—you've got it made!

Knowing the Merchandise

Retail people live with thousands of different items. *Someone* has to know them intimately. Few retail copywriters ever have the chance to gain the familiarity with a product as does an agency person. In retail, someone has to know *all* the intimate facts about the new glassware or the new line of polyester slacks. It's the buyer and merchandise manager who know the facts and work closely with the advertising people to be sure that *they* know.

Knowing the Customers

Retail advertising department people have a wonderful advantage over the agency creative people. They can *see* their customers. They can stand in the aisle of the store and look at them, and they can stand beside them at the counters and listen to them. They can even *chat* with them. Most agency people would give a lot to have that retail-customer instant-survey sample. When the retail ad department puts together an ad, they can *see* the person with whom they are talking—literally.

Economic Considerations

The "house agency," as you may recall, came about because advertisers felt they could get their advertising done more economically by people employed by them and working within the company. In most cases it hasn't worked very well. Again, the reason is economic. Their company salary schedules prevented them from paying their creative people Madison Avenue salaries. But they found themselves competing for attention and sales with the best people in the business. Often they came in second.

The very nature of retailing and its special problems, however, have made the "house agency" the best setup for them. In addition to the considerations mentioned, directly placed retail advertising enjoys a special rate from much of the media. Generally speaking, the salaries paid to retail ad department people are lower than those paid to agency people. There have been some awfully good copywriters forged in the fires of department store advertising departments. They have gone on to great success in the agencies. But it's seldom that a department store will be able to hire away a first-rate agency person.

The Department Store Advertising Department

In Chapter 4, if you recall, we mentioned the department store advertising department. We were discussing the differences between the various kinds of "advertising departments."

In many ways the advertising department in a large department store resembles a well-staffed advertising agency. You'll recognize many of the jobs done in the department store's ad department. There are art directors, copywriters, production people, and media people. But there are no account executives, and there is no research department.

Creatively they do much the same thing as the ad agency. They make

ads for the newspapers and magazines, for radio and TV, and perhaps for billboards and car cards. It's the way they go about doing their job that makes them so different from the advertising agency.

We have already mentioned that department store advertising people work under pressure. The time limitation on producing ads and commercials is much more strict than it is when making ads for nationally advertised products.

Aside from *institutional ads,* almost all department store ads are single-shot efforts designed to promote—right then—the sale of a single product or category of products. The department cannot enjoy the luxury of writing a 12-month campaign and seeing it put to bed. Tomorrow always brings a new ad to be written for a new product. Neither does the department store copywriter have the time to put his or her feet up on the desk, stare off into space, and contemplate a variety of approaches and selling appeals. Five minutes from now, an art director will be screaming for the headline.

The department store people have devised a nice shortcut for their copywriters. They supply them with a "fact sheet" that includes every conceivable bit of information that writer and art director will need in order to prepare the ad. It is the information that in an agency is found on the production *job jacket,* and in call reports, memos, and creative platforms.

The fact sheet is a great time-saver for the department store copywriter. In addition to all the information important to the production department—space, closing date, and so on—it contains the outstanding selling points of the product. Sometimes it even contains information that should be in the headline itself. The department store people don't leave a stone unturned. If an ad says a product comes in strawberry, fuchsia, old gold, and puce, you can be sure that these are the colors —and the *only* colors—in which it comes.

Producing the Department Store Ad

It is necessary to compress the time in which a department store ad is written and laid out into as brief a period as possible. But *production time* of the finished ad is the same as for any other newspaper ad. The only way to speed up typographers and engravers is to pay them high overtime charges. In almost all cases the newspaper itself takes care of typesetting and engraving and matmaking. Proofs are rushed back to the store as quickly as possible. The final proof is okayed by the ad manager and buyer or merchandise manager, and the ad is ready to run.

Follow-up

As you have already learned, no one knows better and sooner whether his advertising has worked than does a retail merchant. The day an ad runs, buyers and merchandise managers anxiously count heads and

sales slips to see what kind of results they got from their advertising
investment. No one is unhappier than they when a travel-inhibiting
storm hits and literally robs them of sales.

Whenever a department store ad works well for a standard item of
merchandise, the store will run the ad again and again at proper intervals. It works, they say, why should we change it? When this result-getting ad is found, it also means that the store will be able to make real
savings in production charges and ad department time.

Department Store Institutional Advertising

A woman in her sixties stood, bewildered, at the foot of a long
fashion aisle in a newly renovated specialty store. Rock 'n' roll music
from a hidden loudspeaker assaulted her ears. "There is nothing
here," she wailed as she surveyed displays of bright knits, printed
shifts, and vinyl raincoats. The store had changed its image and left
her behind.[1]

In a sense, *all* department store advertising is institutional in that it
always tries to reflect the character and personality of the store. Often
this is accomplished through the style of the ads.

Brooks Brothers, for example, is a conservative, high-quality, high-
priced men's wear store with locations in several major American cities.
Their rigidly patterned advertising, which has maintained the same
style for years, certainly reflects the quality and quiet good taste of its
merchandising policy.

In addition to reflecting and building the personality of the store,
Brooks' advertising is also traditionally promotional. Each ad always
carries the price and description of the new item they wish to promote.
But another men's store in New York and its suburbs is Wallachs, with a
famous campaign which disdains "promotional" advertising. They seek
to project, through the style and content of their copy, a good-natured,
relaxed approach to helping men select clothes. These ads, for many
years written by Les Pearl, cheered the readers of New York's morning
papers.

You will also see the character and policies of stores reflected in their
slogans, such as Gimbel Brothers' famous "Nobody, but nobody, under-
sells Gimbels."

Fashion illustrators have a chance to score well with department
stores. The good ones are in tremendous demand because their unique
and eye-catching styles add just the touch of class the store desires to
capture for itself.

---

[1] Annalee Gold, *How to Sell Fashion—What Retailers Should Know About Women's Wear*
(New York: Fairchild Publication, Inc. 1968), p. 30.

Opportunities in Department Store Copy

315

Chain
Department
Store
Advertising

Some of the most interesting, provocative, and hard-selling ads anywhere have been written by department store people. There are advertising people working in the big-name stores in Dallas, Chicago, and New York, whose ability is so bright they would sparkle anywhere.

For thousands of other stores in medium-sized cities the story is different. Most of them can't afford those king's ransom salaries paid by a handful of famous-name stores. They, too, work under the terrible deadline pressure characteristic of retail advertisers. Much of the ad department staff is young and, frankly, some of them are underpaid.

One of those who look upon current department store advertising with a jaundiced eye is a fellow by the name of Stanley Marcus. We had better listen to him because he's the chairman of Nieman-Marcus, one of the world's *great* department stores in Dallas, Texas.

Says Mr. Marcus, "There just isn't that much that's new or innovative about department store advertising. It's in a rut, in other words." Too much of advertising is just plain boring. He says one of the reasons is, "There's just not that much talent around." He also blames merchandise men and buyers who "know little about advertising, and understand less."[2]

My personal gripe with department store copy—mostly department store *fashion* copy—is that it seems to have been written by people from another world. My wife never talks this way. My daughter doesn't talk this way. I've known jetsetters, and airline stewardesses, and lady wrestlers, and none of them talked that way. Maybe the girls say things like that when they're alone in the dressing room. If so, pardon me.

Chain Department Store Advertising

Stores such as J. C. Penney, Sears, and Montgomery Ward can't differ a great deal in the type of merchandise they sell. They go, of course, for more of a mass market than many of the department stores and usually stock merchandise in a lower price range. In your community there may be a department store that is far beyond Sears' or Ward's in price and quality. But you can be very sure there will be another store that is quite competitive with the big names.

Chain Ad Departments

You'll recall we distinguished between the advertising department in a chain store, and that in a department store.

---

[2]*Ad Age*, February 10, 1975, p.10.

Chain store people are not up against the gun quite so often as are the department store people. They are called on much more frequently to prepare full-page newspaper ads, spreads, and newspaper inserts of 10 and 12 pages. These ads and inserts are, in effect, catalogue pages. They show pictures of products, give prices and product descriptions. The ad department's problem is putting this all together neatly and attractively and getting everything in the right place. It is a prodigious pasteup job.

At this point the chain store departs from the usual department store advertising practice.

Chains, being chains, are managed out of a central office; it is here that a great deal of their newspaper, magazine, radio, and TV advertising originates. This advertising is prepared by top-flight agencies, and is of a creative quality that, mostly, the average retail merchant simply can't achieve. Some of their advertising is placed directly by the home office, and is run nationally by them for the benefit of all their stores.

When you see Colonel Sanders on the tube, plugging his chicken, you are watching an example of a home-office produced TV commercial run for the benefit of KFC's everywhere.

A great deal of the centrally produced advertising for the chains is supplied to the local chain store for them to run at the time and in the places to suit their particular need, thus the local chain store is able to run high-quality advertising at the *local rates.*

Store Promotions

In both the chain department store and the traditional department store, advertising is closely tied to department and product promotion, store decoration, and window display. In fact, in many stores all these functions may be wrapped up in the advertising department.

Discount Stores

Here you have to be careful to distinguish between the chain discount store—such as K-Mart (Kresge) or Woolco (Woolworth)—and the local discount store selling clothing, furniture, or appliances.

The Woolcos and K-Marts are the big chain department stores' answer to the competition threat posed by the popularity of the discount operation. Because they are the children of the same parent as the chain department store, their advertising is accomplished in much the same manner. Much of it comes from the home office, and a certain amount of local newspaper and TV advertising is done when featuring a number of items at discount prices.

Your local discount store goes about it differently. It doesn't have a home office to supply it with slick advertising. Neither does it have the volume to compete with the chain's big newspaper space. Some dis-

Agency: Zayre Advertising Department, Jacksonville, Florida.

This is the cover of a 12-page newspaper insert by a retail merchant, displaying literally hundreds of items for sale.

count stores are quite fond of locally produced TV spots. Many of them rely on catalogues that go out at regular intervals to a carefully selected mailing list. For many of them, this is just about *all* the advertising they do.

These catalogues are often supplied by one of several printing firms in the midwest. The art work, copy, and often the complete page, are   **317** supplied by the manufacturers; and the printer takes care of the cover design and printing. Usually these catalogues are mailed out once a year, and may be supplemented by smaller editions seasonally or for special sales events.

Supermarkets are also chains, as are franchise operations such as Seven-Eleven. Here, again, the pattern is the same. Exposure, high-quality ads and commercials centrally done, and the individual's local effort produced at home in newspapers, newspaper supplements, and so on.

The Local Individual Retailer

What we have left is the well known "small businessman." There are hundreds of them in your town. They sell insurance, plumbing supplies, bookkeeping services, and dozens of other products and services.

They are nongiants. They don't have any home office to supply them with newspaper mats and TV prints. There's no battery of artists and writers in the back room, knocking out instant copy on demand. Their advertising budgets wouldn't earn a second glance from the national media. Not so for the local media; *they* love 'em. The local retailers —they may not be big, but there surely are a lot of them!

What the Local Media Can Do for You

Yes, the local media—newspapers, billboard, radio, TV—all love you and want to help you. It's not hard to figure out why. Of your local newspaper's advertising lineage, about 40 percent comes from local retail advertising. Your local radio station, even the network-affiliated stations, carry as much as 60 percent retail. And your nearest TV station, you will find, has a retail advertising manager who is not paid to sit around and twiddle his thumbs.

Yes, the local media love you and hope to see you grow and prosper. No matter how small your market, or modest your business, you will find that they are eager to serve you.

But before we consider in detail some of the things you can expect from them, let us review some of the facts of marketing life that we have already learned.

What Do You Know About Your Market?

If yours is a *new* business, you must be quite sure that you have a clear vision of the profile of your customers and potential customers. Even if you have an established business, you must continually check up on your market. The world changes. Tastes change. *Customers* change.

If you are just establishing yourself in business, the local media can be of immeasurable help to you. They know the market in which they operate. Most of them have accumulated a great deal of information about the buying habits of people in your community. They know, almost on a street-to-street basis, who buys what kinds of products and for how much.

What Do You Know About Your Product or Service?

More particularly, what do you know about the needs, wants, and desires your product or service will satisfy? Here's where young retailers often get in trouble. They often come up with an idea for a product or a service that on the surface looks as if people would fall all over themselves to buy it. If you are smart, you will have talked and tested and surveyed cold-bloodedly in order to discover the answer to the question, "Do the people here really need me?"

Once the growing city of Charlotte Amalie on St. Thomas, in the Virgin Islands, ran ads in the mainland newspapers telling about all the services they needed. They wanted a car wash, and someone who could process and develop film, and another pharmacist, and someone who could repair small machines and appliances, and. . . . It was a good list, and it looked a lot like Main Street in your hometown. It was a retailer's dream come true; an established market just crying for attention. It won't happen that way to you. You will have to use every bit of motivation instinct you possess.

How Much Money Should You Spend?

Earlier we have suggested to you that one place to get a rough rule of thumb is from your trade association or the trade magazine serving your field.[3] They should be able to tell you what percentage of income is customarily set aside for promotional purposes by businesses of various sizes in your field. I'm sure you'll find that if you write to the editor of your trade paper, he or she will be able to supply you with the kind of information you need.

But this will be only a general, industrywide figure. There can be some very wide variations. What you want to know is, "What I can safely invest in promotional dollars, particularly if I am a new business?" The older and well-established retailers in your hometown have learned, by a process of trial and error, what they can do. But not all of them have learned this. Some are still flopping around. They buy radio for a while, and then switch to newspaper. Soon a billboard salesman comes by, mesmerizes them, and off they go into a full showing of boards. Unfortunately every time they flip, they flop; and they haven't as yet found the pot of gold at the end of the rainbow.

---

[3]See *How Much to Spend for Advertising*. Malcolm A. McNiven, (ed.). New York Association of National Advertising, 1969.

If you are a young retailer, this means that you will have to embark on
a systematic and regular plan for testing and recording. There isn't any
shortcut, except for the lucky ones. The idea isn't to find something that
will bring people storming into your store. The idea is to find a marketing mix that will bring you the greatest number of sales for the least
number of dollars.

The sooner you get that magic figure of "cost per sale" the better off
you will be, and the more surely you will be able to make your advertising investment.

To accomplish this, you need take but two basic steps: (1) keep every
ad in every kind of media, so you can measure response; and (2) keep an
accurate and up-to-date record book. After all, horse players spend lives
poring over past-performance charts. So should you. You've already
learned the techniques in the copy testing chapter—split run, coupons,
hidden offers, and others. Remember, too, like the big merchants, you
are looking for *when* things move best.

Retail Media

Newspapers

A glance at your morning newspaper will show you how much the
retailers in your town rely on this medium. It is a tradition to which, in
many cases, the other media are having trouble catching up. It is true, as
we said, that many people regularly look at the department store ads just
to keep themselves up to date on what is going on in the stores.

As a small or new retailer, you will find that you can get all kinds of
cooperation from the retail ad department of your newspaper. They will
make their research department available to you, and all the market
information they possess. They will provide you with free layout service, and submit several layouts to you for your approval. They will even
write the copy for you, if you will explain your selling points to the
representative. All this they can do for you even though you may be
running only a 3-inch ad once a week. They can also supply you with
some pretty good suggestions for the merchandising of your advertising—ways you can get more mileage out of your advertising.

Radio

We have already touched on the big benefit of radio for the retail advertiser: the considerable creative ability radio people are able to bring to
you in the making of commercials. These commercials can also be dirt
cheap. As often as not, the rep may do the announcing for you and charge
you nothing. Remember, too, that in radio you have a wonderfully
selective medium that can pinpoint the kind of audience you most want

to reach. Radio can be a relatively inexpensive medium. If you are
dealing with one of the smaller locals in a medium-sized city, you will
find that you can buy daytime spots for as little as, for example, $7.10 (on
a 52-time rate) and $7.65 for a one-time spot at WTTS, Bloomington,
Indiana.

Television

Many smaller retailers have been frightened away from TV because of
the supposedly high production costs. Recent developments, particularly in the area of video tape, have made it possible to do low-budget
commercials of a very respectable creative quality. Local spots are not as
expensive as you may think. At WPRS, Kansas City, Missouri, you can
buy a 30-second daytime spot for $13.00 and, when it is available, a
prime-time spot for only $16.00.

If you are retailing a product or a service in which appearance, design,
or color are factors, or one that lends itself to demonstration and has a
fairly broad market, you should look seriously at television.

Car Cards

If you are a downtown retailer in a city that has bus lines serving the
shopping area, car cards might be a very good buy for you. For example,
you can buy a 50 percent showing for a month in 150 buses in the
Jacksonville, Florida bus system for only $316.00.

The interesting thing about transportation advertising is that you are
buying "the last word" with the customer. There she is, comfortably
seated in the bus, on her way to the store. Mentally she is probably
reviewing her purchases and the stores she intends to visit. And then,
boom, she looks up and there, right in front of her eyes, you are remind-
ing her that she ought to drop by your store and see the latest thing you
have for sale. For a downtown merchant with lines that don't change too
drastically (say, a shoestore) transportation advertising can be very
effective and very economical. We mention "standard lines" because
this means you will not have to incur additional production costs involved in changing your cards frequently.

Direct Mail

You've just finished a chapter on direct mail, and you know the advantages and shortcomings. There is no medium that holds quite so much
potential for the small retailer as does direct mail or mail order. Remember, we mentioned the little "gift shoppe" in the New England town that
suddenly discovered it was merchandising nationally because of mail
order? Though the cost may be high per message, you are able to zero in
on your market very accurately through the use of mailing lists.

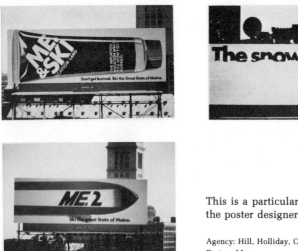

This is a particularly good example of
the poster designer's art.

Agency: Hill, Holliday, Connors, Cosmopulos, Inc.,
Boston, Mass.

But, remember: direct mail is *tough*, probably the toughest and most demanding medium there is. If you're going to get profitable results, your letter or mailing piece has to be good—very good. Insurance agents, franchise operators, and others connected with big companies are often supplied with mailing pieces prepared by specialists in the mail order field (of which there are not too many). But as a young retailer, you will have to tread with some caution in this area. There simply aren't very many people around who can do this sort of thing. If you can find one of them, cling to him. He could make you rich.

Dealer Cooperative Advertising

"Co-op" advertising is advertising supplied by the manufacturer to the retailer and is paid for by the manufacturer, either in part or entirely.

"Co-op" advertising is often part of a *deal* made by the manufacturer's salesperson with the retail store. "Mr. Jones, to show you how much we appreciate the fine order you have placed with us, my company has authorized me to give you an advertising allowance of five hundred dollars. We'll supply you with the mats of the ad, in addition to other promotion pieces such as brochures and floor and counter displays."

The salesperson will also make it clear that the company will appreciate it very much if the retailer will run a total of $1,000 worth of space. That is, the retailer will agree to pay for *half* the advertising. There are, of course, a number of variations on this deal.

When the retailer accepts the manufacturer's proposition, he is usually asked to supply *tear sheets* (page proofs) and copies of invoices as proof of performance before the manufacturer gives him his rebate.

With co-op advertising, you have to be careful not to violate the provisions of the Robinson-Patman Act, which has to do with discriminating between retailers in promotion advertising help.

There are disadvantages as well as advantages to dealer co-op advertising. It gives the retailer a source of high-quality advertising that he might not otherwise be able to call on. He also receives financial aid in running advertising with his name well displayed. If he is small his advertising efforts might otherwise be severely limited.

Some retailers wish they could simply have the manufacturers' contribution to use for advertising as they choose. This is especially true where a store carries numerous lines. They find themselves, with the co-op ad, promoting only one among the many.

Co-op advertising allowances are sometimes misused as disguised hidden rebates. The retail business is by no means in agreement as to the usefulness or the desirability of co-op advertising and its allowances.

Outdoor

Outdoor advertising includes not only the traditional "outdoor"—the 24-sheet billboards—but anything that appears outdoors that can help you sell. A great many poster locations in your town are already taken by the long-contract national advertisers—Coke, Pepsi, cigarettes, and beer ads. You should be particularly interested in picking up a few locations near your place of business.

Painted signs come in all shapes and colors, and there are specialists in your town who do this work. (Look under "Signs" in the Yellow Pages and you will find companies listed who do signs in a variety of materials for all kinds of locations.)

There are other forms of outdoor advertising, and you might look around to see what is available in your community. Benches at bus stops sometimes carry advertising, and it is very cheap. Some taxicab companies sell space on the back or the top of cabs. Trash receptacles have been known to carry advertising messages. Some of these can be difficult to find, but they may prove just the thing for you.

I suggest that you go back and reread the story of The Movin' Dude and how he solved his media problems. The Movin' Dude, a retailer of men's wear, with a very limited budget, had to face exactly the same kind of promotional and advertising problems you will face as a young retailer.

WHERE YOU ARE

---

1. You understand how the retailer's unique marketing requirements affect the character of his or her advertising.

2. You are familiar with the way local media serve local retail businesses.

3. You are now familiar with the workings of department store advertising departments. You know how other retailers can go about having their advertising messages created.

4. You know the factors to take into consideration before you launch a retail advertising campaign.

5. You understand the various media that retailers use, and the possibilities each one holds for the local retailer.

QUESTIONS FOR CLASS DISCUSSION

1. How many retail failures were there in your town last year? How many retail successes?

2. Does your spouse or friend have an opinion about the best retail advertising being done in your town? Who is it, and why?

3. Retailing has changed considerably since the days of the pack peddler. What do you think might be the next popular form of retailing in your community?

4. Define the most important basic difference between retail advertising and national manufacturer's advertising.

5. In your community, what would you consider a unique and economical advertising medium for a new retail store?

SOMETHING FOR YOU TO DO

There may be a very real opportunity for a new and different kind of retailing operation in your community. See if you can figure out what that business might be, where you would establish it, and what your policy might be, so that you might have the greatest chance for success.

Advertising Calendar.   A chronological list of advertising and promotional events kept by the store.

Chain Discount Store.   A discount type of operation that is part of a chain of similar operations, e.g., Woolco.

Coop Ad Allowance.   Money contributed by the vendor for retail advertising purposes.

Cost Per Sale.   Total costs involved in completing one transaction.

Dealer Coop Advertising.   Advertising that the dealer runs with the help (money, cuts, illustrations, etc.) of his or her suppliers.

Event.   Basis for a promotion, e.g., "Back to school."

Fact Sheet.   Information supplied to the retail advertising copywriter about an article that is to be featured.

Fashion Illustration.   Illustrations for advertising that feature fashion items—dresses, coats, etc. Correctness of fashion features is of utmost importance.

Local Discount Store.   Single outlet store with a discount policy.

Production Time.   The amount of time it takes to get an ad ready to publish.

Retail Fashion Advertising.   Store advertising (usually in newspapers) that features fashion items.

SELECTED READINGS

Charles, Edward M. Jr., and Brown, Russell A. *Retail Advertising and Sales Promotion* (3rd ed. Englewood Cliffs, New Jersey: Prentice-Hall, Inc., 1959.) This is a very complete book on the subject, and would provide any young retailer with a ready reference book.

Gold, Annalee. *How To Sell Fashion* (New York: Fairchild Publications, Inc., 1968.) This one zeros in on the problems of the women's wear business. Practical, readable, and published by the people who know *all* about women's wear.

Hower, Ralph M. *History of Macy's of New York, 1858–1919* (Cambridge, Mass.: Harvard University Press, 1942.) There are several excellent books of history of department stores and the men who built them. You ought to read at least one if you are interested in a career in retailing.

Robinson, Preston O., Robinson, Christine, and Zeiss, George H. *Successful, Retail Salesmanship* (3rd ed. Englewood Cliffs, New Jersey: Prentice-Hall, Inc., 1961.) This is not about advertising but about retail salesmanship. I think it could be helpful to any retailer, particularly if you are thinking of going into business for yourself.

Fitz-Gibbon, Bernice. *Macy's Gimbels and Me* (New York: Simon and Shuster, 1951.) Largely autobiographical by an irrepressible lady who came from a small town and made it big in retail advertising. Read it, you'll like it.

chapter fifteen

The Promotional Push

In this chapter we show you how merchants and manufacturers use promotional techniques to put an extra "push" behind their selling efforts.

We will look at the different types of promotions as they are carried out by retailers and by manufacturers.

You are going to see that promotion starts with ideas, and where these ideas come from.

We will discuss the major factors in a promotion, and how they relate to one another.

We will examine all the different promotional techniques and devices that can be used in putting together a promotion.

You will become inspired, I hope, to go forth and dream up your own promotion that will sweep the counters clean.

I must warn you now, before we get started on this chapter, that you may be entering an area of some confusion. Here's why.

When a manufacturer puts out a special effort behind the sales of one of his products, it's called a *promotion*. When a store is all geared for the back-to-school buying time, it's called a *promotion*. When a soap manufacturer puts a free tea towel in every box, he's going in for a *promotion*. And when you find a coupon worth 10¢ in the next carton of breakfast food you buy, that's a *promotion*.

Moreover, there is a multitude of things called *promotional items*. There are people called promoters (including the promoters of heavyweight boxing bouts) and there are textbooks written on sales promotion. In your college you might even find a separate course by that name.

Let me unconfuse you.

In this chapter we are talking about the different kinds of *pushes*—the *extra* pushes that retailers and manufacturers put behind their sales efforts *in addition to* the formal kind of advertising we have been studying. These pushes don't take the place of advertising; they *work with* advertising. No matter what form the promotion takes, advertising is usually an integral part of the effort.

Many companies spend almost as much on these *promotional pushes* as they do on their publication and broadcast advertising. It has also been demonstrated that without the extra promotional pushes, selling **329** can be far less effective than when "push" and advertising work together.[1] Moreover, "promotional push" is a game anyone can play, from giant corporation to the smallest retail store. It's an area that holds great promise for the local merchant. Often all it takes is a little nerve and a little imagination—two qualities, of course, that we should all cultivate.

So we will start talking about retail promotions in local stores. These are the kind with which you are most familiar. They are all around you right now, and you can check them out for yourself. If you work in a retail store, then I hope that by the time you finish this chapter you will be thinking up a promotional push of your very own.

Retail Promotions

Retail promotions are the most fun of all, because it is the person with the most uninhibited imagination who often wins the game. Retailers tell me there's no quicker way to promotion and pay than to establish yourself as a promotional idea bank. They'll love you, particularly if your promotions work. Once I had a student in a retail merchandising class who had a part-time job in a department store. Each morning we would all devote ten minutes in an effort to dream up a promotional idea for Yvonne. Our great day came when the buyer in costume jewelry accepted one of Yvonne's ideas, and they sold a ton of the stuff.

But if you don't happen to have a great promotional imagination, don't let that bother you. There are plenty of good retail promotional gimmicks around, and retailers are absolutely shameless about stealing them for their own use. In fact, really fresh ideas are rare. Most of what you see are variations on old themes.

The Idea

Good retail promotions start with great ideas. They are born when someone says, "What if the. . . ." Or, "Why don't we. . . ." Or, "Let's try this. . . ."

Once someone down on 34th Street in New York said, "Why don't we put on a parade this Thanksgiving to kick off the pre-Christmas buying season?" *A parade?* Ridiculous! But for that Thanksgiving, and for a lot of Thanksgivings to come, the Macy's Thanksgiving Day Parade will march down to 34th Street with umpteen million kids and their parents watching it. All the Disney characters will be in it, plus characters from the kids' books, plus floats and bands, elephants and camels. New York wouldn't quite be New York without it. *That's* a promotion.

---

[1]See Otto Kleppner, *Advertising Procedures*, p. 485.

Agency: Fawcett-McDermott Cavanagh, Inc., Honolulu, Hawaii.

This Hawaiian island produced a 4-color brochure by making tie-ins with several different advertisers.

The "Tie-in"

When you start thinking about a promotional idea, you should think of all the promotional *tie-ins* that might fit in with it. A *tie-in* is any other force or factor that you might add to your promotion on a mutually beneficial basis. Sometimes it is known as the "you-scratch-my-back-and-I'll-scratch-yours" technique.

Here's how it works. Let's say you are planning a winter resort fashion promotion. The first thing you should think of is, "Whom can I get to play ball with me who might help make my promotion more interesting and exciting?"

One of the first things you'll probably think of is a little promotional cooperation from travel agencies and the resort public relations offices. You pick up the phone and call the Jamaica Tourist Bureau, and say, "We're putting on a promotion of resort and travel wear. We have the use of one of the largest windows for the entire week. We could use any materials you can let us have for window and department decoration. We'll give you an exclusive on the window, and feature only Jamaica in return for your cooperation."

You will probably find that the Jamaica people will jump at the opportunity. A week's display in the window of a leading department store is a great publicity break, and it costs them next to nothing. You will also find that they can supply you with posters, resort brochures, calypso drums, steel guitars, and maybe even some white sand, sea grape, and palms.

Where Promotional Ideas Come From

Aside from those which seem to have been pulled out of the air, such as the L'eggs idea for packaging pantyhose, you will find that starting points for promotional ideas are all around you.

Holidays

Let's start with all the holidays. Christmas, Easter, and Thanksgiving are the obvious ones. Washington's Birthday and St. Patrick's Day are also popular. If you are a department store, the January white sale and the back-to-school time in late August are favorite times for promotion.

Events

Another very good place to hang your hat when looking for a promotion idea is on some local event. Your city's symphony orchestra may be putting on a membership drive—a ready-made tie-in for your promo-

tion. If your town is football-mad or basketball-mad, you can certainly
build a promotion around a let's-get-out-and-support-the-team theme. In each of these promotions, you'll notice, the tie-in would afford you lots of help with display material.

Personalities

A very effective way to build a retail promotion is through the use of some well-known, accomplished, or interesting personality. When an author spends the day in the book department autographing his or her book for each purchaser, that is a *personality promotion*.

Sports stars, either local or national, make good promotion figures if you are selling equipment or sports clothing. Here, again, you might have some excellent opportunities when your hockey, basketball, or baseball team is putting on its drive to sell season tickets. Just give them a table from which to sell their season tickets in your sports department, and they'll supply all the athletes you want to sign baseballs or show Johnny or Jane how to hold a hockey stick. Again, for the window display person, they will be glad to make available all sorts of equipment.

A great promotional gimmick for the kitchenwares department is the cook who gives omelet-cooking demonstrations—and lets the customers eat the omelets.

I know a store that used the London Town Crier. They were putting on a storewide promotion of British-made goods. Of course they tied in with British Overseas Airways Corporation, and got lovely pictures and posters from them. And then somehow they came up with the London Town Crier. He wandered up and down the aisles, costumed in his scarlet coat, ringing his bell and shouting store news. It added quite a bit of excitement.

Now let's hear *your* suggestions. What would you do, as a retailer, if your local high-school basketball team came out of nowhere and won the state championship? What would you do if your town was playing host to the annual chicken-raising festival? What if you are celebrating the centennial of the founding of your town, and all the men are bearded, and the ladies are wearing bonnets?

Sales

One of the oldest and most common forms of promotion is the *special sale*. Here, again, it is the promotional *idea* behind the event that will make it pick up and go. Apparently the public is no longer motivated simply by getting something a little cheaper than it used to be. The event has to be surrounded with an aura of excitement, if possible.

Of course you've heard of "fire sales." This comes under the heading of "My bad luck is your good fortune," and includes all sorts of disasters, such as rain and wind damage, and the night the roof blew off the store. Train or truck wrecks, or anything else that makes it possible for the retailer to give away his merchandise at but a fraction of its original cost, make this promotion possible.

A first cousin to the "damaged goods" promotion is the vendor of factory *rejects* or *overruns*. This is really a separate form of retailing in itself, and is fairly common in men's and women's wear. The retailer buys the distress merchandise at a slight markup, and passes along the savings to his customers. Somethimes the savings on really fine men's and women's garments are quite spectacular.

For a *sale* promotion, it is often customary to give the impression that (a) you have gone out of your mind; (b) have panicked; (c) fallen afoul of a terrible piece of bad luck. One of the most common devices is a variation of the "moonlight madness" theme. Usually this is a simple end-of-season clearance, but the promotional idea is in the name. The "moonlight" part means that the store is going to stay open until midnight, or until everything is sold. The "madness" implies that the store must be completely off its rocker to be giving away all its merchandise at such ridiculously low prices.

"Madman Muntz" was a very successful vendor of television sets on the West Coast. I'm sure, if you'll look around in your community, you'll find at least one "Crazy Otto" who is driving himself into quick bankruptcy with his ridiculously low prices. He's crazy—like a fox.

Closely related to this is the "I let my brother-in-law, the idiot, do the buying." The thrust here is that, through an act of utter stupidity, they have made a purchase of merchandise that simply won't sell. "Everything must go"—they will practically pay you to take it away.

Under the *panic* type of sales promotion we have headlines such as the "Business Has Been Lousy" promotion, or the "My Creditors Won't Take No for an Answer" push.

The Rules of the Game

We have descended the ladder, you may have noticed. We have started with the kind of promotion *you* will put on—clever, original, and honest. Then we came down to a point at which it may have occurred to you that there was no fire, or a dumb brother-in-law. This sometimes happens, you know, and the Better Business Bureau and several federal agencies are quite touchy about it. Since it's possible for a retailer to get into a peck of trouble with *too* imaginative a promotion, let's look at some of the do's and don'ts.

1. You must be very careful that the savings you represent in your sale are *legitimate* savings. If you advertise "25 percent off," it must be 25 percent off your normal usual retail price for that item.
2. You cannot advertise an article for sale at a low price when you don't stock *that* article but one similar to it.

3. Do not misrepresent the reason for the sale. If there is a "fire sale," there must have been a fire. If it is a manufacturer's closeout, that's what must have happened. In your town you may have seen stores that for years have carried "Going Out of Business" signs. This is not considered a legitimate promotion, since the company evidences absolutely no intention of going out of business.

4. If your promotion says that you are offering goods at "10 percent above the wholesale price," you may be called on to prove exactly what the wholesale price was for each item.

5. "Two for the price of one" must be two for the same price as one normally costs. Same for the "1¢ sale"; it must be priced at 1¢ above the *normal* retail price.

When you consider the number of "special sales" held in your town, and the fact that it is necessary to protect the consumer with legislation, it would seem to indicate that the effectiveness of this kind of promotion is being badly diluted. In fact, the economists suggest that there may be something called *diminishing marginal impact*.

This means that someone has been threatening to kill the goose that laid the golden egg. That's quite likely, especially in situations in which the customer has been badly burned or misled by illegitimate claims. But for the vast majority of honest retailers, the natural human desire to get "something for nothing" or to purchase a "bargain" is still a very strong attraction.

In our town we have a shopping center that every now and then puts on a Moonlight Madness Sale. By the end of the evening the stores have cleared their shelves of merchandise, and the aisles look as though Attila the Hun had just ridden through.

Display

A very important and necessary part of every retail promotion is the window and point-of-purchase or in-store display. A promotion that does not include effective and carefully thought-out display is starting off with two strikes against it. Some retail stores think nothing of spending more for their promotion displays than they do for the promotional advertising support.

Windows

Store windows have been called the "face" of the store.[2] You might even think of them as the reflection of the personality of the store. They reflect not only the kind of merchandise the store has for sale, but much of the character of the store itself.

---

[2]Charles M. Edwards, Jr., and William H. Howard, *Retail Advertising and Sales Promotion* (Englewood Cliffs, N.J.: Prentice-Hall, Inc., 1943), p. 520.

Certainly few retailers underrate the importance of their windows.

Just think—many of them have audiences or circulation that may be as great as the circulation of their newspaper. Intense rivalry and competition exist between retail stores in the creation of windows. In many large cities, at Christmas time people will make special trips to gaze at the beautiful windows depicting holiday or biblical scenes.

Most chain retail stores and department stores have a resident *decorator* or *dresser*. The dresser has a workshop in the store, and there he or she plans the windows and constructs the in-store displays. The ingenuity and "make-do" of store decorators is astounding. Using what to the layman appears as just some odd and beat-up scrap lumber, fabric, and paper, they can often transform a department overnight.

The decorator has a stock of male and female mannequins to rely on, as well as busts and legs and hands. In addition, there are certain kinds of shelving, brackets, and display holders that can be used. But what the decorator mostly has going for him or her is a boundless ingenuity and an encyclopedic knowledge of where to find odd things; for example, a ship's wheel, a fisherman's net, a bucket of clams, at a moment's notice.

Manufacturers, too, are aware of the importance of windows, and award prizes to the window dresser who comes up with the most interesting and attractive window display.

Earlier we mentioned the "tie-in." You can imagine what the right kind of tie-in can mean to the window dresser. Here the dresser is presented with a ready-made source for material to enhance the appearance of the window. In the case of the Jamaican tie-in, mentioned earlier, they would be happy to supply the dresser with everything from white sand to sea-grape leaves. Maybe they could even dig up a limbo dancer. Who knows?

Point of Purchase

Usually referred to simply as POP, point-of-purchase promotions can be defined as "all those promotional devices that appear at or are near where the product is purchased or paid for." Much of this material is supplied by the manufacturers.

One of the best places I know of to study POP material is in a bar or restaurant. The next time you are in one, you might play a game by seeing how many promotional pieces you can identify within five minutes. You'll find the list longer than you might think. Clocks, calendars, napkins, glasses, beer taps, cigar boxes, thermometers. . . . The list goes on and on. In retail stores, POP can be broken down into several recognizable categories.

Counter Displays. These can range from elaborate cutouts or posters to a simple arrangement of merchandise on the counter. In departments where there is an opportunity for the "related sale"—such as shoes and socks, or shirts and ties—the related item will often be placed on the counter. Small "impulse items," such as chewing gum and mints, are often given display at the checkout counter.

Mobiles. Any display that moves is, by definition, a "mobile." But what retailers generally mean is a *hanging* display piece. For a long time retailers had a tendency to leave untouched all that nice space in the store above the customer's head. Then someone, no doubt inspired by the Chinese mobiles that tinkle musically in the breeze, decided to hang a promotion piece from the ceiling. Many of them move, and are therefore eye-catching.

Catch-All Displays. These are first cousins to the pyramid displays. Both are frequently found in drug and food stores. The *catch-all display* utilizes a barrel, market basket, food cart, or some other kind of container. Often a variety of the same type of merchandise will be dumped, helter-skelter, into the same container. There is a nice little psychological twist here. The careless jumbling of the items seems to imply that the store is practically giving them away.

Carefully piled-up cans and bottles make eye-catching displays. But there's nothing a store manager hates more than a jangling crash that tells him one of his customers has brushed a little too close to the display.

Cut-Case Displays. These are packing units that are self-contained displays. By simple cutting and bending, the storekeeper is able to convert a shipping carton into a display unit. Retailers are happy to use them because they save them time, conserve shelf space by concentrating the item, and provide a colorful display of the items. Candies, tobacco products, and many other small items found around the cash register often use cut-case displays.

Display Stands. An elaborate, very desirable, and also more permanent kind of display is a stand shaped like a tree that carries a number of items on it. Often the display can be rotated by the customer. Bookstores often feature paperbacks this way. The L'eggs stand merchandising unit may be seen in many food stores.

This kind of display has several advantages. It is large enough so that, with the merchandise in place, it makes a good-looking unit. Because it is round and vertical, it manages to store a lot of merchandise in a relatively small space. It enables the retailer to take an unused part of his floor space (say, a corner of a department) and convert it into profitable use.

Department Displays. These may be attractive shelf units supplied by the vendor. A wine wholesaler, for example, who is the supplier for a retail outlet, will lend and install an attractive unit, suitably decorated with grape leaves, in which will be displayed his foreign and domestic brands of wine.

Shelf Dividers, Talkers, Extenders, and Loaders. These are, as the names indicate, devices that utilize the shelf space for display. *Talkers* carry a line of copy in the slot at the edge of the shelf. *Dividers* have pieces on which to display the merchandise at a favorable angle. *Extenders* can be fastened to the ends of shelves for more space. A *spring loader* holds merchandise in place by means of a spring that automatically adjusts the shelf as merchandise is removed.

Posters. These are familiar to you as the paper-display pieces that may be put up on windows or behind counters.

Advertising

Earlier in this book you have learned about a category of advertising referred to as *retail promotional.* As with a number of promotional terms, this one can be confusing. Retailers, and particularly department stores, regard all merchandise advertising as promotional advertising. They also differentiate their institutional, or image-building advertising. The kind of advertising we are talking about is the kind that advertises the *promotion.* This kind of ad can and usually does carry merchandise advertising. But it is an integral part of the promotion, and features the theme of the promotion.

One of the things you will do when you plan your retail promotion is to sit down with your advertising people and plan the ads that will *promote the promotion.*

Merchandising the Advertising

More mileage is obtained from advertising by promoting the advertising itself to the dealer and to the consumer.

Very often sales representatives who call on their accounts will carry with them brochures or presentations of the company's advertising. These presentations are designed to show the dealer the kind and the amount of advertising support the company is putting behind their products. The presentation will contain proofs of ads and story boards of TV commercials. Sometimes these presentations are quite elaborate. Companies often use slide-film presentation of their advertising programs, with a recorded voice making the pitch.

In the case of important accounts or groups of dealers, executives from both the company and the company's advertising agency will put on a complete "dog and pony show" in which ads and commercials are screened before an audience.

If you have noticed, in a retail store, a counter display that is a reproduction of an ad for a product, and that says "As advertised in . . ."

this is usually a service by the publication to the advertiser to enable him to merchandise his effort to the retailer. At the same time it gives the retailer another promotional display piece to help him.

A close relative of this kind of advertising merchandising is the "Seal of Approval" awarded by a publication to a product whose advertising it carries and that has been tested by them. This seal of approval is merchandised by everyone—by the publication to the advertiser, by the advertiser to the dealer, and by the dealer to his customers.

Dealer Promotion by Manufacturer

Let's leave the retail stores of your hometown now, with the kinds of promotion you bump into every day. We're going to take a look at the kind of promotion the *manufacturer* originates and plans for himself and his own products.

Promotion is a big item in the budget for many advertisers. For example, the great Procter and Gamble, with its many products, spent

A couponed ad from the manufacturer to the trade.

Agency: Stanley Advertising Agency, New Castle, Del.

about $310 million in 1973. Of that, $76.5 million was spent for promotion.[3]

The main idea in this mix of promotion, which we are going to examine, is to get, keep, and encourage the dealers' support and enthusiasm. You may have everything else; but if you don't have the dealers on your side, you are going to have a tough time. If you support the dealers, they'll support you—literally. So every manufacturer is out to make the selling of his or her product just as easy and profitable as possible. There's no better way to keep a retailer satisfied and cooperative. Let's look at some of the ways it is done.

An interesting kind of dealer promotion was once performed by a major oil company. It actually goes a step further than most dealer promotion. Here the problem was to *induce an action* that would lead to a sale. Gasoline companies have historically had the problem of getting the dealer and his help to *get under the hood* when you pull up to the gas pump. They don't want them to just *ask* if everything is all right; they want them to look—especially at the oil level. That's what makes oil sales, and oil has a good profit margin.

The big oil company's solution to the problem was to inform all its dealers that cars would be pulling into their stations with *golden dip sticks*. And anyone who pulled out and wiped off a golden dip stick would receive a reward of $25.00 on the spot. Oil sales *boomed*.

Point of Purchase Display

We have already talked about POP in terms of the retailers. If you will take a walk downtown and look into some of the drugstore windows, you will undoubtedly see a display piece supplied to the store by one of the national drug, cosmetic, or appliance manufacturers. Often these cut out lithographed displays are costly and elaborate, with moving parts operated by a tiny electric motor. They are designed to help the store sell, and to enhance its reputation. The manufacturer hopes that *his* display is good enough and striking enough to stay in the window for a long time.

Representatives from drug houses, food manufacturers, liquor distributors, and tobacco companies, loaded down with display material, regularly call on their accounts. There is often fierce competition to gain a window or a favorable spot in the store for the displays to get the other fellow's display down, and yours up.

Retail Clerk Cooperation

Manufacturers cultivate their dealers, but they don't neglect the dealer's salespeople—those on the firing line who are responsible for the ultimate sale. This is done in several ways.

---

[3]*New York Times*, March 4, 1975.

When the manufacturer has a new, different, or unusual product he will often send out representatives to train the store personnel. They will be taught selling technique, shown the selling points of the item, and carefully taught the ways to operate and demonstrate the merchandise.

Often the manufacturer will also provide sales incentives for all the retail clerks through sales contests and prizes. This is what is often called "PM'ing." (The PM stands for "push money.") By this device the manufacturer, through a ticketing arrangement, pays the clerk a certain amount for each one of his items that is sold. When you come right down to it, this means that you are paying the clerk a small "bribe" to push *your* product instead of your competitor's. Many retail stores frown on "PM'ing."

Special Shows and Demonstrations

The demonstrator who cooked the omelets in the kitchenware department earlier in this chapter *could* have been supplied and paid for by a big manufacturer of pots and pans. Skilled demonstrators of all kinds are often made available by manufacturers. The woman who sews fancy hems at a mile a minute on her sewing machine, or the fellow getting a carpet clean with a vacuum cleaner, may be one of them. Often demonstrators are also dispensers of samples and free goods. You may have encountered a young person in a food store who pressed a new kind of cheese or peanut butter on you and urged you to take it home to try it. These demonstrators are employed by the manufacturer.

Fashion Shows. A very popular kind of dealer promotion are fashion shows. In these, a designer or manufacturer will package an entire fashion show—models, music, fashion coordinator, and all—and send it to various accounts. Manufacturers will also participate in trade shows, such as "Boataramas." These are designed to gain new retailers and to keep the manufacturers' current customers.

Advisors and Consultants. A close relative to the demonstrators are the experts who are made available by manufacturers to the store's customers for advice and guidance. These are often used in the areas of homemaking, styling, decorating, and makeup.

Sampling. As a promotional technique, sampling is usually out of the question for all but the largest manufacturers of nationally distributed brands. It can be a very costly effort. I'm talking about "sampling" as it is generally conducted in a promotional effort. There is no reason why, if you run a cheese store, you shouldn't be prepared to slice off a bit and let your customers try it.

Sampling is often carried out by the big cigarette, cosmetic, or food companies; and on a very broad scale. You may receive your sample through the mail, find it hanging from your front doorknob, or have it offered to you by an attractive young person in a store.

Sampling constitutes a *forced introduction* that speeds up the rate of familiarity with the product. It seems to be at its most effective where a new taste or use are concerned.

Aside from its costliness, sampling has another drawback—it discloses your hand to your competitors. There have been cases where a small competitor has closely observed the sampling, seen the way the wind was blowing, and beaten the sampler into the national market with a similar version of the product.

Dealer Co-Op Advertising

In our chapter on retailing you have already learned how manufacturers will supply their dealers with ready-made ads in mat form. They also make deals in which the manufacturer, on proof of performance, will assume all or part of the cost of the advertising.

Manufacturers are very generous in supplying dealers with cuts, engravings, and photographs of their merchandise for the dealer's use in putting together his own ad. When you see in your newspaper a full-page ad done by one of the big chain merchandise stores, you can be sure that most of the illustrations were supplied to the store's ad department by the manufacturer.

The dealer can get a great deal of subsidiary advertising material from his or her suppliers. These may range from elaborate *slide-film presentation* to *direct mail material*. The latter might be something as simple as an *envelope stuffer* that can be sent out in the same envelope as the invoice, or an elaborate brochure.

Many dealers who are specialists, but who carry the lines of a number of manufacturers, will receive *catalogue sheets* from them. A dealer specializing in school furniture, for example, will have on his desk a bound volume illustrating all the lines he carries. These sheets are almost always on glossy paper and feature fine color photography.

Consumer Promotion by Manufacturer

Often, in order to stimulate the sale of his product, a manufacturer will promote directly to the consumer. Just as with his national advertising, he is using devices that will raise the demand for his product generally throughout his entire marketing area. It will be reflected, of course, in retail sales.

There is an important exception to this manufacturer-consumer promotion, however, and you are so familiar with it that we will look at it first.

Trading Stamps

The trading stamp promotional device is not handled by the manufacturer, but by *trading stamp companies who sell their services* to the company and its retail outlets. You have collected trading stamps in service stations, in chain food stores, and in other retail outlets. Trading stamps seem to appeal to the collector's instinct in all of us. Psychologically, there seems to be a lot of satisfaction in carefully keeping your books of stamps and finally trading them in for a toaster or a set of dishes.

Trading stamps are controversial. Some retail outlets use them and promote them; others won't have them around the place. But although most consumers are aware that the retailer isn't exactly "giving" them anything, many still enjoy the fun of collecting. Maybe some of them even get "hooked" on the idea.

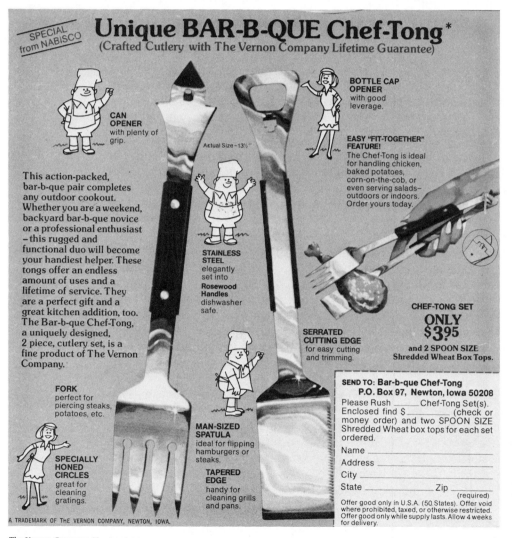

SPECIAL from NABISCO

Unique BAR-B-QUE Chef-Tong*
(Crafted Cutlery with The Vernon Company Lifetime Guarantee)

CAN OPENER with plenty of grip.

Actual Size–13½"

BOTTLE CAP OPENER with good leverage.

EASY "FIT-TOGETHER" FEATURE! The Chef-Tong is ideal for handling chicken, baked potatoes, corn-on-the-cob, or even serving salads—outdoors or indoors. Order yours today.

This action-packed, bar-b-que pair completes any outdoor cookout. Whether you are a weekend, backyard bar-b-que novice or a professional enthusiast – this rugged and functional duo will become your handiest helper. These tongs offer an endless amount of uses and a lifetime of service. They are a perfect gift and a great kitchen addition, too. The Bar-b-que Chef-Tong, a uniquely designed, 2 piece, cutlery set, is a fine product of The Vernon Company.

STAINLESS STEEL elegantly set into **Rosewood Handles** dishwasher safe.

SERRATED CUTTING EDGE for easy cutting and trimming.

CHEF-TONG SET
ONLY $3.95
and 2 SPOON SIZE Shredded Wheat Box Tops.

FORK perfect for piercing steaks, potatoes, etc.

SPECIALLY HONED CIRCLES great for cleaning gratings.

MAN-SIZED SPATULA ideal for flipping hamburgers or steaks.

TAPERED EDGE handy for cleaning grills and pans.

A TRADEMARK OF THE VERNON COMPANY, NEWTON, IOWA.

SEND TO: Bar-b-que Chef-Tong
P.O. Box 97, Newton, Iowa 50208

Please Rush _____ Chef-Tong Set(s). Enclosed find $_____ (check or money order) and two SPOON SIZE Shredded Wheat box tops for each set ordered.

Name _____
Address _____
City _____
State _____ Zip _____
(required)
Offer good only in U.S.A. (50 States). Offer void where prohibited, taxed, or otherwise restricted. Offer good only while supply lasts. Allow 4 weeks for delivery.

The Vernon Company, Newton, Iowa.

Back panel of spoon-size Shredded Wheat carton with a self-liquidating premium offer. Note that the manufacturer of the item gets a good advertising break.

Premiums

The premium promotional device has been around for a long, long time. Your granddad probably collected pictures of baseball stars that came with his favorite candy and traded them with his friends. If you have ever found a tin whistle in a Cracker Jack box, *that* was a premium. Same thing when your mother discovers a dish towel in her box of soap.

A premium, of course, is that little *extra* something that comes with the purchase and makes it just that much more attractive. It's a little added inducement to *buy.*

Frequently premiums are associated with the product with which they come, such as the soap and the towel. Others, particularly where kids are concerned—as with breakfast foods or candies—are anything the manufacturer thinks may strike a youngster's fancy.

Self-Liquidating Premiums and Direct Premiums

Very often premiums are tied into proof-of-purchase. You send in so many labels or box tops and in return get your premium. There may be a small cash requirement along with the proof of purchase "to cover cost of mailing, packaging, handling," and so on. This may be a *self-liquidating* deal in which the manufacturer recovers the cost of the premium.

Direct Premiums. These you receive directly at the time of purchase, such as the magic ring in the box of Post Toasties. Direct premiums can take several forms: they can be *in the package,* such as the towel we mentioned; they can be *attached to the package,* such as a free toothbrush with a tube of toothpaste; and sometimes the premium is the package itself. Producers of bottled goods will make an especially attractive bottle that can be converted into a lamp. Food manufacturers often design their packages to be reusable as containers or drinking glasses.

Come-Back Premiums. One of the very best ways to make a premium work hard for you is to have one that almost *forces* the consumer to return for more. This is often accomplished by offering sets of items, such as steak knives or juice glasses. After all, what can you do with *three* steak knives? So the consumer keeps purchasing the item with the premium until the set is completed.

Here are some suggestions about the use of premiums from the people who know more about it than anyone else—the Premium Advertising Association:[4]

---

[4]As quoted in Kleppner, *Advertising Procedure,* p. 496.

1. Give the complete specifications about your premium in the advertising. Give sizes, colors, and any other details that will help to visualize what you are offering.
2. Deliver premiums as quickly as possible. This applies especially to children's premiums.
3. If you charge anything at all for your premiums, be sure that your customer will feel that his money was well spent.
4. Be sure that premiums offered to children are such as to have the approval of their parents.
5. If in order to get a premium it is necessary that a coupon must be filled in, provide room enough for writing the average name and address.

Coupons. Coupons can either accompany the item, or appear as part of newspaper ads. The package coupons may have a value toward the next purchase; or, like the trading stamps, may be redeemable for merchandise. If you will look at the food ads in your paper, you will no doubt find several coupons entitling the bearer to a discount when purchasing a particular item. Stand in almost any fried-chicken place between 5:00 and 6:00 P.M. and you'll see plenty of people presenting their clipped-out coupons with their fried-chicken orders.

Contests and Sweepstakes

One of the greatest sweepstakes in the world is the Irish Hospital Sweepstakes. It raises millions of dollars each year. Manufacturers use our dreams of sudden riches to help them promote. Again, to a great extent the success of this promotion hinges on the ingenuity of the idea behind it.

Contests are much more fun. There is an element of skill and the spirit of competition. When it comes to prizes, the wilder the better. Contests can range all the way from guessing the number of pennies in a jar, or naming a puppy dog, to solving a whole set of puzzles. Sometimes the prizes are simply wonderful, such as three nights on the town—all expenses paid—with the movie star of your choice; or an uninhabited tropical island paradise. And have you seen the one where you get to take home all the groceries you can pile in a shopping cart in 3½ minutes?

Often manufacturers can get some good marketing ideas from these contests, such as recipes or new uses for their products. I once attended the annual fair of the Delmarva (Delaware, Maryland, Virginia) Poultrymen's Association. (I think you can guess what they were promoting.) As part of the week-long fair, there was a chicken cooking contest that had been heavily promoted through homemakers' magazines and newspapers for six months prior to the fair.

For the fun of it, I cut out one of the entry coupons and sent it in with my chicken recipe. Thousands of entries arrived from all over the world, but somehow I made the finals. They were held in the high-school gym, next to the Fair Ground in, I think, Laurel, Delaware. The organization supplied the chicken; you brought everything else. There we were, on the big day of the finals, cooking up a storm, bending over hot stoves, stirring, measuring. I couldn't believe my ears when the judges announced *my* name as one of the winners.

In this kind of promotion there's a lot of back-scratching done, too. Many prizes are contributed by local merchants; as a result, they get a free publicity ride in the program.

Legal Problems in Sweeps and Contests

Before you plan a sweepstake or contest promotion, it would be a very good idea to sit down with a lawyer who is familiar with the *Federal Trade Commission's* rules and regulations, particularly if you are operating on the local level. You can save yourself some grief. When the big national advertisers put on a contest they usually retain someone who will conduct the entire operation for them, guaranteeing complete fairness and legality. Your state, and indeed your community, may have laws of their own pertaining to sweeps and contests.

Here is some information the FTC requires that you disclose in your ad in a "clear and conspicuous manner."

1. The exact number of prizes available in each category and the odds of winning each prize. If the prizes are worth $25.00 or more, this information must be revised each week after the game has been running 30 days.
2. The geographic area covered by the game.
3. The total number of retail outlets participating in the game.
4. The scheduled termination date of the game.[5]

Putting It All Together

In Chapter 8 we discussed the way in which the agency production department keeps everything straight and on schedule by means of a job jacket. We talked about management tools known as Gantt charts, and PERT systems—a scheduling of "events" so that all the various elements in a job get done at the proper time.

Much of the same thing must happen when you plan a promotion. Every single element in your promotion must be carefully thought out, down to the last detail, and *scheduled* so that everything is in its proper place when the curtain goes up on your event.

---

[5]As quoted in Mandell, *Advertising*, p. 597.

When your big kitchenwares promotion is all set to open, and the person who cooks the omelets is decked out in a chef's apron, ready to go, and it is discovered that someone either forgot or was never asked to order the eggs—I think you can see what I mean.

When you plan a promotion, make yourself a flow chart, and be sure that every "event" in your promotion is given a starting and a completion date. Don't leave out anything, because everything is interdependent: the merchandise, the store window, the samples, the displays, the "tie-ins," the advertising, the salespeople, and who's going to the airport to meet the person who cooks the omelets, and who's going to make the hotel reservation and confirm it. . . .

Lots of luck.

WHERE YOU ARE

---

1. You now know what a promotion is, and how you go about getting the ideas on which promotions may be based.

2. You recognize the difference between promotions put on by retail merchants, by manufacturers in support of their dealers, and by manufacturers promoting products to the public on behalf of their dealers.

3. You understand how cooperative advertising works.

4. You know the part played in promotion by windows, store decoration, and point-of-purchase displays.

5. You are familiar with the manner in which various promotional techniques may be used, such as demonstrators, shows, consultants, and other special events.

6. You know about contests and sweepstakes, and some of the rules governing their use.

7. You have seen the importance of coordination and scheduling in the planning of a promotion.

QUESTIONS FOR CLASS DISCUSSION

---

1. What is the most interesting and original store promotion you have seen lately? Describe it, and tell why you think it was good.

2. The circus is coming to your town. If you were a local merchant, name the ways you could "tie-in" with the circus for a store promotion.

3. Have you ever entered a contest promoted by a manufacturer? What is your opinion of contests as a promotional device?

4. Do you save trading stamps? When you open your retail store, will you offer trading stamps or not? Defend your position.

5. Do you sample new products when they come on the market? Have you switched from one brand to another, as a result of this sampling?

SOMETHING FOR YOU TO DO

Select a type of local retail store that is in a business that interests you. Dream up a promotional idea for the owner.

Put down in detail each step and each device to be used in the promotion. Show a complete schedule for each "event."

Take your promotional plan to the merchant, and offer it to him or her in return for money or merchandise.

KEY WORDS AND PHRASES

Catch-all Display. Sometimes called a "jumble display." Items are thrown together helter-skelter in a box or basket.

Come-back Premium. A premium whose nature impels the buyer to seek to get more of same. A set of glasses, for instance.

Consultant. Adviser who offers guidance in the use of a piece of merchandise (bridal advisers or consultants on home decoration).

Contests. Entrants (usually as the result of having made a purchase) are awarded prizes for a successful performance.

Counter Display. Promotion piece that stands on store counter.

Cut-case Display. Shipping container that is so constructed that it can be made into a display piece.

Department Display. Display constructed within a particular part of the store.

Display.   A promotional device or arrangement.

Display Stand.   Permanent piece constructed so that merchandise can be displayed on it.

Dresser (Decorator).   Person who is responsible for building, designing, and placing store and window displays.

Extenders.   Display pieces that can be attached to ends of store shelves.

Fashion Show.   Display of garments using live models and a "talker."

Loader.   Display with a spring that holds the merchandise in place as each item is removed.

Mannequin.   A figure or model on which merchandise can be displayed. Full body, torso, head, arm, etc.

Manufacturer's Consumer Promotion.   The maker promotes his merchandise directly to the ultimate consumer.

Manufacturer's Dealer Promotion.   The manufacturer promotes his goods to retail merchant.

Merchandising of Advertising.   The reproductions of the advertising are adapted to display or promotional pieces.

Mobiles.   Hanging movable promotional pieces usually suspended from ceiling of store.

Point-of-Purchase.   Display at the place or department where the transaction will take place.

Poster.   Printed piece for window or back-counter display.

Premium, Direct.   Premium that comes with the merchandise.

Premium, Self-liquidating.   Premium that recovers its original cost in the transaction.

Promotion.   Any activity that helps to sell an item.

Promotional Item.   Pieces used in a promotion.

Rejects.   Merchandise that has not passed inspection or has been refused for some reason.

Retail Clerk Cooperation.   Means by which more support from the sales personnel of the store may be gained for an item.

Retail Promotion.   Activity at the retail level.

Sale.   An event at which merchandise is offered at reduced prices.

Sampling.   A promotional method by which consumers are offered an opportunity to try the merchandise free.

Shelf Divider.   Device that can be used to display shelf merchandise at a good angle.

Shows and Demonstrations.   Displays of the product in use.

Sweepstakes.   Another form of contest, usually not requiring skill.

Talker.   Brief copy inserted in slot on leading edge of shelf.

Tie-in. Promotions in which organizations or their merchandise are used cooperatively to each one's benefit.

Trading Stamps. Stamps that are given to the purchaser in proportion to the amount of the sale.

SELECTED READINGS

Tillman, Rollie, and Kirkpatrick, C. A. *Promotion-Persuasive Communication in Marketing* (Homewood, Ill.: Richard D. Irwin, Inc., 1968). This is a standard and popular text on the broad field of promotion. See particularly Part V, "Elements of Persuasive Sales Promotion," and Part VI, "Management of the Promotion Program."

Marcus, Stanley. *Minding the Store* (Boston, Mass., Little, Brown, 1974). Every retailer in America will eat this one with a spoon. If you are a merchant, or about to become a merchant, you shouldn't miss this story about one of the world's great department stores.

Manger, Emily M. *Modern Display Techniques* (New York: Fairchild Publications, Inc., 1964). Excellent and complete work on the subject, particularly suited to the small retail establishment.

Kasper, Karl. *Shops and Showrooms—An International Survey* (New York: Frederick A. Praeger, 1967). The emphasis here is on the big interiors. Good idea source.

Engel, James F., Wales, Hugh G., and Warshaw, Martin R. *Promotional Strategy* (Homewood, Ill.: Richard D. Irwin, Inc.). See Part 1, "Problem Analysis," for a good exposition of the preliminary work that must be done in promotion planning.

chapter sixteen

Industrial and

Agricultural Advertising

In this chapter we shall look at some advertisers who
have a different set of problems. They are the people
who make things for agriculture and industry.

You will see how their problems differ from the
problems of those who direct their efforts toward the
consumer market.

Specific areas of promotional activity in the farm-
industrial field will be examined, and we will make
suggestions about what contributions you, as an
advertising executive, might make in this field.   **351**

When in the very bloom of my youth, I was a thirty-five-dollar-a-week cub copywriter, I worked for one of the World's Great Advertising Agencies. They had one of the World's Great Petroleum Accounts. I wrote the industrial advertising for that account. All of it. Does that tell you something?

The fact of the matter is that on Madison Avenue, among the "100 biggest agencies," an industrial or farm account is as rare as the Whooping Crane. There is nothing particularly sinful about this. It's just another peculiarity of our business. The reason, of course, is economics. It often takes just as much effort to handle a $300,000-a-year industrial account (and sometimes a good deal more) than it does to handle a $3 million consumer account. It would take an awful lot of farm and industrial accounts to pay the salaries demanded by big agency writers, account executives, and art directors.

The economics of the thing work the other way too. It's hard to make it big on Madison Avenue when your reputation is based on the smashing campaign you have just done for the Acme Screw and Bolt Company. What you go to sleep dreaming about is that one Big Chance at a national TV spot for a consumer product that is going to establish your reputation—and your fortune.

If the top agency's big consumer account happens to do some industrial advertising (as mine did) they'll be taken care of, if for no other **353** reason than to keep the opposition from getting its nose under the tent. Very seldom will one of the resident copy geniuses write the ads, though; usually these are given to the younger people. And great training it is, too, as we shall see.

There are several very good big-city agencies that for years have specialized in industrial accounts, but they are the exceptions. Unless the accounts are quite large, or come with a nice fee attached—which most of them do not—Madison Avenue leaves farm and industrial advertising strictly alone.

Not so with the other 95 percent of the advertising business—let us say everything west of 8th Avenue, New York. Out *there* farm and industrial advertising is a way of life. Throughout the country there are hundreds and hundreds of agencies whose very existence depends on the way they handle accounts whose billing may range from $200.00 a month to $500,000 a year (one of the *big* ones).

Take a look at the client list for almost any local or regional agency, and I think you'll know what we are talking about. Here's Conley, Knollin, and Strain, of San Francisco. Their clients include manufacturers of gas cylinders, solar glare and heat controls, commercial cooking equipment, incubators and hatchers, and pipe line and process pumps.

Ray Cooley and Associates, of Houston, Texas, handle sound and vibration control equipment, water pollution equipment, gas detectors, industrial kilns, and laboratory instruments.

One more, just so you get the idea: Juhl Advertising Agency of Elkhart, Indiana. They do advertising and promotion for pressure-sensitive tapes, pressure and temperature gauges, school and office furniture, and equipment for metal casting and pouring.

All this should come as no surprise to you when you realize that the largest number of advertising accounts in the U.S. falls into the farm and industrial category, with only a small percent being classified as non-retail consumer accounts. Understand: we are talking about the number of *accounts*, not promotional dollars.

This fact carries a lot of significance for you as a student and as a young business executive. It means that when you get mixed up in advertising, whether at the agency or at the client level, the chances are better than even that you will become involved with advertising problems either farm or industrial in nature.

Maybe you'd like to hear it from the horse's mouth. Here is the creative director of a relatively small West Coast agency speaking:

I hope your text will point out that in the "real world," outside New York and Chicago, agencies face creative challenges far more important than coming up with a catchy slogan or some dazzling modern art work. Smaller agencies are concerned with making the most of their client's limited budgets—creating messages that sell first, and entertain second. We are faced with the problem of getting four-color effects on two-color budgets, with creating industry TV spots using

MIXER FEEDER

1200-B

Proven in dairy and feedlot. BJM has a Mixer-Feeder designed and engineered to match your feeding requirements. Precision "on the go" mixing of the total ration cuts feeding time, saves labor costs, and increases profits. The BJM 1200-B Mixer-Feeder is the answer for dairies, feedlots, farms and ranches without mill mixing facilities. BJM has the biggest, fastest discharge in the field! Discharge controls are mounted in the cab for easy release of the exact amount of feed in one pass. BJM offers a choice of four Mixer-Feeder models with the widest variety of optional equipment anywhere. See page 11 for specifications and optional equipment.

Optional Electric Clutch Drive. Allows gear shifting while mixing.

Proven Speed Reducer Drive. PTO Drive is standard. All 3 drive options connect to Shaft "A".

SHAFT "A"

Optional Hydrostatic Drive. The ultimate for performance.

Adjustable Auger Clearance. Set at factory to fit your feed requirements.

Seamless auger core, heavy duty auger shafts, and a heavy duty speed reducer drive give you reliable performance load after load.

Auger Couplers. Remove in minutes.

Agency: The High Plains Advertising Agency, Dodge City, Kansas.

A page from a brochure prepared for a manufacturer of farm equipment.

355

three slides and a voice-over instead of filming exotic scenes in a helicopter over the Grand Canyon. Further, smaller agencies are frequently involved in trade or specialized farm and industrial markets, for instance, which lack the glamour and flash of "consumer" advertising. Yet without this specialized advertising, the economy would come to a halt.[1]

A Different Kind of Ball Game

We will now examine a different kind of advertising. Everything you have learned so far is involved in it; yet it concerns certain meaningful differences, and unless you are aware of them you will be lost. In fact, many good advertising executives *have* become lost when they suddenly found themselves in a world for which they were not quite prepared.

Let us take a look, then, at some of the differences you will have to contend with when you get into this kind of advertising.

The Market

The industrial and agriculture advertiser is addressing himself to an audience far different from that of the consumer advertiser. We, and you, know quite a bit about what makes the consumer tick. Company purchasing agents, however, march to the beat of a different drum. They have a different set of motives. Their job is buying. They are professionally equipped to find the materials their companies need, to insure their availability, quality, and competitive prices. Purchasing agents are seldom moved by emotion; they are always moved by value and the best interests of their concerns. They are not moved by claims, but by proofs. Their days are spent in interviewing sales representatives, and they are not exactly naïve about the role of a salesperson. Purchasing agents will give polite and careful attention to anyone who calls on them. They hope that your product will be able to do all it was designed to do—perform a better task at a more economical cost.

The Product

Most of us have never *heard* of the products purchased by agriculture and industry. These are not the products you have known since you could talk—the clothes, cosmetics, smokes, drinks, and foods that make up so much of consumer advertising. What we are talking about in these

---

[1]Quoted from a letter to the author from Harry S. Mindlin, Creative Director, Pettler Advertising, Inc., Oakland, Cal.

fields are carefully engineered and conceived tools, instruments, chemical compounds, and devices that have emerged from laboratories and from the minds of scientists. In many cases, their very uses are confined to a relatively small group of people who are experts in their particular fields.

To promote and sell products such as these requires the kind of expertise that isn't acquired overnight.

The Advertising

Because agricultural and industrial products are different, and are destined for a special kind of market, it follows that they require a special kind of advertising. You are now talking to profit-and-efficiency-oriented business people, whose concern may be the operation of *their* product on the moon or on the ocean floor.

They are not turned on by beautiful four-color illustrations, or tricky headlines, or mouth-watering claims. They are interested in newsworthy products in their field, in performance, and in technical facts. They prefer their facts, not in fulsome generalities but in cubic centimeters, ergs, and millimeters.

You won't have too much trouble getting their attention because they want to know what is going on in their field. If you have something even mildly interesting to say you can be assured of careful readership. Neither do you have to be too concerned about that old cliché, "short, punchy, selling copy." If you have something to say about a product that may save them money or increase their production, they don't want the copywriter to be reticent about it. They want you to tell them *everything*.

This brings us to the copywriter. We've already talked about advertising writers and what it takes to be a good one. But the person writing on the agricultural or industrial account must have an extra dimension. Somewhere along the line this writer must have picked up enough knowledge of science so that he or she knows what the client's people are saying. Remember we said that most good advertising people have the faculty of quickly grasping the details of a client's business? It's not too tough when you are dealing with packaged goods for the consumer. But if your account makes agricultural fertilizers and plant sprays, or gadgets for steam boilers, it is to be hoped that you have a nodding acquaintance with organic and inorganic chemistry and some of the basic principles of thermodynamics.

The Media

Every now and then, in the world of consumer media, a great edifice will come tumbling down. The fatal cracks of advertiser disinterest begin to appear. The doctors prescribe a change of page size and space rates, but the patient keeps losing weight. And then one day the inevitable happens and we have lost an old friend. *Life, Look, Colliers, SEP* —*requiescat in pace.*

This practically never happens to the "trade press." Whether it is *Grit* or the *Georgia Farmer*, or the *Fisherman's Gazette*, or *Coal Age*, they go trudging along, year after year, getting stouter all the time. The field keeps growing, too. Even if you are involved in space travel or ocean-ography, you will have several publications that are devoted to your interests.

I don't pretend to know why *Life* should have died, and the *Game Bird Breeders, Pheasant Fanciers, and Agriculturists' Gazette* survived. This I know. Some of the best edited publications in the U.S. are industrial and farm magazines. For the most part, they are highly effective advertis-ing media because they give their readers more of what it is they need to know and give it to them authoritatively. It has been said, and I am inclined to believe it, that the most knowledgeable people in a special-ized industrial field are the editors of the "trade press."

As a young advertising man or woman, these are the people to whom you can turn. They will open up the world to you.

Back in the $35-a-week days I was trying to grope my way through the mysteries of how do you sell cutting oils to machine tool manufacturers, and what is a steel mill looking for in lubricants. There was, it turned out, a big green building down on 42nd Street called McGraw-Hill, with a big list of trade and technical publications. I'm glad I found it. They were wonderful.

The Clients

For the most part, on the big national consumer accounts, you are dealing with people who have considerable advertising sophistication. This is not always so in farm and industrial advertising. Many accounts in these categories don't even *have* an advertising manager; the top marketing executive often makes the advertising decisions. The result is that life is not always easy for the agencies that handle accounts of this nature. The people who must pass on the advertising are often good engineers and chemists, but their ideas about advertising may be rather primitive.

For a person like you, this offers a challenge and an opportunity. If you should go to work in an industrial company's sales department, look *around* you. After a short time you may discover that you are the only person on the premises who has a firm grasp of advertising techniques and methods. If so, you are in a position to make a real contribution to your company as well as to your own future.

By the same token, if you should find yourself working for a regional advertising agency with several farm and industrial accounts, your future with them can be very interesting and exciting. Far greater opportunities, in terms of needs to be filled, exist with accounts of this kind than with any others.

In this country today there still are a great many manufacturers who are yet to have their eyes opened. They have not discovered what can happen to them when a complete promotional effort, carefully thought out and controlled, is put behind their products.

How You Can Help the Farm-Industrial Advertiser

There are at least eight major ways that you as an agency executive or a company ad manager can contribute to the selling effort of your client or company. Let's examine them.

Writing the Advertising

You may discover that the company has not as yet sat down and seriously considered its advertising goals; they may still be in the "Let's-keep-our-name-before-the-public" stage.

It may be that what is called for is "institutional" advertising. But in this case it is image-building advertising directed to a far narrower market than is true with the big national accounts. Consistent, interesting advertising in the proper "trade papers" can give your company and its products a foundation of solid reputation basic to all selling effort.

Perhaps your company, in "keeping its name before the trade," has overlooked one of advertising's most useful jobs—that of identifying key buyers and prospects. By offering a free copy of important information, engineering details, government studies, or laboratory results, *and other pertinent information,* you can identify interested customers and decision-makers from the requests you receive. The latter are important to the industrial advertisers. Often this is the only way to induce them to reveal themselves.

As you have seen, the company purchasing agents have a specific task to perform. But often their decision to buy is controlled or influenced by people somewhere else on the corporate ladder. It is very difficult for your sales representative to see these executives without endangering his or her relationship with the purchasing agent. Here's where your promotional aids can be of tremendous help to your sales department —by identifying and reaching the decision-makers who might otherwise be out of reach.

In addition to identifying prospects for the sales force, your couponed or offer advertising can perform another important service—that of broadening your company's market. The variety of trade media enables you to put your message before some very specialized and fragmented markets. This means that you can bait your advertising hook and drop your line in some fresh and unexplored ponds. You just might get a big

bite.

Trade advertising can be especially important when your company has a new product that represents a real technical advance in the industry. Unlike most consumer publications, your advertising will be accompanied by lots of editorial support. If your company has come up with a newsworthy advance, you can be sure that every publication in your particular field will be interested in publicizing it. It will be your job to see to it that they get not only the advertising schedules, but all the information they need to do the proper kind of stories on your product.

The Media

If you have never had an opportunity to explore the great big wonderful world of trade publications, it's time for you to start. By all means visit a nearby advertising agency and ask them to let you look at their *Standard Rate and Data* for farm and industrial publications.

In the trade media you will find publications that carve the market into much finer segments than can ever happen with consumer publications. Here you will not only find farm publications that are specialized geographically (*The Alabama Farmer*); you will also find those directed toward particular areas of agriculture, for example, *Holstein-Fresian World*. You will discover industrial magazines that are concerned with whole industries (*Coal Age*); and others that cut horizontally through many industries such as *Electrical World*.

Trade advertising presents the advertiser with a host of interesting media combinations that may prove very productive. Since space costs are far lower in the trade media than in consumer media, you will feel much more free to try new combinations. As already mentioned, media experimentation may tap some unexpected markets for you.

It is worth emphasizing again that the trade media are valuable and almost indispensable sources of information. It is well to remember that nearly everything of importance that has gone on in your field has been recorded in your particular trade publication. Their files are storehouses of knowledge such as few companies have the time or the facilities to collect editorially, for they are in the business of knowing what is going on and what is about to go on.

Like their sisters in the consumer field, the trade publications have gathered considerable information about their readership. They will gladly share it with you. This is of particular importance to the industrial advertiser. As you have seen, the buying decision may rest in the hands of several executives, some of whom may be very hard for your sales department to reach. On the other hand, you may wish to call your company to the attention of people who are not necessarily decision-makers. In any case, it is vital for the industrial advertiser to be able to zero in on the exact *kinds* of people to whom he or she wishes to address

Nothing succeeds like Successful

When a magazine gets results for its advertisers, the business seems to take care of itself.

This past year our livestock demographic advertising was up 39%. Mail order advertisers increased their orders by 31% over a year ago. Total ad revenue was up by $877,361 . . . a gratifying 15% increase.

Thank you.

SF Successful Farming.

in a class by itself

Agency: Creswell, Munsell, Schubert, and Zirbel, Inc., Cedar Rapids, Iowa.

A "trade" magazine promotes itself to a significant part of its market demographics.

Agency: Altman-Hall Associates, Erie, Pa.

Agencies with industrial accounts are expected to provide a variety of material for their clients.

the selling message. The trade press will help you do that, often with great efficiency.

The *Scientific American* might be termed a semitrade magazine. It is read by a variety of people—from young children to corporation executives. All its readers have a scientific bent. This magazine once ran a very impressive campaign for itself by featuring its individual readers in four-color ads. It told about the subscriber—the subscriber's tastes, job, and his or her particular reason for taking the magazine. As you see, the demographic information usually used to aid the advertiser was used to help the publication itself.

Salespeople's Literature

Another great contribution you can make when you are involved in a trade or technical field is in the printed sales tools carried by your salespeople.

I am sure you can see why selling and information literature is so important to the industrial salesperson. The product he is selling is often highly technical and sometimes complicated. Often it is new, unfamiliar, and unusual. The sales prospect needs to know and grasp all the technical facts he possibly can. To *reinforce* the sales story after the salesperson has called and left is vital. Good, clear, informative literature is indispensable to most industrial salespeople.

This may take, as you have seen, the form of sales literature reinforcing and detailing the original sales presentation. It can also be literature of an informative nature which the company supplies *after* a sale has been made. Whatever it is, every bit of creative effort you can summon should go into it. You will be writing for a tough, demanding audience. Remember, they are going to look at your brochure or booklet with wise and critical eyes.

Direct Mail

Your company should maintain and keep up to date lists of customers and prospective customers. It is quite possible that direct mail can be a very productive medium for you. You should be able to compile a list of key people whom you wish to reach regularly by mail. Unlike so much of the direct mailings that come to the consumer, you may find that your particular list is a relatively short one.

As we have discussed in an earlier chapter, the trend in direct mail merchandising is to more elaborate mailing pieces. And that means more expensive mailing pieces. Fortunately you probably won't have that problem. Because of the very nature of your market, you are going to find that a well written informative letter that gets right down to the benefits it can offer the prospect—minus the frills—will do a very good job for you.

As Grosse points out:

Although men in industry receive many mailings, "Letters" are read and acknowledged. Because it is accepted practice for companies to exchange information by letter, personal letters, sent first class will attract far more interest and get far more attention than even the most highly imaginative direct mail pieces—all other factors being equal. A good letter written specifically to you, personally and correctly addressed, can be most compelling. One that betrays itself as a device obviously loses its effect.[2]

Trade Show Exhibits

If you are a firm selling to the trade, or if you are a firm's agency, production of a trade show exhibit is likely to fall into your lap. At least you may be *responsible* for the exhibit.

The trade show is a direct descendant of the ancient bazaars or "markets" where merchants gathered on appointed days to display their wares. For almost every industry, the trade show plays an important role in marketing plans. Sometimes the trade exhibit is part of a state fair, where many manufacturers of farm equipment will show their products. Sometimes they are one of the features of an industry's annual convention. Sometimes, like the boat show, they appear in several large cities across the country.

Your company and its products are going to be on exhibit, cheek by jowl, with a number of other people from your business and related industries. During the course of the show thousands of people will pass by your particular booth, many of them dazed by the variety of exhibits competing for their attention.

Building and staffing an exhibit booth is a real art. The design of the booth, its eye-catching devices, and unusual interest-arousers must be outstanding. If they are not, you will be just one of the crowd.

The sales literature you have on hand has to be well thought out too. The wise exhibitor usually has a smaller, less expensive piece for the "collectors," and a more elaborate brochure for the serious prospects.

Probably there is a firm specializing in exhibit and booth building in your community, or in one of the large ones near you. They can do the whole job for you, from design to construction. But if you are striving for individuality you should participate in the design process yourself. You know the characteristics of your product and your company, and you can translate these to the exhibit builder. But remember—he's built an awful lot of exhibition booths in his time and knows what everybody else is doing. Don't try to tell him how to do it. Let your ideas help him. You know your product and your market. What is it that will be most interesting and appealing to your prospects? As we have said about

---

[2]W. H. Grosse, *How Industrial Advertising and Promotion Can Increase Marketing Power* (New York: Amacom, 1973), p. 25.

How our distributors give you more than just a full line.

First they give you a full line. Flint & Walling submersibles, jets and other pumps, water conditioning equipment, accessories and repair parts. All top performers.

Our competition? They'll give you good products, too. Probably a full line of them.

An F&W distributor, however, does not stop there.

Every one of them carries a balanced inventory. The things you need most are the things they stock ahead. So when you want them, you get them. Fast.

Next, they stay in close touch with us. So the things not in great demand are just a phone call away.

Which means they give you service as good as the product. If they didn't, they wouldn't be selling Flint & Walling.

Finally, they can give you competitive prices. Performance, delivery, service, as well as a full F&W line.

With someone else, you may just be getting a line.

F&W

Flint & Walling, Inc. • Water Systems Division
Kendallville, Indiana 46755

An industrial manufacturer uses trade advertising to promote his distributors.

retail display windows, *an exhibition booth is there to do a selling job.* There is just as much creative-selling ingenuity involved in constructing an exhibition booth as there is in building a newspaper campaign.

Don't let your exhibit just *be* there. Moving parts, moving pictures, and moving people get attention. Get names and addresses, with free offers of literature and samples. Staff your booth with persons who really know how the product works.

Sales Meetings

Very often the planning of a regional or national sales meeting will become the responsibility of the marketing director's staff. As an agency or ad department person, you can make a real contribution. Aside from the cocktail party around the pool, and the company golf tournament, the sales meeting has some very serious work to accomplish in a relatively short time. It's a chance to show new products, to exchange information, to introduce new plans, and to enthuse and inspire.

There is a certain amount of show business involved in all this—in staging, writing, designing, and setting up the presentation. You can make it your job to see that whatever the sales department is pitching, they pitch it under the best possible circumstances. You might be surprised at the money and effort some companies put into their sales meetings. Some of the bigger ones have produced complete musical shows for their dealers and salespeople. These have special musical scores written for them, and are performed and directed by professional people.

But even if your company is small, there is no reason why your sales meeting should be dull. Just remember that *anyone* who gets up before an audience is into show business. There are dozens of ways you can use "props" and sound and light and action to enhance the performance.

If you should ever find yourself in the position of taking over some of the responsibility for putting on a sales meeting, find a theater-oriented person in your community to give you some help and advice. If there is a Little Theater or a Dinner Theater in your community, their director will probably be glad to act as consultant for a reasonable fee.

Audio-Visual Sales Tools

The well-written and produced audio-visual presentation can be a most valuable weapon in the salesperson's arsenal. It lends itself particularly well to products and processes of a technical nature. Of course, we are back in "show business" again. You have an audience, and a screen on which their attention is focused. It's a golden opportunity for your sales organization to score some points. But like any other show, it ought to be done right—or not at all.

general specifications

GRADE-AID Mobil-Pak cabinets and parts are fabricated from 16, 18, and 20 gauge cold rolled furniture steel, resistance welded throughout. All steel items are degreased and cleaned by application of a 60-90 mg. per sq. foot phosphate coating and chromic acid rinse. Final paint coat is high temperature baked, self-texturing, low lustre, alkyd coating and formulated to produce a suede-like finish on all metal surfaces. All doors and drawers are double-wall construction with sound insulation. All casters are furnished as outlined in each item description. All plastic laminated counter tops carry a 1/16" thick melamine plastic surface bonded to water-resistant, resin sealed, phenol overlay particle board with backer sheet. Edges are trimmed as called for in each item description.

For complete information on Grade-Aid's complete line of movable and fixed cabinetry systems, indicate area of interest below.

Name_____
School Dist./Archt._____ Date_____
Address_____ Title_____
City_____ State_____

PRODUCT INTEREST:
Fixed Classroom Cabinets
Movable Cabinet Systems
Movable Library Concept
Tote Stools
Stack Rack
Home Ec. Cabinets
Art Room Cabinets

TYPE OF SCHOOL:
Elementary
Junior High
High School

ACTION
Send Catalogs
Have Salesman Call
Want Planning Service
Will be bidding equipment
Date_____

double-sided tote tray cabinets | base storage cabinets | double-sided book and supply storage | wardrobe & general storage | mobile panels chalk/tack | mobile book carts | mobile utility cart | portable demo science table | stack-rack

double-sided cabinets

GRADE-AID continues its program of stocking the more popular models in its line of movable cabinetry. All items shown are delivered completely assembled, packed in cartons, and kept in inventory for immediate shipment. GRADE-AID hopes that you will find the Mobil-Pak Stocking Program convenient in supplying you with your immediate cabinetry needs.

QC541CDS-30TT
48" Wide x 38" High x 24" Deep
This double-sided, counter-height, tote tray storage cabinet offers a storage capacity of 30 trays (15 per side) for easy accessibility. The counter top provides an excellent work surface, demonstration surface, or display facility. Tote trays are provided with name-tag holders. Tray size is 14½" x 11" x 4¼". Tray color is tan. Cabinet body, black; cabinet shelves, gold nugget; counter top, Teak with vinyl bull-nosed edge. Carpet casters 5" – 4 swivel, 2 with brakes.

QC70JDS-54TT
47" Wide x 67" High x 23" Deep
This double-sided visual-barrier cabinet provides storage for 54 trays (27 per side). Carpet casters 5" – 2 tracking, 2 swivel with brakes. Tote trays furnished with label holders. Tray color is tan. Tray size 14½" x 11" x 4¼". Cabinet body, black; shelves, gold.

42TT
High x 23"
42 tote an in-barrier. trays (21 kes. label tray

GRADE·AID

Agency: Spencer, Bennett, Nowak, Inc., Providence, R.I.

mobil-pak now in stock

An excellent example of an industrial salesman's aid brochure. It contains "specification sheets," and a return inquiry card.

Don't let yourself be trapped into the "homemade" kind of slide film presentation. Unless you really have a special talent for it, the results will not justify your time and effort. Find an audio-visual production house that can handle the whole package for you, from on-location filming to final editing. As an advertising person, your role is to help in the preparation of the script, to make sure the goals and selling points are understood and expressed. You can also fill the role of technical adviser.

The costs of audio-visual presentations vary widely, according to the techniques used, the number of screens, and so on. You will probably find that a good audio-visual house can do a 15-minute presentation for about $4,000. As a sales tool, particularly when you are selling a high-cost item to a relatively limited number of decision-making people, a good slide presentation can pay for itself many times over.

Presentations

Sales presentations range all the way from the simple flip chart to the full-dress "dog and pony show" of Madison Avenue fame. Your department can make a very significant contribution here, too.

The flip chart should never be a crutch or canned sales pitch that the salesperson simply reads as the pages are flipped. The sales flip chart is designed to reinforce and emphasize the sales story through words and pictures. Moreover, a flip chart, whether an 8½" x 10" for desk presentation, or a larger size for easel presentation, has a quality every salesperson appreciates—it is an attention-getter and holder.

Flip-chart presentations require the services of a good copywriter and a good art director. The copy must be short and direct. The illustrations should be plain, simple, and illustrate the sales points being made.

Putting together the full-dress presentation is a far more difficult task. In this kind of presentation, the event is important enough so that a number of the top executives of your company will be appearing before a number of top people from other companies.

Although audio-visual material and flip charts may be used, the very stature of the people involved calls for a restraining hand. A great deal of "show biz" is neither needed nor desired in this case. You, as an advertising person, have a somewhat different kind of contribution to make here. It may call for some diplomacy on your part.

Not all the executives of your company, you will discover, are great speakers. Oh, they can get by at a local banquet; but this is a far tougher job. Moreover, protocol and the company pecking order may dictate that if executive "A" is to have five minutes for his "remarks," executive "B" will expect seven.

You may be able to make a very worthwhile contribution to the selling effort if you can contrive ways to keep some of these people off their feet. Many company executives believe that what they have to say about their department and its work is of overwhelming importance. They get carried away. Two minutes stretches to twenty, while the prospect's president keeps glancing at his watch and wondering if the Friday afternoon foursome will tee off without him.

Pick out the best speaker on your team and let this person carry the ball. Use your president to make the introductions and a few graceful remarks. *Write the whole presentation.* Make sure that everyone involved knows exactly what each has to do and say and for how long. Put it all on a schedule, and make it work like a clock. Hold *rehearsals*—the hardest job of all.

Reminder Presents

When I was a kid, my Dad worked for a big oil company. He called on chief engineers and steamship-line executives. Our house was always full of "gifts" that he left with the engine-room crews on the ships, just so they'd remember him and his company. He had inexpensive watches, straight and safety razors, sets of dice, playing cards, pens, pencils—the list was almost endless. And each little gift was resplendent with the name and trademark of his company.

As discussed earlier, the marketing of "premiums," "gifts," "reminders," or whatever you want to call them, is big business. Undoubtedly there is someone in your town who can supply you with a catalogue offering you thousands of items. Your name can be embossed or printed on them, and your salespeople can mail or take them to their customers.

The average regional manufacturer has a relatively limited list of customers, and their interests tend to be specialized. (A manufacturer, for instance, has a relatively limited list of customers of coal-mining equipment.) This means that you can afford to spend more money per present, and your ingenuity may lead you to come up with some desirable and useful ones.

Suppose you are working for a company that makes an audioelectronic gadget for people who are involved in offshore mariculture, mining, or exploration. What kind of a little reminder present would you choose to leave with their engineers?

Or, let's say that you are a manufacturer of a machine that automatically separates the male chicks from the female chicks, and is of particular interest to every large-scale poultry raiser. What do you leave with a poultry raiser who already has everything?

I think you see the point. You *can* come up with something that is so useful, or unique, or handy that your prospect can find it continuously useful. When you do, you will certainly be getting full mileage from your "reminder present."

How Much to Spend

If you find yourself in a manufacturer's advertising department, or you are working for an agency with industrial accounts, you are bound to encounter some spending problems.

As in the case of many retail stores, some manufacturers are very uncertain about the proper amount to budget for promotion. As a result, they often don't invest the proper amounts. (Note: Not *enough*; but the *proper* amounts.)

The big consumer accounts have become very sophisticated about their promotional budgets. The sheer weight of their dollars makes it possible for them to demand and get all kinds of market information not always available to the smaller spender. The importance of their budgets, often in the millions, demands that these are managed by promotion specialists with considerable expertise.

Sometimes this isn't the case in the industrial field. There are many regional manufacturers, as we have said, who don't even *have* an advertising manager. Some of them feel they can get along even without an agency.

A brand advertising manager for one of the big food processors, or a corporate advertising manager, is usually pretty well up there on the corporate ladder. Not so in many manufacturing concerns; there the marketing director is usually the big shot.

Most salespeople for consumer goods don't have to be convinced of the value of advertising. They know they couldn't get along without it. Many sales organizations in the industrial and farm fields aren't quite so convinced. Deep down in their hearts they believe that with their charm and personality and native selling ability, it might be much better if the advertising appropriation were devoted to the annual picnic or put on their expense accounts.

It is to be hoped that when you get the opportunity you are going to change all this. We have already suggested several ways by which you might make a contribution to your company. Here's another one: the proper setting up and controlling of the promotional budget.

Setting the Sights

Your management people, you will find, are familiar with the EPCC system of control. Whether it is production, quality, or costs, there is undoubtedly some form of EPCC practiced at your plant. EPCC stands for Expectancy (Goals), Performance, Comparison, and Correction. You set an expected goal, you perform in a manner to reach that goal; after a period of time you compare your performance with the goal you have set, and if necessary you take the corrective steps to help you reach your goal. This is probably beginning to sound familiar to you. Applied to promotion, this is the DAGMAR system we have already discussed. You should have no trouble selling the idea of using a variation of EPCC to your management. Let's see how it can be applied to the budgeting and control of a manufacturer's promotional dollars.

There are a number of jobs the promotional dollars can accomplish for a manufacturer. You should make it your responsibility to see that your company has these tasks clearly in focus, and knows what the priorities are in accomplishing them.

Some of the things the promotional dollars can do:

1. Help to build a good reputation for your company and its products.
2. Gain response from potential customers; stimulate inquiries, requests.
3. Pave the way for your sales representatives by preinforming the prospect about your product.
4. Reduce the number of calls necessary to consummate a sale.
5. Cut down the number of "service" or "courtesy" calls necessary to maintain good relations with the account.
6. Influence difficult-to-reach key decision-makers.
7. Identify and locate potential new customers.

These are not all the ways promotion can contribute to selling, but they are most of the major ones on an industrial account. Which of them are essential to your overall marketing plan? Which can contribute most to the selling effort?

When you have decided on your objectives (your Expectancies)—the kinds of jobs you want to accomplish by promotion—there is a next question for you: By what *methods* will you accomplish your ends?

If you examine points 1 to 7 again, you will observe there could be several promotional methods by which your goals might be achieved. Number 1 might call for a series of ads in the leading publication in your field. Perhaps, however, circumstances might dictate that the job could be done better by sending a personal letter from the president of your firm to each of your customers and prospects.

Number 6 would seem to be the place where a detailed, carefully illustrated brochure might do the job best. But maybe not. Maybe your major customers are near enough so that a few dinner-plus-slide-film presentations would do the job most effectively.

The point is that *you* can make a real contribution by helping to *define the objectives* and *devising the most effective and economical tools* for accomplishing them.

Measuring Promotional Effectiveness

Go back to Chapter 12 now, and review what you have learned about copy testing and the second part of DAGMAR. If you set promotional goals, you can determine promotional results. Or, in other words, *what did your company get in return for its promotional investment?* This is a question the executives of any manufacturing concern would love to have answered. You are in a position to do it.

Does your company wish to "reduce the number of calls necessary to consummate a sale?" The sales department, by reviewing the salespeople's reports, should be able to supply you with an average figure. You now have your bench mark.

The next step is to sit down with your marketing director and set a realistic goal. A 15 percent reduction in calls-per-sale? Get it in writing, and make sure that everyone is aware of it. The next step is up to you. What promotional technique, or combination of techniques, will you use to attain the goal? You know where your choices lie—publication advertising, direct mail, slide-film presentation, and so on.

Inevitably you must come to the question of how much to spend. But now an interesting thing happens. The question is no longer how much money is available in the promotional budget, but *how much do we care to invest to try to buy ourselves the advantages of reducing the number of calls-per-sale by 15 percent?* If through your efforts you have persuaded your company to think in this direction then perhaps you have made the greatest contribution of all.

There now remains, as you know, only one more step—to measure, after a 6- or 12-month period, the *performance.* In the case of which we have been speaking, it would simply mean going back to those sales department records and getting an accurate figure for the current number of calls-per-sale. You would then compare your original bench mark figure with your present figure. Did you make the goal? Did you fall short? Did you go over? Whichever it was, you now have the starting point from which your department can continue to search for the proper ingredients in the promotional mix that will help insure your company's sales success.

Earlier in the book we indicated to you that the setting of promotional goals and the measurement of results is something that is practiced too infrequently by marketing people. If this is so in the consumer field, it is doubly so in the fields of agricultural and industrial advertising.

Let's make the point once more. In a vast section of American industry there is a need for better, more accountable kinds of promotion. The need spells opportunity in thousands of America's regional agencies and manufacturing plants.

It may be that you are another Mary Wells, or a David Ogilvy with an Iowa accent. But these days the jobs are few and far between in the big advertising centers and in the ad departments of the great corporations.

Wasn't it Horace Greeley who said something about young people turning their footsteps westward?

WHERE YOU ARE

---

1.   You understand what an important place farm and industrial advertising plays in a great many of America's advertising agencies.

2. You know something about the vast number of publications—both horizontal and vertical—that are available to the farm and industrial advertiser. You know how they, with their storehouses of accumulated knowledge in their fields, can be of great help to you.

3. You have learned how, in a number of important aspects, farm and industrial advertising markedly differs from consumer advertising.

4. You now know a number of specific areas in which the farm-industrial advertising executive can aid his company. You are aware of the kinds of contributions you could make in each one.

5. You are in possession of a method by which a promotional program can be set up for your company, and by which the return on its promotional investment can be measured.

QUESTIONS FOR CLASS DISCUSSION

1. If the salary scale for farm-industrial advertising people is often lower than that for those working on consumer products, what are some of the positive arguments for getting into a career in the farm-industrial advertising field?

2. How many farm-industrial type businesses can you identify in your area?

3. Farming today is big business. If you live in a farming area, what would you say the capital investment is in the farms in your marketing area?

4. If you were to start your own agency, specializing in farm and industrial accounts, what selling points would you present in soliciting business for your agency?

SOMETHING FOR YOU TO DO

Select a manufacturer in your area who makes products for use in agriculture or industry.

Ask for an interview with their marketing director or advertising manager.

Analyze, in writing, what this company does in each of the areas of promotional opportunity you have identified in this chapter.

Specify how, as an advertising executive, you feel you could contribute to the promotional efforts of this company.

KEY WORDS AND PHRASES

Audio-visual Sales Aids. Equipment that tells a sales story by means of tapes or recorded narration accompanied by moving or still pictures.

Brand Advertising Manager. Advertising manager of a single line within a company. Found frequently in large food companies with diverse brands of popular products.

Decision-makers. Key people in an organization who are responsible for making final decisions.

E.P.C.C. System. One of the management-by-objectives systems.

Exhibit Booth. Display booths that are set up at trade shows, conventions, etc.

Farm Press. Publications that are directed to the interests of farmers and farm families.

Industrial Account. An advertising account that sells in the industrial and manufacturing market.

Key Buyer. One who makes the ultimate buying decision.

Presentation. Formal meeting at which an agency either presents itself when soliciting an account, or presents work it has done for a client.

Purchasing Agent. Executive who is responsible for the buying of goods and services for a company.

Reminder Presents. Gifts that bear company's name or other advertising message.

Sales Meeting. Formal gathering of a company's sales force—usually annual, though they may be held more often.

Sales Person's Literature. Printed material used by the salesperson to help secure sales and customers.

Service Call. Calls on accounts made by salespeople to keep contact, receive complaints, requests, information, and render "services."

Trade Press. Publications whose editorial and advertising content is directed toward the interests of a particular business or professional group.

Trade Show. Shows, conventions and exhibits devoted to the interests of people in, or serving, a particular field, e.g., Boat Show, Hotel Show.

Note: The publication section of your college or public library contains a great number of papers and magazines published in the farm and industrial fields. There is no better way for you to get the flavor of this kind of advertising than to select some of these books and carefully read them through, both for their advertising and for their editorial content.

Grosse, W. H. *How Industrial Advertising and Promotion Can Increase Marketing Power* (Amacom, New York: A Division of American Management Association, Inc., 1973). If there is a better book on the subject, I haven't as yet found it. If you are an agency or an ad department person in this field, this book should be on your desk. I have leaned on it heavily in this chapter, and have enjoyed every minute of it.

Mitchell, Robert J. *What to Do 'Till the Salesman Comes.* (Unpublished manuscript.) The author is an executive with Force Creative Advertising, Inc., of Santa Barbara, Cal. He was good enough to let me see Chapters 9 and 10. Great stuff by a man who really knows the field and can write like a whiz. The agency has found it a most effective new-business getter.

chapter seventeen

Some Legal and Moral Aspects of Advertising

In this chapter we talk about how people think about advertising.

We'll see some of the rules and regulations that apply to our business.

We will discuss some of the areas where you might get into trouble, and how to avoid them.

And lastly we'll talk about you, and your personal integrity, and the kind of advertising executive you want to be.

377

Somewhere along the line, advertising picked up a guilt complex that simply is not justified by the facts. We've done a great job of building reputations for other people; but until recent times we have somewhat neglected our own. This is not going to be a "How You Can Answer Those Nasty Critics of Advertising" chapter; rather we will help you arrive at a place where you can determine what your own moral stance, as an advertising person, should be.

Advertising has its high-powered lobbyists and "spokesmen" who at every opportunity will trumpet our purity and the "why-don't-they-just-leave-us-alone" theme. Chances are that you'll never meet one of them, although if you attend a national convention you might hear one. Those are the generals. *You* are an infantryman, and your battle will have to be fought on a lonelier field.

The Rules of the Game

Over the years a body of laws has emerged to protect both buyer and seller. We no longer live in the free-wheeling "anything goes" days of a hundred years ago. As an advertising person, when you write a campaign, or supply your agency with facts, or approve an ad, you are taking on a big responsibility. It's up to you to know the laws that apply to your particular case. Here are some of them:

Sherman Antitrust Act of 1890. Prevents monopoly and restraint of trade.

Pure Food and Drug Act of 1906. Meat Inspection Act of 1907. To keep food, cosmetics, and drugs from being adulterated or mislabeled.

Clayton Act of 1914. To encourage competition and prevent monopolies.

Federal Trade Commission Act of 1914. Established the famous "FTC" to reduce unfair methods of competition.

Robinson-Patman Act of 1936. To prevent price discrimination on products sold to retailers. Designed to protect small businesses. Under attack at present time.

Miller-Tydings Act of 1937. Allows manufacturers in interstate commerce to make minimum retail price contacts with their outlets.

Wheeler-Lea Act of 1938. Gives FTC authority over deceptive business practices, including false or misleading advertising.

Anti-Merger Act of 1950. To prevent large companies from gobbling up little ones.

Fair Packing and Label Act of 1966. To prevent misleading or missing information on packages.

Consumer Credit Protection Act of 1968. To enforce truth in revealing credit terms.

Unfair Trade Practice Laws. Most states have a variety of laws prohibiting unfair trade practices. These laws regulate competition and protect the consumer. Also there are laws affecting special groups, such as the Alcohol Administration Act, and the Automobile Dealers Franchise Act.

In addition to these and other federal laws, your state has on its books laws regulating business activities.

Non-Government Regulation

The laws are formal ways of regulating business; but as we shall see, there are a number of other ways in which promotional activities are controlled and influenced. You need not regard the laws and regulatory practices as punitive. In many cases references to these laws and consultation with the regulatory body can save you, your company, or your

client a great deal of grief and trouble. We are going to examine some of **381**
the controls in detail. But first . . .

What to Be
Careful About

What to Be Careful About

If you are the one who writes the advertising, or okays it, there are some basic trouble areas you can look for. Get into the habit of checking them over mentally before you release any kind of promotional material for use or publication.

First, *are you telling the truth—the whole truth?* This one seems obvious, doesn't it? But it isn't. The big, bold, blatant lie is easy to detect and relatively easy to stop. Anyone who tells the Big Lie in advertising has got to be crazy, for I know of no quicker way to alienate customers, ruin your reputation, and be sent to jail.

It isn't the big lie you have to look out for—it's the little lie. It's the tiny almost-truth that will make trouble for you. It is the fact that gets itself so surrounded by qualifications that it disappears. *These* are the lies that do you and our business a great disfavor.

You should get into the habit of judging a piece of copy not by what it actually says, *but by what the reader is most likely to think it says.* We have wordslingers in our business, I regret to say, who can shuffle the language the way a riverboat gambler can manipulate a pack of cards. Here's what I mean:

The headline or commercial announcer blares forth, "Now you can get blessed relief from the nagging pain of fallen arches," and persons with fallen arches, who are within the sound of the announcer's voice, slide forward to the edge of their chairs; their feet hurt them—they *want* relief. But if you will read the fine print at the bottom of the page, or listen carefully to the announcer's muffled voice, you may become aware of the following statement: "This product is suggested for use, and may be helpful in the temporary relief of some of the symptoms commonly associated with fallen arches."

Yes, they're within the law. The weasel words, such as "may be," and "temporary relief," and "symptoms associated with," have helped put 'em there. But a lot of people didn't read carefully or weren't listening, and so they hurry down to the nearest store and pay $2.00 for a bottle of Father Danaher's Fallen Arches Balm and hope for "blessed relief." I hope you won't associate with people like that.

In advertising, it doesn't pay to kid others; moreover, it doesn't pay to kid yourself. Whenever you find yourself mixed up with people who write with their fingers crossed behind their backs—run, do not walk, to the nearest exit. You wouldn't like these people anyway. They'll explain to you that most Americans are just dumb clods who read at a sixth-grade level; and if they didn't exploit them, then someone else would. So why not get in on the action? Look at all the money you could make. All it is going to cost you is a little piece of your soul!

I can't think of an ad or a commercial I've ever seen that was downright dirty or obscene. Considering where motion pictures are today I'd say that, for the most part, advertising numbers itself among the innocents.

Compared to British and French advertising, we are in fact downright prudish. For some reason, the British seem to take delight in being a little vulgar when they can. The French, bless 'em, don't seem to be quite so reluctant as we are about showing the human figure. Until quite recently we Americans never illustrated a bra on a live model on TV. And, if you have noticed, whenever a guy is shown shaving, he always wears his undershirt.

On the other hand, in a Paris Metro station I once saw a wonderful poster for Levis. It was a beautiful shot of a boy and girl lying, stomach down, on a sand dune. They are, of course, wearing Levis. *Only* the Levis.

So with all the restraints we are going to mention in a moment, I don't think that you will have to worry about anyone pulling anything particularly raw in an ad or in a commercial.

But *good taste* is something else again. It is quite frequently violated in advertising, and you might ask yourself why. To start off, we had better define "bad taste." I suppose it might be called anything we do or say, deliberately or not, that offends someone. We've had some stand-up comedians in this category. They'll go along for 20 minutes being hilariously funny, and then suddenly open their mouths and come out with something that is so offensive it makes you want to crawl under your chair.

And that—the unintentional one—is what you, as an advertising person, will have to look out for. An ad that says something that is offensive to people, *turns people off.* When you use the wrong word in mixed company you not only offend and embarrass a certain number of people, but you may not be asked back there again.

Games and Contests

We've already mentioned these in the chapter on sales promotion. Anything involving a game of chance or a lottery is illegal in interstate commerce in most states. If you are planning to run some sort of a promotion locally that involves a game or contest, better have a lawyer at your side; otherwise turn the whole thing over to a professional contest house, and let them worry about your legal headaches.

Releases. In an ad or in a commercial, never use anyone's name. picture, or attributed statement, without a formal, signed release. Be particularly careful if you are using crowd shots. The release, of course, covers professional models as well as anyone else you might use.

Comparisons.   If you are going to compare the performance of your product to that of your neighbor's—a practice that is becoming more and more popular these days—you had better have all your facts and figures notarized and authenticated by an outside independent source, if possible.

Copyrights.   It is not only a good idea to copyright your own material, but you must also be very careful about using material submitted by someone else. With all the best intentions in the world, people will send you ideas, slogans, or jingles that they think will do a great job and should be worth a lot of money. Avoid everything of this nature. Make it a hard-and-fast rule that anything submitted to you must be accompanied by a release.

Unfortunately, advertising minds often operate along the same track. Sometimes it is very easy to suspect that someone may have been peeking over your shoulder. I know of two agencies that came up with exactly the same theme for their clients who were in the same business. In a case like that, about all you can do is sit down for some friendly negotiation.

Trademarks.   I'm sure you know that you can't use even an approximation of someone's registered trademark. You must be particularly careful not to step on the toes of something not quite so obvious as the Coca Cola signature. This includes musical themes, certain sounds, slogans, characters (if you go into the fried-chicken business, you should avoid the temptation of featuring an elderly gentleman wearing a string tie and white beard) and other distinctive features.

Special Products.   From time to time you'll encounter some products that are surrounded by certain limitations. You are probably aware that cigarettes are barred from TV, and that they are required to carry the Surgeon General's warning statement in their print ads. A liquor account can drive you crazy, since different states have different advertising regulations. Some publications simply do not accept liquor advertising. (The *Saturday Evening Post* barred liquor ads for years.) Most publications, as we shall see, exercise a degree of control over the kinds of products advertised in their pages. Most TV stations are particularly sensitive in this area.

The Ways Advertising Is Controlled

Aside from the federal and state laws already mentioned, there are many other ways in which advertising is regulated. The big sensational headline-making cases may be initiated by the FTC, but thousands of sins are never committed due to the influence of the advertising business itself. Advertising *is* sensitive to what people say and think about it, and makes a real effort to keep its own house clean.

One of the formal ways this is done is through the National Advertising Review Board, which was initiated in 1971, and is a self-regulatory instrument. Complaints about misleading or deceptive advertising come to it through the Council of the Better Business Bureaus. The NARB reviews these complaints and works with the advertiser to correct them, when necessary.

The Better Business Bureau

There may be a Better Business Bureau in your community. Quite possibly there is a Better Business Division in your Chamber of Commerce; there are some 600 of them around the country. Either one will be able to supply you with its own advertising code of ethics. It might be a good thing for you to have these on hand if you are just starting out in business. You are much more likely to encounter one of these regulatory bodies than one of the big federal agencies. Their intent, of course, is much less punitive and is designed, mostly, to keep you from wandering too far off the reservation.

A citizen in your community can initiate a complaint with a Better Business organization simply by picking up the phone. These complaints range over a wide spectrum of business practices, with advertising complaints generally in the minority. These Better Business organizations are not federal or state regulatory bodies, but are independent organizations supported by the business people in your community. It is to be hoped that when you set yourself up in business you will become a member of one of them.

There is also a National Better Business Bureau that keeps an eye on business practices on the national scene. If your agency or your client is a member, you can call on them for advice and counsel. Their *Do's and Don'ts in Advertising Copy* is a helpful guide.

The Media

We've already noted that certain publications have had a policy of not accepting particular kinds of advertising. This quiet policy of controlling advertising content has to some extent always gone on in all media. Some are a lot tougher than others. Newspapers and magazines continually screen the advertising submitted to them for claims and type of sponsor. Generally speaking, the big-city press is likely to be more strict than the smaller papers.

TV and radio are especially sensitive about the kind of advertising they carry due, in part, to their federal licensing. The networks have "acceptance departments," which keep a close watch on all broadcast content. Your local station manager keeps close tabs on locally produced and placed commercials. The National Association of Broadcasters has a Television Code Review Board that sets the standards for the industry.

Seals of Approval

Some publications have their own laboratories in which they test their advertisers' products before accepting them. The *Good Housekeeping Seal of Approval* is one of the more famous. In addition, the Seal is a very nice merchandising device.

Associations

Wherever there is an association of any kind—whether agency, advertiser, or media—you are almost certain to find a regulating body. Each one has adopted, and attempts to enforce, its own code of ethics. Many of them feel that they are faced with a "if we don't do it, someone else is going to do it for us" situation. Naturally they'd rather play policeman themselves.

Ad Agencies

One of the responsibilities every creative director has is to keep an ethical control over his or her agency's output. In a moment of wild enthusiasm, one of the writers may submit a campaign that looks just great—except that it throws a couple of below-the-belt punches. Despite the copywriter's anguished cries, it's the copy chief's job to get those punches out of the ads.

If you have an Ad Club in your town you will discover, on becoming a member, that they too have an "ethics committee." They may be able to bring considerable pressure to bear on local advertisers because their membership will include representatives from all levels of your advertising community. Some of these ad club ethics committees are more active than others. Many work very closely with the Better Business organization in their town. Keeping the friendship and respect of one's fellow advertising practitioners often acts as a powerful deterrent against wrongdoing.

Publications

Regional as well as national advertising trade publications, such as *Advertising Age,* are conscious of their roles as "watchdogs of the industry." They are in a particularly good position to do an effective job of maintaining advertising's standards of good taste and honesty. Since their whole thrust is the ultimate good of the advertising business, they are listened to with respect. Through their editorial columns, "features," and letters-to-the-editor, they have quick, powerful and widespread means of appealing to the intelligence and decency of the great majority of advertising people. *Ad Age*, particularly, has never been at all reticent about calling attention to what is bad in our business—whether it is completely out of bounds, or something that is just silly or dumb. The "power of the press," and the possibility of public ridicule have kept a lot of advertisers in line.

Ombudsmen

The word is Swedish. An *ombudsman* is someone who intercedes for you. Your community may have one under any one of several names. Sometimes they work in a branch of the city government called "Consumer Affairs." In any case the ombudsman is a good person for you to know, and is usually listed in the telephone directory.

Anytime a consumer has a beef, he can pick up the phone and call the Consumer Affairs office and speak with the *ombudsman*. Generally they are more concerned with the misrepresentation of merchandise, or hit-and-run house repair and driveway builders. If there is any question in your mind about an advertising claim you are making, or the kind of service or product you are offering, it might be a very good idea to call them first and get clearance from that office. A letter of approval from this city official could be very handy for you to have in case any questions should arise later.

This office will also know all about city vending regulations, such as door-to-door direct solicitation. Some communities are very particular about this and will arrest vendors without proper licensing. And they also know just about everything that is going on around town, particularly in the retail field. If you are new in business, and just getting into your first promotions, a phone call to the Consumer Affairs office can save you trouble.

"Consumerism"

The consumer and the so-called consumer movement have been around for quite some time. They are a lot older than Ralph Nader.

There are advertisers who bristle at the very mention of the word "consumerism." I suppose this is understandable, particularly when a group of consumers has looked at your product and found it wanting.

Both Consumers Union and Consumers' Research have been getting out reports for years. You can probably find copies at your public library. These reports subject various products to tests in their laboratories, and report the results to their subscribers. Based on quality as shown in the tests, and relative price, they make recommendations as to "best buys" and "not acceptables."

Subscribers to these services are relatively limited in numbers, though perhaps not in influence. But what *does* have a very real effect on the marketplace is the growing knowledge and sophistication of buyers.

The world changes, marketing and advertising keep changing, and in your career you are going to see a lot of it happen. You will be dealing with a much better-informed consumer than anyone has ever had to deal with before. Today, in many schools, consumerism is a *required* course.

The day is really not long gone (the Patent Medicine Era, Chapter 1) when you could put almost anything in a bottle, make almost any curative claim for it, and happily pocket the dollars without an iota of interference from anyone. But don't feel too complacent; there are still some little beauties on the market that are good for man and beast, or whatever ails you. I know of one very popular nonprescription medicine the Federal Trade Commission has been trying to nail for years. Actually the stuff isn't much good for anything, but the medicinemen seem to have some awfully good lawyers and scientists on their side.

The market of the last quarter of the 20th century is more sophisticated in its buying habits than were the buyers of the first 25 years. We are a far better educated people than we were then, and that means we are more wary and less gullible. One reason is that we have gone to much trouble and expense to educate ourselves and our children *as consumers*. This education has taken place in the schools, of course; but it is interesting to note that it has also taken place in the marketplace *through advertising*.

As various products stress their differences competitively, consumers become more and more knowledgeable about their potential purchases. In many ways, advertising today caters to the greater sophistication of its market. The "blue-sky" approach has been replaced by "reason why" and "proof of performance." Very often the "reason why" assumes a grasp of knowledge on the part of the consumer he was never accorded before.

There has always been a school of advertising thought that held that the consumer is a fairly stupid clod who moves his lips when he reads, and wouldn't pay attention to you unless you shouted at him through a voice box. Fortunately that idea was put to bed, though not completely to sleep, by the advertising people themselves. They have proved that treating the consumer with respect and deference is very good salesmanship after all. They hit on something the psychologists have been aware of for some time—that sometimes the average Joe may have trouble pronouncing all the words, but he has an uncanny ability to catch on to issues and concepts and ideas. There are some politicians who might still be politicians if they had only discovered this principle in time. There are some ex-businesspeople who never found out, either.

Stanley Marcus, the great retail merchant, once wrote a letter to a customer whose complaint had been adjusted. Mr. Marcus pointed out that his store was doing what they'd always done—giving the customer the satisfaction he expected from his purchase.

He then went on to say, "It didn't take Ralph Nader, or Bess Myerson, or any governmental agencies to make us aware of our responsibility to sell satisfaction. As a matter of fact, consumer protection has a long history—at least as far back as Biblical days . . . Talmudic law rejected the theory of "caveat emptor" and unlike the law of the frontier, the seller was required to inform the buyer of all defects. Overcharging or undercharging was deemed to be fraudulent practice, an offense punishable under the law. Free competition . . . was given full support . . . I hope it is of interest to you. Sincerely, Stanley Marcus." I hope this letter is of interest to you, too. Maybe what you have just read is part of the reason for Mr. Marcus's success.

Changing Tastes and Standards

We have already talked about how, in marketing, nothing is static. You can count on change. This should be of particular interest to you as an advertising person. We are not talking only about changes in taste in cars and food and clothes; rather we are talking about man's values—what is good, what is desirable.

In the 1960s and 1970s we have seen great changes take place in the way people feel about their possessions and acquisitions. We have seen a real shift in the perspective with which man regards his life. This comes as no surprise to the historian or the anthropologist who sees it as part of man's ascent. What is surprising, perhaps, is that today it is happening so fast.

More and more people, particularly more and more young people, are asking themselves, "What do I want to do with my life? What is really important to me? Where do the true values lie?" Searching for the answers, and getting them, often involves a change in symbols.

The appurtenances of status and position no longer have the meanings they once had. All of life's appurtenances are available in the marketplace, you know: A can of beer, a ticket to the play-offs, a course of study, a book of poems, an afternoon of quiet contemplation on a deserted beach, the sounds of a symphony. . . . But the best things in life are not free. One of your greatest challenges as an advertising person will be to comprehend (what an assignment!) the way the world is changing.

What They Say About You

You will not be long in advertising before you discover that it has its critics in high places. I've never yet been in a library that didn't have several well-thumbed copies of Vance Packard's social commentaries including *The Hidden Persuaders*. (Vance was a great kid. I remember him with admiration as a college newspaper editor.) I doubt very much that until you become a big shot yourself, you will be called on to debate these people. At the end of this chapter, I will suggest some reading to you. It will familiarize you with some of the arguments, pro and con, that go on in and about advertising. I hope you are fairly well grounded in

History, Sociology, and Economics before you get into the subject too far.

In the meantime you will have to cope with your mother's friend, Mrs. Murphy. When the word gets out around the neighborhood that you have decided against a career in the ministry, and have refused to follow your father into the plumbing-supply business, you'll hear from Mrs. Murphy. At the first opportunity she is going to fix you with a beady stare and say, "I can't *stand* advertising!"

After you have gotten over the shock of that one, try to help Mrs. Murphy compose herself enough to tell you just what it is she doesn't like about advertising. It turns out that one thing she doesn't like is advertising that resorts to wild exaggeration—and who's to blame her? *I* don't like advertising that blows up its claims all out of proportion. And neither do you. When I see an ad for a "health salon" that says it will reduce me by 20 pounds or 20 inches in two weeks, my first inclination is to call a cop. And maybe I'd be doing us all a favor if I did.

Actually Mrs. Murphy doesn't see very much of this kind of advertising. The trouble is, she has seen some. It will do you little good to point out to her that she spent an hour and a half last night checking over the food ads in her evening paper for the best buys, or that she found absolutely nothing exaggerated about the ads for the 47 different products happily in use in her bathroom, her kitchen, and on her dressing table.

You'll find another thing Mrs. Murphy has a beef about: "silly" TV commercials. Odd, no one ever accuses a newspaper ad or a billboard of being "silly"—only the TV commercials. And do you know, Mrs. Murphy is right. There *are* some awfully silly TV commercials. Sometimes they portray people who couldn't possibly have ever existed in real life. Sometimes they portray *us* as simpletons. And sometimes their selling arguments are so idiotic that it is obvious they think we must be—well—"silly."

So put your arm around Mrs. Murphy's shoulders and say, "Mrs. Murphy, you and I are going to start an antisilly campaign. Every time we see a silly commercial we'll sit down and write a letter to the sponsor, saying, 'Congratulations, you have just sponsored one of the year's silliest commercials. It was so silly I went downtown and bought ten dollars' worth of your competitor's product.' "

You'll find, too, that your mother's friend is downright *annoyed* by a lot of advertising. Being a gentle lady, she doesn't like the idea of being shouted at either by an announcer or a headline. She doesn't like people who force their way into her living room and discuss their irregularity, their body smells, or their loose-fitting dentures. And there are certain other things she would just as soon *not* be reminded of, particularly before she has had her second cup of coffee in the morning.

You can't argue with Mrs. Murphy because, for the most part, she is right: she *does* have a beef. All you can do is try to remember that you work in a glass house.

And you can tell her, "Mrs. Murphy, I refuse to die for someone else's sins. And I'll promise you one thing. The kind of advertising I'm going to be associated with won't be the kind that bothers you so much. The kind *my* company is going to do may sell hard, but it will also help the ordinary guy to reach a sensible buying decision based on facts.

"I hope I can do something more in my advertising than just *tell* people. I want to inform them, too. The more sophisticated and informed my public is, the better I'll like it.

"And I hope I never forget that I have an obligation to the people who stop to listen to me, or read me. I'll never be dull, if I can help it, or pretentious, or phony. I'll keep my wits about me, and my sense of humor. I'll try to be exciting and rewarding, and worth every moment they give to me. I'll keep my own self-respect, and, in doing so, I'll keep theirs, too."

If you can do this, you'll be doing yourself a favor. You'll be doing us all a favor.

WHERE YOU ARE

1.   You are aware of the major laws that govern much of what goes on in advertising and marketing.

2.   You understand some of the pitfalls that await the careless advertiser, and how to avoid these legal and moral trouble-makers.

3.   You have been introduced to the various bodies within the business whose job it is to oversee advertising and to help both advertiser and agency to stay out of trouble.

4.   You are now conscious, I hope, that this is an ever-changing world, and that lately it has been changing at an ever-faster pace. You'll be prepared for it.

5.   You are ready to accept the fact that, as an advertising person, there are a lot of people out there who may not exactly love you. You are determined, I hope, to shape your conduct accordingly.

QUESTIONS FOR CLASS DISCUSSION

1.   Suggest three ways you might bring your pressure to bear on an advertiser you feel is offensive.

2. What are six things advertising can do *for* people? What are six things advertising can do *to* people?

3. What place do you think advertising techniques should play in political campaigns?

4. Recall, if you can, the last time you were led into making a purchase of something you did not want or need. Cite the exact circumstances.

SOMETHING FOR YOU TO DO

Keep a file of news stories recording indictments and convictions of advertisers accused of breaking the rules. It will remind you that the business world is not without sin, and what the wages are.

KEY WORDS AND PHRASES

Advertising Code of Ethics. Guidelines set down by industry organizations such as Better Business Bureau and the Ethics Committees of ad clubs.

Better Business Bureau. Organization designed to help business maintain standards of conduct and performance.

Blue Sky. The big, impossible promise.

Comparison. As in "comparison shopping" done by retail stores. The hard look at competing brands.

Consumer Affairs Department. Body at local and state level that looks after interests of consumers.

Consumerism. Name given the movement that actively seeks to protect the consumer against unfair or unethical business practices.

Consumer Research. Organization that does the above.

Consumer's Union. Same as *Consumer Research*.

Copyright. An exclusive legal right to publish, reproduce, etc.

Do's and Don'ts of Advertising Copy. A guideline published by the National Better Business Bureau.

Ethics Committee.   Most ad clubs and professional organizations have one. Oversees member's performance.

Good Housekeeping Seal of Approval.   Awarded by the publication to its advertisers who meet certain standards.

National Advertising Review Board (N.A.R.B.).   A self-regulatory body.

National Association of Broadcasters (N.A.B.).   Trade organization.

Ombudsman.   State or local official designated to review and investigate complaints by citizens, or to cut bureaucratic red tape.

Proof of Performance.   Test results usually compiled by an independent organization.

Reason Why.   Term for a particular kind of copy that states explanations behind its claims and promises.

Release.   A legal form, usually used by actors, models, etc. freeing the purchaser from responsibility in using their name, picture, or statement. A statement of permission in return for a consideration.

Surgeon General's Statement.   Warning copy by Surgeon General's office required on all cigarette ads and packages.

Television Code Review Board.   Industry watchdog of taste and ethics.

Trademark.   Identifying design of a brand or business.

Voice Box.   Device used in TV and radio to achieve an echo effect.

SELECTED READINGS

Alexander, George J. *Honesty and Competition: False Advertising Law and Policy Under F.T.C. Administration.* (Syracuse, N.Y., Syracuse University Press, 1967).

Diamond, Sidney A. Valuable articles on the legal aspects of advertising often appear in *Advertising Age, Journal of Marketing* and other professional publications by this gentleman. See the Business Periodicals Index.

Kintner, Earl W. *An Anti-Trust Primer: A Guide to Anti-Trust and Trade Regulations for Businessmen* (New York: The MacMillan Co., 1964).

_____. *A Primer on The Law of Deceptive Practices: A Guide for Businessmen* (New York: The MacMillan Co., 1964).

Sandage, C. H., and Fryberger, Vernon, (eds.). *The Role of Advertising* (Homewood, Ill.: Richard D. Irwin, Inc., 1960). This valuable book contains 49 articles that pretty well cover the whole subject, pro and con, of the role of advertising in the economy. Despite the fact that it is tilted in favor of advertising, and was compiled before some of the more modern critics and consumer advocates came on the scene, there is much of value in it for you. I highly recommend to you the opening article by James W. Carey, which traces the steps, in a fascinating philosophical manner, by which modern promotion and marketing came to be where it is. Brush up on Galileo, Newton, Locke, and the Industrial Revolution before you tackle it.

Index

395